THEO-LOGIC
Volume III

THEO-LOGIC

Volumes of the Complete Work:

HANS URS VON BALTHASAR

THEO-LOGIC

THEOLOGICAL
LOGICAL THEORY

VOLUME III
THE SPIRIT OF TRUTH

Translated by Graham Harrison

IGNATIUS PRESS   SAN FRANCISCO

Title of the German original:
Theologik: Dritter Band: Der Geist der Wahrheit
© 1987 Johannes Verlag, Einsiedeln

Cover by Roxanne Mei Lum

ISBN 0-89870-720-x
Library of Congress Control Number 00109331
Printed in the United States of America ∞

CONTENTS

CONTENTS

CONTENTS

ABBREVIATIONS

BGPhThM   Beiträge zur Geschichte der Philosophie und Theologie des Mittelalters

BKAT   *Biblischer Kommentar zum Alten Testament*, Neukirchen

C   Louis Bouyer, *Le Consolateur* (Cerf, 1980)

DTC   *Dictionnaire de théologie catholique*

DSp   *Dictionnaire de spiritualité*

EE   *Église et Esprit: Actes du Symposium organisé par l'Académie internationale de sciences religieuses* (Fayard, 1969)

ES   Yves Congar, *Je crois en l'Esprit-Saint*, 3 vols. (Paris: Cerf, 1979–1980)

GL   Hans Urs von Balthasar, *The Glory of the Lord: A Theological Aesthetics*, 7 vols. (San Francisco: Ignatius Press, 1982–1989)

GG   Walter Kasper, ed., *Gegenwart des Geistes: Aspekte der Pneumatologie*, QD 85 (Herder, 1979)

GP   Heribert Mühlen, *Der Heilige Geist als Person*, 2d ed. (Münster: Aschendorff, 1966)

HM   Claus Heitmann and Heribert Mühlen, eds., *Erfahrung und Theologie des Heiligen Geistes* (Hamburg: Agentur des Rauen Hauses; Munich: Kösel, 1974)

HThG   *Handbuch der theologischen Grundbegriffe* I–II (Munich: Kösel, 1963)

KS   Walter Kasper and Gerhard Sauter, *Kirche–Ort des Geistes* (Freiburg, 1976)

KuD   *Kerygma und Dogma* (Göttingen)

LSE   F. J. Lienhart, ed., *Le Saint-Esprit*, Publication de la Faculté autonome de théologie de l'Université de Genève (1963)

MES   Henri Cazelles, Paul Evdokimov, Albert Greiner, *Le Mystère de l'Esprit-Saint* (Mame, 1968)

NRTh   *Nouvelle Revue théologique*

NTD   Das Neue Testament Deutsch

ÖKÜ   C. L. Vischer, ed., *Geist Gottes—Geist Christi: Ökumenische Überlegungen zur Filioque-Kontroverse* (Frankfurt am Main: Otto Lembeck, 1981)

QD   Quaestiones Disputatae (Freiburg, Herder)

QS   *Sektenkommentar* (Dead Sea Scrolls)

RAC   *Reallexikon für Antike und Christentum*

RGG   *Religion in Geschichte und Gegenwart*, 3d ed. (Tübingen)

RSR   *Recherches de science religieuse* (Paris)

SC   Sources chrétiennes (Paris)

T   W. Breuning, ed., *Trinität: Aktuelle Perspektiven der Theologie*, QD 101 (Freiburg, 1984)

TD   Hans Urs von Balthasar, *Theo-Drama*, 5 vols. (San Francisco: Ignatius Press, 1988–1998)

ThKNT   *Herders Theologischer Kommentar zum Neuen Testament*

ThQ   *Theologische Quartalschrift* (Stuttgart)

ThW   Kittel et al., eds., *Theologisches Wörterbuch*

TL   Hans Urs von Balthasar, *Theo-Logic*, 3 vols. (San Francisco: Ignatius Press, 2000–2005)

TU   Texte und Untersuchungen zur Geschichte der altchristlichen Literatur (Leipzig and Berlin)

UMP   Heribert Mühlen, *Una Mystica Persona*, 3d ed. (Paderborn: Schöningh, 1967)

ZKTh   Zeitschrift für Katholische Theologie (Innsbruck)

ZNW	Zeitschrift für neutestamentliche Wissenschaft und Kultur der älteren Kirche (Gießen and Berlin)
ZThK	Zeitschrift für Theologie und Kirche (Tübingen)

PREFACE

This volume concludes the *Theo-Logic*. The difficult task here was to preserve, within the limits imposed by the concept of "logic", the superabundant fullness of what could be said about the Holy Spirit; for is there any article of faith in which he is *not* present—patent or latent—in manifold ways? The Spirit is the indispensable guide who "leads" us "into all truth"; so it is in this context that we must discuss the seemingly endless array of things that fall under the heading of "all truth". As a result, many a topic that would have required a whole book is here compressed into a meager paragraph. It was essential to allow our discussion of everything concerned with salvation history to emerge according to the fundamental trinitarian dimensions of the Spirit; this meant taking up topics developed in the earlier volumes and drawing out their consequences.

In a substantial book (*Streben nach Vollendung. Zur Pneumatologie im Werk H. U. v. Balthasars*, Freiburger theologische Studien 125 [Herder, 1983], 556 pp.), Kossi K. Joseph Tossou has already dealt with this same topic, distilling it from my widely scattered theological writings; the present volume does not render his labors superfluous.

There has been a veritable flood of writing on the Holy Spirit; it was possible to take account of only the most important works, often giving them no more than a bare mention. Our guiding principle throughout was Jesus' promise that the Spirit "will not speak of himself, he will take what is mine and declare it to you"; and when he says "mine" we must remember that all that the Father has also belongs to the Son. Here we discern the unity of the trinitarian work of salvation in the Church and in the cosmos, a work that is only the outward expression of the inner, personal wealth of God, indivisibly one and sole.

Hans Urs von Balthasar
Solemnity of All Saints, 1986

PRELUDES

I

WHAT HAS THE SPIRIT
TO DO WITH LOGIC?

Faithful to the Johannine approach of the previous volume, we can answer this question quite straightforwardly with the promise of Jesus that, "when the Spirit of truth comes, he will guide you into all the truth." But "he will not speak on his own authority . . . , for he will take what is mine and declare it to you. All that the Father has is mine; therefore I said that he will take what is mine and declare it to you" (Jn 16:13–14). The Spirit's entire role is to guide us into the truth and to declare it: all the other, manifold utterances concerning the Spirit that we find in John and in the Scriptures of the Old and New Covenants come back to this fundamental role. As we have seen, the Son, become Incarnate, was the adequate declaration of the Father, but this declaration remained closed to men so long as the Spirit "had not been given" (Jn 7:39).

> This took place in a visible manner at Pentecost. For, prior to this day the apostles had no awareness of this infinite meaning in Christ; they did not yet know this to be the infinite history of God: they had believed in him, but not as in One who is this infinite Truth. His enemies saw him, heard his teachings; they were cognizant of it all; they even saw miracles, and so they were brought to believe in him. But Christ himself vehemently rebuked those who desire miracles from him. "The Spirit", he said, "will guide you into all truth."[1]

Therefore, the Fathers will conclude, the Spirit himself must be God. How else could he, the "Spirit of truth", declare the "truth" that resides in the Son's revelation of the Father? He must have been already present within this very Word-event, for the Son's words—and he was all Word—were themselves "spirit and life" (Jn 6:63). In part 3 of this volume we shall have to give a thorough exposition of this inseparable relationship of Logos and Spirit in the event of revelation. Nonetheless, the

[1]Hegel, *Geschichte der Philosophie*, III (1836), 134.

17

human destiny of Jesus had to be brought to its "con-summation" (Jn 19:30) before the Spirit could be breathed forth out of him (ibid.) and breathed into the world (Jn 20:22). The thrust of the lance, too, was necessary to open the heart of the revelatory body, so that now the Spirit—always together with the water and the blood (1 Jn 5:6)—can bear its testimony to the truth of the Father's love as revealed by the Son.

We have shown in some detail that the incarnate Son was the Revealer of the Divinity not only in his words but in all the phases of his flesh.[2] This means that the Spirit will not simply interpret a teaching (let alone the mere letters of "Scripture"), but will guide us to the vital depths of what takes place between Father and Son, introduce us into the hypostatic realm. Nor will this be a kind of guided tour for a group of tourists visiting an as yet unknown landscape or a fascinating underground grotto: we can only be introduced to the christological reality if we are prepared to be assimilated to it. This unveils the central Pauline aspect of this "guiding" by the Spirit: it makes us to be sons in the eternal Son, *filii in Filio*. This can be expressed in Paul's "in Christ", "in the Spirit", or in the Johannine, "We will come to him and make our home with him" (Jn 14:23). So in essence it is already clear why the Spirit is called "Holy Spirit", and why he who elsewhere is always witnessing to the truth and guiding us into it—and so can be called the "Spirit of truth" (Jn 14:17; 15:26; 16:13; 1 Jn 4:6)—can also be actually identified with the truth: "the Spirit is the truth" (1 Jn 5:7): the space between Father and Son, into which the Spirit introduces us, is in a certain respect the Spirit himself. As we shall see, he is the love between Father and Son by being simultaneously their fruit and hence their witness.

We must never forget, however, that the interpreting Spirit operates by taking "what is mine", and the Son's "mine" is and remains an incarnate "mine". Thus the Spirit's witness is never

---

[2] "In John, *alētheia* is the divine reality that is manifested in Jesus. Jesus' self-identification with *alētheia* in 14:6 is central to the Johannine concept of truth. . . . Whereas in 14:6 *alētheia* is what Jesus *is*, 16:13 speaks of 'all truth' as what Jesus *has*. But both expressions mean practically the same thing: Jesus *is* what he *has* and *brings*" (Wilhelm Thüsing, *Die Erhöhung und Verherrlichung Jesu im Johannes-evangelium* [Münster, 1960], 146, 148).

given apart from water and blood. The Spirit may be spoken of as a divine water that we must drink, a spring that wells up unto eternal life (Jn 7:38; cf. 4:10–14), but at the same time we must also drink the living blood of Christ (Jn 6:54f.). This leads to a further panorama in the Spirit's declaring of, and leading into, the truth, for it takes place preeminently in a particular realm that Paul calls the Body of Christ, or the Church. Here, effected essentially by the "Spirit of God" and the "Spirit of Christ" (Rom 8:9), the Holy Spirit manifests himself as truth: "Where the Church is, there is the Spirit of God; and where the Spirit of God is, there is the Church and all grace; and the Spirit is truth."[3] We can leave it open for the present how "Church" is to be defined and what boundaries she has, since we are only giving a preliminary adumbration of her dimensions. However, by way of anticipation we can indicate that two emphases are possible here. Ecclesial man's introduction into the realm of truth in the Godhead can be interpreted predominantly as his transmutation into the realm of the divine; in this case the Spirit's operation will be understood more as purification, illumination, union, and "divinization"—both through insight and through virtue: this is the way of the Greeks. Or this "guiding into all truth" can be interpreted more as incorporation into the Body of Christ, the ultimate analogy being the "one flesh" of Bridegroom and Bride, or the one Body with many members; thus Christ loves himself in his own Body (Eph 5:28f.): "*Ipsi sunt ego*",[4] taught Augustine and his followers in the West. These two perspectives are so complementary, however, that neither in isolation from the other can yield a comprehensive doctrine of the Spirit. This is true even if the first view begins in a more theological mode (thus Basil says that the Spirit belongs to God because he sanctifies in a divine manner), and the second in a more anthropological mode (Augustine says that the Spirit of divine freedom wrests us from slavery and makes us free children of God in Christ—which is in the Church). Historically, furthermore, the two perspectives fuse, as we see in Cyril of Alexandria's emphasis on the "life-giving pneumatic flesh" of Christ that no

---

[3] Irenaeus, *Adv. Haer.* III, 24, 1.
[4] Augustine, *Tr. 108 in Joh.*, c. 5.

"divinization" can bypass; conversely, Augustine insists: "You cannot receive the Spirit as long as you continue trying to know Christ after the flesh, 'for if I do not go away, the Comforter will not come to you.' "[5] We recognize the congruence of these two views in Basil's address on the Spirit:

> And when, by means of the power that enlightens us, we fix our eyes on the beauty of the image of the invisible God, and through the image [Christ] are led up to the supreme beauty of the spectacle of the archetype [the Father], then . . . is in him (the Son) insepa-rably the Spirit of knowledge, *in Himself* bestowing on them that love the vision of the truth the power of beholding the Image, not making the exhibition from without, but *in Himself* leading on to the full knowledge. . . . "In thy light shall we see light," namely by the illumination of the Spirit. . . . It results that in Himself He shows the glory of the Only begotten.[6]

However, if the dimensions of the Spirit's operation are to correspond to those of the Son, and the Son's operation can-not be confined to the Church, the question arises: How far does the Holy Spirit act even outside the Church in declaring the trinitarian truth? The question arises initially in respect of the Old Covenant, where the "word of God" and the "spirit of God" are closely paralleled and often equated; our Nicene Creed deliberately stresses the fact that the Spirit spoke through the prophets. The Old Covenant contains what we might call preliminary sketches of the trinitarian mystery revealed in Christ. Yet neither the Old Covenant nor (most particularly) the New Covenant is self-enclosed: they have a missionary openness to-ward all peoples. So, just as there is a *logos spermatikos* among the latter, we must assume that there is something like a *pneuma spermatikon* that corresponds to it. Finally, over and above the perspective of world history, there opens up the panorama of the Spirit's activity in the whole of creation. In this context we shall have to ask whether, in this united operation of the divine Hypostases in the work of creation, it is permissible to discern,

---

[5] *Tr. 94 in Joh.*, c. 4.

[6] *De Spiritu Sancto*, c. 18 (PG 32, 153AB). Translation adapted from *Nicene and Post-Nicene Fathers*, 2d series, ed. Philip Schaff and Henry Wace (Grand Rapids, Mich.: Wm. B. Eerdmans, 1996), VIII, 29.

in some way, the distinctive contribution of each Hypostasis. The question will be addressed in part 6 of this volume.

These are peripheral issues. If we return to the center and consider the Spirit's role in declaring the truth—which means that he is essentially involved in *theo-logic*—we become aware of the ultimate purposes of his operation. If the truth that has appeared in Christ is infinite, since "in [him] are hid all the treasures of wisdom and knowledge" (Col 2:3), it will be impossible to come to an end in declaring this truth all down the ages, for although this truth resides in an apparently limited spatio-temporal phenomenon, it is nonetheless "the whole fullness of deity [dwelling] bodily" (Col 2:9). Nor is it the case that first of all the main points are clarified (for example, in conciliar definitions) and then the more and more partial issues come up for treatment. No, it is rather that new vistas are continually being opened up on the infinite whole, which is not vague, but supremely particular. These new perspectives can be discerned or lived out sometimes in a more intellectual way and sometimes by the way of love. Sometimes, if the Spirit wills, we can suddenly become aware of entirely new aspects of the infinite truth as they come under the spotlight, aspects that always had their place within faith's spiritual horizon but were somehow neglected. The oft-repeated dictum is true: There is much more truth in Christ than in the Church's faith and much more truth in the Church's faith than in the formulated dogmas. People with great charisms, like Augustine, Francis, and Ignatius, can be granted (by the Spirit) glimpses of the very center of revelation, and these glimpses can enrich the Church in the most unexpected and yet permanent way. Insight, love, and discipleship are always inseparable in such charisms, which shows us that the Spirit who declares the truth is at the same time divine Love and divine Wisdom: he is by no means mere theory, but the inspirer of a lived faith.

There is one final trait that is typical of the Spirit: in broadcasting the divine fullness into an infinity of time and space, he constantly and increasingly imparts unity to it. He unveils no detail without causing the totality to light it up from within. A theology that became dissipated in details, or a practice that one-sidedly concentrated on one aspect of Christian life, could not regard itself as animated by the Spirit. We have just referred to the fact that the "hidden treasures" in Jesus Christ are simultaneously spread abroad and gathered into one: this is entirely dependent on the uniqueness and specific nature of the hypostatic union; from it the riches are distributed, and into it they are gathered. The Lord says of the Spirit that "he will take what is mine". That is also why Christ's Church has a missionary thrust "to the end of the earth" (Acts 1:8), but she can only pursue this expansion if simultaneously she returns to and concentrates on the goods she has to squander. This is equally true of the pattern of Christian existence and of the form of theology taught by the Church; by this christological paradox we can see whether Christian existence and theology are inspired by the Holy Spirit or not.

Since the Spirit of God and of Christ is always at work here and now, there can only be a "relative eschatology", not an "absolute eschatology", in Christianity.[7] The latter is present in all forms of Jewish (utopian) messianism; here the truth is to be hoped for and realized only in the future, by changing the current situation of alienation.[8] Liberation theology seems to have a fateful tendency in this same direction. The dynamic advantage of "relative eschatology", by contrast, is that the foundational saving fact was and is present and that the Spirit's presence is powerfully pressing the world and history toward the *eschaton*. Thus Romans 8 speaks of the Spirit's "sighs too deep for words" that give unfulfilled "hope" all its intense yearning; and "the Spirit and the Bride say, 'Come'" (Rev 22:17). When it is said that the Spirit will "declare to you the things that are to come" (Jn 16:13), what is meant is the totality of what for the

---

[7] This distinction is drawn by Michael Theunissen, *Hegels Lehre vom absoluten Geist als theologisch-politischer Traktat* (Berlin: W. de Gruyter, 1970), 366–86.

[8] Theunissen shows this with reference to Marx ("painstaking studies no longer leave room for doubt that Marx is rooted in the radical eschatology of Judaism", ibid., 356) and in detail with reference to Bloch, "and the same could be said in principle of Walter Benjamin or Georg Lukács, and even of Horkheimer, Marcuse, and Adorno" (ibid.). "Nor is Jakob Taubes (*Abendländische Eschatologie* [Berne, 1947]) listing mere brute facts when adducing the 'names of Moses Hess, Karl Marx, Ferdinand Lassalle, Rosa Luxemburg, Max Adler, Otto Bauer, Eduard Bernstein, and Leon Trotsky' to illustrate the astonishing part played by Jews in the 'revolutionary movement'" (ibid., note).

present can only be grasped obscurely and in riddles. According to Deutero-Isaiah, it is a sign that the true God, he who governs the future, is at work, whereas the false gods are incapable of giving true instruction about the future.[9] In the New Covenant it is the Holy Spirit, the third divine Hypostasis, imparted to believers, who has the task of leading them from the truth they have embraced in faith and hope into the coming complete truth of the covenant between God and the world.

Here, in a preliminary adumbration, we see why the Spirit has his inalienable place in *theo-logic*. Christian truth is trinitarian because Jesus Christ, the Father's Son made man, incarnate through the Spirit and accompanied by the same Spirit through his life, work, and suffering, is the revealed Word and hence "the truth" (Jn 14:6) in that—unto death—he gives an adequate* portrayal of the Father's love. This was the central theme of the preceding volume. The Father wills, ratifies, and accompanies the truth that (in the Son's mission) reveals him: so the Father can be called "true" (*alēthinós*). "I have not come of my own accord; he who sent me is true" (Jn 7:28). The lapidary, albeit puzzling, conclusion of the great Letter of John gives us the word "true" three times in the same verse: the first time it no doubt refers to the Father, the second time to the Son, whereas the third time it seems to refer to both at once or to one of them—probably the Son: "And we know that the Son of God has come and has given us understanding, to know him who is true; and we are in him who is true, in his Son Jesus Christ. This is the true God and eternal life" (1 Jn 5:20).[10] Thus to say that the Son is

---

[9] "Tell us what is to come hereafter, that we may know that you are gods" (Is 41:23). But Yahweh says, "I am the first and I am the last. . . . Who has announced from of old the things to come?" (Is 44:6-7; cf. 42:23; 45:11). Cf. F. Porsch, *Pneuma und Wort: Ein exegetischer Beitrag zum Johannesevangelium* (Frankfurt, 1974), 297-98.

Adäquat does not have the rather grudging sense that "adequate" has acquired in English. Here it means "equal to, matching" and, hence, "true" and "dependable".—TRANS.

[10] For a discussion in particular of the third occurrence here, cf. Raymond Brown, *The Epistles of John*, Anchor Bible, vol. 30 (Garden City, N.Y.: Doubleday, 1982), 624-26. With regard to the first "true" (assigned to the Father), Brown refers to John 17:3: "That they know thee the only true God, and Jesus Christ whom thou hast sent". As to the connection between the first and second occurrences, Brown

"true" is to say that he faithfully declares the Father, not only by reproducing his Logos exactly in human words, but also by being "the true light" (Jn 1:9), "the true bread" (6:32), the "true judgment" (8:16), and the "true vine" (15:1). In all this he is the truth of God in earthly form. All this, however, would be closed to us if "the Spirit of truth" (Jn 14:17; 15:26; 16:13; 1 Jn 4:6) were not entrusted to us so that, together with the Spirit, we can know what Paul calls "the depths of God" which the Spirit alone can search; "we have received not the spirit of the world, but the Spirit which is from God, that we might understand the gifts bestowed on us by God" (1 Cor 2:10, 12). Accordingly, we are also able to discern the spirits: "the spirit of truth and the spirit of error" (1 Jn 4:6), and recognize Jesus' abiding in us: "By this we know that he abides in us, by the Spirit which he has given us" (1 Jn 3:24). Negatively and positively, therefore, the Spirit is the indispensable Declarer of trinitarian truth; in all the functions attributed to him he is the final and concluding object of *theo-logic*.

---

gives the following "probable" interpretation: "We are in the God who is true by being in his Son who is the truth." With regard to the third occurrence, Dodd had suggested taking the unity of Father and Son ("God known in Christ") as the subject, which is hardly likely in Johannine thought. It is possible to regard it as referring back to the Father (cf. Jn 17:3), but a reference to Christ is more probable, since elsewhere too (at the beginning and end of the Gospel, 1:2; 20:28) Christ is termed "God" (here even with the definite article!). In agreement with Brown and many others (ibid., 625) is R. Schnackenburg ("Johannesbriefe", ThKNT 1953, 261–62).

2

IS A THEOLOGY OF
THE SPIRIT POSSIBLE?

Initially, when asking this question, we do not need to consider whether and how far the Holy Spirit can be designated a Divine Person. We shall address this issue in part 2. Scripture speaks about the Holy Spirit in many ways, portraying him now as an impersonal power, now as a subject with personal qualities; our question is this: Does the Spirit ever appear "objectivized", or is he not rather that which (or he who) mediates something or "Someone" else (first and foremost, of course, Jesus Christ)— rendering it (him) the "object" of spiritual understanding? Ultimately this "object" is the Father, who is "seen" (Jn 14:9) through and in Christ, and only in him, for the Father "dwells in unapproachable light" (1 Tim 6:16). Basil, in his seminal treatise on the Spirit, describes him as the One by whom we are enabled to see God. So it is clear to him that the Spirit belongs on the side of God, as, shortly thereafter, the First Council of Constantinople will declare: "qui cum Patre et Filio simul adoratur et conglorificatur".[1] Basil, too, ascribes these indubitably divine attributes to the Spirit, but, no more than the Council does he call the Spirit "God".

> Wherefore even in our worship the Holy Spirit is inseparable from the Father and the Son. If you remain outside the Spirit you will not be able even to worship at all; and on your becoming in Him you will in no wise be able to dissever Him from God;—any more than you will divorce light from visible objects. For it is impossible to behold the Image of the invisible God [that is, Christ] except by the enlightenment of the Spirit, and impracticable for him to fix his gaze on the Image to dissever the light from the Image,

[1] On the preparation for this Council and what the expanded Nicene Creed owes to it, cf. Adolf Martin Ritter, *Das Konzil von Konstantinopel und das Symbol: Studien zur Geschichte und Theologie des II. ökumenischen Konzils* (Göttingen, 1965). On pp. 182ff. Ritter finds it probable that the Council produced the expanded form without intending to change anything in the formula of Nicaea. On pp. 202ff. he explains why the latter enjoyed no great currency prior to Chalcedon.

because the cause of vision is of necessity seen at the same time as the visible objects. Thus fitly and consistently do we behold the "Brightness of the glory" of God [Heb 1:3] by means of the illumination of the Spirit, and by means of the "Express Image" we are led up to Him [that is, the Father] of whom He is the Express Image and Seal, graven to the like.[2]

Earlier, Basil had written,

For just as objects which lie near brilliant colours are themselves tinted by the brightness which is shed around, so is he who fixes his gaze firmly on the Spirit by the Spirit's glory somehow transfigured into greater splendour, having his heart lighted up, as it were, by some light streaming from the truth of the Spirit. And this is "being changed from the glory" of the Spirit "into" His own "glory".[3]

It follows from this that the Spirit

wishes only to breathe through us, not to present himself to us as an object; he does not wish to be seen but to be the seeing eye of grace in us. . . . He is the light that cannot be seen except upon the object that is lit up: and he is the love between Father and Son that has appeared in Jesus. . . . The One through whom we "behold" God is the Spirit, that least objective mystery that breathes eternally beyond all objectification but in whose light everything that is at all capable of being illuminated becomes clear and transparent.[4]

At this point, however, we must recall what was said in volume 2, namely, that what is "graspable" in God, the incarnate Logos, cannot be separated as such from his twofold transcendence toward the Father and toward the Spirit. As we shall show

---

[2] *De Spiritu Sancto*, c. 26 (PG 32, 185bc). Translation from *Nicene and Post-Nicene Fathers*, 2d series, ed. Phillip Schaff and Henry Wace (Grand Rapids, Mich.: Wm. B. Eerdmans, 1996), VIII, 40.

[3] Ibid., c. 21 (165bc); Schaff and Wace, *Nicene and Post-Nicene Fathers*, VIII, 34. Of course there is a reference here to 1 Corinthians 3:14–18, particularly to the statement "the Lord is the Spirit"; but it is not necessary to follow Basil and take "the Lord" as an attribute of the Spirit; "the Lord" can equally be the spiritualized Christ, who, by the Spirit's power, takes possession of those who are his.

[4] H. von Balthasar, "The Unknown Lying beyond the Word", in *Explorations in Theology*, vol. 3, *Creator Spirit*, trans. Brian McNeil (San Francisco: Ignatius Press, 1993), 111–12.

in part 3, the Incarnate One, in all stages of his "graspability", is utterly permeated by the Spirit; he can never be understood as a mere brute fact: only the faith that is likewise permeated by the Spirit can grasp him as the "objective" reality he is. So it is right to say that "no Christology can ever be developed without an *indirect* Pneumatology, and conversely no Pneumatology can be developed except as a way into Christology; Christology must be the measure of Pneumatology." We could say that this "indirectness" reveals the Spirit's striving to remain "anonymous". In iconography, for instance, the Spirit is not given a face. "The contradiction in the fact that a Person is represented *impersonally* (as a dove, as wind and fire) shows our inability to lay our hands on the Spirit." "He is, for us, the giver of divine presence", which points to the Spirit's "selflessness". There is thus no theological "discourse *about* the Spirit, because the Spirit is primarily the divine *subject* of theology and of church life".[5]

This is confirmed by the words addressed to Nicodemus, where the breathing of the pneumatic wind (which is a tautology since, both in the Old and the New Testament, *pneuma* means both breath and wind) cannot be tied down: "The wind blows where it wills, and you hear the sound of it, but you do not know where it comes from or where it goes" (Jn 3:8). And this applies, as the text goes on, not only of the *Pneuma*, but to "every one who is born [again] of the Spirit". Paul confirms this when he says that the one who has received the Spirit, while he does speak of God, does not do so "in words . . . taught by human wisdom but taught by the Spirit, interpreting spiritual truths to those who possess the Spirit. The unspiritual man does not receive the gifts of the Spirit of God, for they are folly to him, and he is not able to understand them because they are spiritually discerned. The spiritual man judges all things, but is himself to be judged by no one" (1 Cor 2:13–15). This is a speaking about God (*theologia*) in the Spirit, which is evidently grasped as such—and not rejected as "folly"—only by those who themselves have

---

[5] Jean Yves Lacoste, "Zur Theologie des Geistes", *Internat. Kath. Zeitschrift Communio* 15/1 (1986), 1–7. The same view is put forward by Sergeï Bulgakov, *Le Paraclet* (Aubier, 1946), 167–69, and by Louis Bouyer, *Le Consolateur* (= C): "L'Esprit de Dieu . . . ne pourra jamais être à proprement parler l'objet de notre vision puisque c'est par lui que nous verrons Dieu" (Cerf, 1980), 451.

been endowed with the Spirit. But in this case, how can there be any objective and hence intelligible discourse? The answer is this: Such discourse must arise from that very center where the divine Logos (*Theo-Logos*) is *flesh* and so can translate God's speech into human speech. Volume 2 was concerned with this; it also pointed out that this Logos cannot be separated from the Pneuma. This applies equally to every "theology", whether put forth in terms of life or in concepts.

What we have just said can be illustrated by the two great liturgical hymns to the Holy Spirit. He who is "worshipped with the Father and the Son" can naturally be asked to exercise his functions, and this, together with the listing of the scriptural images and symbols for the Spirit, is the entire content of the hymns "Veni Sancte Spiritus" and "Veni Creator Spiritus". He who is "the highest gift of God" is asked to fill the "minds" and "hearts" of those who are his, healing their weakness, emptiness, restlessness, poverty, dejection, weariness, wretchedness, filth, rigidity, sickness, coldness, and waywardness through his coming, through his "heavenly radiance", his "most blessed light", his "sevenfold gift". The stanza is fashioned most carefully: "May we by thee the Father learn, / And know the Son, and thee discern, / Who art of both; and thus adore / In perfect faith for evermore."* This fully preserves the trinitarian formula, "in the Spirit through the Son to the Father".

Nonetheless, our prayer to the Spirit is not possible apart from the "conglorification" defined by the Second Council of Constantinople: "The triune God is worshipped and adored for his own sake. Thus in the trinitarian doxology the Spirit, too, becomes an 'object' of our worship."[6]

On this basis it is possible to get a first glimpse of the essential shape of Christian theology. The God who is initially "the unknown God", that is, the Spirit, causes his light to fall on the "known" God, the Incarnate One, bringing out the latter's significance as the Signifier, the Interpreter, of the invisible (and to that extent "unknown") Father. The Son can only be under-

---

*Translation in the *Yattendon Hymnal* (London, 1920).—TRANS.

[6] Jürgen Moltmann, "Die Einheit des dreieinigen Gottes", in *Trinität: Aktuelle Perspektiven der Theologie* (= T), QD 101 (Freiburg: Herder, 1984), 105.

stood as "the truth" (Jn 14:6) insofar as he is acknowledged to interpret the Father as the "other" (Jn 5:32) with whom he is yet "one" (Jn 10:30). Only in this way can the Son's truth be grasped; only thus can the Son be truly understood. With his light, therefore, the Spirit illuminates simultaneously the distinction and the identity between Father and Son. We see, but do not fully understand, the unity of distinction and identity; through the Spirit's act of interpreting, therefore, something both interpretable and beyond interpretation comes to light in the Incarnate One. What *can* be interpreted must be able to be grasped —to a certain extent—even by man's natural powers of insight; then it seems possible to isolate it and find a place for it, albeit an extraordinary one, in the human sphere. Jesus will then appear as a highly unusual man, a religious genius and the founder of a religion; he will be regarded as "the one imbued with grace", who succeeded in understanding God as a Father (so Harnack and all forms of Christian liberalism). While this *seems* to be part of the truth, it is no part of what Jesus calls truth or of what the Spirit wishes to show us. "The flesh is of no avail; the words that I have spoken to you [and my deeds and my whole being] are spirit and life", and it is only "the spirit that gives life" (Jn 6:63). Every exegesis of Jesus that fails to see that his very essence is to interpret the Father is nothing but "the letter that killeth" (2 Cor 3:6 AV). Here, in the interpretation of Jesus, we find the abyss between *sarx* and *pneuma*, or between *gramma* and *pneuma*, resulting in the christological gap between the mere *littera* and the *allegoria*. (This gap exists, in a somewhat different sense, between the Old Covenant as *littera* and its truth in the New Covenant. Origen regards the New Covenant as the enspirited letter; to that extent it is an "otherwise speaking" [*allos + agorein*], uttering the same thing but in a different and deeper sense.) In Christ himself the *littera* is the *flesh* (which on its own is "of no avail"); yet we may not jump over the flesh to reach the Spirit's interpretation: "Unless you eat my flesh, you have no life in you." In fact, that flesh that is illumined by the Spirit and, in Christ, actually contains the Spirit is an inalienable part of the "truth". This truth, since it is the living Christ, cannot be understood theoretically but only by being lived; hence the "tropological" sense of Scripture, the *littera-sarx*. We must live

it, and live it together with Christ, going with him, through his
death, to the Father; this is the "anagogical" sense of Scripture.
No theology can do without these dimensions, otherwise it will
get stuck in the *sarx-littera*, which are "of no avail". To speak
of Christ merely interpreting the Father without appropriating
the *content* of this interpreting is to fail to rise to the level of
Christian theology.

The illuminating Spirit (*lux beatissima*), takes complete possession of the theologizing human subject (*cordis intima*). Through
his own mystery, the Spirit grants insight into the mystery of the
Son who interprets the Father, insight into him and his relationship with the Father ("We have received . . . the Spirit which is
from God, that we might understand the gifts bestowed on us by
God" [1 Cor 2:12]). Thus liberal theology, which thinks itself so
wise but in reality is foolishness, is led farther toward insight into
"God's secret and hidden wisdom" (1 Cor 2:7). This wisdom,
with regard to its human recipient, can be described neither as
knowledge nor as ignorance, nor even as a partial knowledge
and partial ignorance: rather, it is what Paul calls—in many cir-
cumlocutions—"knowing that which surpasses knowledge" (cf.
Eph 3:19), a being "fully understood" (1 Cor 13:12), or a being
already known by God (1 Cor 8:3; cf. Phil 3:12). It is a being
overwhelmed by a knowledge that is too great for our capacity;
hence it can be termed neither apophatic nor kataphatic, neither
in this life nor in eternal life, when we shall see and know God
through God himself, though not in any comprehensive way. It
is not that God holds back something of himself from us; on
the contrary, his very nature is always to give more than we can
grasp. J. Pieper speaks of the "bottomless chalice of light" (*Das
unaustrinkbare Licht* [2d ed., 1963]): "There is so much light that
a particular finite faculty of knowing cannot drain it; it eludes the
attempt to grasp it" (32). Adrienne von Speyr makes bold to say
that this "excess" is inherent in God's nature: In his trinitarian
life he is continually being surprised by the "ever-greater" that
he is. For the theologian, all this is precisely the interpretative
work of the Holy Spirit: making the Son and the Father known
in this manner, he also makes himself known as God's "excess".

It cannot be said, therefore, that we are condemned to a gnostic
or mystic silence concerning the Spirit, like many non-Christian

religions that feel obliged to embrace an apophatic silence. The liturgy says of the Spirit: "Scientiam habet vocis",[7] which can be interpreted as meaning that the Spirit both recognizes the voice of God in the Son's Word—and causes it to resound through the whole world—and also imparts the correct meaning and tone to the answering human voices. This indicates that it would be wrong to develop a theology of the Spirit in parallel to that of the Son or of the Father; it also implies that an authentic theology, however simple or learned it professes to be, can only be developed *in* the Holy Spirit. We shall demonstrate this later, in speaking of the relationship between the Spirit and the Christian in the Church (part 4). By way of anticipation we can say that, since every grasp or "experience" of the Spirit is indirect, we are forbidden to prescribe any anthropologically normative mode of access. Neither the forms of "enthusiasm", which can be highly ambivalent (in their pagan days the Corinthians were "led astray to dumb idols", 1 Cor 12:2), nor certain ecstatic phenomena in early Jewish prophecy nor the lofty utterances of secular wisdom (which are shown up as mere folly in God's sight, 1 Cor 1:21) nor the courage shown at the hour of death by martyrs for some religious or secular ideal can be reliable signs of the presence of the divine Spirit. The Spirit never points to himself or places himself in the limelight; he is always the Spirit of the Son and the Father, and it is on their love—without revealing its source as such—that his light falls.

[7] Introit for the preconciliar Mass of Pentecost, cf. Wis 1:7 (LXX and Vulgate). The authentic sense is that God's Spirit of wisdom knows the voices (the speech) of men.

CAN THERE BE A
SPIRIT-CHRISTOLOGY?

This question, which will be taken up in part 3, needs closer definition if it is to find a meaningful answer within dogmatic theology. It is not a matter of casting doubt on the enterprise of Christology as such or of changing its fundamental premises; the only question is whether it could or should be given a broader context in the framework of a Pneumatology. While, from the point of view of salvation history, the revelation of God's trinitarian essence begins with the Father and is accomplished objectively in the Son's Incarnation, in fact such revelation is not brought to its conclusion until the outpouring of the Spirit, who interprets to subjects of all times and places what has objectively been made known. And is it not true that the *ultimum in executione* is necessarily *primum in intentione*? All his life, Karl Barth had tried to come to grips, at a profound level, with Schleiermacher, a man whose followers had come nowhere near his "calibre"; in a much-quoted afterword to an edition of the selected writings of Schleiermacher, the old Barth had admitted to a certain "painful embarrassment" in his regard: he found himself wondering whether Schleiermacher might not perhaps be understood in the context of a comprehensive "theology of the third article", the Holy Spirit. Should he, Barth, without giving up his own position, have perhaps written his work with the Spirit in mind? Then:

> All that is to be believed, reflected upon, and said concerning God the Father and God the Son, in the sense of the first and second articles, . . . should be shown to depend on God the Holy Spirit, the *vinculum pacis inter Patrem et Filium*. One would have to show God's whole work for the sake of his creature, for and with man, in its single teleology, excluding all chance. . . . But in that case would not justification, sanctification, and vocation have to be located under this sign? Not to mention the creation as the Father's *opus proprium*. Would not Christology itself, which governs

33

everything (*conceptus de Spiritu Sancto!*), receive illumination from this quarter?[1]

Barth concludes with a warning: "To set forth and develop a theology of the third article, we shall need only 'learned Thebans', people who are solidly grounded, spiritually and intellectually."[2] In what follows we shall see that at least *one* learned scholar, in the long series of defaulters, took up this task, but that he too failed. After him we find only fragments indicating what might deserve to be called a Catholic Spirit-Christology. Such a Spirit-Christology could in no way "get beyond" the central place occupied by the Incarnation of the Logos, but, taking its cue from the "conceptus de Spiritu Sancto" referred to by Barth, it would consider whether the Spirit was not already involved, not only as the agent of the Incarnation, but also as the One who acts in the Old Testament—*qui locutus est per prophetas*[3]—prior to the Incarnation (where he had the initiative). This would be the place to revisit the "trinitarian inversion" we spoke of in *Theo-Drama* III, 183f. and to reconsider its validity, presuppositions, and consequences.[4]

---

[1] *Schleiermacher-Auswahl*, afterword by Karl Barth, Siebenstern Taschenbuch 113/114 (1968), 311.

[2] Ibid., 312.

[3] The words "who spoke through the prophets" inserted in the Creed of Constantinople, "which of course had a long history in creeds and went back to the primitive kerygma of Christendom, recalled the verse of 2 Peter 1:21, 'For no prophecy ever came by the will of man, but men spake from God, being moved by the Holy Spirit": J. N. D. Kelly, *Early Christian Creeds* (London, 1950; 2d ed., 1960), 341. Cf. also 1 Peter 1:11. "In 1 Peter, accordingly, it is an accepted teaching that the Spirit speaks in the prophets": K. H. Schelkle, *Die Petrusbriefe* (Herder, 1961), 40. But the Epistle of Peter calls this "Holy Spirit" (v. 12) who speaks in the prophets the "Spirit of Christ" (v. 11), which many take to be "an assertion of Christ's pneumatic pre existence", while others (the majority) take it to refer to "the Spirit, who was manifestly given in New Testament times as the Spirit belonging to Christ" (ibid., 41 n. 2.). Schelkle gives a thorough treatment of the relationship between Old Testament prophecy and its fulfillment in Christ in his book *Die Passion Jesu in der Verkündigung des Neuen Testaments* (Heidelberg, 1949), 81–104 (with bibliography).

[4] So Bulgakov (see n. 5 above), 237f.: "L'ordre des agissements des hypostases dans le monde est l'inverse de leur *taxis*: l'action de la Troisième hypostase précède la descente de la Deuxième. . . . La Pentecôte de la Mère de Dieu précède

Three main topics need to be discussed here, although in this chapter we shall devote closer attention only to the second. The first topic will be considered in connection with Scripture, and the difficult, third topic will be discussed in a special section concerning the relationship between the Logos and the Spirit in bringing about the hypostatic union.

First it must not be forgotten that God's whole address to the world—seen from the point of view of the New Testament—was trinitarian right from the beginning. This is indicated, though darkly, in the very first verse of the Bible: God (the Father) brings forth the world by his very utterance (the Son), while the Spirit, brooding over chaos, imposes order on formless nothingness. As the Old Testament moves toward the New it becomes clearer and clearer that God not only brings the world into being, but also rules it and finally redeems it "with both his hands" (Word and Spirit, according to Irenaeus): these two, inseparable, operate together in the Old Covenant, though not yet recognized as "Persons"; in the New Covenant they are equally inseparable, but now distinct. Ultimately, God's self-surrender and self-giving, understood as "gift", will be given the name "Holy Spirit": this means, notwithstanding the trinitarian periodizing of salvation history,[5] that this Spirit must have been at work from the very beginning in creation and in the establishing of the covenant.

Secondly we must address what we have termed the "trinitarian inversion". Understood in its whole breadth, this means that the christological center of the economy of salvation is framed by a Pneumatology that precedes and succeeds it. First we shall have to unpack a number of naïve, early Christian "Spirit-Christologies" and analogous theologoumena, before examining the greatest attempt (Hegel's) to construct a "Spirit-

---

l'Incarnation. . . . C'est seulement par la vertu de cette descente de l'Esprit que s'est manifesté la venue du Verbe."

[5] First stated explicitly in Gregory Nazianzen, *Or.* 31 (*theol.* 5), 26—27 (PG 36, 161C—164C). If the highest revelation of God—the Holy Spirit who interprets all things—was to be borne and assimilated, it required a long period of maturation in mankind.

Christology" and assessing its greatness and its limitations. Next we shall devote some attention to the "Spirit dimension" in Christology as categorically demanded by contemporary Catholic theology, without one-sidedly setting Spirit-Christology against Logos-Christology. This second topic will be discussed in somewhat more detail in the present chapter.

A *third* issue has occupied the christological treatises since medieval times. Initially, even if the Father and the Spirit are conceived as collaborating in it, the hypostatic union of a human nature with the divine "Person" of the Logos seems to concern the Son alone, to such an extent that a direct involvement of the Spirit (who, after all, does not become man) seems excluded. However, since Christ's humanity, united to the divine Word, must simultaneously possess all holiness and be the source of all human sanctification, we cannot say that it is not equipped with the gifts of the Spirit. The question, therefore, will be this: Does the sanctification experienced by the humanity of Christ in the hypostatic union (that is, his "substantial holiness") include *eminenter* every subsequent, "accidental" sanctification by the Spirit or not? And if not, does Christ's humanity need a special, indispensable sanctification (*gratia creata*) effected by the Spirit, enabling him, as *caput*, to exercise his mission? This series of problems is related to the second issue, since it seems to presuppose that, as many Fathers say and some modern theologians (Scheeben) repeat, the Logos himself "takes" his human nature, which cannot be completely reconciled with the principle "conceptus a Spiritu Sancto". We must defer discussion of this third issue until later.

Here, considering the concept of Spirit-Christology in its more strict sense, we are addressing only the second issue. We shall present it in four parts: (1) The alleged Spirit-Christology of the apostolic Fathers. (2) Hegel's Spirit-Christology. (3) The role of the Spirit in the Incarnation of the Logos according to Scripture and the Creed. (4) The theological requirements of a contemporary pneumatic Christology.

a. Primitive Christian Spirit-Christology

On the one hand, the apostolic Fathers embrace the biblical concept of the Spirit simply and ingenuously, seeing it as a divine totality. They understand it not only as the *ruah Yahweh* in its manifold forms of revelation—and the utterances of the prophets constitute one particularly clear and important form[6]—but also as that unity of spirit and wisdom which is emphasized in the Book of Wisdom.[7] On the other hand, they are confronted by the Johannine axiom that God is spirit (Jn 4:24), the Pauline statement that the risen "Lord [Christ] is the Spirit" (2 Cor 3:17) and a "life-giving spirit" (1 Cor 15:45), and the Lucan promise that the "Holy Spirit" will come down upon Mary to effect the Incarnation (Lk 1:35)—whereby the Man who thus comes into being is denoted by John as "flesh" (*sarx*). It is no surprise, therefore, that the divine sphere from which Jesus comes is called "pneuma" and the human is called "flesh", with no reflection as yet on the distinction between Pneuma and Logos in God. In 2 Clement 9, 5, is it clear that "Spirit" refers to the sphere of the divine but also that of Christ and of the Church, while at the same time Christ is called "Spirit" and the Church is called "flesh"; the Church "was made manifest in the flesh of Christ, showing us that if any of us guard her in the flesh without corruption, he shall receive her back again in the Holy Spirit. For this flesh is an anti-type of the Spirit; no one therefore who has corrupted the anti-type shall receive the reality" (2 Clem 14:2f.).* Several biblical ideas intersect here; the latter analogy between flesh/anti-type and spirit/reality prevents this theology from sliding into gnosticism. Ignatius of Antioch speaks equally ingenuously of the "undivided pneuma, which is Jesus Christ" (*Magn.* 15);

---

[6] Two New Testament passages very clearly asserted that the prophets spoke in the Spirit: 2 Tim 3:16; 2 Pet 1:19–21; cf. also 2 Pet 3:2. Similarly Clement of Rome 45, 2; 16, 2; 8, 1; 13, 1; Ignatius of Antioch, *Magn.* 8, 2; *Philad.* 5, 2; Theophilus of Antioch I, 14; II, 9; II, 30, 33; Irenaeus, *Adv. Haer.* III, 21, 4; IV, 11, 1; 14, 2; 20, 8; Justin, 1 *Apol.* 39.

[7] Irenaeus, *Adv. Haer.* II, 30, 9; III, 24, 2; IV, 7, 4; 20, 1–4, 9; V, 36, 3. Theophilus of Antioch, *Ad Autol.* 1, 7; cf. 2, 18.

*Loeb Classical Library, vol. 1, trans. Kirsopp Lake.—TRANS.

Melito of Sardis says that "through his passible flesh he put an end to the suffering of the flesh, and through his immortal spirit he killed that death which destroys men";[8] and the Letter of Barnabas describes the body as "the vessel of the spirit" (7, 3; 11, 9). Theophilus of Antioch, too, can equate God's Word with his Spirit, his wisdom and power (*Autol.* II, 10).[9] No one is thinking in terms of adoptionism here. Things are more difficult in the confused Christology of the *Shepherd* of Hermas, which first speaks of a "servant" who is termed the "son" (in Sim. V, 5); but Similitude V, 6:5–7, introduces a "body" that merits, on account of its good life, to be "chosen" by God "as a fellow of the Holy Spirit". However, Similitude IX, 12:1f., supersedes this construction in the direction of an orthodox Christology: The Son exists from all eternity but has manifested himself in the end-time as the Door through which everyone may enter into the Kingdom of God.

W. Pannenberg has observed that every Christology that begins with the presence of the Spirit in Christ inevitably falls into the trap of adoptionism,[10] since it cannot make the qualitative dis-

---

[8] *Peri Pascha*, SC 123, 96–97.

[9] On this, cf. F. Loofs, "Theophilus von Antiochien Adversus Marcionem", TU 46, 2 (Leipzig, 1930). Loofs constructs a systematic Spirit-Christology from this, against which A. Grillmeier rightly protests, in his *Christ in Christian Tradition* I, 2d ed. (London, 1975). Theodor Rüsch, in his *Die Entstehung der Lehre vom Heiligen Geist* (Zürich, 1952), correctly observes that the authors in this "childhood stage of pneumatic teaching" (13) are "witnesses" who "speak and write in the Spirit" (12; cf. 129ff.). This does not mean that they are charismatics in the Corinthian sense but that they are familiar with the "decisive movement of the *pneuma* toward the word" (39); in them the "concept of the Spirit is moving in the direction of the subsequent trinitarian profession of faith" (56). Cf. Ignatius, *Magn.* 13, 1–2. In Irenaeus, "spirit" is primarily God's *dynamis* by which Christ has accomplished his entire work of salvation (*Adv. Haer.* II, 32, 5); the spiritual man actually is given an insight into this (IV, 33, 1 and 7). From here there is an inevitable road to the Spirit's *homoousia* (124), but also to an analogy (!) between the christological assertion "of Chalcedon and the assertion of the Spirit's undivided and unconfused indwelling in believers" (133). See also H. Opitz, *Ursprünge frühchristlicher Pneumatologie* (Berlin, 1960), D. W. Hauschild, *Gottes Geist und der Mensch: Studien zur frühchristlichen Pneumatologie*, Beiträge z. Ev. Theol., 63 (Munich, 1972). The best book on the true meaning of Spirit-Christology in the earliest Fathers is A. Gilg, *Weg und Bedeutung der altchristlichen Christologie* (reprint, Munich, 1955), 18–20.

[10] *Jesus—God and Man* (Philadelphia and Westminster, 1968), 120–21.

tinction between a prophet and Christ. Evidently this is not yet true of the "naïve" Spirit-christology of the Apostolic Fathers, but it shows itself, as we have seen, in certain passages in the *Shepherd* of Hermas. Once the Church's Christology was aware of this, it quickly changed its model from Pneuma-sarx to Logos-sarx. We may find hints of a conscious Spirit-Christology in the heterodox Jewish-Christian Ebionitism, which regards Jesus as no more than a prophet illumined by the Spirit,[11] but later adoptionism, beginning with the elder and younger Theodotus and continued in Artemon of Rome, is not part of this current of thought: for them, Christ no longer consists of Pneuma and flesh. This applies too, of course, to Paul of Samosata, a strict Monarchian, whereas the great Antiochenes—who held fast to Nicaea—were drawn into the wake of a "christology of separation" that came to a head in Nestorius.

It is well known that the theology of the Holy Spirit was not worked out until the period between Nicaea, where Logos-Christology finally asserted itself without subordinationism, and Constantinople I, although the Matthean baptismal formula and the trinitarian liturgical prayer had long since established themselves.[12] One reason for this late theological development may be the fact, already noted, that the Spirit cannot be objectified; there is a certain reticence to pry into the Spirit's mystery. As Cyril of Jerusalem says, "You should not be curious to search out the Spirit's nature and essence. We should not dare to speak of things that are not in holy writ."[13] Gregory Nazianzen, when asked whether we worship the Spirit, replies, "The Spirit is he in whom and through whom we worship. So to pray and worship in the Spirit means nothing other than this: By him we bring prayer and worship to him."[14]

---

[11] J. Daniélou, *Théologie du Judéo-Christianisme*, Histoire des doctrines chrétiennes avant Nicée I (Desclée, 1958), 75.

[12] It was Jules Lebreton, in his *Histoire du dogme de la Trinité* vol. II, bk. III 4th ed. (1928), 133–247, who pointed out that these two ideas had a decisive role in shaping the doctrine of the Trinity.

[13] *Catech*. XVI, 2.

[14] *Fifth Theol. Oration*, 12 (PG 36, 145C).

b. A "Speculative Pentecost"

This expression comes from Hegel,[15] and there can be no doubt that Hegel produced the most comprehensive outline of a Spirit-Christology, that is, a theological philosophy in which the Spirit is that which is the all-embracing, the Alpha and Omega, yet in such a way that it is centered in a Christology that alone renders it intelligible as Spirit. It is well known that Hegel understood his philosophy to be coextensive with the essence of Christian theology; it is also well known that he despised all theology that could not rise to the level of a philosophical consideration of its content, regarding it as "salt that has lost its savor", spirit-less exegesis springing from Enlightenment rationalism, "arrogant, self-satisfied barrenness".[16] To avoid this, he said, religion should "take refuge in philosophy".[17] Not only the "Hegelian right" of those days, but also many protagonists of modern Protestant and Catholic theology—Barth, Jüngel, Pannenberg, Moltmann, K. Rahner (though he is perhaps closer to Kant and Fichte), Küng, Bruaire, Chapelle, Brito, A. Léonard, G. Fessard—are unthinkable apart from Hegel. It is beyond doubt that Hegel wanted, as a philosopher, to think through the Christian idea; for him, philosophy had no new subject matter beyond Christianity.[18] Likewise it is clear that, for him, the divine Trinity is central to his theological philosophy. There is no question of presenting his system here; we can only raise two questions that are relevant to our topic: Does Hegel have a Spirit-Christology? Is Hegel's "Spirit" the Holy Spirit?

---

[15] *Berliner Schriften*, ed. Hoffmeister (Hamburg: F. Meiner, 1956), 327 (= B1).

[16] *Philosophie der Religion*, ed. Lasson (3d reprint, 1974), II/2, 230 (= PR). "Thus God is the one and only object of philosophy. . . . This means that philosophy is theology and that to be concerned with it, or rather in it, is worship": ibid., I/1, 30.

[17] Ibid., 231.

[18] *Geschichte der Philosophie*, in *Sämtliche Werke*, ed. Glockner (1949–1968), XIX, 8.

α. On Hegel's Spirit-Christology

The central question we must ask Hegel is this: Does he acknowledge an immanent Trinity? Or is the abstract concept of God as the Infinite and Absolute filled with reality only when it changes over into finitude (nature and history), becoming Spirit in becoming aware of this distinction—the highest instance being in the God-man Jesus and in his death on the Cross? Is it only in this way that the Spirit, poured out upon the Church and the world, brings about (for the first time) God's fullness? There is only one answer to this: Yes, Hegel has an immanent Trinity in view, but it is an immanent Trinity that "sublates"* the economic Trinity in itself, by moving through time and "erasing it".[19] This comes at the conclusion of the *Phenomenology of the Spirit*, which follows the Spirit's manifold ascents to the Absolute; but the end of these ascents (which is the vital divine Spirit) shows itself in philosophy of religion to be the absolute beginning.[20] This does not, however, put an end to the forward march portrayed in his great *Logic* and in the *Phenomenology*; so it is undeniable that "Hegel's trinitarian speculation does not unfold, as in Greek theology, according to the principle of magnanimity that knows no envy, but rather according to the principle of lack:

---

* Hegel uses the word *aufheben* in a technical sense in his philosophy; it means "to supersede—and hence abolish—by taking to a higher level in the dialectical process."—TRANS.

[19] "Time is that concept which *is there*, offering itself to consciousness as an empty perception; thus the Spirit necessarily appears in time, and it appears in time as long as it has not *grasped* its pure concept, that is, as long as it has not erased time": *Phänomenologie des Geistes*, in Glockner, *Werke*, II, 612.

[20] "The Idea gives itself existence in *nature* and, thereby coming to itself, makes itself Spirit, that is, knowledge of itself. Thus God is the result of philosophy; yet not merely the result, but that which eternally brings forth itself and, hence, is prior. The one-sidedness of the result is sublated in the result itself . . . , namely, that it thus knows itself to be the absolute First": PR I/1, 32. This does not mean "that Hegel has [failed to] distinguish God's internal trinitarian life from the world process", as Pannenberg suggests, quoting from section 244 of the Enzyklopädie: "The absolute freedom of the Idea, however, is that it does not simply *pass over* into life, or cause the latter to shine forth in it as finite knowledge, but *resolves*, in its own absolute truth, . . . freely to propagate itself as nature" (*Gottesgedanke und menschliche Freiheit* [Göttingen, 1972], 99–100).

the latter causes the primal Lack of the Abstract Universal and the innate lack of particularity to sublate each other reciprocally in the Spirit's ultimate consent to be torn asunder—as a necessary stage in making reconciliation freely available."[21] There is no way of getting beyond this two-sided system: one can think "from God's viewpoint" or "from man's viewpoint";[22] one can conceive of God's concrete fullness as cradling and sublating all finitude in its infinity, or as the process of this sublating through nature and history, as the unfolding concretion of the fullness that is to be filled. The second aspect predominates where the "creation" of the world (as God's "Other", or the "Other" in God) is equated with the Son, who only at the end of the world process steps forth as the concrete Son of God in Jesus Christ. One could object that the Son's eternal *processio* already and always contains his *missio* and that he is brought forth from all eternity as the One-who-becomes-man; but such an identification would fail to respect the distinction between generation and creation. And if one were to assume, like the Greek Fathers, that all the ideas of the world (*ennoiai*) were really contained in the Logos from all eternity, one would be brought, within the Hegelian system, to the Cartesian notion that, since in God there is a unity of thinking and willing, there can be no other ideas but those that are realizable; this would put a question mark over God's creative freedom. Finally, since for Hegel it is nonsense to speak of a continuation of life once the finite being has been sublated in death, it must be asked whether, for him, the Christian "image" of Christ's Resurrection and Ascension can be anything other than "the outpouring of the Spirit, which could only come about . . . once the physical, immediate presence [of Jesus] had ceased".[23]

---

[21] A. Chapelle, *Hegel et la religion* (Paris: Éditions Universitaires, 1963–1966), II, 106.

[22] PR I/1, 200–201.

[23] Ibid., II/2, 194. "The finite is not true being; within being it is the dialectic whereby it sublates and negates itself, and its negation is the affirmation as infinite" (PR I/1, 218). Ultimately, therefore, resurrection and ascension are nothing other than what will be portrayed in the Spirit-community, subsequently, as the cultic "lifting oneself to God" (PR I/1, 228ff.), as "self-consciousness". Here God is not merely the "object of consciousness" but "the witness of the Spirit" (252), making it clear that the believer's knowledge of God is to be understood "only

This physical presence, however, has already come to an end with the death of Christ; thus this death, the negation of the negation of the finitude of the man Jesus, is as such the true origin of the Spirit. "The death of Christ is the center around which everything turns; the way it is conceived distinguishes the external conception (as in Socrates, for instance)[24] from that of faith, that is, as viewed with the Spirit, by the Spirit of truth, by the Holy Spirit."[25] For Hegel, the Cross is "the highest pinnacle of finitude", "the divine self-emptying, yet in such a way that, in this very self-emptying, it remains itself", and, "to that extent, it is the highest love. . . . The monstrous union of these extremes [identity and otherness] is love"[26]—and precisely this is the Spirit. "Spirit is only Spirit in that it is the negative of the negative, which therefore contains the negative within itself."[27] It is simultaneously reconciliation in the most extreme pain. For, according to Hegel, the "highest pinnacle of finitude" experiences its ultimate nothingness in evil,[28] so that by his death on the Cross, Christ has "taken upon himself the pain of evil and of his own alienation" and "simultaneously abolished it in his death".[29] Hegel affirms the "for us", the "satisfaction" aspect of this death, and rejects Kant's objection that it is only the individual who can atone for his own sins: this death "represents the absolute history of the divine Idea".[30] This only makes sense if this "life of Christ", which seems merely "natural and ordinary",[31] always and already possessed the (eternal, holy) Spirit in a unique way. Only thus could Christ's life have brought forth or set free the Spirit at his death. This brings us directly to the

---

as a knowledge of God within him" (253). Or as Meister Eckhart says, "the eye with which God sees me is the eye with which I see him; my eye and his eye are one" (257). When we "lift ourselves to God", we "pass over from the finite to the absolute infinite" (206).

[24] Ibid., 109.
[25] Ibid., 170.
[26] Ibid., 157–58.
[27] Ibid., 163.
[28] Ibid., 173.
[29] Ibid.
[30] Ibid., 159.
[31] Ibid., 157.

second problem of Hegelian Spirit-Christology: Is the Spirit who was in Jesus prior to his reconciling death, and hence was already in the world throughout the entire prehistory that looked toward Jesus, the "Holy Spirit"?

β. Spirit and Holy Spirit

What does the Holy Spirit bring with him when he is poured out upon the community? It is that "this objective Spirit should posit itself, realize itself, in the community; just as, at first, it was posited objectively, so now it posits itself subjectively."[32]

> It is only in the mode of thought that history attains the form in which it attracts the absolute interest of the Spirit. On the one hand, this "Third" (after Father and Son) is *what had always been in the Son*, namely, the Spirit's self-objectification as the unity of the First and the Second, with the result that this Second, this "Other", is sublated in the eternal love. . . . On the other hand, contrariwise, . . . it is true that the infinite Spirit does not indwell him objectively, but brings the Spirit forth in him; it brings itself forth in self-consciousness.[33]

So it is the community that first discerns that God is Spirit; only the Church, in the Spirit, can interpret Christ's word in its whole depth and understand it, not as mere history, but as something "absolutely present".[34]

However true this "on the other hand" is, it does not help us to cope with the meaning of the antecedent "on the one hand". For Hegel, of course, God is spirit, and his entire logic and philosophy of nature and of history is (in a more comprehensive sense) a genesis or phenomenology of spirit. What Hegel describes as the national spirits that unite in the world spirit, what he portrays as the spirit of the (pre-Christian) state—all this is *objective* spirit, and even if it is understood as the "agent of Absolute Spirit", it is not (yet) subjective spirit but only a moment in the "history of God".[35] (We are entitled to speak of a "history of God", since

[32] Ibid., 196.
[33] Ibid., 197.
[34] Ibid., 198.
[35] Ibid., 54.

God freely chooses to engage with historical man and, as Karl Rahner says, while remaining immutable in himself, chooses to be mutable in the "Other".)[36] This brings us back, however, to that "enclosed circle" of Hegelian philosophy to which we have already referred, "in which the First is also the Last, and the Last also becomes the First."[37] If the Father is "the eternal Universal" and the Son "the infinite Particular", then "the Spirit is individuality as such, but all three are Spirit. In the Third . . . God is Spirit, but the latter has a presupposition, namely, that the Third is the First. . . . It is the same in love given and love returned: where love is, its utterance and all its actions are only ratifications of it, simultaneously bringing it forth and sustaining it. But what is brought forth already is; it is a ratification; nothing comes forth but what already is. The Spirit, similarly, presupposes itself: it is that-which-begins."[38] "The Last is the First."[39] If this principle, presupposing the dialectic of positing and sublating, applies at all stages (or preliminary stages) of Spirit, for example, in "natural religions" with a dying and rising god "as in the death of Adonis in Syrian religion and the death of Osiris in Egyptian religion"; that is, if the element of conflict and pain is present everywhere here,[40] then it follows that "the element of spirit" is part and parcel of religion, even if only "indirectly" and "in the form of naturalness". This being so, we would have to ask whether Christ's death on the Cross is qualitatively different from these dialectical spirit-"conversions" and, hence, whether it is appropriate to attribute a special indwelling of the Holy Spirit to the consciousness of the historical Jesus, even if he proclaims the "Kingdom of God" and brotherly love.[41] Hegel seems to do this,[42] but he ultimately contradicts his own assertion that the

---

[36] "On the Theology of Incarnation", in *Theological Investigations*, vol. 4 (London and Baltimore, 1966). Cf. W. Kern: " 'Geschichte Gottes' als Geist-Geschichte", in W. Kasper, ed., *Gegenwart des Geistes: Aspekte der Pneumatologie* (= GG), QD 85 (Herder, 1979), 70–90.

[37] *Wissenschaft der Logik*, ed. Lasson, 2d ed. (1966) I, 56.

[38] PR II/2, 72–73.

[39] Ibid., 62; cf. I/1, 32.

[40] PR I/II, 213–15.

[41] PR II/2, 143.

[42] He adduces sayings such as "I and my Father are one" or points to the scene

(Holy) Spirit is identical with the reconciliation between heaven and earth that takes place in the absolute disintegration of death on the Cross.[43] Thus Hegel's Christology can be called Spirit-Christology only in a very general (philosophical) sense.

Here, however, a further question raises its head. Hegel may speak of divine "persons", but is his spirit to be understood in any sense as a third Person in God? L. Oeing-Hanhoff has studied this question and come to a negative answer.[44] This throws a good deal of doubt on Hegel's "speculative Pentecost". For Hegel, Being is necessarily self-presentation: Spirit, conceived as thought, is always both what thinks and what is thought. Thomas would call it the "inner word". Hegel, however, holds the identity of these two (Father and Son, in Christian terms) to be the Spirit. "This makes Three: the One, the Other, and the Unity of Both. This concrete Idea is known to us . . . as the Trinity-in-Unity."[45] In contrast to this definition of Hegel's, "according to the traditional doctrine of the Trinity, the third Divine Person is by no means constituted by the unity that is maintained in the distinction and otherness of the Persons."[46] The merely reciprocal love of Father and Son only yields a binity. What is missing is the miracle of fruitfulness, of "gift" above and beyond (in nature, the image here is the child); this points us back to an earlier remark, namely, that the Hegelian God has no sovereign freedom in creating. "Hegel, the philosopher of spirit, has forgotten the Holy Spirit, or, more precisely, he has failed to advert to the Spirit's distinctive, personal mode of being and has completely reinterpreted what the Church says about him."[47]

---

with the woman taken in adultery: "Here his elevation of spirit (becomes) visible, . . . this tremendous majesty of spirit that can reverse all that has taken place and pronounce it to be so reversed": ibid., 148.

[43] "Death is *above all* . . . this element whereby the spirit is reconciled with itself, with what it itself is. . . . This negative element, which belongs only to the spirit as such, is its inner conversion, its inner change": ibid., 158–59.

[44] "Hegel's Trinitätslehre: Zur Aufgabe ihrer Kritik und Rezeption", *Theologie und Philosophie* 52 (1977): 378–407.

[45] *Phänomenologie des Geistes*, ed. Hoffmeister, 6th ed. (1952), 534.

[46] Oeing-Hanhoff, "Hegels Trinitätslehre", 371, n. 30.

[47] Ibid., 334–35. The "personal character of the Holy Spirit is seen primarily in the fact that the *spiratio activa* whereby Father and Son act as 'we' is not itself a

Hegel's utterly serious intention of making the divine Trinity the central plank of his theological philosophy—which he pursues unrelentingly to the very end, in opposition to the past (the Enlightenment, Kant) and the present (Schleiermacher)—threatens to turn into a version of modalism because of his universal application of the dialectical method. Since the creation is imported into the immanent Trinity, the place of the *personal* Other (*der Andere*) in God must be taken by the *impersonal* Other (*das Andere*); this means that, in the Incarnation, when the Son steps forth as the personal Other (*der Andere*) he does so as the apex of the creation (the impersonal Other, *das Andere*), but if there had been no evolution of the world, there would have been no divine Son, either. Hegel's method presupposes that between the Divine Persons there is not only a contrast, but a "contradiction" (albeit one that is constantly being sublated), which Karl Barth terms "Hegel's boldest and most weighty innovation."[48] One consequence is that "Error, lying and sin, with Hegel, can only signify obstinate one-sidedness, a blind lingering and stopping which represents a departure from obedience to the self-movement of the concept."[49]

Yet: "His doctrine of the Trinity, unsatisfactory as it may be from the theological point of view, is anything but a retrospective adaptation of his philosophy to comply with the wishes of the theologians. . . . In propounding it Hegel was theologizing in his own way, alone and acknowledging no master, against the philosophers *and* against the theologians."[50]

Person", although it is possible to say that the common *actio* of Father and Son, as the *actio* of both of them, is "the *actus purus* in its personal aspect". H. Mühlen, *Der Heilige Geist als Person* (= GP) 2d ed. (Münster, 1966), 156–57; see the whole context in 143–67. Astonishingly, Oeing-Hanhoff discovers the same form of Trinity in Karl Barth (*Church Dogmatics*) I/1, 304ff., and IV/2, 43f. Cf. also section 67, 614–840), which confirms my own view that Barth's mode of thought is Idealist (see my *The Theology of Karl Barth*, trans. Edward T. Oakes. [San Francisco: Ignatius Press, Communio Books, 1992], 220ff.).

[48] *Die protestantische Theologie im 19. Jahrhundert* (Zürich: Zollikon, 1947), 359. [Selected chapters in *From Rousseau to Ritschl* (London: SCM, 1959); here 285.] The origin of this "contradiction" is discussed in the chapter on Luther in volume 2 of *Theo-Logic*, trans. Adrian Walker (San Francisco: Ignatius Press, 2004).

[49] *From Rousseau to Ritschl*, 286.

[50] Ibid., 298.

c. Biblical Starting Points for a Spirit-Christology

Hegel's great plan presented a comprehensive doctrine of the Spirit with a christological center but no biblical doctrine of the Holy Spirit. Next, therefore, we must look for a starting point for a biblical Spirit Christology before (in the next section) going on to consider the position of the Spirit in the entire corpus of Scripture. The starting point is to be found in the event of Incarnation that has already been characterized in some detail in *Theo-Drama* III, 165–91, by two basic concepts: the "a priori obedience" of Jesus, who does not "take" his humanity but "entrusts himself" to the Spirit who makes him man; this involves an "inversion" in the transition from the immanent to the economic Trinity. Thus, without endangering or abolishing the immanent Trinity (TD III, 190), and in order to secure the a priori mission-obedience (which is "no mere passivity" but demands the highest degree of involvement: TD III, 186), the Spirit takes over the role of the active mediator: "Cette troisième personne, ne produisant rien d'éternel et d'incréé, produit le Verbe Incarné." "Vous faites en la terre cette opération d'Amour qui joint l'Être créé à l'Être incréé. Béni soyez-vous de cette sainte opération qui accomplit l'Incarnation du Verbe et la Déification suprême de la nature humaine."[51] In this "act" of the Spirit we can discern the fulfillment of his activity in the Old Covenant, an activity that, though pre-christological, has Christ as its goal: "qui locutus est per prophetas".

If we hold fast to the idea that the Son's Incarnation is already an act of his personal "economic" obedience, it becomes impossible to understand the overshadowing of the Virgin as an act common to all three Divine Persons; it must be a personal act of the Spirit.[52] One might counter the idea that the Logos

---

[51] Bérulle, *Grandeurs de Jésus*, in *Oeuvres Complètes* I (1646), 173.

[52] Bonaventure (3, d. 4, a. 1, q. 1) would like to attribute the *missio* personally to the Father, the Incarnation (*assumptio*) personally to the Son, but the *conceptio* to the common action of the three Persons; it is only *appropriated* to the Spirit. There are several reasons for this: First, he wishes to exclude the unholiness of fleshly conception, but then—which is more important—because the Holy Spirit comprehends the unity and community of the other two Persons. And, finally, because the Incarnation is the highest outpouring of divine goodness. "So the

does not himself take his human nature by citing Philippians 2:7, which speaks of a "taking" (*labōn*) "the form of man". But this statement is preceded by the one that says that the preexistent Christ "did not count [his divine form] a thing to be grasped, . . . but emptied himself" (v. 6) and "humbled himself and became obedient unto death, even death on a cross" (v. 8). This not-grasping, which is primary, governs the entire attitude of the Son in becoming man: in the obedience that has Incarnation as its goal, he *allows* himself to be transported into the womb of the Virgin; accordingly, the One who transports him there cannot be himself but only the Spirit.

The weightier objection to this thesis comes from exegesis: "Holy Spirit will overshadow you", we read, where "Holy Spirit" appears without the article and so indicates the traditional Old Testament meaning of "the spirit of Yahweh", that essentially impersonal power of God which belongs to his knowledge; this meaning is immediately added by way of explanation: *dynamis hypsistou* (Lk 1:35). Not until the Baptism of Jesus does "the Holy Spirit" (this time with the personalizing article) come down upon Jesus (Lk 3:22). In what follows we shall make many objections to this attempt to distinguish an impersonal power in God and a personal Holy Spirit when we come to discuss the Spirit's specific personhood. For the present it must suffice to point out that the article can be absent even where the Person of the Holy Spirit is clearly meant. Thus, for instance, when the risen Lord breathes on his disciples, he says: "Receive Holy Spirit" (Jn 20:22), namely, the same Spirit he had "breathed forth" in death along with the mission he had accomplished in

---

conception is appropriated to the Holy Spirit: first on the basis of what is his own, since he is the unity of both; and then on the basis of what is appropriated to him, since he is the goodness of both." This mere appropriation must be rejected for christological reasons. Nor does it lose its force as a result of Aquinas' distinctions in *S. Th.* III, 32, 1c and ad 1–2: Aquinas says that, in the common action of the three Persons, the mission is appropriated to the Father, the assumption of flesh is appropriated to the Son, and the "preparation and fashioning of the matter of Christ's body" is appropriated to the Spirit. This draws a distinction between mission and conception, which, "while they are one as concerns the subject (the Son), . . . are notionally distinct: the mission is attributed to the Father, the conception to the Holy Spirit, while it is the Logos who takes flesh." Cf. also *Contra Gentes* 4, 46.

the Spirit: "And he bowed his head and gave up *the* (Holy) Spirit" (Jn 19:30). And when, at his first sermon after his Baptism (Lk 4:18), Jesus claims as his own the anointing with "spirit of the Lord"—without article—(Is 61:1-2), there can be no doubt that he is also referring to the Spirit he received at his Baptism. Moreover, the descent of the Spirit at Pentecost, which Jesus promises his disciples ("you will receive the power *of the* Holy Spirit"—Acts 1:8) clearly parallels his descent upon Mary. Further, in John 7:39, at the promise of "living water", when we read "as yet spirit had not been given", this refers without any doubt, in spite of the absence of the article, to the personal Holy Spirit whom Jesus would give to the Church after his glorification. He himself, while on earth, possessed the Holy Spirit as a personal "power": he "rejoices in *the* Holy Spirit" (Lk 10:21); he begins his preaching "in the power *of the* Holy Spirit (Lk 4:14, and so on); but this does not prevent Peter from saying to Cornelius that God had "anointed Jesus of Nazareth with Holy Spirit" (without article) "and with power" (Acts 10:38).[53] So too, in Luke 24:49, "power from on high" that Jesus promises his disciples is the same Holy Spirit whom Luke, as the author of Acts 1:8, calls "the power *of the* Holy Spirit".

This is sufficient to show, in a way that faith can grasp, that the Spirit who overshadows Mary really is the "Holy Spirit" as a Divine Person.[54] The concept of "power" that is added to the Spirit in the "overshadowing" of Mary underlines the unique character of the Holy Spirit as the divine Executant, powerful in action.[55] It is true, of course, that the New Testament does not reflect on the formulated issue of the Spirit's Personhood

---

[53] This same anointing (on the basis of Is 61:1f.) is the theme in Acts 4:27 and Hebrews 1:9. On this, cf. F. Hahn, *Christologische Hoheitstitel*, 3d ed. (1966), who cites I. de la Potterie, NRTh 8 (1958): 225-52.

[54] In the circumcision account (Lk 2:22ff.) there is an alternation between *pneuma* with and without the article without any change in meaning.

[55] H. Schürmann (*Lukas* I, 34, n. 55) points out the frequent connection between pneuma and dynamis in Luke: 1:35; 4:14 (in contrast to Mark); 24:28; Acts 1:8; 6:8, 10; 10:38. Cf. also Rom 1:4; 15:13, 18f.; 1 Cor 2:4; 5:4; 1 Thess 1:5; 2 Tim 1:7. Of course there are links with Old Testament ideas, but in the overshadowing of the Virgin (for christological reasons) the Personhood of the Spirit comes to the fore.

within the Trinity,[56] but it does distinguish him, as divine, from the Person of the Father and from that of the Son: both Father and Son can "send" him, according to the Farewell Discourses (Jn 14:26; 15:26). An impersonal power cannot be "sent". This means that the Incarnation event is trinitarian: the Spirit bears the "seed of God" (1 Jn 3:9), the seed of the Father, that is, the Son, into the womb of the Virgin; the Son, in his "a priori" obedience, allows himself to be carried, and so begins his mission. He is not "thrown" into existence as we are; his very existence is obedience.

Clearly, this biblical starting point, restricted though it may seem at first, has the most far-reaching consequences for Christology and so for dogmatics in general. If this personal activity on the part of the Holy Spirit applies in the event of the Son's Incarnation, his whole human existence will remain marked by it. We see it—prescinding for the moment from all questions of exegesis and textual chronology—in the Baptism scene, where the Spirit's visible descent upon Jesus is portrayed both as an entering *into* him (*eis auton*: Mk 1:10) and as a hovering *over* him (*ep'auton*: Mk 3:16; Lk 3:22; and most clearly in Jn 1:32: "and it remained on him"). Initially this *in-and-over* is a baffling riddle, but it prompts us to deeper reflection; such reflection can be developed on the basis of authentically theological starting points for a Spirit-Christology, and this in turn is only possible within the framework of a doctrine of the economic Trinity. All the time we must remember that the Spirit cannot be objectivized: he is not only the fruit but always the ever-new source of the love between Father and Son, and he will always attain his greatest manifestation or personalization where he is able to manifest this ineffable unity in the most profound way.

d. *Themes in Modern Christology*

This section is concerned simply with a few fruitful stimuli in the process of forming a Spirit-Christology, that is, not systematic presentations (such as that of Heribert Mühlen), to which

---

[56] As H. Mühlen correctly observes, GP 197.

we shall return later, but themes thrown into the discussion, grains of corn that seem to bring promise of harvest. What we are *not* doing is lamenting the fact that the topic of the Spirit has remained too underdeveloped hitherto[57] or that the Latins are in the grip of a "Christomonism";[58] we are not issuing a general summons to push ahead with a Pneumatology,[59] nor are we offering simultaneously both promises and warnings[60] or listing models that are unacceptable in principle;[61] nor are we suggesting that we go back to historically less developed stages.[62]

Despite its wealth of material, *Yves Congar's* great three-volume work, *Je crois en l'Esprit Saint*[63] has only two central themes: the experience of the Spirit (throughout the Church's history and in particular in the charismatic movement, which he criticizes), and the problems associated with the *filioque* in the relations between East and West (together with his suggestions toward a reconciliation). *J. M. Garrigues*, in a subtle manner, has taken the

---

[57] G. S. Hendry, *The Holy Spirit in Christian Theology* (Philadelphia and Westminster, 1965), 53–71.

[58] Y. Congar, "Pneumatologie et 'christomonisme' dans la tradition latine?", in: *Ecclesia a Spiritu Sancto edocta: Mél. G. Philips*, Bibl. Eph. theol. Lov. 27 (Gembloux, 1970), 41–62.

[59] Klauspeter Blaser, "Vorstoß zur Pneumatologie", *Theol. Studien* 121 (Zürich: TVZ, 1977).

[60] Philip J. Rosano, "Spirit Christology: Ambiguity and Promise", *Theol. Studies* 38 (1977): 423–49.

[61] Cf. J. A. M. Schoonenberg, "Spirit Christology and Logos Christology", *Bijdragen* 38 (1977), where he presents the Pentecostal Christology of Edward Irving (1792–1874). Here the Logos adopts a sinful body and a soul filled with the Holy Spirit: these fight the human battle for attachment to God. See also an adoptionist Christology ("The Holy Spirit and the Person of Christ", in Sykes and Clayton, *Christ—Faith and History* [Cambridge, 1972], 111–30), in which, once the Logos is disengaged, the man Jesus "possesses" the Spirit of God. The latter is a preliminary stage on the way to Schoonenberg's own theory (see n. 91 below).

[62] Thus Harry A. Wolfson, *The Philosophy of the Church Fathers* (Cambridge, Mass., 1964), 154–91, who points out that, in John, the preexistent Christ is equated with the Logos and in Paul with the Spirit. Wolfson shows that the two are, at least, implicitly equated, both in the New Testament and in the apostolic Fathers.

[63] Vol. 1: *L'Esprit Saint dans l'"Économie"*; vol. 2: *Il est Seigneur et Il donne la Vie*; vol. 3: *Le Fleuve de vie coule en Orient et en Occident* (Paris: Cerf, 1979–1980). The German edition, *Der Heilige Geist* (Herder, 1982), is abbreviated.

second question farther,[64] whereas *Ludwig Weimer, Die Lust an Gott und seiner Sache*,[65] endeavors to do justice to Congar's first question within an all-embracing doctrine of grace (not a doctrine of the Spirit): Only through the mediation of the Church can the problem of grace and freedom be solved.

The first comprehensive contribution to a Catholic Spirit-Christology was made by *Louis Bouyer* in volume 5 of his double trilogy *Le Consolateur: Esprit Saint et Vie de grâce*.[66] Leaving aside the chapters on Church history, two themes emerge: the first is a kind of transposition into theological terms of Schelling's later philosophy concerning mythology and revelation and of certain of his Russian followers (Soloviev, Bulgakov). According to him, in world history and salvation history we discern the operation of Irenaeus' "two hands of God the Father"—Logos and Spirit—an operation that is common to them, yet distinct in each case, and that is moving toward a point of convergence. The pagans had "intimations of the Spirit"[67] in myth, poetry, and inspiration, which constituted a confused and obscure premonition of the Logos; in the Old Testament this mythology is clarified and becomes genuine prophecy in the Spirit of wisdom, in which the divine Word comes close and exercises its purification,[68] right up to the point where both of them meet in the Virgin Mary,[69] who, as the highest flowering of the Spirit's wisdom, is ready to receive into herself the Word who is drawing near.

[64] *L'Esprit qui dit "Père!" et le problème du filioque*, preface by L. Bouyer (Paris: Téqui, 1981).

[65] Herder, 1981.

[66] Cerf, 1980.

[67] "Pressentiments de l'Esprit", C 19–35; "De l'inspiration mytho-poétique à l'inspiration prophétique": ibid., 365–80.

[68] "Plus d'Israël se rapprochait donc la Parole, se faisant de plus en plus instante, l'Esprit devenant de plus en plus intime aux anciens justes, et mieux ils pressentaient le visage de l'amour": ibid., 396f.

[69] She is termed the fulfillment of prophecy, following many Fathers (cf. A. Grillmeier, "Maria Prophetin: Eine Studie zu einer messianisch-patristischen Mariologie", in: *Mit ihm und in ihm: Christologische Forschungen und Perspektiven* [Herder, 1975], 198–216). Rupert of Deutz continued to dwell on this Marian title: *De operibus Spiritus Sancti* I, 9 (PL 167, 1578); he regards all Old Testament prophecy as moving toward Mary, its fullness and fulfillment.

"The countless renunciations, settings-forth, and banishments of Israel" had purified and reduced the "poor of Yahweh" down to her, the pure Virgin; in her we see the meeting of the ascending Spirit-wisdom and the descending Word; "created wisdom" (Augustine)[70] becomes the eschatological Spouse of the Word, who becomes flesh of her,[71] while Mary becomes the Church, both Bride and Body.[72] The return to the Father takes place in this union of Spirit and Word. Thus the incarnate Son expresses his indebtedness to the Spirit and to the perfected work of the Church—which simultaneously goes forth from the Son.

Bouyer's second theme is inner-trinitarian. Marius Victorinus, one of those who inspired Augustine's treatise on the Trinity, conceived the nature of the biblical God in terms of motion ("esse est moveri"); in that movement in God which is three-fold (tridynamos), his being corresponds to the status, his life corresponds to the progressio, and his insight to the regressio. Here the Holy Spirit becomes not only the copula between Father and Son, but God's perfect return to himself.[73] Here there emerges the terrifying problem of the holiness of the Divine Being vis-à-vis the Holy Spirit, which first oppressed Augustine[74] and has perplexed us ever since. He thought he had solved it with his many-faceted concept of appropriation: What the three-personal God does as sole God can be "ascribed" to one of his Hypostases on the basis of their distinctness. Augustine likes to quote Romans 5:5: "God's love has been poured into our hearts through the Holy Spirit": Is this Spirit God's essence or the third Person? Or, perhaps, is there a more intimate relation between "God is love" and "the Holy Spirit is the bond of love between Father and Son"? In this case, if the "essence" is not thought of as some fourth thing, something neutral behind the Persons, might the Spirit not be the expression of what is deepest in God? Could he not be the "motion" (Victorinus) that drives the Father to go out from himself and generate the Son (and so become Father); the "motion" that moves the Son to gratitude to the Father

---

[70] Cf. *Confessions* XII, 12–13.

[71] "Vers les Noces de la Sagesse et du Verbe": C 444ff.

[72] Ibid., 448.

[73] Ibid., 216ff.

[74] *De Trin.* 7, 4 and 6.

for everything and drives him to give it all back to the Father (thereby becoming Son)? Is the inherited distinction between love as essence and love as personal "inevitable"?[75] Should we say, therefore, that "love—which is the life of God himself, the Father in his Fatherhood, the Son as the Beloved and the One who returns love—is perfected in this Spirit of the Father that can only be the Spirit of Sonship and rests upon the Son as the free Spirit of reciprocity, so that the same Spirit is both utterly loving and utterly beloved"? If such be the case, "the Spirit, as his name implies, would be the breath of the divine life or, which is the same thing, the heart of the divinity, as it were, the heart of the Father and equally the heart of the Son, the Gift that gives life by giving itself away."[76]

At this point *F. X. Durrwell*, in his last book, *L'Esprit Saint de Dieu*,[77] makes a tentative step forward. From his highly concentrated pages, which sum up the entire doctrine of the Spirit, we select just two issues that are *leitmotifs* found throughout his work. First: "God is love, and the Spirit is love. All God's attributes are hypostasized in the Spirit; he is God himself in his innermost depths."[78] Thus "the Spirit is the personalizing Person in the Trinity-in-Unity. The Father generates in the Spirit and so constitutes himself as Person; the Son is generated in the Spirit and, equally, constitutes himself as Person. In the world, too, the operation of the Spirit is personalized. . . . In the Spirit the man Jesus is personalized as divine, that is, taken up into the Person of the Logos."[79] For the Spirit is "the One who effects the Incarnation"[80] and hence who grounds any Spirit-Christology. In God, therefore (and here we see how close he is to Hegel), the Spirit is "at the end as at the beginning": "The Father's eternal act of

---

[75] C 425.

[76] Ibid., 439. We cannot go into a third question that exercises Bouyer, namely, the attempt to reconcile Palamism and a Western doctrine of the Trinity based on Aquinas: ibid., 316ff., 428–32, 448.

[77] Cerf, 1983.

[78] Ibid., 32. In confirmation he cites 2 Peter 1:14: the grace of the Holy Spirit makes us "partakers of the divine nature"; also Augustine's dictum, "God's gift is God himself, for God's gift is the Holy Spirit" (*Sermo* 128, 4: PL 38, 715).

[79] Durrwell, *L'Esprit Saint*, 54.

[80] Ibid., 79, also 161.

generation is the Father's act of love, and this love, in operation, is the Spirit. . . . The Spirit is *at* the origin, in the generating Father, and he is *at* the end, in the generated Son. Although he proceeds from both, he comes neither after the Father nor after the Son, for it is in him that they are Father and Son."[81]

> John Damascene says, "the Spirit is the breath of God's mouth, the utterance of the Word." So the generation of the Son and the procession of the Spirit mutually co-inhere, though they are not identical: the Spirit proceeds in the Son's generation; he is the Spirit of the Father in his Fatherhood. The generation of the Son is the Father's entire work, and although the Father does not generate the Spirit, it remains true that his Fatherhood is the source of the Spirit. . . . If the Spirit proceeds from the Father, whose whole work consists in generating, and if he is not the Son, he can only be this process of generation.[82]

He is "the fullness whence everything springs forth, in which everything is bathed and perfected".[83] "In God there is no nature to develop and show itself fruitful in Persons: it is God's nature to be Trinity. Of these Persons, one is the Holy Spirit; he is the bond of unity between Father and Son; God's attributes are personified in him."[84]

It follows—and this leads us to the second theme—that the Son is only Son *in the Spirit*; in the Spirit he gives himself back to the Father. He does this as the Incarnate One, and the highest act of this "giving back" in "the eternal Spirit" (Heb 9:14) is his death on the Cross. It is clearly seen that this giving back of himself is the Son's Eucharist both to the Father and to the world.[85] ("Water", Spirit, and "blood" are inseparable.) How-

---

[81] Ibid., 160; cf. 50: in the Spirit, the man Jesus grows into what he already is.

[82] Ibid., 154–55.

[83] Ibid., 36. "At the origin of all personalization" lies "self-offering; relation is what is most original; it constitutes the pinnacle and the ground of being" (151).

[84] Ibid., 162, cf. 149. Cf. GP 162: Thus "it is in the Holy Spirit, the We in Person, that the Actus Purus attains its plenitudo." In him it reaches "its ultimate fullness".

[85] Durrwell, *L'Esprit Saint*, 67, 54, 111. Durrwell's thesis is not as new as one might think. The young Augustine found himself confronted with it: "Many people have wanted to see the Holy Spirit as the communion itself (*ipsam communionem*) between Father and Son, as the Divinity itself, so to speak (which the

ever, if Jesus' death is the pinnacle of his Incarnation, if this
death is simultaneously the highest revelation of his relationship
of love with the Father, it is also that act of his which is most
filled with life; accordingly, it is an act that cannot be left behind
(as something past) when his humanity is rendered "eternal" by
the Spirit. Hence these astonishing assertions: "The Spirit raises
Jesus without wrenching him from the clutches of death, . . .
he does not take him beyond that highest surrender of love,
namely, death. Death is the mystery of the Incarnation in its ultimate depth, and death and glory are aspects of a single mystery:
the Lamb stands upright 'as it had been slain', in a glory that does
not follow death but consecrates it."[86] "Jesus does not return
after his death but in it, for the Spirit glorifies him in death."[87]
"Jesus rises, but without abandoning the mystery of his death."[88]
Durrwell indicates the consequences that flow for the Christian,

---

Greeks call *theotēs* . . .); this, which they also situate between both as their reciprocal love and *caritas*, they call the Holy Spirit" (*De fide et symbolo* 19: PL 40, 191).
Here Augustine may have been thinking of Marius Victorinus. Elsewhere he calls
the Spirit "*concordia*", "*communitas*" (*Doctr. chr.* 1, 5; *Sermo* 71; *Trin.* 6, 7). The
idea is very clear in Isidore of Seville: "The Spirit creates unity between Father
and Son" (*Sent.* 1, 15: PL 88, 568). But Augustine himself, in his mature work
De Trinitate, will portray the Spirit as the (personal) reciprocal love of Father and
Son (*Trin.* 6, 7) on the basis of the human *imago* (*memoria-intellectus-voluntas*). He
describes the Spirit's proceeding from Father and Son as from a single, common
Source (*Trin.* 15, 47), which implies that these two are not counterposed; what
else can this Source be, following St. Thomas, but the divine nature itself? "Spiritus Sanctus procedit a Patre et Filio inquantum sunt unum in virtute spirativa,
quae quodammodo significat *naturam cum proprietate*. . . . Neque est inconveniens
unam proprietatem esse in duobus suppositis quorum est una natura. Si vero con-
siderentur supposita spirationis, sic Spiritus Sanctus procedit a Patre et Filio ut
sunt plures: procedit enim ab eis ut *amor unitivus* duorum" (*S. Th.* I, 36, 4 ad
1). "Here the divine *nature* appears as relation, i.e., as the Father's and the Son's
common relation to the Holy Spirit . . . in this sense the *actus purus* appears in
his *personal* aspect" (GP 156). This does not fully correspond to what Durrwell
is saying but goes a long way toward it. In a prespeculative manner Athenagoras
(leg. 10) had said: "The Son is in the Father and the Father in the Son through
the unity and power of the Spirit." Thomas is critical of Durrwell's thesis: *S. Th.*
I, 37, 2c ("quod Spiritus Sanctus sit principium diligendi Patri et Filio . . . est
omnino impossibile").

[86] Durrwell, *L'Esprit Saint*, 56.
[87] Ibid., 112.
[88] Ibid., 173.

that is, his "mortification", his (Pauline) life in death and from death.[89] Basically this only articulates, in fullness, the Johannine "glorification", which is a unity of death and Resurrection. And since the act of death (Heb 9:14; Mt 27:50; Jn 19:30) is a work of the Spirit, as is the act of Resurrection (Rom 1:4; 8:11), we see once again that Christology has a pneumatological form.

One might fear that Durrwell's doctrine of the Trinity could fail adequately to protect the trinitarian *taxis*, in spite of his assurances to the contrary. *Adrienne von Speyr* helps us over this unease by reminding us that the *taxis* must not be understood in any temporal sense whatsoever, because the processions of Son and Spirit are just as eternal as their existence: "The Son even cooperates in his begetting by *letting* himself be begotten, by holding himself in readiness to be begotten", and if we can speak of a "necessary will" in the Father when he begets the Son, and in both Father and Son in the case of the Spirit's procession (*taxis*), this will is always recapitulated, from its very origin, by a "free will". Thus, without abrogating the Father's priority, the Son recognizes

> that as he unveils his purposes the Father counts on the Son's collaboration and on the influence of a third, the Spirit. From this it follows that, in the knowledge that the Father needs him, the Son makes himself available to him for the generation of the Spirit. . . . And as he sees how the Son restrains his free will in favor of the Father and is obedient to him, the Spirit wishes to exercise the same obedience toward both Father and Son. Now it is as though Father and Son observe this restraint, this reserve, this kind of self-abnegation on the part of the Spirit, and immediately cry "No!", definitively bestowing on him complete divine freedom. The Spirit is no late arrival in God, the last of a series originating in the Father.[90]

Rather, it is that "he manifest[s] something of the Father's paramount will and something of the Son's subordinate will in an original and unified way, in which the relationship of superordination and subordination is no longer completely visible. . . .

[89] Ibid., 134f.
[90] *The World of Prayer* (San Francisco: Ignatius Press, 1985), 65, 61.

He can freely do whatever he can devise to promote the love of Father and Son."[91]

This insight, initiated by Bouyer, expounded by Durrwell, and clarified by Adrienne von Speyr, brings out an important theme of the theology of the Trinity. Volume 2 of *Theo-Logic* approached this same theme on the basis of the tradition (and its partial destruction).

The most energetic advocate of a Spirit-christology is *Walter Kasper* in the concluding part of his *Jesus the Christ*.[92] Kasper was partly influenced by Max Müller's *Erfahrung und Geschichte*[93] and very deliberately distanced himself from Hegel, who failed to reconcile God's non-manipulable freedom and sovereignty with his self-giving love.[94] Only where these attributes are united can the Spirit be understood "as the personal bond of the freedom of the love between Father and Son." He is "the medium" in which the Father sends the Son in freedom and out of pure love and in which he finds, in Jesus, the human partner who can respond to the Father in love's free obedience.[95] By "medium" here he means that the Spirit is not only the unity of Christ's humanity

---

[91] Ibid., 63. At this point we can refer to the unacceptable Spirit-Christology of *Schoonenberg* ("Spirit Christology and Logos Christology", 350–75). His starting point is the central role of Spirit-Christology in all four Gospels (apart from the Prologue of St. John), which, however, is initially only the fulfillment of Old Testament pneumatic messianology. He himself acknowledges that, in stopping here, he is exposed to the danger of adoptionism (360). Taking as his basis the Thomist principle that the closer a creature is to God, the more autonomously it acts, he rejects Chalcedon (364). Since the human person enjoys an ever-greater immanence in God, God's immanence in the man Jesus becomes so intensive that it is ultimately the human person who makes the God of the Old Covenant (previously one Person) into a three-personal God. Before the Incarnation, Logos and Spirit were only "extensions" of the one Yahweh, but now, "in uniting themselves with Jesus' human person in this most intimate way, the Logos and the Spirit *become persons* in the trinitarian sense of this term" (368), even if not "in the same way", the Spirit "in a less determined way than the Logos". Both Logos and Spirit become Persons only *after* the Incarnation. A strangely radical form of process theology, giving rise to a Christology "in which Logos- and Spirit-Christology coincide" (374).

[92] Trans. V. Green (London: Burns and Oates, New York: Paulist Press, 1977).

[93] *Grundzüge einer Philosophie der Freiheit als transzendentale Erfahrung* (Freiburg and Munich, 1971).

[94] Kasper, *Jesus the Christ*, 245–46.

[95] Ibid., 251–52.

in the wake of the hypostatic union, "but its precondition . . . the creative principle which sanctifies the man Jesus in such a way as to enable him, by free obedience and dedication, to be the incarnate response to God's self-communication."[96] This response, fruit of the Spirit, is perfected in the death of Jesus: thus the Spirit, after the conclusion of the Son's finite mission, "as it were becomes free". "He is released from his particular historical figure", which means that both the death *and* the Resurrection of Jesus mediate the coming of the Spirit. Kasper's central concern is this: "Thus Jesus Christ, who in the Spirit is in person the mediator between God and man, becomes in the Spirit the universal mediator of salvation."[97] More precisely: only a Spirit-Christology can combine Jesus' uniqueness and peerlessness with the universality of his claim and his Lordship. We discern Bouyer's theme again here: Spirit, right from the first creation, is the One who orders the world of nature; he shows himself to be the natural-supernatural Wisdom of God poured out over the entire world, yearning for the New Creation (Rom 8) that is initiated through the Spirit's overshadowing of Mary and in the divine-human fruit of her womb; in him, its Firstborn, the New Creation is straining toward its eschatological fulfillment. It is the Spirit who imparts universal meaning, in the Church and in world history, to the uniqueness of Jesus, the only Son of the Father.[98]

---

[96] Ibid., 251.

[97] Ibid., 252.

[98] The entire concluding reflection (pp. 413–29 below) is devoted to this combination of uniqueness and universality.

I. THE INTERPRETER

I

APPROACHES

On the basis of what we said about the Spirit of God at the beginning of this volume, we could sum up the Spirit's role—albeit crudely—by saying that he is that by which God discloses himself, as God, to what is not God. This disclosure begins in the Old Testament; but we should note that these instances of God's self-disclosure do not start with numinous generalities or with the experience of the world's createdness or its wise ordering, but with those communications whereby God chooses a "people for himself". In creating, leading, and nurturing this chosen people, God shows a sovereignty that "the poor worm Israel" (Is 41:14) could never have confused with its own powers. Such sovereignty does not need to be expressed, initially, by the word "spirit"; the "word of God", issuing commands in utter freedom and contrary to expectation, can express God's sovereignty with the same authority, as we find in the case of Abraham and Moses. In fact, even in the Old Testament, once the term "spirit" has become usual, word and spirit remain fundamentally linked: word is primarily the content and particular application of God's command, and spirit the divine power with which God executes what he has determined. The two can draw apart where Israel refuses to follow God's word: in that case, God's spirit asserts his word over and in face of the weakness, the objections, and the reluctance of its addressees, at the same time equipping them with powers they could not themselves account for or assume. The first instance of this, illustrating the word "spirit", is found in the choosing and appointing of judges (Judg 3:10; 6:34; 11:29). Later—where the term "spirit" can be superseded by the "word"[1]—in the great prophets: Elijah (2 Kings 2:9), Micah (3:8), Deutero-Isaiah (42:16; 61:1),

---

[1] Even in the great visions of Isaiah, Jeremiah, and Ezekiel the Spirit is not named. This may be because these prophets wanted to distance themselves from the "prophet bands". In point of fact, the great "word" prophecies are so clearly a phenomenon of the Spirit that they are given pride of place in the New Testament creed: "qui locutus est per prophetas".

Zechariah (7:12). "Spirit" can also be used in a more general sense ("the Spirit of God came upon Azariah" [2 Chron 15:1] and upon Jahaziel [2 Chron 20:14]), and, in retrospect, it can be applied to Moses (Num 11:17, 25–26), David (2 Sam 23:2), to gifted artists (Ex 34:3; 35:31), wise judges (Num 11:17), the wisdom of Joseph (Gen 41:38). A somewhat more dubious usage emerges when God's "spirit" is separated from his "word" and applied to the bands of dervish-like prophets who used dance and music to reach ecstasy; this phenomenon was associated with God's power, as in the case of Saul, who, having been anointed king, was invested with divine power through this ecstatic spirit: "Then the spirit of the LORD will come mightily upon you, and you shall prophesy with them and be turned into another man. Now when these signs meet you, do whatever your hand finds to do, for God is with you" (1 Sam 10:6–7). Even here, however, the "word" reappears in the following verse: "Seven days you shall wait, until I come to you and show you what you shall do" (v. 8). In the postexilic period, when great prophecy dwindles and is finally extinguished (1 Macc 4:46; 9:27; 14:4; cf. Daniel's prayer, Dan 9:1–19),[2] the path diverges.[3] On the one hand, the Spirit is associated with Israel's past or—even more—projected into Israel's messianic future: the king of the end-time will be equipped with all the gifts of the Spirit (Is 11); indeed, the Spirit will be poured out on the entire nation (Joel 3:1–2). On the other hand, people learn to recognize and praise God's "spirit" as his "wisdom" in the whole of creation (Prov 8:22ff., Wis 7:22), tracing it right back to the creation of the world, in which God's "spirit", brooding over the chaos (together with God's "word"), began to bring order to the world (Gen 1:1). The whole of nature, in its life and constitution, remains dependent on the "spirit" (the "expiration") of God (Ps 104:30; Jud 16:14). Apocalyptic writers were transported, in the Spirit, to divine regions, but at the same time they assumed the names of long-dead predecessors: Enoch, Abraham, Ezra . . . The rabbis regard the entire Scripture as inspired by the Spirit. All the

[2] On rabbinism, cf. Sjöberg, ThW VI, 384. Individual wise rabbis were said to have the "spirit".

[3] Cf. "The Long Twilight", in vol. 6, Theology: The Old Covenant, of The Glory of the Lord (= GL) (San Francisco: Ignatius Press, 1991), 299–416.

same, we now hear only a gentle echo (*bath-qol*) of God's actual voice.[4] As a result, one of the themes current in the great period of prophecy (Jer 28; Dt 18:9–22) comes to the fore, particularly in the Qumran sect, namely, the discrimination of spirits. Does a prophet or man of the spirit speak from God or from himself? There is a "spirit of truth" and a "spirit of evil": these two struggle for man.[5] Related to this topic is the tendency to personify the divine Spirit that we observe toward the end of the Old Testament. Even in the Wisdom literature it was possible to describe the Spirit, just like the Wisdom of God and the Word of God, as a form of his presence in the world, in Israel, and in individual human beings. The "Hypostases" of God (in strict monotheism, of course) often act very anthropomorphically (thus the "spirit" can cry aloud, weep, threaten, rejoice, be sad, and so on), and often they even speak to God in the person of the world; all these, however, "like the divine *shekhina* that wanders over the earth in banishment, must not be imagined as beings separate from God: they are all forms of his presence and omnipresence." It is inappropriate to see in them a transition to the Christian doctrine of the Trinity.

For, as we move from late Judaism to the New Testament, what comes first is not a doctrine of God, but simply the impression that the man Jesus of Nazareth made on his surroundings. He spoke rarely—or perhaps not at all—of the Spirit of God, but the impression he made on the people—by what he said and how he said it or by his miracles—reminded the people directly of the prophets of old. "Who do men say that the Son of man is?" The answer: "Some say John the Baptist, others say Elijah, and others Jeremiah or one of the prophets" (Mt 16:13–14). In the New Testament there is a way of approaching Jesus via the phenomenon of prophecy,[6] and here the "mighty deeds" of the early prophets (Elijah, Elisha) play their part. New themes coalesce around this center, first and foremost the connection

[4] Strack-Billerbeck, *Kommentar zum Neuen Testament aus Talmud und Midrasch* (Munich: C. H. Beck, 1922), I, 126–27.

[5] 1 QS 3, 18f., 4, 23ff.; cf. J. Maier, *Die Texte vom Toten Meer*, II (1960), 18–19. Similar views in Test. Jud. 20; Test. Ass. 1; Test. Benj. VI, 1.

[6] Franz Schnider, *Jesus der Prophet* (Fribourg, Switzerland and Göttingen, 1973), with refs.

between baptism and the Spirit that came into view with the Baptism of Jesus. Jesus, however, pointed beyond his own earthly existence, most notably in what may be his only reference to the Spirit, when he promised that the disciples would be "delivered up", but that they should not be anxious about what they should say to the court: "for what you are to say will be given to you in that hour; for it is not you who speak, but [Mk] the Spirit of your Father [Luke: the Holy Spirit] speaking through you" (Mt 10:20). This promise points ahead to the time after the Resurrection, when the young community will have a wealth of spiritual experiences: not only will the whole gamut of Old Testament aspects of the Spirit be recapitulated and collected, the latter will be surpassed by new ones (such as the apostles' Pentecost addresses and that glossolalia with which it must not be confused). In the Acts of the Apostles there seems to be no overall concept for this wealth of aspects,[7] yet Paul himself will find one in his doctrine of the Church as the Body of Christ in which every member is given a special gift of the Spirit for the benefit of the whole. Now this fullness is the very opposite of a scattering: it is the necessary unfolding of a unity; Paul will expressly call it the unity of the Spirit, the unity of Christ as the Lord of the Church, which is ultimately the unity of God (the Father) himself (1 Cor 12:4–6). The multiplicity that the Apostle will develop elsewhere in his doctrine of the Spirit is welded together here into an intelligible unity that is both theoretical and practical. In this unity all that is pneumatic is closely knit to the incarnate and risen Logos, while, behind the latter, we discern the face of the Father revealed in the Son.

This vision of unity, which presents itself initially as ecclesiological and then, at a deeper level, as trinitarian, enables us to proceed to a final simplification in John; this simplification,

[7] G. Trocmé, "Le Saint-Esprit et l'Église d'après le livre des Actes", in *Église et Esprit: Actes du Symposium organisé par l'Académie internationale de sciences religieuses* (Fayard, 1969) (= EE), 19–44. In the discussion of this lecture, H. de Lubac says: "(In Luke) I do not look for a rounded doctrine (of the Holy Spirit), nor am I disappointed when I do not find one. What seems more important than a rounded theology is the fact that, in the story he sets forth, Luke presents so many aspects of the Holy Spirit. He gives us such concrete, rich, naïve, puzzling, complex, and objectively profound aspects . . . that this seems more interesting to me than a rounded theology" (ibid., 36–37).

however, is simultaneously an opening out into the highest fullness. Features that, in Paul, had not yet been integrated into his synthesis, such as his personal experiences as an apostle in a discipleship that joined him to the sufferings of Christ, find their true place in the concluding Johannine formula.

2

"HE WILL GUIDE YOU
INTO ALL THE TRUTH"

If we are to grasp this statement in its proper context, we must reflect on the Johannine starting point set forth in volume 2 of *Theo-Logic*. Logic is concerned with truth; in theo-logic, truth consists in the interpretation of God given by the incarnate Logos: "I am the truth" (Jn 14:6). "For this I was born, and for this I have come into the world, to bear witness to the truth" (Jn 18:37). The man Jesus addresses does not know what he is talking about: "What is truth?" (v. 38). He is one of those who "cannot bear" what Jesus has said and has yet to say. "I have yet many things to say to you, but you cannot bear them now. When the Spirit of truth comes, he will guide you into all the truth; for he will not speak on his own authority, but whatever he hears he will speak, and he will declare to you the things that are to come. He will glorify me, for he will take what is mine and declare it to you" (Jn 16:12–14). This penultimate one of the five "Paraclete" sayings of the Farewell Discourses contains a summa of all that the Holy Spirit does and thereby, indirectly, reveals his essence. On the basis of this saying, we can understand the others as supplementary clarifications; it sheds light on the meaning of the "Paraclete" sayings seen as a totality (in the "Book of Signs", chaps. 1–12).

From a philological point of view, one can examine the individual sayings separately and ask about the origins of the terms used (for example, "Paraclete"), but from a theological point of view, all of John's statements about the Spirit are so integrally connected that to isolate them is to obscure, rather than to clarify, the author's synthesis. His central assertions concerning the Spirit are so clearly convergent that they must be seen as complementary perspectives of a single reality.

a. Making God Known

In the text we have quoted the word "declare" (*euangellein*) occurs three times; this can be given (in the second saying) simply as "teach" (*didaskein*) and as the more specific "bring to remembrance" (*hypomimnēskein*) (14:26), but the best term is "guide", "set on the right path" (*hodēgein*) (16:13). The realm into which we are to be guided is unimaginably vast, namely, "all (or the whole) truth". If, in Johannine terms, truth means the "making known" (1:18) of God (the Father) by the incarnate Son, then he who makes this truth known can rightly be called the "Spirit of truth" (14:17; 15:26; 16:13), at various levels: he utters the truth and can "witness" to it because he knows it; and he knows it because he is internal to it, that is, internal to the relationship between the Father (who allows himself to be made known) and the Son (who makes him known). The Son's making known is "true" (*alēthinōs*) because, unlike the false prophets, he does not make himself known but is sent from the Father to make *him* known; since the Father is not merely passive in thus allowing himself to be made known, but actually effects this *exegesis* by sending the Son, the Father is himself called "true" (Jn 7:28; 17:3); it is with this self-revealing truth in mind that Jesus says that the Jews have no knowledge of God. Returning to 1 John 5:20, we note that in the first place it is God the Father who is "true"; through the Son we have been given understanding to know him; immediately thereafter it is the Son who is "true" ("we are in him who is true, in his Son Jesus Christ"). The third statement, "this is the true God and eternal life", again refers to the Son but can also refer to the unity of Father and Son. The concluding warning against idols, namely, the Antichrist,[1] firmly sets this theoretical truth and ethical truthfulness in the context of genuine incarnation.

But why is the Son not sufficient to make the Father known? Why is the sending of the Spirit needed as well? The question is particularly apposite in the case of John, since even prior to the promise of the Spirit, Jesus' proclamation both demands faith in his divine origin and also, in part, effects it. Should it not suffice

---

[1] Cf. J. L. Ska, in NRTh 101 (1979): 860–79.

that he himself has received "the Spirit without measure" from the Father beyond all the prophets (3:34) and that this Spirit came down upon him according to the Baptist's testimony (1:32) and "remained on him", thus choosing him as the Pneumatic One? Would not this be enough to make him the Spirit-giver? And does not the Baptist himself say that Jesus, in contrast to himself —who baptizes "with water" (1:26)—is the one who "baptizes with the Holy Spirit" (1:33, here in the present tense, whereas the Synoptics have the future tense: Mk 1:8 parr.)? Against this we have the clear statement in 7:37–39, where Jesus offers the thirsty streams of living water, referring to "the Spirit, which those who believed in him were to receive; for as yet the Spirit had not been given, because Jesus was not yet glorified." Two periods are distinguished here: the time prior to the glorification on the Cross and the time after it. The Johannine understanding would be very much inclined to begin the second period at the point when the crucified Son bowed his head and "gave up his spirit" (*paredoken to pneuma*, 19:30). This would have explained why Jesus, prior to the promise of the Spirit, says to the disciples, "I have yet many things to say to you, but you cannot bear them now" (16:12): these "many things", in fact, *most things* that he will still have to tell mankind—and these things are precisely what it cannot yet bear—are the consummation of his being (his being as Word) on the Cross, for which Paul coins the lapidary formula "the word of the cross", God's highest wisdom in the form of the sheerest folly (1 Cor 1:18, 25).

Thus we can also see how there could be an initial, inchoate faith understanding of Jesus prior to the Cross. If Jesus baptizes "in the Holy Spirit", it is because, on the basis of his own fullness of the Spirit, he is and has always been the Spirit's source.[2] Thus, at his first miracle, his disciples saw his glory and were able to "believe in him" (2:11); thus the Samaritan woman, after all her misunderstanding of the "living water", finally believes and comes to some understanding of what is meant by the worship of the Father "in spirit and truth" (4:23); thus the

[2] Felix Porsch, *Pneuma und Wort: Ein exegetischer Beitrag zur Pneumatologie des Johannesevangeliums*, Frankfurter theol. Studien, 16 (Knecht, 1974): "This expression [i.e., 1:33] characterizes him as the abiding source of the Spirit" and "defines his essence" (49).

"official" becomes a believer (4:53), the chief priests' officers are close to faith (7:46), the blind man who is now cured professes his faith (9:35ff.), as does Martha (11:27). When Jesus speaks of himself as the "bread of life", he provokes a genuine decision between faith and unbelief, and Peter ("we believe and know", 6:69) chooses him who has "the words of eternal life". Undoubtedly, all these people have made an authentic journey, even if the post-Easter faith understanding is largely absent. (It is not until after the Resurrection that the disciples understand and "believe" that Jesus was speaking of the "temple of his body" in connection with his cleansing of the Temple [2:22]; the same is true of the entry into Jerusalem [12:10].) Jesus' hearers are, after all, Jews, who are party to a covenant with God; and such a covenant is unthinkable apart from a certain communication of the divine Spirit. In fact, this is the very reason for the accusation against them: "You always resist the Holy Spirit. As your fathers did, so do you" (Acts 7:51). On the basis of this covenant with God, Jesus can expect that Nicodemus will understand, not only what "being born again of the Spirit" means, but also that Jesus himself is the authoritative Revealer of the Father (Jn 3:3ff.) and hence the One who baptizes with the Spirit, as John the Baptist had described him. If we look at Luke for a moment, he regards the announcement of the birth of the Baptist as part of the preamble to the account of Jesus' life and work, and this event is in continuity with the Old Covenant, promising that the Child to be born will be filled with the Holy Spirit (Lk 1:15, 17). So too Zechariah "prophesied, filled with the Holy Spirit" (1:67); Elizabeth does the same in response to Mary's greeting (1:41), as does Simeon (2:25–27).

This does not obliterate, of course, the vast gulf created by the Passion of Jesus: only when Jesus disappears can the Spirit come. This is affirmed in different ways by all passages that speak of the Paraclete. They speak of the sending of the Spirit as something that will take place in the future (Jn 14:16, 26; 15:26; 16:13f.); the fourth is very explicit: "If I do not go away, the Counselor will not come to you; but if I go, I will send him to you" (16:7). The reason for this is not that Jesus' bodily presence must disappear so that his "spiritual being" can be made present, but, as we have said, the incarnate Word of God can only be interpreted

in all his fullness ("all truth") after this Word has been uttered
to his very end, that is, in his death and Resurrection. John and
Luke have different approaches here, but now these differences
are immaterial: John regards the death of Jesus as the highest
glorification of the Father and sees the Spirit welling forth from
the Cross so that he can be breathed forth into the Church and
the world on the Resurrection day itself. Luke divides the event
of glorification into Resurrection and Ascension; for him, the
promise of the Spirit is not fulfilled until Jesus returns to the
Father (and the giving of the Spirit confirms this return)—Acts
2:33. At all events it is only the fulfillment of the mission of the
Incarnation that can provide an overview and an interpretation
of it. Only now has "all the truth" in the Johannine sense been
realized; only now is it ready to be interpreted. How does the
Holy Spirit interpret "all the truth"? This can only be set forth
after we have gained an insight into what "all the truth" means.

b. "All the Truth"

When Jesus tells his disciples, "I have yet many things to say
to you, but you cannot bear them now" (Jn 16:12), this does
not mean that his teaching on earth was incomplete and had to
remain so for extraneous reasons, that is, the disciples' poor understanding. In fact the teaching activity of the Spirit, the Interpreter, is essentially that of "bring[ing] to your remembrance all
that I have said to you" (14:26). It is not straining the text, when
we read that the Interpreter will speak "whatever he hears . . . ,
and he will declare to you the things that are to come" (16:13),
to take "the things that are to come" to refer initially to what
will shortly happen to Jesus, his glorification through the Cross
and Resurrection—for it is only in the wake of this that the
Word can be interpreted in its totality. "The things that are to
come" are not matters of temporal prediction but rather (as in
Deutero-Is 41:23; 42:23; 44:7) the inauguration of the eschatological dimension, by which the Gospel means the ability to read
the signs of the time, to recognize the nearness of the end (Mt
24:32f.).[3]

[3] Ibid., 102f.

Thus "all the truth" does not mean a synthesis of a given number of individual truths but the one truth of the Son's interpretation of God in the inexhaustible fullness of its concrete universality. This fullness is present when the Son, in all his incarnate existence, interprets the truth of the divine love: this interpretation is the glory "full of grace and truth" (1:14, 17), it is a "true testimony" (5:31; 8:14). Analogously, the Spirit, too, will not only expand on this interpretation, but also "bear witness" to it (15:26), which means staking his entire being on it. In theological terms this "testimony" is not given *in the presence of* someone, or *for* someone, but as a disclosure and surrender of what is one's own *to* someone, which, if it is accepted, becomes a *movement into* someone. "Truth" (in 1:14) is simultaneously "grace". The milieu of love between Father and Son is opened up in the Son as a result of his self-surrender to the world; so too the Spirit's introduction into this milieu of love, which is truth, is also the Spirit's self-surrender to the person who receives his testimony.

In this context we must always remember that the Spirit is simultaneously the (objective) attesting of this love between Father and Son (as the third Person, dogma would say) *and* the inner fruit of this reciprocal (subjective) love; thus he can be called the Spirit of love of the Father and of the Son (cf. Rom 8:9). So his "leading into all truth" is initially something quite different from the imparting of information; rather, he leads us from inner participation into inner participation. He also has the power, since in Paul *dynamis* is often paired with *pneuma* and is practically its equivalent. Through him who "searches the depths of God"—and he is communicated to us precisely in these terms (1 Cor 2:10, 12)—we come to recognize who this God the Father is, who "so loved the world that he gave his only-begotten Son" (Jn 3:16), and also who this Son is, who accepts the task of manifesting this love on the Father's part, a task that culminates in the glorification of this love on the Cross and in the opening of his heart. Thus we are not only introduced to an "economic" Trinity in its external relations; we are introduced to its immanent truth, otherwise we should not be introduced to "all the truth"; something of the mystery of God would be left in the background, uncommunicated to us. We are introduced, not to God's "energies", but to the incomprehensibility of his essence, which *is* manifested and communicated to us, yet in a way that is beyond our grasp.

According to Jesus' word, the Spirit takes "what is mine"; but since this "mine" is also the Father's, when the Spirit "leads us" into all truth he also causes us to participate in the divine realm of the Father-Son relationship (thus this initiation can be called a "divinization") and to participate in the Incarnation. Our participation in the Incarnation actually becomes deeper and deeper and more and more effective, because the divine realm never discloses itself to us except in the self-offering of Christ's flesh and blood (6:53–57). These two dimensions of the truth are inseparable; it will appear, therefore, that the different emphases of Western and Eastern theology are complementary. In other words, the unity of both sides clearly shows us why the truth (as W. Kasper said) cannot be abstracted from the historical, concrete event: it is precisely through the Spirit's work of declaring and interpreting that the truth shows itself to be what is universally valid, that which embraces every partial truth in the world, just as the self-disclosing Father-God is inseparable from the divine Son who *is* this disclosure.

Insofar as the Spirit is the one who explains and introduces us to this realm of truth that is internal to the Godhead, many aspects are brought together here that, in the tradition, are treated more in isolation. The divine realm is the realm of the holy: it can be entered and inhabited only by the sanctified (those who have been justified and made holy): "Be holy, for I am holy" (Lev 11:44). Otherwise no covenant can be concluded between God and man, let alone be perfectly lived out. The Holy Spirit must be a sanctifying Spirit if he is to lead us into all truth.

In the context of holiness the relationship between Father and Son can only be one of prayer—be it adoration, thanksgiving, intercession, or decision[4]—and, since it is through the Son that the Spirit facilitates our entry into the realm of truth, he teaches us the Son's prayer: "Abba, Father" (Gal 4:6; Rom 8:15 = Mk

---

[4] A. von Speyr, *The World of Prayer* (San Francisco: Ignatius Press, 1985).

14:36), which expresses the fact that we are admitted to this realm as children adopted by the Father (Rom 8:15, 23; 9:4; Gal 4:5; Eph 1:5). It is only because we are thus the Father's children that God gives us a participation in things the mere servant cannot know, for the servant serves in the house only for a time, whereas the son "continues for ever" (Jn 8:35). This "continuing" is also an "indwelling" and can also be applied to the Spirit himself (Rom 8:9, 11; 1 Cor 3:16). Again, by this same indwelling of the Spirit we are initiated into that indwelling whereby Father and Son indwell the believer (Jn 14:23). Moreover, if "all the truth" is nothing other than the love that is made manifest in God and his revelation, this love that is lived out in act and being ("God is love", 1 Jn 4:8, 16) must be implemented by those who inhabit the realm of truth, and implemented in both directions exemplified by the Son, namely, toward the Father and, coming from the Father, toward the world. The Farewell Discourses are full of this commandment. Thus John can say unequivocally, "He who does not love does not know God; for God is love" (1 Jn 4:8). Since it is essential for us to be introduced by the Spirit to the truth that is love if it is to be put into practice, we can brush aside any other love that claims to ascend to God from the creature as such; it is of no account: "In this is love, not that we loved God but that he loved us and sent his Son to be the expiation for our sins" (1 Jn 4:10). In all this the Spirit's interpretative operation, leading us into "all the truth", goes beyond all mere theory (even in the sense of the Greek *theoria*); it is "action" (Blondel), self-realizing existence; and since Christ—who is the Father's "action"—lives out this "action" in detail, it is discipleship of Christ.

The essence of this discipleship, however, is union between people in a faith and love centered in Christ: "that they may all be one; even as thou, Father, art in me, and I in thee, that they also may be *in us*, so that the world may believe that thou hast sent me" (Jn 17:21 [emphasis added]). It is only the love between believers that causes the Church to be believable; and, on the other hand, John insists that this Church can only be one in Peter, who appears as the "rock" in the very first chapter of the

Gospel (1:42); in fact the entire "gospel of love" culminates in Peter's commission, on the basis of his "greater love", to pasture Christ's flock. At the center of the Gospel, however, as the dying Lord "hands over" his Spirit, we have the creation of the first living cell of this Church in the unity between Mary and John (19:25ff.). In the First Letter of John this ecclesial community is portrayed as the constant presence of its origin: "That which we have seen and heard we proclaim also to you, so that you may have fellowship with us" (1 Jn 1:1–3), and this presence is the effect of the "anointing" (1 Jn 2:20, 27) of the Holy "Spirit of truth", who through water and blood, baptism and Eucharist, gives witness to the constant presence of the whole truth of God in Christ (1 Jn 5:6, 8). This sacramental work of making the truth present is indicated and presupposed everywhere in John, while Paul unfolds it in all its breadth as the operation—inseparable from Jesus—of the Holy Spirit.

Together with the Spirit there is reference to the *knowledge* that, flowing from faith, is found in those who have been initiated by the Spirit. Peter assures the Lord that "we believe and know" (Jn 6:69); faith, having gained entrance to the truth of Jesus, has acquired the character of unshakeable firmness. And the contrary is true: as a result of the insight acquired through fellowship with Jesus, the commitment of faith has become final: the disciples have "received" the words that the Father gave to the Son, and they "know in truth that I came from you; and they have believed that you did send me" (Jn 17:8; cf. 1 Jn 4:16: "We know and believe the love God has for us"). This inseparable two-in-one of faith and knowledge constitutes the foundation of Christian ethics and of what is called "theology" in the narrower sense. As far as ethics is concerned, the "Paraclete" sayings are so organically woven into the Farewell Discourses that they cannot be separated from the latter's total content; this in turn has a lot to say about Jesus' keeping of the commandments (which means, practically, his being pursued and his path to the Cross) and the command to the disciples that they, too, must surrender their lives (15:13f.; 1 Jn 3:16) and be hated and persecuted without a cause (15:25; 16:1–4). The complete "teaching" (1 Jn 2:27) that is given through the Spirit's anointing provides sufficient

instruction for Christians of all ages (2:12–14), right down to
the most concrete forms of charity to the poor (3:17f.) and inner
dispositions: anyone who hates is a murderer (3:15), whereas if
anyone *does* what is right and righteous, like Jesus, there is no
sin in him because God's seed abides in him; in other words, he
is born of God as a child of God (cf. 3:4–9). Here ethics is again
linked with knowledge: "No one who sins has either seen him
or known him" (3:6).

With regard to theology in our sense, we shall return to it later.
In John there is no particular statement about the link between it
and the Holy Spirit; his entire work is an expression of it. From
the earliest time he was called "the Theologian", which shows
that what he has to say comes from the inner realm between
Father and Son, inspired by the Spirit like no other writer. He
uses the most everyday language, far removed from all glossolalia, and expresses the most unfathomable truth in the fewest
possible terms, thus proving that inspiration by the Spirit and
personal meditation are not only compatible, but mutually beneficial, and that, in order to draw near to God, one must not
move so much as a step away from the Incarnation: "Little children, keep yourselves from idols" (spurious mysticism) is the
concluding admonition of his great Letter (1 Jn 5:21). The hallmark of Johannine theology is that by "truth" it understands
"all the truth", presenting its fullness in outline and in specific
details.

c. The Paraclete

In John the Holy Spirit is referred to variously as the Paraclete,
the Comforter, the Advocate, the Witness; this in no way conflicts with his central role as Declarer of God's revelation in
Christ; rather it only shows this role in greater relief. "The Holy
Spirit's main function in John is his activity in revealing the divine truth and introducing us to it."[5] It does not matter where
John found the term "Paraclete", whether from some preexist-

[5] R. Schnackenburg, *Johannes* I, 187.

ing Late Jewish[6] or gnostic[7] tradition or from the literary genre
of the Farewell Discourse,[8] or whether he was the first to combine the concept with that of the Holy Spirit.[9] In biblical terms
we can get closest to its meaning by attending to two Johannine expressions: first, that in which Jesus himself is called "our
paraclete with the Father" (1 Jn 2:2), our advocate "if anyone sin",

---

[6] Cf. Otto Betz, *Der Paraklet: Fürsprecher im haeretischen Spätjudentum, im Johannesevangelium und in neugefundenen gnostischen Schriften* (Leiden: Brill, 1963).
Betz rejects attempts to find the origins of the "Paraclete" in the Old Testament
(Schlette, Mowinckel, and Johansson), in gnosticism (Bultmann), and late Jewish
apocalyptic (G. Bornkamm, "Der Paraklet im Johannesevangelium", in *Festschrift
Bultmann* [Stuttgart, 1949]) and endeavors to locate the concept in Qumran. However, his attempt to derive the Paraclete from Qumran's "angels of intercession"
(and from Michael in particular, 150f.) is unconvincing: these angels are involved
in a dualistic struggle with the evil spirit—which is not a feature of the Johannine
Paraclete. Furthermore, Yahweh's function as a "witness" in the "court proceed-
ings" against the nations is entirely different from that of the Spirit; and "the spirit
of truth" in Qumran (147) has nothing in common with John's concept of truth.
Similarly, in Qumran (192f.), the "convicting/convincing" of the world by the
Paraclete does not take place against the backdrop of world history, such as we
see in John. The theme of "calling to mind" (94) has no parallel, either, for in
Qumran it is God who is reminded, and in John it is the disciples.

[7] Bultmann, *Johannes*, 437–40, adduces Mandaean texts and, in particular (like
others before him), the figure of Yawar. As has been shown, however, this does
not mean "helper". Cf. the sharp criticism of this by Betz, *Paraklet*, 31.

[8] Thus the view of U. B. Müller (see n. 9 below) and G. Bornkamm (see n.
6 above), which assumes a dualism (taken over from the tradition) between the
Herald (Jesus) and the One who is to come (Spirit). But Jesus is not a herald. Cf.
Betz, *Paraklet*, 128.

[9] Betz, *Paraklet*, 163. On this whole issue, cf. the cautious article by R. E. Brown,
"The Paraclete in the Fourth Gospel", *New Test. Stud.* 23 (1966–1967): 113–32.
His attempt to show a link between the idea of the Paraclete and the death of
the eye-witnesses and the delay of the parousia is, however, unconvincing (121–
30). Other attempts to trace the Paraclete back to the Christian *parakalein* (to
"comfort", "encourage", e.g., J. G. Davies: "The Primary Meaning of Parakle-
tus", *Journal of Theol. Studies* 4 [1953]: 35–38; C. K. Barrett, "The Holy Spirit in
the Fourth Gospel", *Journal of Theol. Studies* 1 [1950]: 1–15; U. B. Müller, "Die
Parakletvorstellung im Johannesevangelium", ZThK, 1974, 31–77) fail to do
justice to the forensic aspect present in the fourth Paraclete saying. For a survey
and further bibliography, cf. R. Schnackenburg, *Johannes*, III (1975), excursus 16,
156–73. There is a good theological summary in I. de la Potterie, "Le Paraclet",
in Ignace de la Potterie and Stanislaus Lyonnet, *La Vie selon l'Esprit* (Paris: Cerf,
1965), 85–105.

because he is "the expiation for our sins", and "not for ours only but also for the sins of the whole world". Here the main point is that the Spirit takes our part and speaks in our defense in an advocacy that embraces the whole world. The second Johannine expression is this: "I will not leave you desolate [orphans] . . . but I will pray the Father, and he will give you another Counselor (*paraclete*) to be with you for ever" (Jn 14:18, 16). This is the first of the five Paraclete sayings; they introduce the word for the first time and thus indicate that the One for whose presence Jesus prays will have the power to take his place and so prevent the disciples from being "orphans", all the more so since it is repeatedly said (14:26; 16:26) that the Spirit comes from the Father, that is, is no less divine than Jesus; thus he will replace Jesus' restricted local presence with an eternal abiding. Furthermore, if we take into consideration the words that immediately follow: "I will come to you" (14:18), it is clear that the Spirit does not replace an *absent* Jesus, but on the contrary renders him present in a new way. Whereas the world can no longer see Jesus because it does not know him, it will be the Paraclete's task to enable the disciples to see him, "because I live, you will live also. In that day you will know that I am in my Father, and you in me, and I in you" (14:19–20). All this is to be understood in the context of the first Paraclete saying; it is evidently an effect wrought by the promised Holy Spirit, for the second saying directly calls the Paraclete the "Holy Spirit" (14:26), with the task we have described in the previous section, namely, to call Jesus' words to mind and to unfold and teach the depth of their meaning.

We must agree with R. E. Brown that the various affirmations concerning the Spirit must not be isolated from one another since they mutually interpenetrate;[10] and that, at the same time, in spite of the close bond between Jesus and the Spirit, they remain distinct. The Spirit's roles as "witness" (15:26) and as "convincer" (16:8–11) interpenetrate: in both roles the Spirit plays his part in Jesus' great trial against the world that persecutes and condemns. He "testifies" that the disciples who witness together with him (15:27) are in the right, and he "convinces"

---

[10] See previous note.

them that the world's condemnation of them is unjust and that the world has already lost its case against God: "the ruler of this world is judged" (16:11). The objection is constantly raised that this testimony on the part of the Spirit is not appreciated by the world but only by the disciples: the world is not aware that it is arraigned before any tribunal, and this judgment is evident only to the consciences of the disciples.[11] But the point is that this is an utterly objective, public, even "cosmic" event, and whether or not the condemned party *now* appreciates its defeat is neither here nor there. "*Now* is the judgment of this world, *now* shall the ruler of this world be cast out" (Jn 12:31 [emphasis added]). The Apocalypse depicts the "dragon" being cast out from heaven on to the earth and attributes his "great rage" to the fact that "he knows that his time is short" (Rev 12:9–12); so too in the Gospel, the persecuting world is not simply unaware that it has lost its cause. The condemnation of Jesus by the Jews and Pilate is turned upside-down, and the Paraclete shows that this verdict is "sin", "because they have not believed in me"; he shows the condemned Man as the Victor, since he has been justified and raised by the Father. Judgment passes from the judging world to the world that is itself judged (Jn 16:8–11). The objective action of "convicting" (*elengchein*) also has a subjective side: "to convince", that is, "to show a person his sin and urge him to repent, to point out the path from sin to repentance".[12]

Now this "forensic" activity of the Spirit vis-à-vis the world is most closely connected with his activity of "guiding us into all the truth". For the believer, the latter signifies positive guidance into the inner wealth of the revealed truth of the Father-Son relationship; for the unbelieving world, it is the definitive unveiling—on the stage of all world history—of the victorious superiority of total truth over hostile untruth. As far as the individual man is concerned, one can still hold on to the idea of a struggle between the good and evil spirits (as, in Qumran, the angel of truth fought against the angel of the lie), but in terms of world history the outcome of the case is already decided. So we can say that Christ reigns "as King [!] until all his enemies

[11] La Potterie and Lyonnet, *Vie*, 98, 102.
[12] Büchsel, ThW II, 471.

have been put beneath his feet" (1 Cor 15:25); but it can also be said that the Victor "waits until his enemies should be made a stool for his feet" (Heb 10:13).

The Farewell Discourses give a blunt portrayal of world history after Christ as a time filled with hatred and persecution of Christians. Like the Synoptics, however, they put this suffering on the part of the Church expressly in the context of Christ's own suffering of hatred and persecution: that is, it is the suffering of the Victor. The Spirit's *martyrein* for Christ is directly associated with the disciples' *martyrein* (Jn 15:26–27), so that, even in the Gospel, this "giving testimony" acquires the flavor it will have throughout the Apocalypse: it is the testimony of those who "have been slain for the word of God and for the witness they have borne" (Rev 6:9).

It would not be right, therefore, to question the title "Paraclete" given to the Holy Spirit on the grounds that his activity does not adequately correspond to his title.[13] Naturally, the Spirit is not like an earthly advocate. Rather, he conducts his case at the level of the divine revelation in Christ; and at this level, for as long as history lasts, he is the One who introduces us into all truth, simultaneously refuting all error.

It remains for us to examine the "Book of Signs" (chaps 1–12) in the context of the Farewell Discourses, in order to see whether it, too, vindicates the Spirit's role as the Interpreter.[14] In order to grasp what these chapters say about the Spirit, we need to keep two things in mind. In the first place, it is Jesus who, from the very first, is the bearer of the Spirit; Jesus himself is the source and giver of the Spirit. Prior to the Cross, the handing over of the Spirit, and the piercing of Jesus' side, there is no possibility of men accepting this offer. Objectively speaking, Jesus' word is, from the very first, "spirit and life" (6:63), and so it *is* always interpreted by the Spirit; but until the Spirit is breathed out in Jesus' death and breathed forth into the

---

[13] On this objection and its refutation: Porsch, *Pneuma und Wort*, 305–24.

[14] Cf. ibid., 25–214: "The Spirit's operation is directed to the reception and preservation of Jesus' revealed word." For a highly compact synthesis, cf. H. Schlier "Zum Begriff des Geistes nach dem Johannesevangelium", in *Besinnung auf das Neue Testament* (Herder, 1964), 264–71.

world in the Resurrection, this word cannot be understood as it was meant to be. In the second place, the Evangelist, living and writing within a community of faith, endowed with the Spirit, looks back to this first phase in grief and what almost amounts to puzzlement: Surely, everything done in the Spirit and said about the Spirit—as he now sees it, fully interpreted —was so clear: How can people possibly still misunderstand it? Jesus' words and signs are such an utterly convincing interpretation of God in the Spirit that he himself seems to expect people to grasp them immediately in their spiritual nature. Hence his baffled question to the "Teacher in Israel", asking why he cannot grasp the simplest fact, namely, that everyone must be born again. As in Paul, however, thinking "from below", from the sphere of the flesh, is inadequate if we wish to understand what is being said about the sphere that is opened to us from above and that can be entered only in the Holy Spirit. The lower sphere consists of concepts that are human, and hence ossified, whereas in the higher sphere the Spirit blows where he will. Below, it is true, we do hear the Spirit, but we cannot locate him because his movement is so free (Jn 3:3–12). "No one can receive anything except what is given him from heaven" (3:27), and this applies also to our entry into the sphere of the Spirit. Jesus possesses the Spirit without measured limits (3:34), his words come from the sphere of the "life-giving Spirit", and he himself is "spirit and life", the Word-made-flesh; but when it comes to knowing him, mere spiritless "flesh is of no avail" (6:63). John's whole account of the Baptism, by contrast with the Synoptics, centers on the Baptist's recognition of him "who baptizes with the Holy Spirit" (1:33). We are given an initial glimpse of what this means when he says that "He whom God has sent utters the words of God" (3:34), and offers "living water" from within himself as the "gift of God" (4:10; 7:37–38); but we are unable to accept this offer until the Vessel on the Cross is emptied to the last drop. To the testimony of the "Spirit of truth" must be added not only water, but also blood, that "greater testimony" that the Father "has borne to his Son" (1 Jn 5:6–9), if the recipient is really to enter into the trinitarian sphere that gives him understanding from within. It is only after Easter that the disciples understand, when the Spirit reminds them of what Jesus said and did. Even the Father's "drawing" to the Son (6:44) will not be effective until the Son's flesh and blood are transformed into food and drink, until the "Lamb of God" (1:29, 36) can be eaten as the Passover lamb (cf. 18:28), having so "consecrated himself" that the disciples, too, can "be consecrated in truth" (17:19). Only now can the Son who "descends"—who in his self-surrender was always one with the Spirit—be understood also as "he who ascends" (6:62; cf. 1:54). What the disciples had hitherto considered a mere "speaking in figures" can now be termed "speaking plainly"—because these words are now understood in the Spirit (16:29). In all this John is very close to what Paul says in 1 Cor 2: we are given a participation in the inner Spirit of God, who searches the depths of divinity; as a result of this, what formerly seemed folly and a stumbling block is now disclosed as the superior wisdom of God. So it is, too, in all the disputes between Jesus and the Jews, who understand nothing because they are not "of God" (8:47).

3

RETROSPECT

Reflecting on the Spirit's role in salvation history as set forth by John, it should be possible to look back and see how it integrates the multifarious aspects of previous Spirit-theology; supplementary insights will enrich the total picture, but the Spirit's function within theology—that is, to be our "guide" and "interpreter"—will be confirmed.

a. Paul

By far the richest and most nuanced is Paul's Spirit-theology. If we wish to assemble all its many facets around a single center and make a single intelligible unity, it is essential to start from the trinitarian plan of salvation. The Father shows us his peerless love by surrendering his Son (Rom 8:32, 39) to that Cross which is the center and turning point of the entire Pauline kerygma (1 Cor 1; Phil 2:8). This Cross means "being made sin for us" (2 Cor 5:21; Rom 8:3). Paul not only proclaims this all-embracing truth: he lives at the heart of it. He exemplifies pure fatherly self-surrender for those who are his and total co-suffering with the Son; and this in turn is only possible because "God's love has been poured into our hearts through the Holy Spirit" (Rom 5:5). Beholding this love, he realizes, without equating Cross and Resurrection under the one concept of "glorification" as John does, that the Resurrection and its "glory" (*doxa*) is inseparable from the Cross; and that the "weakness" of Christ on the Cross (2 Cor 13:4) inexorably moves toward that *dynamis* of the Resurrection which is particularly attributed to the Spirit of God (Rom 1:4; 8:11), whereby the Exalted One himself enters God's sphere of power, spirit, or glory (2 Cor 3:17; 1 Cor 15:45). But while a primitive Christology endeavored to see the Messiah who descended from David elevated to the status of the heavenly and eternal Son only at the Resurrection, Jesus is already the eternal Son, showing himself to be such both through his weakness and through his glorification in the Spirit.[1] Discipleship, therefore, must mean nothing else than "being changed into his likeness" (2 Cor 3:18) by the Spirit who is given to us as a "guarantee" (2 Cor 5:5). If the Spirit's role is to lead even Jesus into ultimate glory, this must be his role for us, too, in a much more radical sense—since, unless the Spirit is poured forth into our hearts, unless we are "saturated" with him (1 Cor 12:13), we will never attain the *understanding* of divine truth, nor will we be empowered to *live* within it.

Let us take this *understanding* first, since the Spirit clearly not only "guides" into the truth but also "explains" it. For Paul, the ability to understand is the prerequisite for the broader instruction he gives with regard to life in the Spirit. Of course he does not divorce such understanding from the decision to open oneself, in baptism (which is the work of the Spirit), to this illumination.[2] It is to baptized believers, therefore, that Paul proclaims "a wisdom [not] of this age", namely, that no one knows the inner depths of God but the divine Spirit, and yet that "we have received, not the spirit of the world, but the Spirit which is from God, that we might understand the gifts bestowed on us by God"; moreover, we impart this, not in words of human wisdom, but "as taught by the Spirit" (1 Cor 2:5–13). Thus, in a thoroughly Johannine sense, we are also empowered to discern the spirits, which the man who thinks in a purely earthly way cannot do (1 Cor 2:14–16). This brings us back to the Johannine teaching of the two spheres, the lower ("sarkic") to which the upper ("pneumatic") has no access—with the result that God's wisdom seems folly to the former—and a divine sphere from which everything else can be evaluated. In John we saw

---

[1] H. Schlier, "Eine christologische Credoformel der römischen Gemeinde: Zu Röm 1, 3f.", in *Der Geist und die Kirche* (Herder, 1980), 56–69.

[2] "We were all baptized into one body . . . and all were made to drink of one Spirit" (1 Cor 12:13). "[God] has put his seal upon us and given us his Spirit in our hearts as a guarantee" (2 Cor 1:22). "You also, who have heard the word of truth, . . . were sealed with the promised Holy Spirit" (Eph 1:13). "God our Savior . . . saved us . . . by the washing of regeneration and renewal in the Holy Spirit, which he poured out upon us richly through Jesus Christ our Savior" (Tit 3:4–6).

the two standpoints in dramatic, polemic opposition, with every dialogue between Jesus and the Jews ending with the casting of stones, threats of murder, and the abrupt breaking-off of discussion ("Why do I talk to you at all"? Jn 8:25). So, too, in Paul we see the sphere of the "flesh", which closes itself off in egoism and enmity against God, taking an irreconcilable stance against the sphere dominated by the Spirit; only the latter, coming down from above, can understand the just claims of the law and fulfill it. (Thus what for the sinner is the *adynaton tou nomou* is replaced by *to dikoiōma tou nomou*; the demand of the law is fulfilled by those who "walk not according to the flesh but according to the Spirit", Rom 8:4.)

This provides us with the transition between the Spirit as "Interpreter" of the truth and the One who "guides us" into *life* according to this truth—and it is only this *life* that gives us real understanding. Only he who in fervent discipleship "is united to the Lord becomes one spirit with him" (1 Cor 6:17), for "any one who does not have the Spirit of Christ does not belong to him" (Rom 8:9), namely, to "the Lord of the Spirit" (2 Cor 3:17), who communicates himself to us through his Spirit and in himself. A spirit not proclaiming Christ to be the Lord would not be a divine Spirit, just as no one can proclaim Jesus as Lord "except by the Holy Spirit" (1 Cor 12:3). This would be the place, properly speaking, to explain in detail how the Spirit's "introduction" into the divine sphere implies both justification and sanctification—we read of Christ himself that he was "justified [vindicated] in the Spirit" (1 Tim 3:16)—and how objective sanctification requires us to walk in the Spirit, who desires to bear fruit in us (Gal 5:22) and wishes us to live so as to manifest his "gifts" (*charismata*). What is remarkable is that these gifts both differ from one person to another and yet are designed with a view to the whole ecclesial Body of Christ; in Romans they are all portrayed as normal social functions. The list begins with the gift of prophecy: this is nothing other than the ability to give a correct and fruitful verbal expression of the Christian faith for the other members of the Church (Rom 12:6); it is followed by the many other ways of integrating personal gifts of the Spirit within the community according to Christ's norm.

None of Paul's letters omits to explain how each individual, in whatever state of life he may be, is to put his gift of grace at the service of the Church.

Paul's detailed observations concerning the situation in Corinthian worship should be regarded as nothing other than a corollary to his doctrine of grace, unless one wishes to assume with W. Schmithals and U. Wilckens that Paul, attempting to interpret such Corinthian phenomena as glossolalia, had underestimated the influence of foreign, gnostic *sophia* speculation.[3] From the pagan point of view, after all, any and every instance of unintelligible babbling could be justified as being "mystical". Crucially, the Apostle only tolerates glossolalia in the Spirit if there are "prophets" present who can translate it into a language the congregation can understand; again, the charism of prophecy is adduced as being among the most important: the triad of "apostles, prophets, teachers" heads the list, clearly demarcated from the others. "The real work of the Spirit in man is . . . to lead him, through his mind and his natural intelligence, to full insight, knowledge, and understanding. That is why glossolalia has the lowest place in the list of 'charismata'."[4] It is not something to be striven for, since one should "desire the higher gifts" (1 Cor 12:31); and even these—even prophecy and *gnosis* (13:2)—are worth nothing without that *agape* which is a "way" that lies beyond all individual gifts of grace (12:31). Nor is *agape* a gift distributed by the Holy Spirit "according to his will", but rather it is his very own presence, "God's love . . . poured into our hearts" (Rom 5:5). It is only when Paul speaks as "a fool" that he mentions miracles wrought by him (2 Cor 12:12) and the raptures he experienced, in which he "heard things that cannot be told" (12:4).[5] Nor should the Holy Spirit's Pentecost miracle (as Luke understands it) be equated with glossolalia: quite the contrary, for then people of all nations understood the one language of the apostolic preaching (Acts 2:11). "Thus, tongues

[3] Walter Schmithals, *Die Gnosis in Korinth* (1956); Ulrich Wilckens, *Weisheit und Torheit* (1959).

[4] Kurt Stalder, *Das Werk des Geistes in der Heiligung bei Paulus* (Zürich: EVZ-Verlag, 1962), 92.

[5] On the pneumatological basis of Paul's many visions: Ernst Benz, *Paulus als Visionär* (Wiesbaden: Akad.d.Wiss. u. d.Lit., Franz Steiner, 1952).

are a sign not for believers . . ." (1 Cor 14:22) but a "speaking into the air" (v. 9).

There is no great emphasis on this in Paul's doctrine of the Spirit; what is essential for him is the Spirit's function of interpreting the revelation in Christ. This takes place in the explanatory word of prophecy but, even more, in the whole of existence, and here the Apostle's own life is the clearest and most comprehensive example: "I urge you, then, be imitators of me [1 Cor 4:16], as I am of Christ" (1 Cor 11:1; Phil 3:17); all the more so when affliction is linked to "joy inspired by the Holy Spirit" (1 Thess 1:6). Everyone in his own way should be an example both for his individual fellow Christians and for the entire community, for, in Paul, the Holy Spirit works toward the perfection of the individual and of the whole Church by liberating believers from the external law and replacing it with the "law" of interior freedom, which is identical with the service of obedience—unto death—that Christ rendered to the Father.

b. Luke

The closer we get to what Jesus himself said about the Spirit, the fewer the sources become. Jesus lived and worked as a man of the Spirit unlike any other; by looking at him it was possible to see what it means to be a bearer, doer, and utterer of the Spirit in every respect; this was so true of his own self that he did not need to discourse upon the Spirit. When he promised the Spirit to his unreceptive and resistant disciples, and when, in the wake of his Resurrection and disappearance, they experienced in various ways that the hitherto impossible discipleship was now possible and real, they were able to understand that this wonderful gift of continuity through their sharing in the Spirit of Christ was in fact the sending of the Spirit from the Father. Thus Luke, in his dual opus, becomes aware that the Church is filled with the Spirit because she is animated by the Spirit of Christ; he is the first to see that Jesus' entire existence—not only after the Resurrection (cf. the early theology of Romans 1:4), not only in the wake of the Baptism with the visible descent of the Spirit (Mk 1:8, 10)

—is grounded on the operation of the Holy Spirit;[6] and in this, though more explicit, he shares the view of Matthew 2:10f.

It follows that Luke introduces the Holy Spirit into his Gospel at several points because of the apostolic Church's experience of the Spirit. Here, for the most part, the Holy Spirit is the ground of bold apostolic preaching. As early as Acts 1:5 we read that the disciples will "be baptized with the Holy Spirit"; at Pentecost the Spirit descends upon the apostles with wind and fire, and they preach "as the Spirit gave them utterance" (2:4), which enables them to recognize that Jesus' promise of the Spirit has been fulfilled (2:33). They urge their listeners to be converted, to be baptized, and thus, having had their sins forgiven, to "receive the gift of the Holy Spirit" (2:38). When the apostles make their profession of faith before the Sanhedrin and are subsequently released, the entire community lifts its voice in thanksgiving, and "the place in which they were gathered together was shaken; and they were all filled with the Holy Spirit and spoke the word of God with boldness" (4:31). Once again the apostles have to stand before the court and profess their faith in the crucified and exalted Lord: "And we are witnesses to these things, and so is the Holy Spirit whom God has given to those who obey him" (5:32). Stephen makes his address to the Jews ("You always resist the Holy Spirit", 7:51) and finally, "full of the Holy Spirit, gazed into heaven and saw the glory of God" (7:55). Paul is thrown down and blinded; subsequently, by the imposition of Ananias' hands, his sight is restored, and he is "filled with the Holy Spirit" (9:17)—evidently for the task of his apostolate. At Cornelius' house Peter reminds him "how God anointed Jesus of Nazareth with the Holy Spirit and with power; how he went about doing good . . ."; as he is speaking, the Holy Spirit comes upon the Gentiles, and they are baptized by Peter (10:45ff.), who avers that it was the Holy Spirit who told him to go to Cornelius (11:12). Ever since the Baptism of Jesus the disciples are aware that Spirit and baptism (or the laying on of hands) go together: so

[6] H. Schürmann, "Die geistgewirkte Lebensentstehung Jesu", in *Festschrift H. Aufderbeck* (Leipzig, 1974); H. Schürmann, *Das Lukasevangelium* I (1969), 39–80; J. Ernst, *Das Evangelium nach Lukas* (Regensburg, 1966), 64–80; G. W. H. Lampe, "The Holy Spirit in the Writings of St. Luke", in *Studies in the Gospels* (Oxford, 1955), 159–200.

it is in the case of the baptism of the eunuch by Philip (8:26ff.),
the imparting of the Holy Spirit in Samaria (8:17), and the baptism of John's disciples in Ephesus (19:1–7). Baptism, however,
is primarily an empowering to preach the gospel. This is true of
the solemn declaration of the Apostolic Council ("It has seemed
good to the Holy Spirit and to us . . .", 15:28), the Spirit's "separation" of Paul and Barnabas for their apostolic task (13:2), and
also of the special guidance of the apostles' paths by the Spirit
who facilitates some things (8:39; 10:19–20; 13:4) and obstructs
others (16:6f.). The gift of prophecy is closely related to preaching and baptism; the "prophet", together with the "teacher", is,
by the Spirit, an interpreter of God's will and word for today and
tomorrow. Without much detailed reflection, Luke can link this
with "speaking in tongues" (10:46; 11:27f.; 13:1; 15:32; 19:6;
21:9f.).[7] All these varied expressions are nonetheless clearly centered on the concept of proclamation; to this extent they are the
ecclesial counterpart to the "Spirit" in the Johannine utterances,
that is, the interpretation, in the anamnesis of the fact of Jesus
Christ, of the meaning this same Jesus Christ has for Christians,
Jews, and Gentiles. The fact that the numerous instances of the
imposition of hands can also have the sacramental significance
of giving the Spirit (consecration for some apostolic task, which
can also become a permanent office) does not deflect us from the
central meaning we are insisting on here: at the commissioning
of a bishop (20:28) or a presbyter (14:28; 20:17) the office of
proclamation is closely allied with the pastoral office.

In evaluating the understanding of the Spirit in Luke's Gospel
we must do so in retrospect, on the basis of the Church's experience of the Spirit. True, the events involving the Spirit in
the Infancy Narratives may suggest that they are echoes of an
Old Testament notion of the Spirit; but when, in his first sermon, Jesus applies to his own person the prophetic promise of
the Spirit (Is 61:1–2, "The Spirit of the Lord God is upon *me*,
because the LORD has anointed *me* . . ."), the Spirit in the entire
Gospel becomes the Spirit of Christ. This is particularly true, as
we have shown above, of his Incarnation. Accordingly, instead of

---

[7] One is inclined to suspect that this stereotyped repetition owes more to
1 Corinthians than to the miracle of Pentecost.

the sober Matthean "Jesus declared" (Mt 11:25: this declaration may be in response to John's question in 11:3 and to the whole misunderstanding of John's mission and prophecy exhibited in 11:7–24), Luke gives us "he rejoiced in the Holy Spirit" (Lk 10:21). As in 1:67, 41, this outburst of holy joy is not psychological in origin but is grounded in the mystery of revelation, which is discussed immediately afterward: that is, the revelation is given, not to the wise, but to the simple, solely at the Son's good pleasure. Once again Luke replaces Matthew's jejune "how much more will your Father who is in heaven give good things to those who ask him" (7:11) with the gift of the Holy Spirit (Lk 11:13), who here epitomizes both the good things that come from God and the gift itself.[8]

c. Matthew and Mark

Three declarations concerning the Spirit are common to all four evangelists. First, at the Baptism of Jesus, there is the warning not to blaspheme against the Holy Spirit and the promise to the disciples that the Holy Spirit will stand by them and inspire them with the right words when they have to give testimony before the courts. In Mark these three passages constitute the only references to the Spirit (1:8; 3:29; 13:11). The event of the Baptism, with heaven opened and the Spirit descending in the form of a dove, is part of the core of the revelation concerning Christ; it is impossible to suggest that Jesus did not utter this promise of the Spirit's assistance: it may be, perhaps, his only mention of the Spirit for the era of the Church, but, according to this promise, the Spirit will be his authentic interpreter in the trials that are in store for believers in the days ahead. All three passages are of the greatest importance for the relationship between Jesus and

[8] It may be correct to follow J. Ernst (see n. 6 above), who points to the baptismal catechesis here; at baptism the Holy Spirit is given as the epitome of all the divine gifts that are mediated through the Church. As Luke sees it, the result of the prayer of intercession would be a challenge to those yet unconverted to enter the community in which the divine Spirit is alive (367–68). In this context Ernst brings out the special significance of prayer (the prayer of Jesus and of the disciples) in Luke's Gospel (368–71).

the Spirit. These various affirmations about Jesus being baptized by the Spirit and being the Spirit-baptizer, placed at the beginning of his preaching activity, constitute an event that has no analogy in the Old Covenant. There *is* an analogy, but only between John's water baptism and Jesus' subsequent baptism with the Spirit (and fire); and again we have nothing in the Old Testament with which to compare the activity of the Baptist: he himself insists that his baptism and that of Jesus are completely different in kind. All the evangelists emphatically underline this difference. The Baptist stresses it from the outset, while he is in expectation of the awaited eschatological "One who comes after me"; and it is confirmed, visibly (to Jesus himself in Mark, to the Baptist in John, and to others, too, perhaps, in Matthew and Luke) when the heavens are opened, the Father speaks, and the Spirit descends.

The Baptist predicts that after him will come One—the ultimate One—who will baptize "with the Holy Spirit and with fire" (Matthew and Luke; Mark omits the "fire"). In the context of the eschatological expectation of a divine fire at the end of time, a fire that will judge, divide, and purify (cf. the other image of the threshing floor), this must be a genuine saying. Confirmation of this is the way Jesus uses the same expression in reference to himself: "I came to cast fire upon the earth . . ." (Lk 12:49); this, too, is an eschatological word, although in a different sense from what the Baptist expects. What distinguishes Jesus from the prophets, whose inspiration was merely intermittent, is that he is equipped by the Spirit of his mission in a definitive way ("[it] remain[ed] on him", Jn 1:32) and also that his status is confirmed by the Father's voice from heaven. The baptismal theophany is explicitly trinitarian at all points, even if those who record these events are not yet thinking in terms of trinitarian dogma. For them the decisive issue is that this event defines who Jesus is right at the beginning of his ministry, prior to any guesses men may hazard about him. At his Baptism, Jesus is defined in the theophany as he who baptizes with the Spirit, in line with the prediction of the Forerunner; that is why the latter—understandably—resists the idea of the more important Baptizer being put in the position of the baptizand: "I need to be baptized by you, and do you come to me?" (Mt 3:14). Jesus'

answer, namely, that this apparent paradox is right, "all righteousness", has far-reaching importance: Jesus must take upon
himself the Old Covenant, of which the Baptist is the culmina-
tion (Mt 11:9), in order to fulfill it from within and so reveal its
preparatory nature; Luke brings this out in the symbolic meeting
of the two mothers, when Elizabeth's child is sanctified for his
mission, in the Spirit, by the Child of Mary. The Father's word
is to be understood as a word of mission and of ratification;
whereas here it is a quotation from the Old Testament (Is 42:1,
which goes on: "I have put my Spirit upon him, he will bring
forth justice to the nations": the Spirit himself becomes visible at the Baptism of Jesus), the voice on Tabor completes the
command: "Listen to him" (Mt 17:5 parr.). In both scenes the
accent is on the inseparability of Word and Spirit; it is the Word
who, as Word of the Spirit, interprets both God and himself.
At Jesus' Baptism the Spirit hovers over him, guaranteeing the
adequate relationship between the One who sends and his sent
Word; on Tabor the Spirit is symbolized by the "overshadowing" "bright cloud" (Mt 17:5; cf. Mk 9:7; Lk 9:34), just as, in
the Old Covenant, the cloud of Yahweh's glory overshadowed
the Ark of the Covenant (Ex 40:35). In the New Covenant this
same cloud, now as the Holy Spirit, "overshadowed" the new
Ark of the Covenant, Mary (Lk 1:35); and in the Apocalypse's
"throne-room vision" this overshadowing dissolves into a rain-
bow with its seven colors, surrounding God and the Lamb (Rev
4:3). But just as in Exodus 40:35 a twofold presence of God is
manifest, that is, *above* the Ark and *in* it, so it is with Mary, and
so it is in the Baptism scene, where the Spirit's "hovering" over
Jesus is also an internal filling of the Son with his (the Spirit's)
entire fullness: "For he whom God has sent utters the words
of God, for it is not by measure that he gives [him] the Spirit"
(Jn 3:34).[9] Ever since his Baptism, however, it is Jesus himself
who is the "Pneumatic One", as is shown by the remark common to all the Synoptics, that the Holy Spirit drove him into
the wilderness (Mark 1:12 puts it more vigorously: "threw him
out"). The assistance of the Spirit does not come to an end with

[9] Cf. *Theo-Drama* (= TD) III, 191: "The Spirit is *in* him in fullness, so that the
Son can surrender himself to the guiding Spirit *above* him without any sense of
heteronomy."

the temptations, as is indicated by Luke, who has Jesus returning "in the power of the Spirit into Galilee" (Lk 4:14), taking Isaiah 61:1–2 as the text for his inaugural sermon and claiming this prophetic Spirit as his own (4:18); at the same time he looks ahead to new temptations (4:13; 22:28). Having made this clear, it would be superfluous if Jesus were continually to make reference to his relationship with the Spirit; only occasionally, if the situation requires it, does Jesus do this (Mt 12:28); here it is in the context of a miracle: people were denying that it came from God, but Jesus had performed it in the Holy Spirit.

The second theme common to the Synoptics is the warning against blaspheming against the Holy Spirit. The simplest form is in Luke: "Every one who speaks a word against the Son of man will be forgiven; but he who blasphemes against the Holy Spirit will not be forgiven" (12:10). This passage stands in isolation and is also in a certain tension with the logion before it, that is, that he who "acknowledges me before men" will be acknowledged by the Son of man at the Judgment, but he who "denies me before men will be denied before the angels of God". These two sayings can only be reconciled if, in the first one, the Spirit is regarded as belonging to the Son of man. Mark, on the other hand, draws a distinction: all blasphemies will be forgiven (by Jesus, who is fully empowered to do so), "but whoever blasphemes against the Holy Spirit never has forgiveness, but is guilty of an eternal sin". Mark goes on to give the reason why: "for they had said, 'He has an unclean spirit'" (3:28–30). They are blaspheming, therefore, against the Holy Spirit who is at work in the miraculous deeds wrought by Jesus and, hence, against the only power of divine forgiveness that now exists on earth. Once a blasphemy has been thrown in the face of grace, there can be no grace of forgiveness until it is withdrawn. Matthew says the same, but whereas Mark puts it in terms of plain finality, Matthew gives more detail: "[neither] in this age [nor] in the age to come" (Mt 12:32), which indicates the thought forms of the Jewish-Christian community for whom he is writing. All three modes of expression, originating in Jesus' mouth and self-awareness, point to the same thing, namely, his certainty, not only of speaking, but of acting in the Holy Spirit. The guilt of those who do not recognize him, who regard him and insult him as a mere man, can be overlooked; but those who have recognized the higher power in him—like the Pharisees, who accuse him of wielding demonic influence —cannot entertain any prospect of forgiveness, for they have blasphemed against that spiritual power they have actually recognized. They are in an inner contradiction. This passage shows us how much Jesus acknowledges the Holy Spirit given to him as a reality coming from the Father, a holy and truly divine reality; he defends it even at the risk of being slandered himself.

Mark's third reference to the Spirit incorporates it into his "little Apocalypse" and sets it within a universal context: "The gospel must first be preached to all nations." Only then do we read, "and when they bring you to trial and deliver you up, do not be anxious beforehand what you are to say; but say whatever is given you in that hour, for it is not you who speak, but the Holy Spirit" (Mk 13:10–11). "Here Jesus himself is speaking to his disciples, giving them the promise that John includes in his discourse on the Paraclete."[10] Jesus speaks with great confidence of the continuance of his gospel after his death; this will be guaranteed by the Holy Spirit's responsibility for its correct proclamation. Scholars disagree as to whether the "universal" context comes from Mark himself, but his conception of a gospel that extends beyond Jesus' lifetime is manifestly present in the words he attributes to Jesus (cf., for example, 8:35; 10:29). Here again, in the Church's proclamation of the Word—a proclamation sustained by the Spirit—the Spirit is the reliable Interpreter.

d. Matthew

Matthew clarifies certain points found in Mark; with regard to the understanding of the Spirit, he occupies a position between Mark and Luke. With Luke he asserts that Jesus was conceived by the Holy Spirit (1:18), an event that is explained and justified in some detail for Joseph's benefit. Where Mark and Luke speak, in the context of Jesus' promise to his disciples, only of the "Holy Spirit", Matthew says, "[it is] the Spirit of your Father

---

[10] W. Grundmann, *Markus* (1965), 264. Cf. the parallels Mt 10:19–20; Lk 12:11–12 and 21:14–15.

speaking through you" (10:20). This means that, for the disciples, the Spirit loses something of his anonymity; he appears
more clearly as the divinely appointed Guardian—a Johannine
theme. In the scene in which Jesus drives out demons, thereby
upsetting some who witnessed it, Luke says that Jesus drives
out the demons "by the finger of God"; here, too, Matthew
speaks of the Spirit: "But if it is by the Spirit of God that I
cast out demons . . .", since shortly beforehand he had quoted
the prophecy in which Yahweh puts his Spirit upon his chosen
Beloved (12:18). Nonetheless it is probable that Luke has retained the more original version. Finally Matthew concludes his
Gospel with the following trinitarian formula that was to have
such immense consequences: "Go therefore and make disciples
of all nations, baptizing them in the name of the Father and of
the Son and of the Holy Spirit" (Mt 29:19), which became the
pattern both for the three baptismal interrogations (which developed into the Creed) and the Church's baptismal formula itself.
On one occasion (together with Mk 12:36) he refers back to
the Spirit of Old Testament prophecy: When the Pharisees ask
whose son the Messiah will be, he quotes David, who "inspired
by the (Holy) Spirit" (22:43) called him Lord, not his "son".

e. The Old Covenant

This brings us back once again to the Old Testament, the ultimate background, where we need only repeat that "Spirit of
Yahweh" and "Word of Yahweh" are largely synonymous. In
strict monotheism there is ultimately only one objective self-
revelation of God, even if it can present itself, and be subjectively assimilated, in various ways. Theologically speaking, the
Word of God and the Spirit of God are not two distinguishable
Interpreters: both refer back to the same divine "truth" (objective) or "truthfulness" (subjective). This is intrinsic to them:
they carry their own credibility within them, whereas the distinguishing of true and false bearers of the Spirit, true and false
prophets of the Word, remains a late and secondary matter. The
equivalence of God's truth and truthfulness points back to his
whole being and to his dealings that express that being. Thus

the Psalms continually link *veritas* with *misericordia* or with *mansuetudo* or *aequitas*, and so on. God's Word and Spirit carry their own credentials. In the New Testament, where the uniquely incarnate "Word" is distinguished from the Interpreter "Spirit", this fundamental relationship is reflected in all those Johannine passages in which the Word, Jesus, speaks of the inner truth of his testimony concerning the Father—whether we think of this as a single testimony of God or as a twofold testimony by Father and Son—and the apostolic and ecclesial Spirit equally carries his truth within him as he bears witness to Christ, as Paul, preeminently, shows in his "demonstration of *pneuma* and *dynamis*" in the "Logos of the Cross" (see 1 Cor 2:4) and in his doctrine of the inner credibility of his ministry of reconciliation (2 Cor 2–6), "to be known and read by all men" (2 Cor 3:2), since his entire existence is "the open statement of the truth [of God]" (2 Cor 4:2). The fact that, in the Old and New Testaments, this self-evidence in the way God reveals himself and thus is "truthful" can be met, and is met, with men's refusal to see and to acknowledge it does not affect its quality.

It is true that, in the Old Covenant, God's Spirit and his Word are initially distinguished as relatively distinct modes of his self-revelation, but even then one must observe that God always gives himself as an indivisible Whole, whether as Spirit or as Word. "What the prophets have to proclaim is *the* Word of Yahweh. It is never *a* word of Yahweh. . . . Thus it is always the whole Word of God that is uttered in each individual revelation."[11] The Spirit of God—however various his manifestations—is always the evidence of a powerful, assertive presence of God, in nature, in the covenant history as a whole, or in particular events of that covenant. Even in the early forms of classic prophecy, when the Spirit of God "overtakes" certain people, putting them into a trance or empowering them to do certain deeds (the Judges), the Spirit is not entirely separate from the Word (cf. the announcements of the Judges' births). In the great prophets of the Word, who never (Jeremiah) or seldom speak of the Spirit, the Spirit is actually more at work than elsewhere, not only in their

---

[11] L. Köhler, *Theologie des Alten Testaments* (Tübingen: Mohr, 1936), 90.

vocations—which overwhelm them—but also in the irresistible
necessity that is laid upon them to utter the Word that has been
put into them (often they have actually to eat it: Jer 15:16; Ezek
3:1ff.); if they attempt to resist this necessity of speaking, a flaming fire burns within them (Jer 20:7–9). Later prophets again
give the name "Spirit" to that *dynamis* which indwells the Word
of God; the word of God's law, experienced and grasped as a
living power in the lives of men, can also be designated as Spirit.
When the author of the "Miserere" implores, "Take not your
holy Spirit from me" (Ps 51:11), or another says, "Let your
good spirit lead me on a level path" (Ps 143:10), what is meant
is not a wordless Spirit but the Spirit who indwells the word
of the Law. The concept of "wisdom", identified partly with
the Spirit and partly with the Word, serves to smooth out the
difference between them even more effectively. Ultimately they
can be named in the same breath: "My spirit which is upon
you, and my words which I have put into your mouth, shall not
depart out of your mouth" (Is 59:21). This invocation of the
Spirit, which refers more to God's personal power to act decisively, becomes more and more necessary in the later period as
the "Word" becomes increasingly ossified into an unchangeable
written law. Thus, in the great prayer of expiation (Nehemiah
9:13, 34), the revelation of the law in the desert is linked with
the gift of the good Spirit (9:20), and the prophetic word is portrayed as having been effected by God's Spirit (9:30). Finally the
entire Torah can be regarded as inspired by the Spirit, and, where
prophecy has ceased, that power which gives life to the Word
of the past and brings it into the present with an immediate and
binding force can be termed Spirit.[12] But "Jewish thought was
never able to make a precise delimitation between them."[13]

This unity of God's Word and God's Spirit in the Old Covenant
is of great significance in the context of our *theo-logical* task. We

[12] W. Eichrodt, *Theology of the Old Testament*, trans. J. A. Baker, vol. 2 (London:
SCM Press, 1967), 69–76. "The community has no difficulty in understanding
God's Spirit and God's Word as a single unity": E. Sell, in *Theologie des Alten
Testaments* (1933), 53.

[13] Eichrodt, *Theology*, 79. On the Spirit in the OT, cf. the many works by P. van
Imschoot, cited in ThW VI, 331.

shall see that their interrelatedness will continue in the New Covenant since, as we have already shown, Jesus' word concerning the Father is in itself a word infused by the Spirit of the Father, a word assimilated and uttered in the Spirit of Jesus; after Jesus disappears from view, the Spirit not only constantly interprets the (total) word of Jesus to the Church, but also, through his operation, makes Jesus sacramentally and existentially present. This takes place in the Body of Christ, which the Spirit builds up as his holy Temple. "The same Spirit inspires the whole Body to the end of time. But each generation receives its own manifestation of the Spirit's presence." The fundamental lines of the New Covenant, which are laid down by the Word, cannot be changed, but the Spirit "leaves to successive generations the task and the joy of pursuing them into new regions of thought and life, as the Divine Guide points the way".[14]

[14] H. B. Swete, *The Holy Spirit in the New Testament* (London, 1909), 360. We have already discussed (above) the special spiritual endowment expected of the Messiah. Cf. on this subject: Robert Koch, *Geist und Messias* (Vienna: Herder, 1950). Here the Messiah appears also as a kind of recapitulation of all forms of spirit-bearer (judge, king, prophet) down through the history of Israel. The Spirit who rests upon him simultaneously extends his influence over the entire people of the end-time.

4

PREVIEW

A brief examination of the patristic period must suffice here, since we are only attempting to show that, in our interpretation of the Spirit's role, we are simply assembling the wealth of aspects treated by the Fathers and focusing them in the Johannine concept, according to which the Spirit's "leading into all truth" means his setting forth all the "treasures of wisdom and knowledge" hidden in Christ (Col 2:3). Two things will need to be kept in mind: first, the difficulty experienced by the first theologians in fashioning a doctrine of the Holy Spirit, given his manifold expressions and also his closeness to the work of Christ (from whom he is yet distinct); and second, the necessity of keeping oneself open to this rich manifold in order, on this basis, to reach a theory that does justice to all the functions of the Spirit.

For the first Fathers, who did not yet have the canon of New Testament writings available to them, the relationship between the prophetic Spirit in "Scripture" (that is, in the Old Testament) and the Spirit who spoke and operated in Jesus and in the early Church must have been an important question. They recognized (and this is itself a Johannine theme, confirmed by 1 Peter 1:11 and 2 Peter 1:19-20) that the prophetic Spirit of the Old Covenant had spoken with a view to Jesus; the Letter of Barnabas insists on this (10:2; 12:8; 9:7; 13:5), as does Irenaeus, who is so concerned to demonstrate the unity of the two Testaments (1:10, 1; 3:21, 4; 4:10, 8; 4:33, 1; 4:36, 2); Novatian follows Irenaeus in this (*De trin.* 29). Later on, Didymus will do the same (with greater clarity than Athanasius) in his book on the Holy Spirit (33-37). Theodore of Mopsuestia will come up with a fine distinction: While the men of the Old Covenant knew nothing of the Holy Spirit as a distinct Person in God,[1] nonetheless the Spirit's operation began long before the Son's

[1] Commentary on Haggai (PG 66, 486).

Incarnation.[2] Cyril of Jerusalem sheds much light when discussing the prophetic inspiration given in anticipation of Christ (*Cat.* 16, 4); and for Leo, too, the whole Old Testament is filled with the Spirit (*Sermo* 76).

It is equally important to note that these first Fathers, following the apostles and the Spirit who is now poured out "upon all flesh" (Acts 2:17), themselves write as Spirit-filled witnesses to the truth of Christ. Here, first of all, we think of Ignatius, but also of Clement, the *Shepherd*, individual apologists, and, of course, Tertullian.

However, the normative formula, to which the post-Nicene Fathers, too, will adhere when constructing a theology of the Holy Spirit, remains that coined by Irenaeus: "God can do everything. Once he was seen in a prophetic manner through the mediation of the Spirit; then he was known through the mediation of the Son when we were adopted as sons; and finally he will be beheld in the Kingdom of God according to his Fatherhood. The Spirit prepares a man for the Son, the Son leads him to the Father, and the Father grants him incorruptibility and eternal life" (*Adv. Haer.* 4, 20, 5). Here the Spirit is acknowledged as the Interpreter and the One who leads us to the Son; the Son, in turn, interprets the Father and leads us to him. This idea is repeated (*Adv. Haer.* 5, 36, 2, and *Epid.* 7), complemented by two important observations: the Spirit is given primarily, not to the individual, but to the Church; only through the Church is the Spirit given to the individual (*Adv. Haer.* 4, 33, 9; 3, 24, 1); thereby the Spirit brings to perfection the work begun by Jesus (5, 8, 1).

When he becomes a Montanist, Tertullian gives a radical shift to the Spirit's "leading"; now the interpreting Spirit unfolds things that Jesus himself mentioned only briefly (*De monog.* 2, 4): the prior rule of faith is maintained, but in such a way that the Scriptures, as God's work, "progress" from the childhood of ancient prophecy to the youth of the Gospel, and are brought to full maturity by the Paraclete. This, according to Tertullian, is the meaning of Jesus' words, "I have much to say to you, but you cannot bear it now. When the Spirit of truth comes, he will

---

[2] Commentary on Nahum (PG 66, 408).

lead you into all truth" (*De virg. vel.* 1)—a thought that points ahead to Joachim of Fiore. Tertullian maintains, however, that the Spirit's interpretation does not overthrow the immutable *regula fidei*: the Spirit is nothing but the Witness to Jesus and ultimately the One who "explains the economy" in its totality, "the One who leads into all the truth that is to be found in the Father, the Son, and the Holy Spirit, according to the doctrine of the Christian faith" (*Adv. Prax.* 30). He is the Son's *vicarius* (*Praesc.* 13; *De virg. vel.* 1), just as the Son is the Father's *vicarius* (*Adv. Marc.* 3, 6).

Avoiding Tertullian's daring, the *Shepherd* of Hermas portrays the Spirit straightforwardly as the One who teaches scriptural truth (*Sim.* 9, 25, 2; *Mand.* 3, 1f.). Hippolytus gives us the formula: the Father commands, the Son obeys, the Spirit gives understanding (*Adv. Noet.* 14). For Novatian, too, the Spirit is the Teacher of all truth, not theoretically, but by communicating eternal life (*De Trin.* 29). Cyprian vividly describes how the Spirit opened closed doors for him and brought him light and how what (before his baptism) had seemed impossible subsequently proved to be easy; he is not boasting, he says, but only manifesting his gratitude to God (*Ad Donat.* 4). For the Alexandrians the Spirit is the One who first introduces us to the *"gnosis* of the truth"* (Clement, *Paed.* 2, 2, 20; *Strom.* 7, 7, 44), and for Origen he is the real Interpreter of the Scripture he himself has inspired (*Ep. ad Gregor.* 3). For Cyril of Jerusalem, the Spirit is the One "who, by the prophets, announced the Messiah and who came down after the manifestation of Christ in order to bear witness to him" (*Cat.* 16, 3). The faithful must not be confused by the multiplicity of scriptural statements concerning the Spirit and the spirits; they must hold fast to Christ, who said, "the words I have spoken to you are spirit and life"; he who comes from Christ and speaks unmistakably to us is the Holy Spirit (ibid., 14). In contrast to the violent, demonic spirits who darken men's minds and put them in a trance, the Holy Spirit aims only at what is good and wholesome. He spreads "rays of light and knowledge"; as when the sun rises, "the man who has been made worthy by the Holy Spirit and enlightened in his soul sees things he was unaware of until now" (ibid., 16). Cyril reverses Irenaeus' formula but uses it in the same sense when he says that "the Father gives all graces to the Son, and the Son hands them on to the Spirit. . . . The Father gives all graces through the Son, in connection with the Holy Spirit. Nor are the graces of the Father any different from those of the Son or of the Spirit" (ibid., 24).[3]

This quotation from Cyril places us in the period during which the theologians will be constructing their theological Pneumatology. What they say about the Spirit as Guide and Interpreter will not differ from what we have here set forth, yet now another problem takes center stage, namely, that of the divinity and "personhood" of the Holy Spirit. Given what we have said so far, we, too, are now faced with this question and must address it before proceeding with our analysis of the Spirit's function in theo-logic.

---

[3] On the foregoing, cf. H. B. Swete, *The Holy Spirit in the Ancient Church* (London, 1912). In conclusion we give the words of Thomas Aquinas: "For the Spirit will not speak of himself, but of me, because he will proceed from me. For, just as the Son does not work of himself, but by the power of the Father, so the Spirit (since he proceeds from others, that is, from Father and Son) will not speak of himself but only of everything he hears. After all, he receives his wisdom, like his being, from eternity, and he utters this (received wisdom), not physically, but by inwardly illuminating the minds [of believers]" (*Lectura in Joh.*, no. 2103).

II. THE HOLY SPIRIT AS PERSON

So far, in envisaging a Pneumatology that would see the Spirit's central, comprehensive role as that of Interpreter of God's self-proclamation in Jesus Christ—and such interpretation had necessarily to operate by leading believers into the realm of the *mysterium*—we have bracketed out the question of "who" the Spirit is. Initially the problem was to know whether this Interpreter was the enabling principle of an inner "understanding" of the divine revelation; even at that stage it seemed worth questioning whether this principle could be simultaneously an "object" of theological reflection. It became clear from Scripture, and even clearer from an examination of the Fathers, that any principle that can introduce us to God must be itself divine; and this meant that we could no longer skirt round the question of "who" the Spirit is. The Old Testament answer did not seem difficult: the Spirit of Yahweh was only a particular aspect or a particular mode of operation of his single, indivisible, divine power or almighty divinity. In the New Testament, however, the question became acute: Is this traditional understanding adequate?

At the outset there seemed to be no objection to this received tradition: Why should not the divine power (be it called *pneuma* or *dynamis*) "fill" John the Forerunner (Lk 1:15) and even his father (Lk 1:67) and mother (Lk 1:41); why should it not "overshadow" Mary (Lk 1:35), inspire Simeon with prophecy (Lk 2:25–26), and finally come down upon Jesus at his Baptism (Lk 3:22), enabling him to perform his deeds in divine strength (Mt 12:28)? Two objections arise, however, against this simple understanding of the question. If, in the event of the Incarnation, God the Father is distinct from Jesus the "Son of God" (Mk 1:1; Lk 1:35), this Spirit of God must pertain essentially to him who is now called Father and who—most clearly in the Baptism scene—sends him (the Spirit) down upon Jesus, the "Beloved Son" (or servant?—*pais?*). Here we discern the outline of the Eastern Church's doctrine of the Trinity, with its assertion that the Spirit proceeds from the Father alone; but at the same moment the danger of adoptionism arises: Does this not mean that Jesus becomes just one of a series of spirit-filled prophets (and, for example, all those who are listed at the beginning of Luke's Gospel as being equipped with the Spirit)? If this is to be avoided, if we are to attribute to Jesus, the Son of God, the same relationship to the "Spirit of God" as to the Father, what happens at the Baptism of Jesus becomes unintelligible. Furthermore we have to ask whether (and in what way) the Spirit of God can still be held to be a force and power of the one, undifferentiated God (as in the Old Covenant), since this image of God has been decisively superseded. So we encounter a question already indicated in our "Preludes": is the divine Pneuma henceforth to be understood as something that expresses the undivided fullness (the "essence") of God, something that is neither Father nor Son, or are we to conceive of this "something" as two things at the same time: a Third beside Father and Son *and* at the same time a kind of recapitulation of the whole (triune) Godhead?[1] This problem cannot be avoided if we are to conduct a theology of the Trinity on a New Testament basis; it is of considerable moment in our theo-logic.

---

[1] F.-X. Durrwell, *L'Esprit Saint de Dieu* (Cerf, 1983), 177: "Tous les attributs de Dieu [sont] hypostasiés en lui."

I

WHAT SCRIPTURE SAYS

In late Old Testament and Jewish writings we find that the Spirit is almost treated as a person; this, however, is of no concern to us here, because in these instances there is no intention of going beyond strict monotheism, nor is this particular "personalization" any different from other personalizations (of wisdom, of the shekhina, and so on).[1] We must interrogate the New Testament alone. Possible derivations such as we have already mentioned, for instance, of the term "Paraclete" from Jewish or earlier Old Testament sources, are of no importance with regard to the problem of the Trinity.

First of all, it must be said that the New Testament has no interest in defining the Holy Spirit's "personhood" more closely, just as it is not interested in systematic teaching on the Trinity. There is a wide field in which the Spirit appears as a quasi-impersonal power of God. (At this stage it does not matter whether this power is attributable to God the Father, either exclusively or preeminently, or can be wielded by the risen Son.) This is the *dynamis* with which God the Father endows his Son for his work on earth, raises his dead Son from the dead, and invests his exalted Son with authority over the same power that belongs to him, the Father. This results in a second problem, which begins to emerge in the New Testament but is not treated with the distinctions we might desire: The Son seems to be so endowed with the power of God that it is (almost?) as if he *coincides* with it: "The Lord is the Spirit" (2 Cor 3:17),[2] even if the writer immediately goes on to introduce a qualification (vv. 17-18).

---

[1] E. Sjöberg, art. "Pneuma", in ThW VI, 385-87. Here the Spirit is characterized as a mode of God's presence for man.

[2] This famous, much-discussed passage could plausibly be remedied by the addition of a single letter, namely, if οὗ ὁ were put instead of ὁ. This was expressed before but was suppressed by the exegetes in the absence of textual support; it has been revived by Alberto Giglioli, "Il Signore è lo Spirito", *Rivista Biblica* 20 (1972 Brescia): 263-76, on the basis of other Pauline passages where "a first sentence is succeeded by a second with the grammatically identical value." In this case the reading would be: "Where the Lord is, there is the Spirit; and where the

The many New Testament passages in which the Pneuma is mentioned in close connection with God's *dynamis*[3] must not be reduced—by wayward speculation—to some "quasi-physical" sphere, possibly influenced by Stoic thought:[4] the simplest recourse to the Old Testament will show that anything of the kind is excluded right from the outset in the case of Yahweh's "spirit" and "power". Yahweh's spirit and power can in no way be termed "impersonal"; he himself is always their subject. Since this personal idea is always in the background of New Testament thought, the *pneuma*, even if it is no longer identical with the Father or Christ, cannot suddenly sink into impersonality. So it cannot be held to be a *metabasis eis allo genos* when the divine Spirit-Power appears elsewhere as a "personal being".[5] Initially we can let this term "personal" stand (it also applies to the Johannine words concerning the Paraclete) since pure "impersonality" is out of the question;[6] on the other hand, the New Testament gives no clear statement of a "personhood", with regard

---

Spirit is, there is freedom." Against such a reading it is of course possible to cite 1 Corinthians 15:45, where Christ, the second Adam, is designated a "life-giving Pneuma". The attempt, in 2 Corinthians 3:17a, to make Pneuma the *subject*—as K. Prümm does in *Diakonia Pneumatos* I (Rome: Herder, 1967) with reference to the preceding passage (Israel's return to the Lord = Kyrios)—must be regarded as a far-fetched failure.

[3] W. Grundmann, *Der Begriff der Kraft in der neutestamentlichen Gedankenwelt* (Stuttgart, 1982).

[4] There is a certain refinement of earlier, cruder ideas where the Spirit is interpreted as an (eschatological) "heavenly sphere", as "the realm of heavenly substance": E. Schweizer, "Pneuma", in ThW VI, 413, 30–31.

[5] Cf. H. Bertrams, *Das Werk des Geistes nach der Anschauung des Apostels Paulus* (Münster, 1913): only at the end does he assemble a few passages illustrating the "personhood" of the Spirit (e.g., Rom 8:16: "the Spirit . . . bearing witness with our spirit . . ."; Rom 8:26: "The Spirit himself intercedes for us with sighs too deep for words"; Gal 4:6: "the Spirit [in] our hearts, crying, 'Abba, Father' "; 1 Tim 4:1: "The Spirit expressly says . . ."). See also F. Büchsel, *Der Geist Gottes im NT* (Gütersloh, 1926), 410ff.; A. Wikenhauser, *Die Christusmystik des Apostels Paulus*, 2nd ed. (Herder, 1956), 54, where further references are adduced for the "distinct hypostasis" of the Spirit. Cf. E. Stauffer, ThW II, 108, 27, where the Spirit (in association with the exalted Johannine Christ) "appears in a certain distinct, personal role".

[6] For Albert Schweitzer (*Die Mystik des Apostels Paulus* [Tübingen, 1930]) the Spirit is simply the reality of the new aeon or the Messianic Kingdom (163ff.). J. Weiss sees "the metaphysical equivalence of the Person of Christ and the imper-

to the Spirit, that would be equal to that of the Father and the Son.

Two issues are pressing here: the Spirit appears as a divine reality located between God the Father and God the Son (it is he, the "Spirit of the Son", whom the Father causes to cry "Abba! Father!" in us: Gal 4:6); at the same time, and precisely because of this role, there remains something elusive about the Spirit: "The wind [*pneuma*] blows where it wills, and . . . you do not know where it comes from or where it goes" (Jn 3:8). This refers, not primarily to the Spirit's (personal) freedom, but rather to the fact that he cannot be held fast as a person either. Heribert Mühlen speaks of "the absolute impenetrability of the Holy Spirit's personal distinctiveness".[7]

This is amplified further in the second problem, that of the unity and distinction between the Spirit-filled Son (particularly the exalted Son) and the Holy Spirit. Here, exegesis has been largely unanimous in speaking of a merely "dynamic identification", since the closest approximation between the two (as in 2 Cor 3:17 and 1 Cor 15:45) always includes a distinction between them. "Christ is the Bearer, Possessor, Proclaimer, and Communicator of the Spirit",[8] but he is not himself the Spirit. In John the distinction becomes completely clear: Jesus must go away so that the Spirit may come, and this Spirit will "take of what is mine" and interpret it to the faithful. When Jesus "breathes" the Spirit upon the disciples at Easter, he shows his right to dispose of the Spirit but by no means his identity with him. Furthermore, it is not Jesus who leads the disciples "into all truth" (and he is truth) but the Spirit. And when the Spirit is called the one who "witnesses" to Jesus (in the third and fourth sections on the Paraclete), the distinction between them simply cannot be overlooked. This evident distinction in John (which yet seems moderated in sayings such as "My words are spirit and life") is less strongly emphasized in Paul's portrayal of the

---

sonal Pneuma" as an idea natural to Paul, who had grown up "in an ancient way of thought", since here "the boundary between abstract concept and personhood" was easily overstepped (ZNW, 1920, 139f.).

[7] GP 166.

[8] A. Wikenhauser, *Christusmystik*, 53.

Spirit; this is because, here, the transfiguration of the Risen One is shown in terms of his perfect participation in the Pneuma: accordingly, as he continually gives believers a share in himself (*en Christōi*), he also gives them a share in the Pneuma (*en pneumati*).[9]

The New Testament, which is primarily testimony and not speculation, has no interest in defining more precisely this mysterious identity-in-distinction. It will set forth in detail the ethical effects and demands of the gift of the Spirit of Jesus and of the Father (Rom 8:9; 5:5); from this we can see what the Spirit of God and the Spirit of Christ will achieve in the Church. If we lift our eyes from these effects to the God of the New Testament, we can certainly find many passages that speak of the Father-Son-Spirit sequence. K. H. Schelkle has listed a great number of these trinitarian formulae found in the Letters and in John; yet he observes that they "lack, as yet, a strict, formal expression, and

[9] It remains a matter of debate whether E. Schweizer's view that "being in the Spirit" is "synonymous with being in Christ" (ThW VI, 434, 24) can be upheld without further qualification. The preexistent Son is never equated with the Holy Spirit. Jesus' earthly existence is brought about, not by himself, but by the Spirit. However close the Spirit and Christ are in Paul, he makes clear distinctions between them. It is Christ, not the Spirit, who is to be formed in believers. The Spirit possesses none of the features of the Crucified One whom the Apostle strives to emulate. On the other hand, it is the Spirit who effects the presence of Christ in the Church of the faithful and binds them to the Lord. It is the Spirit who glorifies Christ (and not vice versa), whereas it can be said that the Father and Son reciprocally glorify one another. It is the Spirit who brings to mind the words and deeds of Jesus and leads believers into all the latter's truth (and not vice versa). Similarly, Paul's extreme formulation, "the Lord [i.e., Christ] is the Spirit" cannot be turned around (in spite of the views of some writers): the New Testament Pneuma, especially in his service of interpretation, never acts as Kyrios. —On this basis we must reject Ingo Hermann's study, *Kyrios und Pneuma: Studie zur Christologie der paulinischen Hauptbriefe* (Munich: Kösel, 1961), as unsubstantiated and one-sided. Hermann regards "the question of a trinitarian or nontrinitarian Pneuma" and "the person/nonperson categories" as "utterly foreign" to the world of the Pauline utterances (13); his view is that "the identity of Kyrios and Pneuma is the basis of *all* Pauline statements about the divine Pneuma" (132) and that *kyrios* can denote both the fullness of "the Old Testament God" (134) and (preeminently) the risen Christ. He thus rejects totally any understanding that sees the Spirit as a "person": "There is no justification for a hypostatic or trinitarian understanding of Pneuma" (138). "Pneuma is the medium of encounter between God and man" (113), or "the dynamic presence of the Kyrios in the community" (51). "Paul would have been completely baffled by any attempts to locate the Pneuma in the Trinity" (53).

they are not framed in strictly dogmatic terms. . . . The eternal Father became manifest in the Son; the Spirit is God's presence in the Church. At the same time the Spirit is liberated from the realm of pure functionality: he is personified and rendered distinct." As for the trinitarian command to baptize, found at the end of Matthew (28:19), it must be only the record of the universal faith of the Church that is professed at the reception of baptism.[10]

When it comes to thinking about, or at least circumscribing, the mighty, life-giving, divine power that is manifest in the Father's sending of Jesus and later in the Son's glorification and the sending of the Spirit upon the Church, the New Testament leaves the question open.[11] It is content to circle around the mysterious reality of the Spirit from many different, often apparently contradictory sides.

The most prominent trait of the Spirit is his freedom, which John expresses (3:8) by saying that we cannot grasp his "blowing" (he blows "where [he] wills"); Acts records his unaccountable visitations and his imparting of instructions and prohibitions; Paul speaks of the Spirit liberating believers from slavery to sin (—sin that the external law actually produces) and empow-

[10] K. H. Schelkle, *Theologie des NT* II: *Gott war in Christus*, 313–22, esp. 319, 320f. On the "essence of the Spirit", ibid., 247–48; see also the same author's "Der Dreieine als Vater, Sohn und Geist", *Bibel und Kirche* 15 (1960): 117ff. Here 2 Corinthians 13:13 is regarded as a liturgical formula, and 1 Corinthians 12:4–6 has a "rhetorical character".

[11] E. Schweizer says, "the metaphysical (?) question of how God, Christ, and the Spirit are related to one another is hardly touched by Paul" (ThW VI, 431, 30f.). We can allow this statement to stand, although Schweizer passes over many subtle points in Paul. However, we cannot accept his assertion that "the question of the Spirit's personhood is falsely posed" (ibid., 432, 6). He goes on: "Paul is not interested in replacing the concept 'power' with the concept 'person'; he *is* concerned to show that this power is not an obscure something, but the way the Kyrios is present to the community" (ll. 9–12). Confronted with this, any believer must ask what this apparently "obscure something" is and whether it can be simply identified with the "how of Christ's presence" or the "creative power of the Risen One". Nor is it sufficient to say, as C. A. A. Scoff does in his *Christianity according to St. Paul* (1927), that Christ "represents the Pneuma for believers"—which would once more reduce the Spirit to an impersonal force. To that extent the gift [*Gabe*] given to the believing community in the New Testament remains a task [*Aufgabe*] that will have to be performed within the limits of a mind that is both believing and reverent.

ering them to have that Christian love which fulfills the whole law through its free superiority (Gal 5:13f.). Insofar as the Spirit is free and makes men free, he cannot be defined in terms of law. Another constant theme is the way the Spirit effects personal relationship. He does this, as the Johannine Interpreter and Guide, in a far deeper sense than a teacher of truths to be learned, as we see from the Johannine "immanence formulae". One can say that, in this work, the Spirit has his place preeminently in Christology,[12] yet he leads us into the very innermost being of Jesus, into his relationship with the Father, and thereby reveals the latter's whole Personhood[13] while bringing us into the personal relationship of the "child" to the Father. Again it must be asked whether such functions can be thought to take place in a purely impersonal way. Particularly as Jesus himself (even as the exalted Jesus) looks up to the Father "who is greater" and urges the disciples to look up with him, which "can only be done through the Spirit whom the Son sends"; in John this is "absolutely analogous to the Pauline findings", but it also accords with that worship "in spirit and truth" (Jn 4:23f.) of the God (the "ever-greater") who is himself "Spirit". Neither of these two can be simply traced back to Christology.[14]

A further tension exists in the distinction, present in all the evangelists, between the full presence of the Pneuma in the earthly Jesus and the outpouring of the Spirit upon the Church, or "upon all flesh" after his Resurrection and glorification (exaltation). The power of divine being that descends upon Jesus at his Baptism (and this power is not identical with him) is "poured out" into the world and into hearts: this power is *both* the Spirit prayed for and received from the Father *and* Jesus' own Spirit; it is a power that is not identical with either Father or Son yet belongs to and unites them both. Again and again the question arises on the basis of the New Testament: What is this power? Why is it only hinted at in the multiplicity of aspects and never named directly? Or is such direct discourse perhaps impossible?

---

[12] Cf. F. Mußner, "Die johanneischen Parakletsprüche", *Biblische Zeitschrift* 5 (1961): 56–70.

[13] W. Breuning, *Jesus Christus, der Erlöser* (Mainz, 1968), 34ff.

[14] W. Thüsing, in K. Rahner/W. Thüsing, *Christologie—systematisch und exegetisch*, QD 55 (1972), 158.

A final point: the Spirit in the New Testament is "the Spirit of holiness" (Rom 1:4; 2:13) and hence "Holy Spirit" (Lk 10:21; 11:13; Jn 20:22; Acts 1:2, 5, 16, and so on), and so, too, as the Fathers will show in detail, he is the divine Spirit. If we are to assume that an "impersonal" divine power can produce personal holiness, we must posit a Binity in God, namely, a Father who possesses nothing but a Son. For the human mind this would be impossible to grasp; moreover, given the demonstration of the *imagines trinitatis* in the preceding volume, it would be also unacceptable, because such a picture of God would render the structure of created reality unintelligible. No Christian theology, Catholic or not, has ever maintained such a view; it would be preferable to reject the Nicene definition and fall back into an Old Testament monotheism. If we are unwilling to do this, we are compelled to go beyond Binity in God and embrace Trinity. And precisely this step faces us with the urgent question: Who or what is the Spirit? This becomes very clear once we have understood that "Person" in God cannot be used (as it is in the secular, or at least human, sphere) as an apparently univocal concept. Is this not indicated, as far as the Spirit is concerned, in the very fact that in Scripture he has no face? Above the earth, which stands firm, the Spirit is symbolized by the three other elements: storm, wind, tempest, flaming fire, flowing water poured forth;[15] all these images express his elusive nature.[16] The three elements also appear in combination: in the promise of baptism the Spirit appears as fire and water (cf. Lk 12:49–50), at Pentecost he appears as stormy wind and fire; or in combination with the Spirit: Baptism is with "Spirit and fire", "rivers of living water" indicate the Spirit (Jn 7:38f.). This "facelessness" of the Spirit compels us to go back to what we said above: an elusive, faceless God causes the glory of God to shine on him who bears God's face; we reflect this glory and are transformed into it (2 Cor

---

[15] On this "facelessness" (and the prohibition against making any iconographic representation of the Spirit), cf. J. Y. Lacoste, "Zur Theologie des Geistes", *Internationale Katholische Zeitschrift Communio* 15/1 (1986): 5–6.

[16] On John 3:8, "You do not know where it comes from or where it goes", cf. Eccles 11:5 (JB): "Just as you do not know the way of the wind . . . , no more can you know the work of God who is behind it all." Billerbeck, *Kommentar zum Neuen Testament aus Talmud und Midrasch* (Munich: C. H. Beck, 1922), II, 424.

3:17f.). This face, then, becomes the interpretation of the God whom "no one has ever seen" (Jn 1:18) because, although he has become accessible, he "dwells in unapproachable light" (1 Tim 6:16). Only in this way can the Spirit lead us into, and interpret, the unfathomable "depths of God" (1 Cor 2:10).

THE FATHERS. PERSON IN MYSTERY

a. Trinitarian Mode of Subsistence

Given the foregoing remarks, it will be understandable that the Fathers go to much trouble, and exhibit great care and reserve, in defining the Spirit's essence. Indeed, their reticence is far more understandable than certain over-hasty formulations of later theology. Here we shall deal once again, not with the earliest interpreters (who were themselves more in the nature of inspired witnesses than technical theologians), but with that time in the wake of Nicaea when, once the substantial equality of Father and Son had been established, a statement about the Spirit could no longer be delayed.

First of all, one must be aware of the unanimous statements of the Fathers, testifying to their perplexity when endeavoring to say anything about the "Person" of the Spirit. On the threshold we can see Cyril of Jerusalem, who finally committed himself to the Nicene party in 381. A single, central thought goes through his two catecheses on the Holy Spirit (16 and 17): In Scripture there are a great number of statements about the Spirit, but one must not be confused by this multiplicity, for the Spirit is one (16, 3, 24; 17, 2–3). But even if "we truly need the gift of the Spirit in order to speak of him, the fact remains that it is impossible to speak of him as is appropriate to his lofty being" (16, 1); all one can do is to follow the words of Scripture. In the face of the many words, "Do not forget that what is divisible is, not the Spirit, but the grace he effects" (17, 12). It is impossible precisely to define his hypostasis; we must be content to protect it against various errors. "Let this knowledge be enough for us. You must not be curious to know the nature or the essence of the Spirit. . . . If something is not written, we should not dare to speak of it" (16, 24).

Athanasius, in his first letter to Serapion, opens up the way to the idea that the Spirit is of equal substance with Father and Son (1, 27), his emphatically respectful statements carefully avoiding anything rash. Basil, however, in his chief work on the Holy Spirit, proceeds resolutely toward a theology of the Spirit. Like Cyril he knows that it is only "in the Spirit" that we can speak of him (27, 66) and that anything we say must be based on his effects. When we speak of "the breath of God's mouth", this certainly means "a living wisdom, the mistress of sanctification, indicating an inner nearness to God, but the mode of this subsistence (*tropos tēs hyparxeōs*) remains ineffable" (18, 46). This dictum, which is also found in Athanasius,[1] will be handed on to later generations. "But the [Spirit's] communion [with Father and Son] and the distinction apprehended in them are, in a certain sense, ineffable and inconceivable", adds Basil (letter 38, 4). Here again it is the unity of the Spirit in the vast multiplicity of his gifts that impresses Basil just as much as Cyril of Jerusalem; yet it is this very unity that he equates with the unity of the Father and the unity of the Son: it is through this unity that the Spirit, who "completes the most praiseworthy and blessed Three", remains a mystery that cannot be unlocked.

Basil is acquainted with the divinizing power of the Spirit but wisely refrains from directly calling him God. Gregory Nazianzen is not so reserved, but he, too, knows that he has not explained the mode of the Spirit's divine being. He holds fast to the scriptural expression that the Spirit "proceeds" from the Father (Jn 15:26); but what does this mean? It is certain that the Spirit is not a creature. "Do you tell me what is the unbegottenness of the Father, and I will explain to you the physiology of the generation of the Son and the procession of the Spirit, and we shall both of us be frenzy-stricken for prying into the mystery of God" (*Oration* 31, 8).[2] No worldly metaphor or image can touch the reality of the Spirit; only simple, persistent faith can carry us beyond everything worldly into the trinitarian mystery (ibid., 31, 33).[3]

---

[1] *Letter to Serapion* (PG 26, 565c–580b), *Letter 4* (ibid., 641c–645a). The expression "tropos tēs hyparxeōs" seems to have been used as a *terminus technicus* for the first time by Amphilochius of Iconium (PG 39, 112). More details in Holl, *Amphilochius* (1904), 240f., cf. 160f.

[2] PG 36, 141b. [This translation in *Christology of the Later Fathers*, ed. E. R. Hardy (Philadelphia, 1954), 198.]

[3] PG 36, 172ab. Cf. *Oration* 31, 8: We do not know what the "procession" (ekporeusis) of the Spirit is, for it remains "high above our words and concepts".

It is no different in the book on the Trinity ascribed to Didymus: "It is futile to ask what is the distinction between being generated and proceeding; just as the mode is unknown, so is the distinction—if anything at all can be apprehended of this mode and uttered in words. It is arrogance to try to give reasons for things that are beyond all substantiation and beyond our power to grasp them."[4]

This same tradition is continued in Maximus the Confessor, when he says of the Spirit that "he proceeds in his essence from the Father through the generated Son in a way that is ineffable";[5] it becomes established in the Greek Fathers in John Damascene, who, in his profession of the Divine Trinity, knows "that there is a distinction between the generation (of the Son) and the procession (of the Spirit); yet we know absolutely nothing about this distinction".[6]

The Latins are no less eloquent; the difference here is that the ineffable procession of the Spirit is also *from the Son*, for as Augustine says: "In generating the Son, the Father also gives him the Spirit's procession from him." Although he proceeds from both, he is not the Son of both,

> but proceeds from both. But as for the distinction between being generated and proceeding, in connection with the Most High, who could explain it? Not everything that proceeds is generated, even if everything that is generated proceeds. For not everything with two feet is a man, although every man is two-footed. I know this; but I do not know—I have not the ability—how to distinguish between this generation and this procession. Both of them are ineffable—as the prophet says of the Son: Who can tell his generation? (Is 53:8)—so it is equally right to say the same of the Spirit: Who can tell his generation?[7]

---

[4] PG 39, 281b.

[5] *Quaestiones ad Thalassium* 63 (PG 90, 672). Cf. also Leontius of Byzantium: "We need not trouble ourselves to inquire how the One [the Son] is generated and the Other [the Spirit] proceeds" (*De sectis* 1: PG 87, 1196).

[6] *De fide orth.* I, 8 (PG 94, 821–24).

[7] *Contra Maximinum* II, 14, 1 (PL 42, 770–71). The final book of *De Trinitate* closes with a pathetic admission of the inability to distinguish intellectually between generation and procession (XV, 27, 48 and 50; PL 42, 1095, 1097). Cf. also *De Trin.* V, 11, 12: "ineffabilis est quaelam Patris Filiique communio".

Hilary takes the same line when he admits that it would be better to be silent about this issue: it is only the erroneous teachings that compel one to speak.[8] As far as the Spirit is concerned, "I regard it as false to discuss his manner of existing; he exists (for us) insofar as he is given, received, and retained."[9] It is best to hold fast to the words of the Gospel.[10] At the end of his twelfth book on the Trinity, he says, like the Greeks: "I hold fast to it in ignorance; I possess the reality although I do not comprehend it."[11] Finally we quote Nicetas of Remesiana: "Even if it is rash to dispute about him who is with the Father and the Son, . . . we must give an account of it. We believe that the Holy Spirit, the Paraclete, proceeds from the Father, that he is not the Son, not even the Son's Son, but the Spirit, of whose procession no man is permitted to know the mode and dimensions. The Spirit exists in his own, true Person, . . . bound to Father and Son in all his operations. It is pointless to deny him the name of God or the veneration he deserves as God."[12]

Why do we delay so long on this issue of ignorance? The reason is this: what the Fathers call *tropos tēs hyparxeōs*—the divine mode of "personal" existence—is different and specific in the case of each divine Hypostasis, and so it is theologically impossible to define this "specificity". Even Basil's and Gregory of Nyssa's battle against Eunomius (with his rationalistic fixing of the Father's mode of being with the concept of *agennesia*—which was supposed to render his essence intelligible and discernible)[13] shows in exemplary fashion that the "specificity" that grounds each Hypostasis in God, while it is intended by the words of Scripture, is by no means discerned in its essence. Thus the term *tropos tēs hyparxeōs* (and other terms such as *idiotēs, idiōma*)

---

[8] *De Trin.* II, 2.

[9] Ibid., 29.

[10] Ibid., 33–35.

[11] Ibid., XII, 55.

[12] Ed. Burn (Cambridge, 1905), 18, 21–22. In spite of its speculative bent, the Middle Ages speaks no differently. For Anselm, the Spirit proceeds "quodam inerrabili modo" from Father and Son (*Monol.* 57) (PL 52, 852–64).

[13] F. Diekamp, *Die Gotteslehre des hl. Gregor von Nyssa* I (Münster, 1896); P. Stiegele, *Der Agennesiebegriff in der griechischen Theologie des vierten Jahrhunderts* (Herder, 1913).

is used to indicate three different modes of being God, but not in the sense of a generic term that would subsume the various cases univocally.[14] In order to illustrate the concrete unity of the divine nature, Gregory of Nyssa had elsewhere used the image of the unity (which for him was somehow concrete) of human nature existing in several independent persons;[15] but he goes so far as to reject this very image lest the three Divine Persons be understood in the same way that one understands three human beings. Scripture, he says, is like a children's nanny who sometimes babbles along with her children, attributing eyes and ears and other bodily parts to God. "It is in our opinion for the benefit of the weaker brethren that it speaks" of three Persons, whereas it would be more germane to speak of the unity.[16]

b. Trinity and Number

Here is a daunting problem, the relationship between the divine Hypostases and number, which cannot be avoided any longer. First let us listen to Basil asserting, against the Arians, that when Christ commanded the apostles to baptize, he did not list Father, Son, and Spirit in numerical order; he did not call them "first, second, and third, or one, two, and three". An essence (Basil continues) is not changed by the addition of a numeral.

> But, O wisest sirs, let the unapproachable be altogether above and beyond number, as the ancient reverence of the Hebrews wrote the unutterable name of God in peculiar characters, thus endeavouring to set forth its infinite excellence. Count, if you must; but you must not by counting do damage to the faith. Either let the

---

[14] Examples of the use of *tropos tēs hyparxeōs*: Amphilochius, *Frag.* 15 (PG 39, 112s); Didymus (?), *Adv. Eunomium* IV (PG 26, 681); Basil, *Ep.* 235, 5 (PG 32, 871c); Basil, *De Spir. Sancto* 46 (PG 32, 152B); Gregory of Nyssa, *Contra Eunomium* VIII (PG 45, 793a); Pseudo-Cyril of Alexandria, *De Trin.* 8 (PG 77, 1136D); Maximus the Confessor, *Mystagogia* 23 (PG 91, 702b).

[15] PG 45, 117d–120c. This assertion can be understood, on the one hand, as polemic against Eunomius, who wanted to deduce, from the distinction between the Divine Persons, that their natures exhibited a descending order of rank; and, on the other hand, as a view arising out of Gregory's concrete concept of nature (borrowed from the Stoa), which is also presupposed in his *De hominis opificio*.

[16] Morell edition (Paris, 1638), II, 86cd.

ineffable be honoured by silence; or let holy things be counted consistently with true religion. There is one God and Father, one Only-begotten, and one Holy Ghost. We proclaim each of the hypostases singly (*monachōs*); and, when count we must, we do not let an ignorant arithmetic carry us away to the idea of a plurality of Gods. For we do not count by way of addition.[17]

Basil evidently has in mind a plurality that cannot be expressed arithmetically; it has been shown that he was influenced by Plotinus,[18] who insisted that his three hypostases (the One, the *Nous*, and the Soul) should be understood as a threefold, but noncountable, unity.[19] It is evident, however, that behind Plotinus there lurks the problem of the "ideal numbers" (*arithmoi eidētikoi*) in Plato (according to Aristotle, *Met*. A 6, 987 b), since we know that, in his old age, Plato tried more and more to equate the Ideas with numbers, which (crudely put) were supposed to arise from the union of (absolute) Unity with the Infinite (*apeiron*). However this speculation may be,[20] it is certain that Basil, through the mediation of Plotinus, had something like the "ideal numbers" in mind when hesitating to introduce number into the Trinity.[21]

---

[17] *De Spir. Sancto* 18 (SC 17, 192). [This translation from *Nicene and Post-Nicene Fathers*, 2d series, ed. Philip Schaff and Henry Wace (Grand Rapids, Mich.: Wm. B. Eerdmans, 1996), VIII, 28.]

[18] Here he is clearly influenced by the treatise "On the Three Fundamental Hypostases" (*Enn*. V, 1, 7–8). Cf. P. Henry, S.J., *Les États du texte de Plotin*, Museum Lessianum (Paris: Desclée de Brouwer, 1938), 160, 184; B. Pruche, O.P., introduction to Basil's treatise in SC 17 (1945), 57f.

[19] In this treatise he means that the individual soul, in its own depths, is to come to know its participation in the All-Soul, the *Nous*, and finally the One. Cf. the analysis in Bréhier's introduction to *Enneads* V (Paris: Belles Lettres, 1965), 7–14.

[20] Julius Stenzel, *Zahl und Gestalt bei Platon und Aristoteles*, 3d ed. (Darmstadt, 1959).

[21] The paradox is that it was precisely the Plotinian understanding of ranked hypostases that influenced the Eunomians. Basil sees this clearly, for, on the one hand, he stresses that "no essence is changed by the addition of a numeral", while, on the other hand—"if we are not to keep silent" about the Divine—insisting that we must "count religiously and with reverence".—We can see that Plato's problem (of a noncountable multiplicity in the sphere of Ideas) was very serious: for the Greek "One" was understood in Christian terms as the sovereign, living God, and the question was asked whether his "Ideas" of creatable worlds ("Ideas" that are identical with his divine essence) are arithmetically countable or not.

On the basis of this text we can see that the patristic period will search for a solution along two paths. One will be to make use of Basil's quasi-permission to introduce number into the doctrine of the Trinity, particularly in connection with the order (*taxis*) of processions; the other will share Basil's reticence, which points ahead to what Thomas Aquinas will term "transcendental number".

Gregory of Nyssa can be taken as a representative of the first path. In fact he objects, against Eunomius, that "the difference of natures does not arise from the arithmetical *taxis*; countable things retain their natures unchanged, whether we really count them or not; but number is the signifier for the quantity of things."[22] Yet it is clear that this "quantity" is nothing other than the "actual particularity of the individual" (*idia perigraphē*)[23] and that Gregory, by speaking of number in the Trinity, means simply the *taxis* of the processions in the one, indivisible nature.[24] Tertullian can serve as a representative of the second path; on the one hand, he refuses to connect the divine Unity with the number one[25]—Ambrose will follow him in this[26]—and, on the other hand, he regards the counting of the Persons in the *oikonomia* as a mere expedient.[27] Gregory Nazianzen understands that the unity of God is fulfilled through the Trinity, "a perfect Trinity of three Perfect Ones. A mere monad is to be overcome on the basis of the richness of the real; a dyad is superseded (for it goes beyond matter and form, the two constitutive elements

---

[22] *C. Eunom.* I (PG 45, 312b). On the other hand, Gregory Nazianzen can say quite unabashedly that the Divine Persons are "distinct by number, not by nature": *Or.* 37, 16 (PG 36, 236).

[23] "Quod non sunt tres dii" (PG 45, 132a).

[24] Cf. *Adv. Maced.* 6 (PG 45, 1308ab; cf. 1317c: "Ektos tēs kata taxin kai hypostasin diaphoras").

[25] "Ad substantiae unitatem, non ad numeri singularitatem" (*Adv. Prax.* 25). "Numerus incipit post unum" (*De exhort. castit.* 7).

[26] "Quomodo pluralitatem recipit unitas divinitatis, cum pluralitas numeri sit, numerum autem non recipiat divina natura?" (*De Spir. Sancto* III, 13 [PL 16, 799ab]). "Non quantitatem in Deo ponimus" (*De Fide* I, 2 [PL 16, 533ab]). Cf. also Hilary, *De Trin.* IV, 19 (PL 10, 110c–111a).

[27] "The principle of economy . . . introduces numeration in order that the Father may not be believed Himself to have been born and to have suffered" (G. Prestige, *God in Patristic Thought*, [London 1936; this ed., SPCK, 1952], p. 105).

of physical things). It is held to be a Trinity because of its perfection, for, being first, it surpasses something composite such
as the dyad, lest the Divinity should be restricted (as monad) or
dissolve into the infinite (as dyad)."[28] Gregory's pupil Evagrius
puts it formally: "We confess the unity of God, not according to
number, but according to nature. For whatever is called 'one' by
number is neither really one nor is it by nature simple."[29] Maximus the Confessor will draw the ultimate consequences: "Even
if we celebrate the Most High Divinity as Triad and Monad,
it is neither triad nor monad in the way we are accustomed to
reckon by numbers."[30] "The Monad is in truth a Triad, for thus
it exists, and the Triad is in truth a Monad, for thus it is."[31] "For
the unity of the Triad is not something common and generic that
could be distinguished by an abstract analysis of its constituent
parts. The Oneness does not unfold into a Threeness",[32] and it
would be even less true to say that the Threeness combines into
a Oneness.[33]

The problem is taken up by Thomas, who, unconsciously
building on Plato's ideal numbers, distinguishes quantitative
unity and multiplicity from transcendental unity and multiplicity: only the latter is applicable to God, and it has room in itself
for a plurality. This plurality, however, has nothing to do with
separateness (*divisio*) but rather negates it.[34] Just as being or its
transcendental qualities cannot be separated, whether they are attributed to one or more than one, so it is with the (inseparable)
qualities of the divine essence *and also* with the divine (personal)
relations;[35] they pertain to the plurality of the divine Unity but
refuse all separateness. In his own way, Hegel will represent the

[28] 23. *Or.* 8 (PG 35, 1160c).

[29] Pseudo-Basil, *Ep.* 8 (PG 32, 248). Cf. also (Pseudo?-)Didymus, *De Trin.* II:
"'out' anechetai e arithmos prosagoreuetai, tès henados ousias on" (PG 39, 492B).

[30] *Div. Nom.* 13 (PG 4, 412c); *Ambig.* (PG 91, 1185c, 1188ab).

[31] *Ambig.* (PG 91, 1036c).

[32] *Exp. or. dom.* (PG 90, 892cd).

[33] *Mystag.* 23 (PG 91, 701a).

[34] *S. Th.* I, 11, 2, and 30, 3.

[35] Expressly in *S. Th.* I, 11, 30, 3 ad 1. The problem of transcendental number
appears in the Council of Toledo, XI: "Trinitas non recedit a numero nec capitur
numero" (DS 528) or even in Augustine's dictum that "Two Divine Persons are

end of the line insofar as, for him, counting is a matter of common sense, not of reason,[36] which grasps the speculative unity as motion, relation, union. The externality of number remains in the anteroom of the Spirit (which is ultimately triune Life).[37]

If, looking back to the fourth-century doctrine of the Spirit, we want to say something positive about the emphatic hiddenness of the Spirit's *tropos tēs hyparxeōs* (the manner of his "procession"), something that characterizes him as a divine Hypostasis, we shall find the Alexandrians (Athanasius and Didymus) and the Cappadocians pursuing the same paths.

1. The first is fundamental and self-explanatory and is based on the tradition of the baptismal profession (Mt 28:19) and the Church's liturgy. All speculation, ultimately, rests on this.[38]

2. The second is closely connected with it: here the starting point is the effects of the Spirit attested in Scripture; these effects allow us to conclude to the Spirit's hypostatic distinctness. Athanasius who, in the Letters to Serapion, acknowledges the

---

not more than one" (*De Trin.* VI, 10, 12; PG 42, 932, citing Hilary). Thomas Anglicus rejects all attempt to count the Divine Persons (Schmaus, *Liber propugnatorius* II, BGPhThM, vol. 29 [1930], 276f.). The question remains, however, whether it is possible to say "transcendental number" in the same sense as the *transcendentalia entis*, the attributes of the divine essence and the divine hypostases. Does *negatio divisionis* (I, 30, 3c) mean the same thing in all three cases? Earlier studies of number and Trinity produce few results: Ulrich Horst, O.P., *Die Trinitäts- und Gotteslehre des Robert v. Melun* (Mainz: Grünewald, 1964), 152ff.; J. Schneider, *Die Lehre vom dreieinigen Gott in der Schule des Petrus Lombardus* (Munich, 1961), 189ff.

[36] *Enzyklopädie*, sections 99–102.

[37] Texts in A. Chapelle, *Hegel et la religion* III (1967), 82–94. "Numbers, as the Pythagoreans observed, are unsuitable means of grasping ideas. . . . The Three appears at a deeper level in the religion of the Trinity and as a concept in philosophy" (*Einleitung in die Geschichte der Philosophie* [1933], 106; in more detail in the *Einleitung* published by Hoffmeister, 3d ed. [1959], 214). On the problems associated with number and Trinity, cf. also A. Manaranche, *Le Monothéisme chrétien* (Cerf, 1985), 228f. ("méta-mathématique"); Stanislas Breton, *Unicité et Monothéisme* (Cerf, 1981)—a Hegelian approach.

[38] Most fully in Basil, who goes through the entire liturgical and theological tradition: *De Spiritu Sancto* (PG 32, 113, 127, 129, 188–93, 201–9).

Spirit's distinct Hypostasis, sees him in "economic" terms, in the closest bond with Christ, whose radiating brilliance he is (according to Paul); together with the Son he achieves men's divinization.[39] Didymus sees the same intimate connection ("where the Holy Spirit is, there is the Son");[40] "The Son, who comes in the name of the Lord, bears the special quality and name of the Father and is thus called Son of God. But the Holy Spirit is sent in the name of the Son and of the Father and has the special quality of the Son, insofar as the Son is God, but not the Son's sonship, otherwise he would be his Son; this shows that he is bound to the Son through unity."[41] By leading us into all the truth brought by the Son, the "Spirit of truth" manifests his divine being. He can conduct us "from the dead letter to the life-giving Spirit, who alone contains the truth of the entire Scripture; this he does by continually adding new things to the old. Thus he will guide us into all the truth."[42] He is "the Lord of the teaching" and "the fullness of the gift";[43] even when he is poured into our hearts, he shows his divinity, for only God can dwell in hearts.[44] Basil, too, is acquainted with the intimate bond between Son and Spirit: "Only in the Spirit is the Son visible, for the image cannot be separated from the light."[45] "Just as the Father is seen in the Son, so the Son is seen in the Spirit."[46] The "Spirit of truth glorifies the Son by revealing the truth in utmost clarity in himself, and, as the Spirit of wisdom, he manifests Christ, who is 'the power and wisdom of God', in his own [the Spirit's own] sublimity. As the Comforter he characterizes the kindness of the Comforter who sends him, and in his dignity he manifests the majesty of him [the Father] from whom he proceeded." "As [the Son] says of himself: 'I glorified you [Father] on earth, having accomplished the work

---

[39] *Ep. 1 ad Serapionem* (PG 26, 588a).

[40] *De Spiritu Sancto* 28 (PG 39, 1057).

[41] Ibid. (PG 39, 1061a), cf. 40: "Wherever the Holy Spirit is, there is Christ; and wherever the Spirit of Christ disappears, Christ himself disappears" (1069b).

[42] Ibid., 32–33 (1061–62).

[43] Ibid., 19 (1050).

[44] Ibid., 24 (1045).

[45] Ibid., 26 (PG 32, 185bc).

[46] Ibid., 185a.

which you gave me to do', so he says of the Holy Spirit: 'He will glorify me, for he will take what is mine and declare it to you.' "[47] We have already quoted the following:

And when, by means of the power that enlightens us, we fix our eyes on the beauty of the image of the invisible God, and through the image [Christ] are led up to the supreme beauty of the spectacle of the archetype [the Father], then . . . is in him (the Son) inseparably the Spirit of knowledge, *in himself* bestowing on them that love the vision of the truth the power of beholding (*deixein*) the Image, not making the exhibition from without, but *in himself* leading on to the full knowledge . . . "in thy light shall we see light," namely by the illumination of the Spirit . . . It results that in himself (*en heautōi*) he shows the glory of the Only begotten.[48]

Gregory of Nyssa, in the same context, speaks of a ceaseless round of reciprocal glorifications[49]—with which he concludes his proof of the Spirit's divinity.

3. A third theme runs through all the treatises on the Spirit written by these Fathers, namely, that the divine Hypostases work together in the world, yet each according to its personal character. Athanasius attributes this to the common procession from the Father, shared by Son and Spirit; thus "the operation of the Trinity is one";[50] while Didymus emphasizes this common operation within the distinct missions of the Persons, and the Spirit is he who completes the divine acts.[51] Basil, too, underscores this,[52] as does Gregory Nazianzen.[53]

Along these three paths, which rise from *economia* to *theologia*, from the effects of the Spirit to his divinity, the Fathers succeed in demonstrating—as they were obliged to do in their struggle against Arianism—the "consubstantiality" of the Spirit with

[47] Ibid., 152cd.
[48] Ibid., 153ab. Translation adapted from *Nicene and Post-Nicene Fathers* VIII, 29. [Note the different readings: Father von Balthasar translates "then . . . is in him (the Son)" where the Eerdmans St. Basil says "then . . . is in us".—TRANS.]
[49] *Adv. Maced.* (PG 45, 1329b).
[50] *Ep. I ad Serapionem* (660c–661a).
[51] *De Spiritu Sancto*, 16 (PG 32, 1048c–1049a).
[52] Basil, c. 16 (136bc, 140b).
[53] *Sermo* 31, 9 (PG 36, 141c).

Father and Son, without having to express themselves concerning the essence of the Spirit's procession from within the Godhead.

c. Trinity or Energy?

We can only give the briefest note here on the problem of Palamism. This could lead to renewed interest insofar as the distinction Palamism makes between God's essence (*ousia*) and his "energies" seems to recall, in two ways, the modern view of the person. First, God is seen both as a subject reposing in himself and his mystery, and also, since he is in real relationship with the world he has created, he is already turned in anticipation toward "the other", to what is other than himself (*kinēsis pros ti*). He is both God for himself and God for others. And even if, according to Palamas,[54] no necessity is involved in the creation of the world, and God's "energies" are independent of his free decision to create, they nonetheless have always belonged to his divinity since they render God essentially knowable. Secondly, however, there is our experience as persons: in communicating himself to another, a man can go to the limit, giving all he is able to give (and this "all" implies the intention of giving himself). Yet the very thing he intends to give—himself—cannot in fact be given away, and so for the recipient its free self-giving remains a mystery. Do we not find a pre-echo of this idea in late Neoplatonism (Proclus), when it speaks of "communication in the incommunicable", a formula that was introduced into Christian thought by the Areopagite (*Div. nom.* 11, 6)? Palamas radicalizes and systematizes this formula by saying that the creature, even in eternal bliss, only sees God's "energies", not his essence.

The fundamental question here is this: How is God's communicability—and the communication he has actually achieved—

---

[54] The works of Gregory Palamas (insofar as they have been published) are in PG 150–51; *Défense des Saints Hésychastes*, Greek/French ed. by J. Meyendorff (Louvain, 1959), 2 vols, and others in: Meyendorff, *Introduction à l'étude de G. Palamas* (Paris: Seuil, 1959); Meyendorff, *St. Grégoire Palamas*, Maîtres spirituels 20 (Paris: Seuil, 1959). Cf. H.-G. Beck, *Kirche und theologische Literatur im byzantinischen Reich* (Munich: Beck, 1959), with a survey of works: 712–15; bibliog. on Palamas: 322f.

in his energies (grace, love, insight, all the virtues) related to the economic Trinity, particularly as the energies of all three Persons are common to them all?[55] Palamas, who does not develop an original doctrine of the Trinity, often quotes traditional trinitarian passages in his defense. Together with Gregory Nazianzen, he, too, can say that God was manifest, in his energies, at three different times in his trinitarian Persons; but these do not impress a trinitarian stamp on God's activity, and, on the other hand, Trinity and the "energies" seem so closely linked that one is reminded of Eckhart: Trinity as the face of God turned toward the world, behind which the unknowable abyss of God's unity remains hidden.

J. Meyendorff and, subsequently, E. Jüngel and L. Bouyer[56] urge a reconciliation between trinitarian theology and energy theology, while the unswerving analysis by Dorothea Wendebourg[57] comes to the conclusion that the Palamite energies "rob the Trinity of all soteriological function".[58] In this framework the entire trinitarian God expresses himself in the totality of world-ideas, and the "divinized" created subject participates in their totality; the revelation of God in Christ constitutes no exception—as the *aparchē* ("firstfruits") of our divinization, he becomes only the highest instance of the union between God

---

[55] PG 150, 1197b.

[56] In *Le Consolateur: Esprit Saint et vie de grâce* (Paris: Cerf, 1980)—a work criticized by Y. Congar—he tried to see the Trinity and the "energies" as a single unity (321, but the passage in which he equates the Holy Spirit with the love poured into us—in an Augustinian sense—is an isolated case in Palamas). On pp. 430f. Bouyer acknowledges the problems involved in Palamism, but he regards them as balanced by those of the Western theology of grace. The Palamites "should have no difficulty in recognizing that, in denying that the creature can participate in the divine essence itself (in spite of the clear expression in 2 Peter), their meaning is no different from St. Thomas when he says that this participation can only be imperfect, however real it may be. . . . If this is borne in mind, it seems that we are here . . . in a situation where it is impossible to choose between the Oriental affirmation of an uncreated grace that, however, allows us to participate only in the divine energies and not in the ultimate essence—and the Western affirmation of a created grace that, nonetheless, actually makes us participate in the nature or essence of God" (C 431).

[57] *Geist oder Energie? Zur Frage der innergöttlichen Verankerung des christlichen Lebens in der byzantinischen Theologie* (Munich: Kaiser, 1980).

[58] Ibid., 10.

and world that is envisaged by creation and the gift of grace.[59] Finally, that "turning outward" which pertains to God's inner essence is so ordered to a world that God's free will in creating the world (freedom lies in the *ousia*, the bond with the world in the energies), which was originally so emphasized, cannot lead to God freely binding himself to his world: "God is always a non-participant, standing aloof above his participation."[60]

Karl Barth rightly took issue with this teaching, which undermines the triune God's economic self-communication. He compared it to the condemned teaching of Gilbert de La Porrée in the West, which said that "the Godhead, the fullness of the divine attributes, is really distinct from God"; thus Barth identified himself with Palamas' opponent, Nicephorus Gregoras. However, the Synod of Constantinople (1351) approved Palamas' teaching, and "Eastern Orthodoxy is committed to [the Hesychasts'] doctrine to the present day."[61]

The two questions with which we began do not have to be solved in a Palamite way: they can be solved by trinitarian theology. With regard to the individual Hypostases, their self-transcendent relation lies in themselves, since each one is essentially relative to the other two. As regards the Holy Spirit, who, within the Trinity, is already *donum*, no *donatum* needs to be added to his essence. The triune God's self-transcendent relation lies, not in his essence, but in his freedom. And it is a sophism to say that a finite person can only give himself in "another self", whereas he himself cannot be given: in self-giving, it is the person himself who intends to give, for if he were able to give himself away as giver, the giving would eliminate itself. Some may wish to see in this an ultimate inability, conditioned by finitude (since according to Scotus the finite person is *ultima solitudo*); but it remains true that the person is the *imago* of the Divine Persons, whose relationality means that, in their self-giving, there is no remainder that is not given—as in the *Amethekton* of the Platonists and of Gregory Palamas.

[59] Cf. the entire analysis of Christology, ibid., 25–29; and, on the relationship between Trinity and the energies in Palamas, ibid., 44–62.

[60] Ibid., 42: the energies, from all eternity, are so ordered to participation that God's free action does not enter into the discussion.

[61] *Church Dogmatics* II/1 (Edinburgh, 1939), 331n.

3

THE MIDDLE AGES

The topic of this section is the Personhood of the Holy Spirit. However, we cannot meaningfully discuss this topic in its context in the Middle Ages without first taking note of the struggle that went on at this period to reach a concept of "person". Very briefly, what ultimately governed this struggle (which henceforth seems to slip into the philosophical field) was the fact that, from the patristic period on, two theological approaches to the "person" had been inherited. One was trinitarian (in Nicaea), and the other, presupposing the first, was christological (in Chalcedon). The necessary unification of both aspects produced the innovation whereby, as Lonergan observed, people began to ask "what the person is".[1] While there are here seeds of a later, purely philosophical questioning, the concern of the Middle Ages in this area of study is primarily theological; and it is astonishing to find that medieval theology hardly moves away at all from the mysterious, patristic *tropos tēs hyparxeōs*, even when, alongside the trinitarian and christological aspects, it includes the anthropological in its considerations. It is precisely when the human person is irradiated by the twofold theological light that its uniqueness (which eludes all definition) shines forth; but this lasts only as long as the light from above continues to illuminate it.[2]

[1] "Apud Boethium, Richardum, S. Thomam illud est novum quod interdum quaeritur non particulariter quid tres, seu quid sit persona divina, sed generaliter quid sit persona" (*De Deo Trino*, 3d ed., II [1964], 154).

[2] "The theologians of the first centuries formed the concept of 'person', not for the sake of man's own understanding of himself, but rather in order to clarify the mysteries of faith, that is, the Trinity and the Incarnation in Jesus Christ. . . . Thus, even where the Christian origin of the concept of 'person' is not recognized or is denied, the philosophy of the person still draws nourishment from its hidden or unacknowledged Christianity. . . . Furthermore, the Christian concept of 'person' will be in balance if it admits its provisional character, which awaits its fulfillment, in the Christian revelation, through the gift of grace" (A. Guggenberger, "Person", in HThG [Kösel, 1963], II, 295).

a. Origins

The first strand of meaning comes from the Greek word *hyposta-sis*, meaning the "reality", initially, of the individual things one encounters and, later (in Middle Platonism), of the foundations of being that bring these things into reality; ultimately it leads to the Plotinian teaching of the ranked hierarchy of fundamental realities, which the Arians adapted to the three Hypostases in the Christian God. Athanasius, after long battles and corrective work, liberated this concept for service in an orthodox doctrine of the Trinity: the one divine reality expresses itself in a threefold way (or "reality"), but the (Platonist) subordination of rank, which seemed necessary to explicate the distinctions in being, is excluded.[3] Of course, in the background of this process of definition there was always the biblical picture of the living God, who, in the New Testament, shows his inner vitality in his self-manifestation as Father, Son, and Spirit. In continuity with the Nicene *homoousios*, the Cappadocians raised the Hypostasis of the Spirit to the same level as Father and Son; initially, no doubt, against the later Arians and Pneumatomachi,[4] but then influenced (both positively and negatively) by currents of thought that were inclined to exaggerate the effects of the Spirit.[5]

The christological definition of Chalcedon adopts the trinitarian language concerning the *hypostasis* in order to apply it to Christ, notwithstanding the fact that the term could also signify the ultimate facet and uniqueness of every worldly being (even

[3] Heinrich Dörrie, "Hypostasis, Word und Bedeutungsgeschichte" (1955), in *Platonica minora* (Munich: Fink, 1976), 1–60.

[4] The reticence found in Basil, and (in a different way) at the definition of Constantinople I, must not be interpreted as a concession to the Pneumatomachi: Hermann Dörries, "Basilius und das Dogma vom Hl. Geist", in *Wort und Stunde* I (Göttingen, 1966), 118–24; this is rejected by A. M. Ritter, *Das Konzil von Konstantinopel und sein Symbol* (Göttingen, 1965), 296–99.

[5] On monasticism as a positive influence on the definition, cf. L. Bouyer, C, chap. 10, 193–214; Dörrie, "Hypostasis", 137f. Kretschmar thinks he detects negative influence (in Basil, against Eustathius and his wild monks; in Gregory of Nyssa, against the Messalians): *Studien zur frühen Trinitätstheologie* (Tübingen, 1956), 95.

subspiritual being). Damascene, however, restricts the meaning of *hypostasis* to the personal "Who".[6]

Less clear is the adoption of the Latin (and pre-Christian) term *persona*. It meant the actor's mask, and then, via the actor's role, it came to mean "the human being" and, more specifically, his "dignity" and (in the case of a free citizen) his ability to be the subject of juridical process.[7] It was then adapted for use in theological, that is, trinitarian and christological, debate. It was in Tertullian that the term first acquired its exact theological meaning.[8] Carl Andresen[9] and Marie-Joseph Rondeau[10] have traced the trinitarian use of *persona* back to a prosopographical or prosopological prehistory,[11] which has maintained an exact theological (trinitarian and christological) meaning in Christian literature. Thus, a common grammatical term is available for the Divine Persons, yet the term says nothing about their ontological constitution. It should be noted that the pre-Christian association of *persona* with "dignity" survives into the Middle Ages, in both Bonaventure[12] and Thomas.[13]

[6] *Dialectica* 17 (PG 94, 581c).

[7] H. Rheinfelder, *Das Wort "Persona": Geschichte seiner Bedeutungen mit besonderer berücksichtigung des französischen und italienischen mittelalters* (Halle: Niemeyer, 1928), 10–18.

[8] On the (hesitant) adoption of this vague concept for use in theology, cf. Rainero Cantalamessa, *La Cristologia di Tertulliano*, Paradosis 18 (Fribourg, 1962). With reference to *Adv. Prax.* 27, 11: "Videmus duplicem statum, non confusum, sed coniunctum, in una persona, deum et hominem", Cantalamessa interprets "persona", not in the sense of Chalcedon, but as "in una persona Trinitatis". But cf. M. Simonetti, "Persona Christi, Tertull. *Adv. Prax.* 27, 11", *Rivista di storia e letteratura religiosa* 1 (Florence, 1965): 97–98. On the trinitarian use of the term: *Adv. Prax.* 15: (Patrem et Filium) "deprehendo sub manifesta et personali distinctione conditionis utriusque".

[9] "Zur Entstehung und Geschichte des trinitarischen Personbegriffes", ZNW 52 (1961): 1–39.

[10] *Les Commentaires patristiques du psautier*, 2 vols, esp. vol. 2: *Exégèse prosopologique et théologie*, Orientalia Christiana Analecta 220 (Rome, 1985), 481 pages.

[11] It is in Tertullian that the Spirit is first really called "Person" and not merely "Role": Andresen, "Zur Entstehung", 18, 38.

[12] "Proprietas supereminentis dignitatis", "dignitatis et excellentiae": 3, d. 10, a. 1, q. 2, concl. 4; ibid., q. 3. The definition of the person requires "singularitas", "incommunicabilitas", and "supereminens dignitas": 3, d. 5, a. 2, q. 1 c.

[13] Cf. *S. Th.* I, 29, 3 ad 2: Boethius, in his definition of the "person", is acquainted with its origin in the theatre; Thomas takes this up and asserts that

b. Ways of Thinking

With the Creed as the basis, the Holy Spirit's "Personhood" presented no problem; but the question remains: How did the Middle Ages apply the concept "person" to the individual divine Hypostases? If one started with Boethius' classical definition of the person ("naturae rationalis individua substantia"[14] from his book *Against Eutyches and Nestorius*—which is thus not purely philosophical but christological in intention), it seemed to lead at best to a monotheistic concept of God; it was not applicable to distinct Persons in God. Unless, of course, *substantia* was understood as *subsistentia*, "manner of being", which would bring us back to the Greek *tropos hyparxeōs*. In order to make this apply explicitly to the Trinity, Richard of St. Victor alters Boethius' definition so that it reads, "divinae naturae incommunicabilis existentia";[15] in this way, *substantia* can be reserved for the substance that is common to the Divine Persons, and *ek-sistentia* can designate the origin of each of them, that is, their relationality. Of course, this only applies to the Son and the Spirit in God, for in this sense the Father has no "ex". This definition is noteworthy, however, in several ways. First, substance is replaced by existence; this points in the direction of a milieu in which personality will no longer be sought along the lines of essence: this begins with Duns Scotus, for whom (as we shall show) even the immediacy of "thisness", *haecceitas*, still belongs to the realm of essence and does not yet express the person; it will apply to radical nominalism and, ultimately, to that trend in modern personalism which will oppose "personalist thinking" to "substance thinking". Second, as we have just mentioned, in using the term *ek-sistentia*, Richard wants to explain that the Divine Persons can only be designated by their relationship of origin (or, in the case

---

"famous men" were first termed "persons" ("personalities") in comedies and tragedies, and thence the concept "person", as used for people in general, kept the connotation of "dignity". "Now the dignity of the divine nature exceeds every other dignity; and thus the term *person* preeminently belongs to God". Cf. *De pot.* 9, 3; *S. Th.* II/II, 32, 5 c. On this whole issue, cf. *Theo-Drama* III (San Francisco, Ignatius Press, 1992), 208–20: "The Theological Concept of 'Person'".

[14] *De duabus naturis*, c. 3 (PL 63, 1343c).
[15] *De Trinitate* III, 18.

of the Father, by the lack of such a relation, that is, by his *agennesia*;[15a] this means that each of them is called "Person" because of a different relationality in each case. Thirdly, a negative note is struck: here, by contrast with the more neutral concept of relation in Thomas, the Divine Person is designated essentially in terms of origin ("where from?"), and not in terms of goal ("where to?"); this will become even more apparent in Duns Scotus, setting the medieval ideas of personhood in opposition to the modern, where "person" always involves relationship toward a thou.

But if every relation in God is utterly unique, does this not raise the question of how the word "person" can be a concept including several things? Did not this question arise, in principle, in Boethius, since in his definition the *individua* also contained Richard's *incommunicabile*, the utter uniqueness that cannot be subsumed under anything else? Thomas, who sticks essentially to the same line as Boethius, noticed this and asked "whether the term 'person' can be common to the three Persons?"[16] His objections hit the mark:

> Nothing is common to the three Persons but the essence. But this term *person* does not signify the essence directly. Therefore it is not common to all three. Further, the common is the opposite to the incommunicable. But the very meaning of person is that it is incommunicable, as appears from the definition given by Richard of St. Victor. Therefore this term *person* is not common to all the three Persons. Further, if the name *person* is common to the three, it is common either really or logically. But it is not so really; otherwise the three Persons would be one Person; nor again is it so logically; otherwise person would be a universal. But in God there is neither universal nor particular; neither genus nor species, as we proved above. Therefore this term *person* is not common to the three.

Thomas answers these objections by first of all setting forth the solutions hitherto proposed. It would be possible to speak of a *communitas negationis*, that is, incommunicability, but this would not yield anything held in common. One could speak of a purely

---

[15a] But cf. Thomas, *Comp. Theol.* 59: "Innascibilitas ad relationem pertinet sicut relationis negatio, nam negationes ad genus affirmationum reducuntur."

[16] *S. Th.* I, 30, 4.

conceptual community of intention (*secunda intentio*),[17] but that which is Person in God is not the goal of this kind of abstract intention: what is aimed at is an entirely determinate reality. It occurs to Thomas that, basically, no human person can be actually defined; he is not an instance of a species and can only be addressed as "something unique and not more closely definable" (*individuum vagum*). It is no help to say that genus and species are possessed in common; in the case of angels even this "community" disappears,[18] but since it pertains to human nature to manifest itself in the individual, and this individual (who can be characterized) signals the non-definable "person", it is possible at least to envisage the "person". Thus it is possible to construct something like a common concept of "Person" in God, too, and for three reasons: (1) "Although person is incommunicable, yet the mode itself of incommunicable existence can be common to many"; (2) because the Persons in the one divine nature (which is not a universal) agree; and, finally, (3) because, even in human affairs, "the community of person [is not] the same as community of genus or species."[19] From what Thomas says about the Divine Persons, H. Mühlen draws the conclusion that their *modus existendi* (*De pot.* 9, 2 ad 2), since it is only definable in terms of relation, each vis-à-vis the other, is always "even greater" in diversity "than it can be thought to be".[20] However,

---

[17] As Thomas does in S. Th. I 29, 1 ad 1, when he says that, while it is true that the singular cannot be defined, "tamen id quod pertinet ad communem rationem singularitatis definiri potest, et sic Philosophus definit substantiam primam. Et hoc modo definit Boetius personam." But the Person in God is *not* "substantia prima", so Thomas has to look for another way.

[18] Only in man are nature and person distinct ("aliud est natura et aliud persona"), which helps to explain why humanity can be redeemed, but angels cannot, since in them nature and person coincide (*Contr. Gent.* IV, 55 [ad 3, objectionem]).

[19] S. Th. I, 30, 4 ad 1–3. Cf. Lonergan, *De Deo Trino* II, 165–66. In S. Th. I, 29, 1 ad 3: "Quia substantiales differentiae non sunt nobis notae . . . , nomina intentionum possunt accipi ad definiendum res, secundum quod accipiuntur pro aliquibus nominibus rerum quae non sunt posita. Et sic (apud Boetium) hoc nomen 'individuum' ponitur in definitione personae ad designandum modum subsistendi qui competit substantiis particularibus."

[20] GP 235. "The distinctness of the Divine Persons is so great that it cannot be thought greater" (ibid., 108). "This means that, instead of using the word 'person' univocally, one would need to have three different words at one's disposal to express both the personhood of the particular Person and its distinctness

we can only speak of this infinite distance between them if at
the same time we observe the correlative absolute closeness they
enjoy in their essence, since each of the Divine Persons is identical in terms of the one divine nature: "The unity of the divine nature [is] always even more intensive than we can actually
conceive it to be. Deus est maxime indivisus" (*S. Th.* I, 11,
4 c).[21] "A description of the *oppositio relationis* within the Trinity
can only be attempted if we try to conceive *both* the closeness
of the Divine Persons *and* their diversity as being so great that
no greater can be thought."[22] For the moment let us set aside
Mühlen's attempt to throw light on these relationships (Father-
Son as "I-thou"; Spirit as "we") and concentrate on this: in
Thomas' view, the Holy Spirit need not and cannot be thought
of as a Person in the same way as we think of Father and Son;
each divine Hypostasis has its own incomparable *tropos hyparxeōs*
or *modus existendi*.

The formulations of Duns Scotus fully illustrate the whole
tension between a conceptual unity that is univocal, the result
of reflection, and a real diversity that is "always greater".[23] The
ineffable uniqueness of the person is pushed to the limit since,
as we have mentioned, *haecceitas* ("thisness") is still reckoned as
part of the order of essence,[24] and hence "person" remains something absolutely unique (*ultima solitudo*).[25] On the other hand,
Richard's *ek-sistentia* is radicalized to such an extent that being
itself, through which the person enters into existence, is understood as *relatio*: in the realm of the creature it is a being's

---

from the other two Persons" (ibid., 107). We have already referred to this in the
"Preludes" at the beginning of this volume.

[21] GP 108.

[22] GP 73.

[23] On what follows, cf. Heribert Mühlen, *Sein und Person nach Johannes Scotus:
Beitrag zur Grundlegung einer Metaphysik der Person* (Werl: Coelde, 1954), and Éti-
enne Gilson, *Jean Duns Scot: Introduction à ses positions fondamentales* (Paris: Vrin,
1952).

[24] Cf. Gilson, *Jean Duns Scot*, 454f. Haecceitas is "ultima actualitas formae"
(464). Thus "differentiae ultimae sunt primo diversae et idea ab eis nihil unum
per se commune potest abstrahi" (*Ord.* II, d. 3, q. 6, n. 14).

[25] *Ord.* III, 1, 1, n. 17, Wadding XIV, 54a: "Quia ad personalitatem requiritur
ultima solitudo sive negatio dependentiae actualis et aptitudinalis ad personam
alterius naturae", which amounts to a rejection of Boethius' definition.

tendency to exist; in the realm of the divine it is the realizing of the most real, Divine Being in its diverse, intellectual, internal relations. From this vantage point we can see that Scotus, going beyond the (very real) analogy between God and the creature, can speak of a univocity that transcends the "theological difference" between God and the creature, *both* of Being *and* of the Persons in God and those in the creaturely realm; this he does in a *secunda intentio* that operates with concepts, not with real things.[26]

If we survey the medieval attempts to define "person" more precisely in relation to God and, in particular, to the Spirit, we find that the patristic *ignorabimus* with regard to the *ekporeusis* has entered a new stage. All Christian theology acknowledges that statements about the "immanent" Trinity can only be reached via the "economic" Trinity. The central achievement of the patristic period was to have demonstrated that the Spirit, on the basis of his "economic" work as the Interpreter of Christ, in imparting genuinely divine gifts to men, must be himself God; the Fathers explicitly renounced the wish to clarify this divine and personal mode of being. Theology in the Middle Ages, following the same path from *oikonomia* to *theologia*, draws the implicit patristic insight into the full light of day: the *tropos hyparxeōs* of the Divine Persons cannot be brought under any general concept, particularly since we cannot even conceptualize creaturely personhood.[27] Augustine seemed to have opened up a new and promising path, on the basis of the *oikonomia*, with his *imago trinitatis in mente*: on the one hand, the procession of the Spirit *ab utroque* was assured, and, on the other, his essence as *amor personalis*, as *donum* (*donabile, donandum* for the world) seemed

---

[26] "Potest dici quod ab individuis non tantum potest abstrahi species quae dicit quidditatem individuorum, sed etiam aliquid quasi proprium" (*Ox*. I, d. 23, q. and n. 8, Wadd. X, 265b). For God: "Relatio importat conceptum communem in quid dictum de paternitate et filiatione; tale non potest esse commune nisi secundum rationem, quia numeratur in inferioribus" (*Rep. Par.* I, d. 25, q. 2, n. 5 [Wadd. XXII, 287b]).

[27] This, too, had certain patristic roots in the anti-Eunomian controversy of the Cappadocians. The latter (contrary to the late-Arian attempt to define the Divine Persons by a clear concept, e.g., *agennētos* in the case of the Father) emphasized that human reason cannot even grasp the essence of a gnat. Thomas will repeat this (*Symbol. apost.*, c. 1).

evident; this was because, according to this *imago*, the Logos is begotten and made a Person under the sign of knowledge, whereas the Spirit proceeds under the sign of the will, *liberalitas* (Bonaventure), "love". However, in the second volume of *Theo-Logic* there arose certain doubts about the propriety of applying this creaturely psychology to God; these doubts only increased on seeing the way it was applied in the Middle Ages. On the one hand, the Father's surrender of the Son cannot but be seen as his highest *donum* for the world; consequently, the Son's gener-ation within the Godhead can only be seen as an act of absolute love. (We already saw, in the second volume of *Theo-logic*, that the Father cannot beget the Son *in order to* know himself; nor can he do so *because* he knows himself.) On the other hand, the entire economic work of the Spirit is described as a work of "understanding" what the Father has given us in the Son (1 Cor 2:12); the whole work of "guiding" us into the divine nature, including everything that, in the school of Bernard, is described as *sapere, sentire, praegustare*, as "tasting and knowing things from within", is unambiguously in the service of "guiding into all the truth" (Jn 16:13)—and thus it strengthens our fundamental the-sis. The connection so emphasized by the Middle Ages between this loving *sapere* and that *sapientia* in which understanding really takes place—which is the fundamental mark of "theology" in its response to God's revelation—confirms this. This period, there-fore, which felt it had to hold fast formally to the Augustinian *imago* and its trinitarian consequences, was, of its very nature, led beyond its own standpoint, as we see clearly in the whole issue (treated from Bonaventure to Thomas) as to which of the two—knowledge or love—has the primacy. For, according to Thomas, the seven gifts of the Holy Spirit that he sets forth with such genius[28] all serve to infuse into our cognitive powers an

---

[28] The basic statement is in *S. Th.* I/II, 68. The gifts of the Spirit "are given . . . in order to conform us to Christ, chiefly with regard to his Passion" (art. 1); they make men "disposed to be moved by God" by "divine instinct" (ibid.). As such they are necessary to man if he is to become a child of God (art. 2). The gifts of wisdom and knowledge can be given in two ways: as gifts of the Spirit available to all true believers or as special mystical gifts (art. 5): Thomas' view here determines the way in which general or special mysticism will be understood. The particular gifts of the Spirit are treated in II/II in the context of his discussion of

instinctus that operates by divine love, imprinting the secrets of faith upon us and assimilating our inner attitude of faith to the mystery; in Bonaventure the *excessus* of love, far from leaving the reason behind, actually implies the highest form of *intelligentia*.[29]

Since Scholasticism devotes such careful attention to the effects of the Spirit's grace in man and traces the manifold operations of the Spirit-Interpreter attested in Scripture, it would be foolish to accuse it of "forgetting the Spirit" or of being an "impoverishment" compared with the Fathers or of getting bogged down in details or of "neglecting the third article of faith".[30] The expansion of "economic" (and hence anthropological) aspects is entirely justified. The question of the Spirit's mysterious Personhood is bequeathed to subsequent generations. We can anticipate the point at which further reflection upon this Personhood will take place: namely, where the reciprocal love between Father and Son can be pondered "according to the analogy of the communion of a *we*" but *is not yet, as such*, the Person of the Spirit; just as, to use an illustration from creation, the union of the parents is *not yet* the child. We must say, rather, that "Father and Son, in an act of their *we* that is strictly common to both, produce the Holy Spirit as that *thou* within the Godhead to which they relate together and in common." In Scholastic terms, "the *spiratio activa* is . . . not a distinct person"; it is rather that "the *spiratio passiva* . . . is the act of the *we* of Father and Son that has become a Person."[31] With regard to the Person of the Holy Spirit, this means that he is simultaneously two things: the love between Father and Son, which (according to Thomas)

---

the particular theological and cardinal virtues, according to the distinction drawn in I/II, 68, 4.

[29] In spite of the influence of the Areopagite's negative theology, Bonaventure speaks of a "cognitio saporativa et experimentalis" of God (*De perf. evang.* I, vol. V, 126) or a "docta ignorantia" (2, d. 23, 2, 3 ad 6, vol. II, 546; cf. *Comm. in Joh.* I, 43, vol. VI, 256). "Actus doni sapientiae partim est cognitivus et partim est affectivus; ita quod in cognitione inchoatur et in affectione consummatur, secundum quod ipse gustus vel saporatio est experimentalis boni et dulcis cognitio" (3, d. 35, and I, concl., vol. III, 774).

[30] So, among others, Christian Schütz, *Einführung in die Pneumatologie* (Darmstadt, 1985), 90, 114. Schütz presents a concise survey and a wealth of references.

[31] GP 149, 155, 157.

is primarily natural, since there is no relational opposition here; and the fruit and witness of this love (as the child's existence demonstrates that its father and mother were united in love). The former aspect brings out the mysterious affinity of divine nature and Holy Spirit (to which we have already referred);[32] the latter indicates the personal distinctness of the Spirit within the common nature. This means that the Spirit is both the expression of what is most "subjective" in the divine love and, at the same time, the "objective" witness of this "subjective" love between Father and Son. As the next chapter will show, he is the unity of these two, the predestined One who interprets divine revelation by leading believers into it.

[32] Cf. our earlier remarks (in "Preludes") on Durrwell. Cf. also GP 159: "The essential divine self-love is shown in the *spiratio activa* in the primal mode of the *we*; this is concretized, as it were, in the Holy Spirit. . . . The *actus purus* (insofar as, from the outset, it has the *we*-aspect) is shown in the Holy Spirit as subsistent *we*-relation." He rightly adds: "The Holy Spirit, however, is not in this sense the 'object' of the Father-Son dialogue; he himself is the bond between them" (158).

4

MODERN TIMES

a. The Tradition

We come to modern times, where there is endless talk of "spirit" in general and of the "Holy Spirit" in particular, and here again the only question is that of the "who", the "Person" of the Spirit. We have just mentioned one of the aspects that has been consciously developed on the basis of medieval insights; we shall return to it in due course. First, however, it is important to realize that, in the many modern questionings of tradition, a few essential insights of the past (in part newly conceived, in part cleansed of accretions) have survived in theology, particularly in Protestant theology. Here we can only select a few characteristic instances from the vast material available.

1. The Reformers did not question the mystery of the divine Trinity-in-Unity or, accordingly, the "Personhood" of the Holy Spirit. It is only the more recent exegesis, against the background of Enlightenment Deism (and perhaps also of Fichte's assertion that "person" always includes the notions of finitude and limitation), that has found reasons in the New Testament texts for seeing the (Holy) *Pneuma* more as an impersonal divine power than as a Divine Person.[1] Much of this writing is based on a naïve, unreflected concept of the person. Quite apart from the fact that, if *pneuma* in Paul really means a divine power, impersonal powers are unimaginable in the Christian God, two decisive arguments can be adduced for the Spirit's Personhood.

First of all there is the perfect complementarity between the Spirit and Jesus, while both are clearly distinct. Both are worshipped in the Church from the very beginning, with the same

[1] A typical reaction against this is the work (already referred to) of H. Bertrams, *Das Wesen des Geistes nach der Anschauung des Apostels Paulus* (Münster, 1923). He concedes that most Pauline references to the Spirit are "impersonal" but concludes by holding on to the Spirit's "Personhood" on the basis of three or four passages. This carefully constructed work is rightly regarded as obsolete.

143

reverence appropriate to God (cf. Justin, 1 *Apol.* 13); to both are attributed the same divinizing effects, which only "persons" can produce (cf. Calvin, *Inst.* III, 1, 1–2), although Jesus must return to the Father if he is to send the Spirit to us. To deny the Spirit's divinity would be the same as denying the divinity of Jesus. The fact that the Spirit cannot be defined does not militate against his consubstantiality, against the *simul adoratur*.[2]

"If the Holy Spirit is destined to operate on human personality, he himself cannot be an impersonal power. He is the Spirit of knowledge, of wisdom and truth. These personal epithets are appropriate to the Holy Spirit since, because of his origin, he is personal."[3] This does not alter the fact, however, that:

2. The way in which the Spirit is Person is beyond our grasp. "There are no words that would enable us fully to express the Spirit's Personhood and role", says the Dominican, Dupuy: He can be understood in his operations, but only "apophatically" in his essence. "His Person transcends all that is personal"; at this point we must refer to Richard's *incommunicabilis*; even if, according to Paul, the Spirit-filled man is judged by no one, "the apophatic element of the Spirit plays its part."[4] T. F. Torrance means the same thing when he says that there can be no *eidos* for the Spirit.[5] G. Widmer calls the Spirit "non-systematizable", "he cannot be enclosed in any definition, any system."[6] In the Jewish realm it is Buber who emphasizes the ineffability of the Spirit, who needs human beings, in their encounter, in order to put himself into words.[7]

3. Modern personalism (we shall not go over this ground again)[8] is or was an attempt to rescue the human person from being de-

---

[2] Gabriel Widmer, "Saint-Esprit et théologie trinitaire", in LSE 107–28. This is formulated to refute Käsemann and E. Schweizer (in ThW).

[3] Gerhard Ebeling, *Dogmatik des christlichen Glaubens* III (Tübingen: Mohr, 1979), 116.

[4] B.-D. Dupuy, "Esprit Saint et anthropologie chrétienne", in EE 307–26.

[5] T. F. Torrance, in EE 268. J. Y. Lacoste, in *Int. Kath. Zft.* 15 (1986): 5–6.

[6] Widmer, "Saint-Esprit", 111, 113.

[7] Cf. B. Casper, *Das dialogische Denken* (Herder, 1967), 301.

[8] Cf. *Theo-Logic* II, 49ff.

voured by rationalistic technology. It emphatically defended the non-objectivity of the person: and if the human person cannot be made into an "object", how much more is this true in the case of the divine Spirit. This conclusion may be valid, but there is a further question behind it: What if things are the other way around? What if philosophical personalism, essentially, is nourished by a theological deposit and, more specifically, a Christian and trinitarian deposit? In this case it will collapse once it has forgotten or denied its origin. This thesis was put forward energetically by Roger Benjamin, tracing the consciousness of the theological origin of "person" to the work of Mounier, Nédoncelle, Maine de Biran, Renouvier, Maritain, Ricoeur, and especially Denis de Rougemont.[9] Tillich shows that, if God is termed a Person in the nineteenth century (and not until then), this is a relic of the formerly trinitarian theology; he could not be addressed as thou at all except in a trinitarian context. Moreover, if the concept of person is originally trinitarian, it is not undermined by the idea that personality involves finitude.[10] Juan B. Alfaro[11] demands a concept of person at the natural level,[12] which is necessary if God's free grace is to bring man to a final, supernatural personhood, since only in virtue of such an elevation can man attain full self-possession, and only thus can he have the ability to give himself completely. Most importantly, the antinomy inherent in the created human being—between the desire to be oneself and

[9] R. Benjamin, *Notion de personne et personnalisme chrétien* (Paris, Mouton, and La Haye, 1971). Denis de Rougemont (*Politique et personne* [Paris, 1934]) equates person and Christian mission; the natural man is an individual: not until there is what Paul calls the "new creature" do we have a "person".

[10] *Systematische Theologie* I (1955), 289 [Eng. trans., *Systematic Theology*, 3 vols. (London, 1953–1964)]. H. Thielicke, in his *Der Evangelische Glaube* II (Tübingen: Mohr, 1973), portrays the doctrine of the Trinity as a "revolution" insofar as it was necessary if man (God's "other") was to acquire positive value and if the Incarnation was to become possible. Outside the doctrine of the Trinity the "Not-One" always represents a diminution of Being.

[11] "Person und Gnade", *Münchener Theol. Zeitschrift* 11 (1960): 1–19.

[12] In this he refers to Hermann Volk, *Gnade und Person*, Gesammelte Schriften I (Mainz, 1967), 107–22. Volk insists that, where we speak of the theological pair "nature-supernatural", nature always includes the human person—if grace is to be communicated at all. But at the same time he warns against separating the person from its nature and limiting it, for example, to a mere I-thou relation (113). Grace cannot elevate a nature-less person.

the thrust toward self-transcendence—is overcome, albeit only in a fundamental choice facilitated by that grace which operates on created freedom. For Alfaro, therefore, "person" represents an inner analogy according to which both statements are true: man is a person because he is capable of being elevated to an I-thou relationship with God; and man is capable of receiving grace insofar as he is a person.[13]

4. Finally it must be pointed out that the Reformers, and in particular Calvin, brought out anew—from all the many aspects of medieval Spirit-theology—the plain meaning of the sending of the Spirit who interprets the revelation in Christ (that is, the love of Father and Son). The Spirit is inseparably united to the Word, but in such a way that "God always works in his elect in a twofold manner, inwardly through his Spirit, outwardly through his Word."[14] The Reformers, of course, understand the Word primarily as Scripture: without the Spirit-Interpreter the latter is dead, indeed, it "kills"; but by virtue of the bond that God has instituted between letter and spirit, it produces a lively cer-

[13] In a second part Alfaro discusses the Personhood of the incarnate Son of God: in virtue of the hypostatic union, the Personhood of the humanity of Jesus is grace (after Thomas, *S. Th.* III, 6, 6: "Gratia unionis est ipsum esse personale quod gratis divinitus datur humanae naturae in Persona Verbi"). It is the grace of the divine Sonship. At this point Alfaro speaks of Christ's "human spirituality", which had to be elevated to the supernatural order so that it would correspond to the Personhood of the Logos (16). For a human "rational nature without personality" would have been incapable of corresponding to divine grace; it was through the *personalizing* of this rational nature by the Logos (through the hypostatic union) that an adequate response could be given to this union.—In *Theo-Drama* III, 203f., we employed a somewhat different terminology: reserving the concept "person" for Christology and the graces of mission that come from Christ, we gave the name "conscious subject" to what today (in philosophy) is generally called "person". Alfaro comes close to this usage by allowing both complementary statements to stand. However, there is no mention of the Holy Spirit in this account of the problem. This will be treated in the next chapter. Cf. A. Guggenberger, art. "Person" (in HThG II, 1963): "Theology rightly says that only grace, i.e., our being drawn into the inner life of God, can make it clear how man is to be a person according to God's plan. . . . In the context of a theology of faith, the concept "person" must actually be shaped in close connection with Christology" (301).

[14] *Op. sel.* III, 303.

tainty.[15] "The Holy Spirit who dwells in our hearts causes us to feel the power of our Lord Jesus Christ, for he enlightens us so that we can apprehend his graces, seals and impresses them upon our hearts, and makes them effectual there; he makes us newborn, so that, in him, we are able to receive all the goods and gifts that are offered to us in Jesus Christ."[16] The inherent strength in Calvin's argument resides in the strict correlation between word (Scripture) and the inner testimony of the Spirit, which, in the objective word of Scripture, convinces the believing Christian of the divine truth over and beyond all the grounds of human reason. Vis-à-vis this testimony, for Calvin, even the Church's authority is only a "door"; the true witness is and remains the Holy Spirit. The Spirit prevents Scripture from being a "paper pope" (in the sense of mechanical verbal inspiration). As Théo Preiß explains, the Spirit is a witness in three respects: first, he utters and interprets what he himself has heard and so makes the living Christ present; second, he gives place to Father and Son in a kind of *kenosis* (which is why he is so hard to grasp as a Person); and third—by contrast with Montanus and all Pentecostal movements—he deflects our gaze away from himself, so that the Spirit's operation cannot be observed by introspection of any kind; the Spirit points to Christ.[17]

Luther's approach is, in general, no different. For him, word (not only the word of Scripture, but also the word of preaching) and Spirit are so indissolubly united that he abandons the traditional fourfold sense of Scripture and refuses to find the Spirit anywhere else but in the "letter". Here, more vigorously than Calvin, he is engaging in polemics against, on the one hand, the enthusiasts who tried to play off the "inner word of the Spirit" against the outer word and, on the other hand, the pope, who, "with his Church, judges and commands and says that this is the Spirit and this is right, even if it is against Scripture and is nothing but oral teaching. . . . In sum, enthusiasm has its root

---

[15] *Op. sel.*, III 84: *Instr.* I, 8–9, 3.

[16] *Catéchisme*, sec. 14. Cf. Gottfried W. Locher, "Testimonium internum: Calvins Lehre vom Heiligen Geist und das hermeneutische Problem", *Theologische Studien* 81 (EVZ 1964).

[17] Théo Preiß, *Das innere Zeugnis des Heiligen Geistes*, Theologische Studien 21 (Zollikon and Zürich: Evangelischer Verlag, 1947).

in Adam and his children from the beginning of the world to its end."[18] By and large Luther's concern is to protect the objectivity of the divine word: "The Holy Spirit . . . wrote neither doubtful assertions nor mere hypotheses in our hearts, but firm statements that are more certain and sure than life itself and all experience."[19]

However, by fixing the Spirit upon the word of Scripture and the word of the Church, the two Reformers effected a restriction, if we compare their approach with the traditional notion of the Spirit as Interpreter. Instead of the interpretation of Jesus Christ, and hence of his relationship to the revealing Father—an interpretation that unfolds freely in all dimensions—we have the single dimension of the word of Scripture (and sacrament), which was bound to lead to a certain ossifying in Protestant orthodoxy.

b. New Departures

1. The most important departure, bringing an advance in Pneumatology within the framework of the whole doctrine of the Trinity, is to be found in certain insights of personalism. (As already observed, we cannot give a survey of the latter here.) The understanding of trinitarian theology since Augustine was that the Divine Persons were only thinkable as Relations; crucially, this understanding has now borne fruit in terms of the human person. It is astonishing that the theology of the Middle Ages missed this aspect, emphasizing (on the basis of Boethius)

---

[18] *Werkausgabe* [Collected Works] 50, 245–46. "No man can see so much as a jot in Holy Scripture unless he has the Holy Spirit; all have a darkened heart, so that, even if they can tell and repeat everything in Scripture, they neither feel nor really know anything of it" (*Werkausgabe* 18, 609, 5). Cf. G. Ebeling, *Luther: Eine Einführung in sein Denken* (Tübingen, 1964), 117f.; G. Ebeling, "Luthers Ortsbestimmung der Lehre vom heiligen Geist", in *Wort und Glaube* III (Tübingen, 1975), 316–48. On the remarkable passages in the late Luther concerning the context of "works" performed in the Holy Spirit, cf. P. Fraenkel, in LSE (Genf, 1963).

[19] *Werkausgabe* 18, 605, 32. Several Lutheran dogmatical works have continued to expound the doctrine of the Spirit as the Interpreter of Jesus and of the Father in this wide sense. Cf. e.g., W. Elert, *Der christliche Glaube* (Hamburg, 1960), 211ff.

the person's internal identity [*In-sich-Stehen*] and (on the basis of Richard) the person's "whence?" [*Von-her-sein*]. The person's "whither?" [*Auf-hin-sein*] was deduced implicitly, at most, and acknowledged primarily in the way the creature is generally ordered to the Creator by whom it exists. Transcendence toward the other person was presupposed but not reflected upon. This is clearest in Scotus: the *ultima solitudo* of the "I" faces it with a final alternative: either it is pure "being for itself" [*Für-sich-sein*] —but this ontological consequence is discerned by Scotus to be a sinful egoism—or else it is "allowing oneself to be incorporated into God" [*Sich-einfügenlassen in Gott*] on the basis of an *aptitudo oboedientialis* and a following of Christ—whose human "I" allowed itself to be taken up into the Divine Person. As a result of individual difference, however, no man can be compared to any other: at the natural level, no interpersonal relationship can be envisaged. Such a relationship is glimpsed by the Idealists (Fichte, Hegel), expressly discussed by Feuerbach, and raised by many personalists to the level of a definition of the person (as an I-thou relationship). Without a thou, the individual person is unthinkable and self-contradictory. Now we can actually say that to speak of a God in three Persons is not "anthropomorphic", since we can only speak of the human person in "theomorphic" terms.[20] What was true of God can now be attributed to man as well: "The undivided sway of thinking in terms of substance is ended; relation is discovered as an equally valid primordial mode of reality."[21] From the very beginning of the Bible, man is responsible for his thou.[22] This emphasis tended to make "relation" absolute, so that on the Protestant side also there appeared a justified reaction, as with Gerhard Gloege,[23] who rejects "pure personalism" as untenable: according to Gloege,

[20] H. Thielicke, *Der Evangelische Glaube* II (1973), 8.

[21] J. Ratzinger, *Introduction to Christianity*, trans. J. R. Foster (San Francisco: Ignatius Press, Communio Books, 1990), 132.

[22] Gen 4:9. "Responsibility" is the central term in Emil Brunner's theology of ethics, cf. his *Wahrheit als Begegnung* (Zürich, 1938), *Das Gebot und die Ordnungen* (Tübingen, 1932).

[23] "Der theologische Personalismus als dogmatisches Problem", KuD 1 (1955): 23–41. Gloege has misgivings about Luther, then about Pascal's concept of person, and particularly about Gogarten, who, he suggests, dissolves personhood entirely into relationship to the "other".

even in the Old Covenant, to say nothing of the New ("*becoming flesh*", "appearing", and so on), behind the ontological there is the ontic; there is no need, in his view, to suspect this of "early Catholicism". He suggests that the great personalist thinkers proceeded on the basis of a given assumption, namely, that ontology and personhood were reciprocally interdependent.[24] Gerhard Stammler's position is essentially no different:[25] he speaks of the primary Existent [*das Seiende*], which determines all the possibilities of being [*Sein*]; to encounter it is to be "overwhelmed"; this concept of the Existent is "imposed" upon us by the message of Christ, since it is something that transcends the world and addresses us out of sheer, free goodness. Every instance of "God-for-me" presupposes "God-in-himself". True, it is only the revelation in Christ that equips us to engage in a "proper" ontology in theology—that is, a personalist ontology. These corrective operations reestablish the balance: just as God cannot be dissolved into mere relations, human interpersonality cannot do without the person's internal identity [*In-sich-Stehen*].

The fullest exponent of a Christian personalism, one who devoted profound reflection to the task of overcoming the apparent contradiction between ontology and person, is Maurice Nédoncelle. It is true that, like Laberthonnière, he started out from an anti-ontic personalism,[26] which takes as its basis the primary phenomenon of "becoming mutually aware",[27] and so from the very outset he turns his back on the solitary subject of Scotus and Descartes. Very soon, however, in coming to know both the "I" and the "I-thou", he acknowledges the necessity of positing *being* as the "substructure" of the personal dimension— since personal being is the highest form of being. Every "I" owes its existence to another human "thou"—and so is also related to it at the level of essence; moreover, since the "I" acknowledges

---

[24] Ibid., 39–41. He rightly cites R. Bonhoeffer's *Akt und Sein: Transzendentalphilosophie und Ontologie in der systematischen Theologie* (1931).

[25] "Ontologie in der Theologie?" KuD 4 (1956): 143–75. Also W. Pannenberg, art. "Person", in RGG V, 3d ed. (1961), 230–32; W. Kasper, *Jesus the Christ*, trans. V. Green, (London: Burns and Oates, New York: Paulist Press, 1977), 130ff.

[26] *La Personne humaine et la nature* (Paris, 1943), corrected later in *Personne humaine et nature: Étude logique et métaphysique* (Paris, 1969).

[27] *La Réciprocité des consciences* (Paris, 1942).

itself to be something posited, and hence something that must freely posit itself, two implications arise: first, the personal "I" knows that it is in a state of virtual openness to every being and existent (which, as we showed in *Theo-Drama* II, 238ff., he must "let be"); secondly, the "I" knows that it is in relation not only to a finite "thou", but also to an infinite "thou" who has called it into existence and entrusted it with a mission. Its mission (as we saw in *Theo-Drama* III, 183–220) is identical with its person.[28] Thus prayer becomes a fundamental act of finite existence. Nédoncelle establishes, at a purely philosophical level, the prolegomena for a theology of Christ's twofold commandment.[29] While as a philosopher of religion he is not speaking expressly of the trinitarian Holy Spirit, Nédoncelle's thought sheds a bright light on the relationship between nature (*esse*) and interpersonality in God; and, on the other hand, he could not have carried out his analysis of human interpersonal relations except by the radiant power of Existence/Truth, by the Interpreter of the revelation of God in Christ, namely, the Spirit.

2. There is, however, another approach to the renewal of Pneumatology in modern times. Once again we are brought back to Hegel. Of course, his ideas require complete transposition if they are to be employed in a Christian doctrine of the Spirit. From his youth Hegel was preoccupied with finding a reconciliation between the finite and the infinite, which he originally called "life" and soon thereafter "spirit".* "Infinite life can be called

---

[28] The convergence between Nédoncelle's fundamental thesis and my own has been keenly discerned by Jean Lacroix, "L'Ontologie personnaliste de M. Nédoncelle", in *La Pensée philosophique et religieuse de Maurice Nédoncelle*, Actes du colloque Strasbourg 1979 (Paris: Téqui, 1981), 99–112.

[29] If, at the purely natural level, the universality of being and, in particular, the spiritual intersubjectivity of the race forms the basis for ontic relation, this possibility of relationship (*communicabilitas*) is transformed, by our common origin in the personal being of God, who gives out of love, into a possibility of "being for and in" one another in love (communion). Cf. *Intersubjectivité et Ontologie* (Paris-Louvain, 1974), 135.

* A particular difficulty arises when translating German nouns, which are all written with an initial capital letter, whereas English usually reserves the capital letter for proper nouns and names. This difficulty becomes acute in the case of the word *Geist* ("spirit" or "Spirit"), since only the context can indicate which form

'one spirit' by contrast with the abstract multiplicity, for spirit is the living unity of the multiplicity, opposed to it as its form, not opposed to it as the dead, mere multiplicity that is separate from it. . . . Thus the individual lives become organs, and the infinite Whole becomes an infinite universe of life", but "the living Whole also involves death, contradiction, and reason."[30] That is why Hegel so hated the Jewish religion with its rigid irreconcilablity between the infinite God and the finite creature: what he was looking for was perhaps less the God-man than the Holy Spirit, the divine Spirit who searches the depths of the Godhead *in us*. Yet his early work, *Die Positivität der christlichen Religion*, after portraying Jesus' attempt to transform Jewish legalism into morality and free ethical behavior, fails to speak of the Holy Spirit and sees the Church as falling back into the old legalism as a result of her preoccupation with rights and offices: "Loosed from the fetters of positive commands, . . . emancipated reason now could have followed its own commands; but it was too young and inexperienced, unskilled in the enjoyment of the freedom it had won for itself, and it was once again subjected to a yoke of formulae."[31] Henceforward Hegel only speaks of the relationship between this denatured Church, fashioned after the pattern of a state, and the secular state itself. However, in the great treatise that Nohl entitles *Der Geist des Christentums und sein Schicksal* (1789–99) [The spirit of Christianity and its destiny], Hegel, attempting—in characteristic manner—a rapprochement between the Greek idea of destiny and the Bible, goes beyond this horizon and, hence, beyond the purely negative understanding of law: "The mountain and the eye that perceives it are subject and object, but between man and God, between spirit and spirit there is no such abyss; only if a person knows the object of his thought to be one [= a whole individual] and another [= other than himself] does this one [individual]

---

is to be employed in English. Since the capitalization "Spirit" is so suggestive of "Holy Spirit", I have opted for 'spirit' (lower case) for Hegel's concept. Similarly, I have opted for the lower-case "church" in the context of Hegel's thought. It must be emphasized, however, that this orthographical distinction is not possible in German.—Trans.

[30] *Hegels theologische Jugendschriften*, ed. H. Nohl (1907), 347–48.
[31] Ibid., 176.

exist for him."[32] This can be seen in the relationship between Jesus and his Father: Jesus "entered into battle equipped with the whole genius of his people" and was brought down by fate; but "the glorification of the Son of Man in his ruin is not what is negative", since "in this ruin" he salvaged his supernatural truth (Hölderlin's Empedocles is not far away here) and, by imparting his Holy Spirit, succeeded in convincing his disciples that he had overcome fate:[33] "In love, man has rediscovered himself in another; since this love is a uniting of life, it presupposes . . . a parting."[34] In Jesus it is not only a case of celebrating a divinized man (as with Heracles on his pyre): "Worship is also offered to him who teaches and walks among men and who hangs on the Cross." Earthly "reality, which weighs the divinized man down like leaden feet", is transformed in Jesus into a hovering between heaven and earth: the battle with fate forms a unity with the victory that is latent within it—because spirit has set its own limit in order to show its power by overcoming it: here, for the first time, we see the full law of spirit. "This two-ness of natures cannot be taken from the soul."[35] Here, at the heart of theology, we see the rise of what, in the *Enzyklopädie*, will be called "objective spirit". (In the *Philosophy of Law* the term is abandoned, but the thing itself remains and in section 26 is called "the absolutely objective will".) Subjective spirit is the individual consciousness, which initially thinks it has set up the sphere of law as something abstract over against itself; gradually (through property, through morality, through ethics in family, society, and state), by means of the renunciation of self-surrender, it discovers the true dimension of spirit and, hence, the authentic freedom proper to it. "Objective spirit" does not mean only the external institutions as such in the abstract, for Hegel includes "morality" in this category (whereby the subject acknowledges these institutions in his conscience: *Enzyklopädie*, section 503); furthermore, all forms of "objective spirit" are objectivizations of spirit as such, which posits them so that, through them and by transcending the opposition and "necessity" they represent,

[32] Ibid., 312.
[33] Ibid., 321.
[34] Ibid., 322.
[35] Ibid., 335.

it can attain to its true, universal, and free essence. Legality and morality (which Kant had taken to be opposites) now become a preliminary stage toward ethical behavior, which is "the perfection of objective spirit" insofar as it has become the unity and "truth of subjective and objective spirit itself" (*Enzyklopädie*, section 513).

It is all the easier to transpose Hegelian philosophy into a trinitarian theology since the former clearly has its origin in the latter. For the young Hegel, for instance, the true meaning of Church as institution was the Pauline view of the Mystical Body of Christ in many members, so that "the many forms of life should harmonize in one life", and "the walls of division excluding other godlike beings should be removed";[36] the true meaning of the Eucharist is not an instituted sacrament but a sharing in the one spirit of the love of Jesus, which penetrates all.[37] Theologically speaking, the ecclesial "objectivizations" (the word, understood as Scripture; sacrament; tradition; office) will be nothing other than forms fashioned by Christ's Holy Spirit in order to guide the subjective spirit of believers through the process of self-surrender toward that purity and universal expansion which it had always signified. The oft-heard (Protestant) reproach, that Catholicism has turned the subjective love of Christ into something legal and institutional can be disposed of on the basis of the Hegelian understanding of what objective spirit is. Of course there remain substantial differences between Hegelian spirit and the Christian Holy Spirit: the two do not become identical in "absolute spirit", although the Holy Spirit who searches the deep things of God is inwardly given to, and infused in, the created spirit; correspondingly, the believing, spiritual soul genuinely found in the Church is not identical with the Spirit that animates the Church —although this soul can be described (with Origen) as *anima*

---

[36] Ibid., 321.

[37] "The significance of the shed blood of Jesus in the context of his friends is not that it is poured out as an objective thing for their good and advantage; rather, as in the expression, 'He who eats my flesh and drinks my blood', the significance is the wine's relation to them as they all drink from the same cup, which is for all and is the same cup; . . . they are all penetrated by the same spirit of love. . . . Love made objective, this subjective reality that has been reified, returns to its nature and becomes, in the meal, once again subjective" (ibid., 299).

ecclesiastica and even (with Methodius) as having a share in the Church's motherhood. This is because the Church, established by Jesus and his Holy Spirit as "objective spirit", always retains the same priority over the soul (which has been privileged to enter it) as God's free operation enjoys vis-à-vis the operation of the creature (who has been thus set free for such operations).

The fact that the Holy Spirit, as ecclesial Spirit, maintains this twofold aspect, arises from its original, trinitarian, and irreducible dual form: it is the highest ("subjective") unity of Father and Son, and it is at the same time the ("objective", "personal") fruit of this love, distinct from Father and Son, its eternal product, result, and attestation.* This brings us back to what was said in *Theo-Logic* II, 132, namely, that we can only speak about things in God by using "two *countervailing* propositions". H. Mühlen wonders "whether relations between human persons might provide a starting point for an analogical understanding of the personal specifications of the Holy Spirit";[38] but in the end he can only say, on the one hand, that the Spirit can be designated as the "we" of Father and Son and, on the other hand, that he is a "thou" for both of Them. He suggests calling "this relation a 'we-thou' relation. Father and Son, in an act that is strictly common to their 'we', bring forth the Holy Spirit as that 'thou' within the Godhead to which they relate together and in common."[39] It is certainly possible to "shed light" on the convergence of both attempts on the basis of the father-mother-child analogy;[40] but what pertains to the creature and the species can only be, after all, a remote metaphor for the mystery of the inner fullness of the absolute, divine Unity.

This attempt to understand the "who?" of the Holy Spirit leaves one question open: For Hegel, as we know, "objective

---

* In German these three words are *Erzeugnis*, *Ergebnis*, and *Bezeugnis*—TRANS.

[38] GP 4.

[39] GP 155.

[40] GP 150. We have already shown, in connection with Oeing-Hanhoff's remarks (see above p. 46), that Hegel misses this twofold aspect by understanding spirit as the mere "we", what he calls "the identity of the one and the other". In spite of this, Hegel loudly insists on the necessity of recognizing the holy spirit. Texts in L. Oeing-Hanhoff, "Hegels Trinitätslehre", *Theologie und Philosophie* 52 (1977): 403.

spirit" is not only law/morality/ethics, but nature as a whole. So far we have only sketched a transposition with regard to the Church; this means that the question of the Holy Spirit and nature (or "world spirit" [*Weltgeist*]) is still an open one. We shall have to devote a special chapter to it.

5

WHO IS THE SPIRIT?

In putting this question once more at the end of this section, it must be firmly borne in mind that the Trinity is and remains an absolute mystery; that is why, as we have just repeated, any approach to the mystery must proceed by statements running in opposite directions. (Nor must it be thought that we can "get beyond" this insight.) The Augustinian picture was of three functions in the one Spirit: what is missing here is the "personhood" of these functions; without it, self-consciousness cannot transcend itself through the communication that grounds persons.[1] However, where there is genuine communication and hence fruitfulness, in the interpersonal realm, what is lacking is the unity of the concrete essence; a doctrine of the Trinity that proceeds from the *purely* "economic" diastasis is always in danger of putting forward a tritheism, where the unity of essence emerges at best, if at all, from the *circuminsessio*.[2]

---

[1] This constitutes an objection to the subtle doctrine of the person put forward by J. Auer, *Person: Ihre theologische Struktur: Ein Schlüssel zum christlichen Mysterium* (Regensburg, 1970), and in *Kleine Kath. Dogmatik* II (1978), esp. 338–55. Auer explains the Augustinian triad decidedly in terms of human experience of the self and then attempts to distinguish, in the univocal concept of "person" (as applied to God, angels, and men), the three elements of subsistence (the ground of being), existence (free self-actualization), and communication (a "precondition for all personal being", 343); in doing so he recalls (with Augustine, *De Trin.* 14, 12, 15) that the created spirit must become aware, in its self-consciousness, that it originates essentially from an infinite Personhood. The weak point, however, in this renewal of the Augustinian triad is where he understands Augustine's "will"/"love" (which, by analogy with self-love, is at best implicitly the love of God) as interpersonal human communication: this concept is taken from the interpersonal metaphor of the Trinity that Augustine rejects. Not until Bonaventure (1, d. 10, 2, 1) is this concept admitted somewhat. And "modern personalism . . . was the first to discover the element of relationality in this concept of the person, that is, that 'self-being' implies 'being over against' and 'being with' " (L. Scheffczyk, in T 72).

[2] J. Moltmann, "Die Einheit des dreieinigen Gottes" (in T 97–113): "Not until we have a perichoretic concept of unity can we have a trinitarian concept of Trinity-in-Unity" (109). A contrary view is found in L. Oeing-Hanhoff,

The need for statements in opposite directions, in what concerns the inscrutable mystery of the Father, is vividly set forth in the Fourth Lateran Council: "For the Father, generating the Son from eternity, gave him his substance. . . . It cannot be said that he gave him a part of his substance and retained a part for himself, since the substance of the Father is indivisible, being entirely simple. Nor can it be said that in generating him the Father transferred his substance to the Son, as though he gave it to the Son and did not retain it himself, for if so he would have ceased to be substance" (DS 508).* Is the divine substance both given and not given? When a man begets, he gives a tiny part of himself but retains his human nature. God the Father gives *everything*—and according to Western theology this includes his ability to bring forth the Holy Spirit—to the Son, but then how can he remain what he was? Or, if this "was" sounds too Arian, we must try to put it thus: From all eternity he "*is*" Father by eternally giving his all. Here the relation seems to coincide with the substance, yet it does not do so completely, because the Son, too, receives the whole substance of "God", apart from the paternal giving. At the same time the Fatherhood (which is not given) is not withheld either, since it is the principle of "giving all". We have been careful not to connect this total self-surrender (in the Augustinian manner) with God's "self-knowledge": we can say neither that the Father begets the Son out of his (essential) self-knowledge (as *Verbum mentis*) nor that he begets him in order to attain self-knowledge. The only alternative is to understand the Father's self-giving as a primal act of love: the Son receives it as such, not "passively" as the Beloved, but (since he receives the Father's substance, his Father's love) actively as a Lover, returning love, as one who responds to the totality of the Father's love and is ready to do everything in love.

"Trinitarische Ontologie und Metaphysik der Person" (in T 143–82): "It is the identity of the Divine Persons at the level of essence that grounds their perichoresis, not vice versa: the unity of God is not the result of the perichoresis of the Divine Persons" (specifically against Moltmann: 159–60). [The terms "perichoresis" and "circuminsessio" (or "circumincessio") denote the interweaving "dance" or mutual indwelling of the three Persons of the Trinity—TRANS.]

* Text in: *The Teaching of the Catholic Church* (Alba House and Mercier Press, 1967), no. 156.

As Adrienne von Speyr has shown,[3] this results in the interplay of reciprocal wonder and worship, of infinite reciprocal gratitude (on the Father's part, because the Son eternally allows himself to be begotten; and on the Son's part, because the Father eternally gives himself) and reciprocal entreaty (on the Father's part, that the Son will carry out all the Father's wishes; and, on the Son's part, that the Father will permit the Son to fulfill his uttermost wishes). It is an interplay of absolute love that would seem to be eternally self-sufficient, yet internally it is characterized by such an excess that, "incidentally" (as it were), and precisely *as* excess, it produces another One: namely, the proof that this loving indwelling has succeeded, just as the human child is both the proof and the fruit of the reciprocal love of the parents. "The third", says Tertullian, "is the fruit that comes from the root of the tree."[4] He [the Spirit] arises from the reciprocity [of Father and Son] while surpassing it and being inaccessible to it; yet his freedom springs from it. The Spirit ("breath", "wind", "ferment") "blows where it wills, . . . you do not know whence it comes or whither it goes" (Jn 3:8). He is this brooding, overshadowing love, which is a phenomenon not only of the world and of nature, not only of human love, but of absolute Being; all notion of purpose and plan must be excluded from it, as it is excluded from reciprocal love; similarly we must banish from it all the talk of trinitarian "spiration" (which, apparently, was first introduced by Anselm) and of the "two who breathe" (*spiratores*) and thus together form a single "principle of spiration" (Council of Florence, DS 1331). Consequently it is pointless to try to puzzle out whether Father and Son, as Persons, constitute a single principle of the Spirit's procession[5] or whether "the love that springs from the divine essence, entering into relationship with the active spiration, becomes a personal trait (*notionalis*)."[6] God, from his very origin in the Father, is the miracle of that love whereby he can *be* himself in *giving* himself. This miracle is performed in the Holy Spirit because he, the excess of love that

---

[3] *The World of Prayer* (San Francisco: Ignatius Press, 1985).

[4] *Adv. Prax.* 8 (PL 2, 163).

[5] As Thomas maintains: 1, d. 11, q. 1, a. 4c; *S. Th.* I, 36, a. 4c.

[6] Cf. GP 152. Similarly Anselm and Alexander, references in ES III, 139, 151, n. 7.

is "always more", is the incomprehensible and unsurpassable peak of absolute love. *Deus semper major* is true, not only for us, but also for God himself. This, however, is no Dionysian inebriation but the *sobria ebrietas* of the God who, in all the three ways of possessing the divine essence *personally*, participates in all the divine attributes: full knowledge, omnipotence, righteousness, holiness, blessedness, and so on.

As we have said, it is impossible to approach the Holy Spirit except from two sides, as the (subjective) epitome of the reciprocal love of Father and Son—whereby he appears as the bond (*nexus*) between them—and as the (objective) fruit that is produced by this love and attests it. These two poles gradually move toward each other. If, in imagination, we were to exclude from the act of love between man and woman the nine months' pregnancy, that is, the temporal dimension, the child would be immediately present in their generative-receptive embrace; this would be simultaneously the expression of their reciprocal love *and*, going beyond it, its transcendent result. It would be wrong, here, to object that the diastasis we have described is purely dependent on the nature of the human species and that in a higher form of love the element of propagation would disappear (hence, not only the current distinction between the purposes of marriage, but also the notion of eros already found in Plato, right up to Soloviev, cf. *The Glory of the Lord* III, 347–49), because it must be said that this form of "excess" and "fruit" (which can be spiritual-intellectual) belongs to every love, including the higher forms. To that extent, perfect creaturely love is a genuine *imago trinitatis*.

From this vantage point it can be said that the Father's self-surrender to the Son intends the "always more" of absolute love, but this can only take place in the *communio* of paternal love and filial (answering) love; to that extent, the Spirit proceeds from the Father through (*dia*) the Son, but this does not mean that the Son is reduced to a mere means and medium. No objection need be made to the Spirit's procession *principaliter* from the Father (Augustine)[7] or *immediate* from the Father, or *mediate* from the

---

[7] *De Trin.* XV, 17, 29; 26, 47; *Serm.* 71, 26; this is found as early as Tertullian, *Adv. Prax.* 3.

Son (Thomas),[8] so long as the Father is not conceived merely as the "cause" (*aitia*) of Son and Spirit—for this would imply that the Spirit's origin was not the love between Father and Son and that only in the Holy Spirit would God step forth as love. One can try to support the denial of the *filioque* on the basis of considerations of salvation history; but behind this denial, ultimately, there is the ancient Greek, pyramidal way of thought that persists despite the rejection of Arianism: the Father's *monarchia* remains analogous to the Plotinian unity, whence proceeds the dyad of Son and Spirit. According to Augustine, however, the *filioque* follows necessarily from the Nicene *homoousion*.[9]

Let us return to the two approaches to the Spirit. He arises from the reciprocal love of Father and Son and so is *relatio*, but according to Thomas the mere relation has a *terminus*, as became clear in *Theo-Logic* II, 129–30. This was also true analogously in the case of the Father: he cannot be naked relation, but must be someone in relation, and to that extent what is his own must logically precede the relation. (Thus Thomas, *S. Th.* I, 40, a 4, c et ad 1: "Quia Pater est, generat".) This shows us once again that the Spirit is more than the mere relatedness of Father and Son (although, in terms of essence, he is this, too): beyond the reciprocal giving, the Spirit is the gift, the *donum*. So we do not need to adopt the view that the Spirit is only called "gift" in virtue of his role in salvation history (where he is utter gift, the dispenser of all divine graces): even within the Trinity he is essentially the Gift, namely, love, identical in each Person and yet, within this identity, realizes himself in ways that are always new (*tropos tēs hyparxeōs*), incomparable, and personal. In this way the "highest point" of the divine being is identical with its "innermost center"; if the Spirit is given to the creature as a gift, it is a gift that contains the whole being of the Godhead; it implies the "divinizing" of the creature. This, for Athanasius, Basil, and Gregory Nazianzen, sufficed to demonstrate the divinity of the Spirit. In this same context we can cite the idea (of Durrwell, Moltmann, and others) that the Spirit concludes

---

[8] *I Sent.* d. 12, q. 1, a. 3.

[9] "The Western *Filioque*, as Augustine states it, is almost a necessary inference from the Homoousion" (H. B. Swete, *The Holy Spirit in the Ancient Church* (London, 1909), 353).

and rounds out God's entire being as love, insofar as the very "first" procession was made with a view to this "last" end—not that God thus "unfolds himself", since, in eternity, the "last" is just as eternal as the "first". Yet it is "absolutely false to say that the Holy Spirit is the principle of love between Father and Son".[10] Nor should we speak of the "fruitfulness of the being of God" apart from the Persons,[11] for, while it is true to say that God is "fruitful", he is not so in such a way that, in him, something abstract can be distinguished from the concrete;[12] his fruitfulness always includes the proceeding of the personal processions.[13] Furthermore, it would be inadvisable to attribute the title *donum* to the Holy Spirit so exclusively that the Father's self-giving in begetting the Son would fail to qualify as a *donum*, which is manifest in the "economic" surrender of the Son by the Father: "For that the Son is given is from the Father's love, according to the words: 'God so loved the world, as to give his only begotten Son' (Jn 3:16)."[14] The Son by no means reveals the Father (economically) only *per modum intellectus*; as John adequately shows, through his absolute love for the Father and for the men whom the Father loves, what the Son reveals is primarily the Father's love. To that extent the Spirit should be called *donum doni*, that is, the Father's love, given to the world in his Son and "poured into our hearts" through the gift of love in the Spirit. Thus, now as seen from within the Trinity, the Spirit is again shown to be the given Interpreter of the divine Gift (which the Father gives us with the Son); and since the gift of the Son was itself already a revelation of love, the Spirit's interpretation can only operate by leading us into love. In view of all this, the two

[10] Thomas, *S. Th.* I, 37, 2.

[11] As several Scholastics tried to do. Cf. M. Schmaus, *Der Liber propugnatorius* II, BGPhThM 29 (1930), 262f., 285 passim; especially Bonaventure, cf. A. Stohr, *Die Trinitätslehre des hl. Bonaventura* I (Münster, 1923), 118f. Thomas speaks of the "virtus fecundatis in Deo" only in connection with the procession of the Persons: *S. Th.* I, 27, 5 ad 3. Bonaventure's tendency to represent the being of God as *bonum diffusum sui*, and hence as the ultimate principle of fruitfulness, owes more to Platonism than to the Gospel.

[12] *S. Th.* I, 40, 1 and 2.

[13] "Potentia generandi significat in recto naturam divinam, sed in oblique relationem" (*S. Th.* I, 41, 5).

[14] *S. Th.* I, 38, 2 ad 1.

"economic" modes of self-giving need imply no primary relation to the creature;[15] the latter is rooted in the loving relations
found within God himself.

It would be well, finally, to refrain from saying that the Son
proceeds *per modum naturae* while the Spirit proceeds *per modum
voluntatis* or *liberalitatis*.[16] Wherever this explanation is given, it
is immediately neutralized by saying that the "freedom" in the
procession of the Spirit is a necessary freedom,[17] which would
ultimately have to be said of the first *processio*, too. As we have
mentioned, Adrienne von Speyr speaks of a "recapitulation" of
the nature-based processions in a divine freedom[18] that goes to
their very origin; this ultimately excludes every ontic priority of
mere necessity over divine freedom, but it also excludes every
arbitrary exercise of will; God is beyond the terms "necessity"
and "freedom".

As regards the two-ness of the processions, we must avoid any
suggestion (in both immanent and economic contexts) that the
first procession, the Son, is insufficient to implement God's purposes, which require the second procession, the Spirit, to fulfill
them. We must hold fast, on the basis of our understanding of
the economy of salvation, to the fact that Jesus' death completes
God's salvific plan ("consummatum est"), precisely because the
Son has always carried it out and brought it to conclusion in the
Holy Spirit; it is this fulfillment that is poured into our hearts and

[15] As Augustine and Thomas assert of the "donum" of the Spirit. Cf. Schmaus,
Liber propugnatorius, 648f.

[16] Thus esp. Bonaventure 1, d. 2, q. 4: "Summa perfectio [exigit] duplicem ema-
nationem, scilicet naturae et liberalitatis": this on the basis of Richard's distinction
between *dilectus* and *condilectus*, cf. 1, d. 10, a. q. 1, concl. and q. 2.

[17] Summary in Schmaus, *Liber propugnatorius*, 652.

[18] *World of Prayer*, 58: "The Father's first, primal purpose is not free. Or rather,
in its absolute sovereignty it is beyond necessity and freedom. Once the Son is
begotten, however, he adopts the Father's will by freely desiring to be what the
Father's purpose has determined. And now, from the vantage point of this free
will, it is as if even the Father's begetting and the Son's being begotten acquire
characteristics of freedom, as if in their freedom Father and Son recapitulate their
natural relationship, in order freely to be what they are of necessity. . . . But in
God necessity is not a blind necessity of nature, preliminary to his qualities of
mind and personhood. It is a divine necessity which expresses his spiritual nature.
It has no parallel among us creatures." Compare this with Thomas, *S. Th.* I, 41,
2: "Utrum actus notionales sunt voluntarii."

minds in the Spirit that is given to us ("taking what is mine"). This raises the issue of the inseparability of Son and Spirit, which will be the subject of the next section. To approach this issue correctly, we need to keep in mind what we have established so far: each of the Persons in God is unique in the mode of personal being; the Persons cannot (in the categorial sense) be counted; and—ultimately the insight of Richard of St. Victor— that shared love is not perfected without an inner fruit (and a *condilectus* cannot be external to this love).

III. "THE FATHER'S TWO HANDS"

I

INTRODUCTION

It was Irenaeus who coined the expression "the Father's two hands" for the Son and the Spirit. Using these two hands, the Father fashions man, saying to them, "Let us create man" in the image of God (*Adv. Haer.* IV, Pr. 4). He did not need the angels to do this, but was "ineffably helped by those who are both begotten of him and his own hands, namely, the Son and the Spirit, the Logos and Wisdom" (IV, 7, 4). "For Adam never escaped the hands of God, to whom God said, 'Let us make man in our own image and likeness.' And so, in the end, it was the hands of God made man, 'not by the will of the flesh and not by the will of man', but by God's free good pleasure, and this is how Adam became God's image and likeness" (V, 1, 3). When it was a case of eternally vivifying mortal flesh, for instance, the bodies of Enoch and Elijah were taken and transported away by the hands of God that had originally fashioned them, "for, ever since Adam, God's hands were accustomed to take what they had fashioned, guiding it, keeping and carrying it, putting it down where they willed" (V, 5, 1). Not only the human spirit, but the entire, bodily human being was fashioned according to God's image and likeness "by the Father's hands, the Son and the Spirit" (V, 6, 1). He who is thus "originally molded into God's image and likeness by God's hands, the Son and the Spirit, is brought, when he believes, into God's threshing floor" (V, 28, 4).

It is all the more amazing that Irenaeus insists on this metaphor, since in him we find no trace of the later, Eastern theology, according to which Son and Spirit proceed with equal directness from the Father. Furthermore, "the Father's two hands" are those with whose assistance he carries out the entire world project—from creation, via the redemption, to its final consummation in God.

We find a parallel here in the *Letter to Serapion* of St. Athanasius, except for the fact that, here, the Son's divinity has first to be established in his relation to the Father, and then an analogous "Binity" is described between Son and Spirit, according to which the Spirit appears as the "image of the Son", just as the Son had been seen as the Image of the Father (*Ad Serap.* III, 4; I, 20).[1] However, here the word "image" only means equality of essence and posteriority in *taxis*; it does not refer to the mode of proceeding (from the Father). Athanasius is exclusively concerned with the close, correlative relation between Son and Spirit. "The Spirit is not outside the Son. For the grace that is perfected through the Son in the Holy Spirit is one grace" (I, 14). "In the Son one can see the Spirit"; "when we are illuminated by the Spirit, it is Christ who illuminates us in him"; "drinking the Spirit, we drink Christ", and "receiving the Spirit, we become sons" (I, 19). When the Son works miracles in the power of the Spirit, Paul speaks of works of Christ (I, 19). "The Spirit cannot be separated from the Logos, for when Christ says, 'We shall come, my Father and I', the Spirit, too—no differently from the Son—comes to dwell in us" (I, 31). "When the Logos dwells in the prophets, they speak in the Holy Spirit" (ibid.). "When the Logos comes upon the Virgin, the Spirit simultaneously spreads himself over her; it was the Logos who formed a body for himself, joining himself to it in the Spirit" (I, 31). "He who sees the Son sees the Father: similarly, anyone who has the Holy Spirit has the Son" (III, 3). Here Athanasius is dealing, not with the creation, but only with salvation history, proving the divinity of the Spirit in the same way that he proves that of the Son; he conceives the Trinity, as a double Binity (as it were); only the second concerns us here.[2]

[1] For the development of this theme, cf. Pseudo-Basil (Didymus?), *C. Eunom.* V (PG 29, 724C, 725B, 732A); Gregory Thaumaturgus (suggestions can be found in *Exp. fidei*, PG 10, 935); Cyril of Alexandria (at least in essence), in his *Dialogue on the Trinity*, bk. 7 (PG 68, 639B and D); *Commentary on John* 11, 10 (PG 74, 541C); 11, 11 (ibid., 553D); John Damascene, *De fide orth.* II, 13 (PG 94, 856B and PG 95, 60D). Also Thomas, *S. Th.* I, 35, 2.

[2] We can hear an echo of Athanasius in Basil's *De Spiritu Sancto*: "As then we speak of the worship offered in the Image of God the Father as worship in the Son, so too do we speak of worship in the Spirit as shewing in Himself the Godhead of the Lord" (SC 17, 231; PG 32, 185b). [This translation: Philip Schaff and Henry Wace, eds., *Nicene and Post-Nicene Fathers*, 2d series (Grand Rapids, Mich.: Wm. B. Eerdmans, 1996), VIII, 40.]

The compiler of these passages from Athanasius is Sergeï Bulgakov. He connects the results with the question of the *filioque* (which we will set aside for the present), which he treats in a very conciliatory manner. The result he comes to, that the Father reveals himself in the two Hypostases of Son and Spirit, can be adopted by Western theology without any reservations, in the sense that it is only the Son and the Spirit who are "sent" for the purposes of salvation history (Thomas, *S. Th.* I, 43).

> With regard to the first Hypostasis, the other two are its dyhypostatic revelation. This involves a particular hierarchy, namely, the freely accepted, loving renunciation that is unique to each Hypostasis of the Holy Trinity; each has its concrete *tropos tēs hyparxeōs*. . . . The center of revelation is the Father; the Hypostases who reveal him take their orientation from him. The two, Word and Spirit, are differentiated as different modes of this revelation but are united as a two-in-one image of the paternal self-utterance; they constitute a kind of dyad, whereby it is impossible to grasp one Hypostasis without thinking of the other at the same time. . . . Personally distinct, they are inseparable.

Bulgakov reminds us that the name "Christ" means "he who is anointed with the Spirit".[3]

It is worthwhile, in the context of the passages quoted from Irenaeus, to ask about the origin of the missions of Son and Spirit. Are they not already in operation, in a certain way, at the creation of the world? And while no one denies the fact that it is the Son alone who took human nature and that, according to *taxis*, he takes precedence over the Spirit, cannot the work of the Spirit in some way be subordinated to that of the Son? If this should prove to be not the case, we would have to reexamine two items of traditional dogmatics: the role of the Spirit in the Son's Incarnation (we adverted to this briefly in "Preludes"), and the

[3] S. Bulgakov, *Le Paraclet* (Paris: Aubier, 1946), 141–43. A large chapter (4) is devoted to the "Dyad of Logos and Spirit" (171–209). Evdokimov recalls this teaching in EE (272), as does Bobrinskoy with a quotation from Gregory of Nyssa (273). Gabriel Widmer, "Saint-Esprit et théologie trinitaire" (in LSE 107–28) speaks of the "complementarity" between Son and Spirit and draws from it an argument for the Holy Spirit's Personhood (111). Also, he suggests that this "complementarity" can indicate that the Spirit is a link between the immanent and the economic Trinity (122).

much-discussed question of the non-appropriation of the Spirit's indwelling in the Church and in souls to whom grace has been given. These speculative questions, however, will once again be preceded by a biblical section.

2

THE DYAD IN THE
ACT OF REVELATION

a. Biblical Aspect

We have already made some brief observations about the Old
Covenant (section I, 1 above). We noticed two things in particular: while there is no separation of the Hypostases at this
stage, yet God's Word and God's Spirit, though distinguishable,
have come so close to one another that they seem almost in-
terchangeable; furthermore, in the great prophecy of the "word
of the Lord", which does not speak of the "spirit" (or only in
its late period, in Ezekiel), the Spirit's inspiration is most tangible. Beside (or between) "word" and "spirit", in the late period, we also have "wisdom", which inclines now toward spirit
and now more toward word, in its own way showing the correlation between these two. (This will continue for a while in
early Christianity, where "wisdom" is sometimes seen as an attribute of the Son and sometimes more as an attribute of the
Spirit.) It appears, moreover, that the dominance of the word
(in the Sinai code) is increasingly interpreted as prophecy (so
that, ultimately, Moses becomes *the* prophet and spirit-bearer),
whereas, conversely, the dominance of the spirit (in early ecstatic
prophecy) develops more and more in the direction of the word
(in the great prophetic writings).

Initially, in the New Testament, the Holy Spirit is the one
who descends upon Jesus and anoints him as Messiah; but, lest
Jesus be equated with a mere prophet, it was necessary to trace
the activity of the Spirit farther and farther back, to the Virgin
Birth and the act of Incarnation itself. According to a straight-
forward reading of the Incarnation pericope, the Word becomes
flesh as a result of the work of the Spirit, who overshadows the
Virgin. The Cappadocians do not hesitate at this point: "Christ is
conceived, the Spirit is the Forerunner";[1] "Is it Christ's advent?

[1] Gregory Nazianzen, *Or.* 31, 29 (PG 36, 165B).

171

The Spirit is Forerunner."[2] Incidentally one could ask whether this antecedent operation of the Spirit in the Son's Incarnation is not also a cause of the universality of the Incarnation's effect on the whole of human nature, which is otherwise (for example, in Gregory of Nyssa and Cyril of Alexandria)[3] attributed more to the concrete unity of the nature assumed by the God-man. With regard to the whole life of Jesus, we quote the same two Cappadocians: after Basil has established the prior working of the Spirit in the Incarnation, he continues,

> In the first place He was made an unction, and being inseparably present was with the very flesh of the Lord, according to that which is written, "Upon whom thou shalt see the Spirit descending and remaining on Him, the same is" [Tit 2:13] "my beloved Son;" [Mt 3:17] and "Jesus of Nazareth" whom "God anointed with the Holy Ghost" [Acts 10:38]. After this every operation was wrought with the co-operation of the Spirit. He was present when the Lord was being tempted by the devil. . . . He was inseparably with Him while working His wonderful works; for, it is said, "If I by the Spirit of God cast out devils" [Mt 12:28]. . . . And He did not leave Him when He had risen from the dead; for when renewing man, and, by breathing on the face of the disciples, restoring the grace, that came of the inbreathing of God, which man had lost, what did the Lord say? "Receive ye the Holy Ghost."

Then Basil moves on to the Spirit's role in building the Church.[4] Gregory Nazianzen follows him faithfully: "Christ is baptized; the Spirit bears witness. He is tempted; the Spirit leads him. He works miracles; the Spirit accompanies them. He ascends; the Spirit follows him. . . . [God's] conception was a work fulfilled by his Word and perfected by his Spirit."[5] The operation

[2] Basil, De Spiritu Sancto 19 (PG 32, 180C).

[3] Cf. Cyril, Comm. in Joh. I, 4, 68BC and X, 1, 320D. On this concreteness of the nature, cf. L. Malevez, "L'Église dans le Christ", RSR 25 (1935): 280ff. Cyril strongly emphasizes the Spirit's role in our union with Christ (E. Mersch, Le Corps mystique du Christ I [1936], 501ff.) but says that Christ's humanity was sanctified at the Incarnation through the operation of his own Spirit (In Joh. 11, 11; PG 74, 557).

[4] De Spiritu Sancto 39 (PG 32, 140cd) [here quoted from Philip Schaff and Henry Wace, eds., Nicene and Post-Nicene Fathers, 2d series (Grand Rapids, Mich.: Wm. B. Eerdmans, 1996), vol. VIII].

[5] Or. 31, 19 (PG 36, 165B); Or. 38, 9 (ibid., 320C).

of the Holy Spirit's presence on the Cross remains mysterious; we must be content with the statement of Hebrews 9:14: "How much more [than the ancient animal sacrifices] shall the blood of Christ, who through the eternal Spirit offered himself without blemish to God, purify your conscience from dead works to serve the living God." The Son's perfect self-offering to God is made both through his blood and through the eternal Spirit, who can be none other than the Holy Spirit who always accompanies him,[6] by the same *dynamis* that, in Hebrews 7:16, is called "the power of an indestructible life". Thus the bloody death, in virtue of the presence of the eternal Holy Spirit, was itself a positive, eternally living act. Blood and Spirit are inseparable, but there is more: "He breathed out the Spirit" (*exepneusen*, Mark, Luke), "he yielded up ['released'] his spirit" (Matthew), "he gave up his spirit" (John); this once again brings out the two meanings of the word *pneuma* (breath, Holy Spirit), particularly in John, where Jesus gives up the Spirit "with bowed head", more toward earth than toward heaven.[7]

We have no way of inspecting Jesus' consciousness of this inseparable bond with the Spirit. It is unquestionable that the Spirit rested *over* him and that he knew that the Spirit dwelt *in* him: this is manifest in the sovereign authority of his deeds and words. He acts "in the Spirit" (Mt 12:27), even if this Spirit of his accommodates itself to the Incarnate One's mission of obedience and even though the Spirit of the Father remains "above" him, bringing him the Father's instructions. When he is "troubled in spirit" (Jn 13:21), we can discern the unity of this "in-and-over": the Spirit, from the Father, announces his coming

---

[6] As most exegetes propose. Not so Spicq (*Hebr.* I [1958], 238), who suggests that this refers to Christ's divine nature. Shortly before, however (9:8), there is mention of the Holy Spirit. Cf. O. Michel, *Hebräer*, 12th ed. (1966), 314: "The eternal Spirit is a circumlocution for the 'Holy' Spirit. . . . In this sacrificial act, too, Christ is governed by the objectivity of the Holy Spirit."

[7] Sebastian Tromp, in his *De Spiritu Christi Anima* (Gregoriana, 1960), has collected a wealth of texts to show that the primary sending of the Holy Spirit into the Church began on the Cross, and not at Easter (John) or at Pentecost (Luke): (55–83). He admits (73f.), however, that the patristic texts cited "do not prove, either explicitly or implicitly, that the Paraclete was given to the Church on the Cross." For Tromp, the fact that "the Spirit was breathed out on the Cross" is the strongest argument for his thesis (84–85).

suffering, and inwardly in Jesus' consciousness the Spirit feels
and responds to these tidings (one recalls the Spirit's "sighs too
deep for words": Rom 8:26). It is worth noticing that, in all
"economic" situations, there is no question of an "I-thou" relationship between Son and Spirit. The Son's only "thou" is the
Father; and he is this "thou" in the Spirit. (So the "we-thou"
formula that Mühlen suggests for the Spirit in God is hardly
tenable.) Here again we can see that the personal being of each
of the Divine Persons in God is unlike that of the other two.

When, on the Cross, the Son returns his Spirit to the Father,
this once-for-all act belongs to the testamentary conclusion of
the Son's mission. Until then, "the Holy Spirit was constantly
receiving, from the Son's hands, the sacrifice of his divine nature,
in order to lay it in the lap and consciousness of the heavenly
Father. The Spirit is the movement that effects and guarantees
this, now causing the hypostatic unity of divinity and humanity to adopt such a form (on the Cross) that the distinction between God and man, between the pure God and the pure Man,
emerges to its ultimate degree."[8] "The Son 'deposits' with the
Father all that is divine in him, so that the Father may 'grow',
may be exalted."[9] It was the Spirit—who is both the Spirit of
love and the objective guarantor—who ensured that the unity
between Father and Son survived in the form of their mutual,
utter abandonment. But what if now the Son also sends back to
the Father "the Spirit, the guarantor of his obedience, the witness both of his Incarnation and of his suffering on the Cross"?

> Until now the Witness of his abandonment was with him, and in
> giving him back he exposes himself to a new form of loneliness:
> out of obedience. No doubt was possible, since the Spirit of the
> Father, the Spirit of obedience, dwelt in him. He gives his Spirit
> back into the Father's hands so that he may be obedient even when
> abandoned by the Witness; so that he may render and suffer this
> ultimate obedience unto death in the absence of the Spirit's confir-
> mation, in the absence of knowledge and understanding. The Son
> knows, also, that he has power to dispose of this Spirit; he knows
> that it belongs to his office to give the Spirit back. Now that the

[8] Adrienne von Speyr, *Passion nach Matthäus* (Einsiedeln: Johannesverlag, 1957),
154.

[9] Ibid., 153–54.

mission is accomplished, the Spirit returns to the Father along with it. By saying "It is accomplished", the Son gave his mission back to the Father, insofar as his mission was more associated with his body (for he bequeathed his dead body to men); now he entrusts what is absolutely immortal in him to the eternally Immortal One, the Father. Only when all this has been done in due order, when he has stripped himself of everything, is he free to die.[10]

"The Lord gives his whole innocent spirit to the Father and keeps only our own sinful spirit back for himself. In this way he can carry sin as if he himself had committed it."[11] All this is beyond our powers of thought. "All things go out into the mystery of eternity. As for the idea of the Son's handing himself back on the cross, we can only follow it for a certain distance, then it breaks off; for of course the Son, in returning his being—and he is the resurrection and the life—to the Father and dying on the cross, does not cease being God. . . . From the perspective of his visible place in the world he seems to act as a separate and finite person vis-à-vis the Father. But the Three-Person God has never ceased being One and Infinite."[12] Again, this does not mean that the mode adopted by infinite love—utter forsakenness—until the Holy Spirit was given back, was, from the standpoint of eternity, mere "appearance": it was no more "appearance" than the human sin that the Son bore.

The Spirit has been sent back to the Father. Having accompanied the Son on earth, the Spirit has acquired a kind of earthly experience. Thus, when the risen Son, keeping his promise, sends the Spirit upon the Church and actually breathes him into his disciples in a bodily gesture, the unity of Son and Spirit is discernible in a new form that unites the bodily and the spiritual. True, a "reversal of competences" seems to take place: at one time it was the Spirit who brought the Son into the world, but now the Son sends the Spirit into the world. The two are "as if seized in infinite movement that requires a constant exchange of roles, while the Father surrounds and clasps the

[10] Ibid., 184–86.

[11] Adrienne von Speyr, *The Passion from Within* (San Francisco: Ignatius Press, 1998), 147.

[12] Adrienne von Speyr, *The Mystery of Death* (San Francisco: Ignatius Press, 1988), 73–74.

whole movement".[13] Yet, "The Spirit's pathway to men always runs through the Son."[14] "Sent by the Son, issued by the Father, the Spirit goes to mankind by bearing witness to the Son, consolingly strengthens the faith of mankind through this witness and thus leads mankind back to the Father in faith."[15] "His mission must be expanded into the universal dimension. . . . [The Spirit] comes to proclaim the whole fullness, the otherworldly richness of the Son and his revelation."[16] But this mission is "a fruit of the Cross" and of the Son's surrender of the Spirit to the Father, which now means that "The Spirit's pathway to men always runs through the Son."[17] Moreover, the Spirit is inseparable from the Son, whose bodily being has become universal: "the Son in the Eucharist, the Spirit in being poured out over the whole world";[18] nor are these merely juxtaposed: in transubstantiation "the role of the Spirit becomes visible", and in the Spirit's bond with "water and blood" in the "threefold witness" (1 Jn 5:7–8), we discern that he has "the form of Christ".[19]

This inseparability of Son and Spirit, which remains true after the Resurrection and in the sending of the Spirit upon the Church, gives us the central theme of a major section of this volume (which is to follow): the mission of the Spirit in no way takes over from the mission of the Son. It is simply that both their missions have entered a new stage in which the infinite wealth of their relationships is revealed in a different manner. But they remain "the Father's two hands".[20]

---

[13] Adrienne von Speyr, *John: The Farewell Discourses* III (San Francisco: Ignatius Press, 1987), 232.

[14] Ibid., IV (San Francisco: Ignatius Press, 1991), 221.

[15] Ibid., III, 213.

[16] Ibid., 232.

[17] Ibid., IV, 221.

[18] Ibid., III, 232.

[19] Adrienne von Speyr, *Die Katholischen Briefe* (Einsiedeln, 1961), 207.

[20] In the stages we have so far mentioned, i.e., first the Spirit "without measure" in Christ, then (in Cross and Resurrection) the Spirit as sent into (or "breathed into") the Church by Christ, we have set aside an essential factor, namely, Mary's Yes. For this consent, uttered entirely in the Holy Spirit (and hence immaculately), was the precondition for the Spirit's overshadowing of her. This means, however, that in Mary's consent (as the image of the Church and representative of all mankind) to the work and suffering of Jesus, a certain element of human

b. Speculative Aspect

The central theme of theological speculation on the Spirit is the mystery of the Incarnation. No theologian can aspire to get beyond its mysterious quality; the most he can do is to try to approach it as correctly as possible, taking into account all the aspects given and suggested in Scripture. This essential approach was indicated in our "Preludes" in connection with the question of a Spirit-Christology.

It is indisputable that even the Fathers were aware of two passages that are in a certain tension with one another and that, prior to any deeper speculation, indicate different paths. Philippians 2:6–8 seems clearly to attribute an active operation to the Logos: *he* empties himself; *he* assumes the form of a slave; *he* humbles himself and becomes obedient. By contrast, the Lucan account of the Incarnation points to an active operation on the part of the Spirit: *he* "comes upon" the Virgin and "overshadows" her. This results in a series of "logological" statements in the Fathers: the Logos "weaves his own human garment" (Melito);[21] "he anointed himself, since divinity is the anointing for the human race" (Nicetas);[22] at the Incarnation the Logos anoints the temple of his flesh with his own Spirit(!) (Cyril of

---

solidarity was always present. Only thus can we do justice to St. Athanasius when he says, "When the Lord was washed in the Jordan as a man, it was we who were washed in him and by him. And as he received the Spirit, it was we who were rendered receptive for the Spirit. . . . With him, we, too, began to receive the anointing and the seal" (*C. Arian.* I; PG 26, 168C–169B). Bellarmine gives the explicitly Marian reason for this: Mary "was present at the founding of the Church, which is the spiritual earth. For she alone cooperated in the mystery of the Passion, when she stood under the Cross and sacrificed her Son for the world's salvation" (*Sermo de Nativ. B.M.V. Op. Orat. Postuma* VI, 295). At this point one can also see what is lacking in Hegel's thesis (with which E. Jüngel largely agrees), namely, that the Spirit arises in the negativity of Jesus' death (absolute finitude negates itself), or "the entire divinity of Christ . . . [is] perfectly defined in the crucified Jesus of Nazareth" (E. Jüngel, "Das Sein Jesu Christi als Ereignis der Versöhnung Gottes mit einer gottlosen Welt" in: *Ev. Theol.* 38 [1978]: 510–17). For a critical view of this, cf. Walter Kern, "Philosophische Pneumatologie: Zur theologischen Aktualität Hegels", in GG 54–90.

[21] *Fragm.* XIV.

[22] *Thesaurus*, 1, 3, c. 3.

Alexandria).[23] These are contrasted with the "pneumatological" assertions such as those of Augustine:

> Jesus Christ not only gave the Holy Spirit as God, he also received the Spirit as man; that is why he is called "full of grace" (Jn 1:14) and full "of the Holy Spirit" (Lk 4:1), . . . "for God anointed him with the Holy Spirit" (Acts 10:38), not with visible oil, of course, but with the gift of grace (*dono gratiae*). . . . However, it must not be thought that Christ was only anointed with the Holy Spirit when the latter descended upon him in the form of a dove at his Baptism: rather, we should understand that he was anointed with this mysterious, invisible anointing when God's "Word became flesh" (Jn 1:14), that is, when human nature, without the merits of any antecedent good works, was united to the Word of God in the womb of the Virgin in order to become one Person with it.[24]

According to Augustine and the entire school that followed him, the Incarnation of the Logos is the highest of all graces for humanity as a whole and, hence, for Christ's humanity, too; whereas, from God's perspective, the question remains whether the Logos (who alone becomes man) lays hold of his own humanity or whether the Spirit gives it to him or, finally, whether the Spirit so elevates this humanity that the Son, and he alone, can make it his own. The aspect of "grace" will not be surrendered in this connection, but it will be emphasized in different ways; as to the result, however, the "union" as such, it will become the chief object of reflection; Peter Lombard is the first to speak of a "gratia unionis",[25] but in such a way that Jesus now appears both Son of God by nature (not by adoption) and by grace. This twofold view leads to the distinction between an "uncreated grace" (which Alexander's *Summa* connects with the Holy Spirit) "implementing the *unio*" and a "created grace" (the term goes back to Gilbert de La Porrée) that transforms human nature

---

[23] *In Joh.* XI, 11 (PG 74, 557). Similarly Hilary: "The Virgin received what she received through his own Holy Spirit" (*De Trin.* 20f., cf. 10, 15f.). Cf. Bonaventure: "Ipsa persona Verbi se ipsam facit humanae naturae hypostasim" (3, d. 2, a. 3, q. 2). Further references in *Theo-Drama* III, 184, n. 31. For Athanasius, cf. pp. 125–26 above.

[24] *De Trin.* XV, 26, 46; similarly in the *Enchiridion* 36, 37, 40 (PL 40, 250–51); *De praedest. sanct.* 15, 31 (PL 44, 982).

[25] III Sent. 6–7.

as such, disposing this nature for union. Thus the Holy Spirit, as "love", is the mediator (*medium*) between the infinitely sublime God and the creature who is so far removed from him. Now the Spirit appears primarily as that power which, by grace (henceforth known as *gratia habitualis*), equips human nature (in general and at its high point in Christ) for union with God.[26] Bonaventure signals a change insofar as he equates the *gratia unionis* (now seen wholly from God's side) with the hypostatic union, which is the work of the entire Trinity; the endowment of grace necessary for human nature is seen no longer as an indispensable prerequisite but simply as something appropriate (*congrua*).[27] This change is complete with Albert: seen from above, the *unio hypostatica* is no longer the highest instance of habitual grace but simply the inclusion of human nature within the being of the Logos, an "infinite grace". In addition to this grace, Albert continues to attribute habitual grace to the man Jesus in respect of his actions.[28] Initially Thomas will follow Albert's path: the grace of union springs from the fact that the Person to whom humanity is united is God.[29] The elevation terminates in the Divine Person: that is the grace bestowed upon it; there is no requirement of prior habitual grace.[30] Finally, in the *Summa*, the absolutely unique and superabundant "grace of union" that transcends all "species", supersedes all distinction between uncreated and created grace. This position is also maintained in the *Compendium* (c. 214).[31]

---

[26] Quar., vol. IV, 99.

[27] 3, d. 2, a. 3, q. 2, no. 6; *In Luc.* VII, no. 56; *Brevil.* 4, c. 5.

[28] 3, d. 3, expos. text. (Borgn. 28).

[29] *Quodl.* IX; it is preceded by a union of various aspects, cf. 3, d. 4, q. 3, a. 2, sol.; ibid., ad 1. Also 3, d. 13, q. 3, a. 1, sol. and ad 2.

[30] *De Ver.* 29 a 2.

[31] *S. Th.* III, q. 2, a. 10; q. 6, a. 6; q. 7, a. 11. "Il ne s'agit donc pas d'un double aspect de la grâce d'union: une grâce créée et incréée, mais d'une seule grâce d'union incréée," which naturally unites human nature in a special way. Cf. *Comp.* 214, where two forms of *gratia gratum faciens* are distinguished: *per caritatem* (for all other men) and *per unionem* (for Christ). Jan Rohof, *La Sainteté substantielle du Christ dans la théologie scolastique*, Studia Friburgensia, N.S., 5 (Fribourg, 1952), 42. We are largely following this study. Cf. also A. M. Landgraf, "Die spekulativ-theologische Erörterung der hypostatischen Vereinigung", in *Dogmengeschichte der Frühscholastik* II/1 (1953), 40–115.

A strange revolution takes place with Scotus. According to him, the *unio* as such imparts no particular distinction to humanity; it is no longer called *gratia*, but, rather, all that distinguishes Christ is attributed to the *gratia habitualis* that he possesses in the highest degree. We shall not examine the proliferating forms of late Scholasticism in detail, but we will group the main positions together. According to Thomas, the grace of union is understood to be of itself sanctifying; in the case of Christ's humanity it is understood to be effected either through the grace of the Trinity or through the Logos alone (united with the divine substance). However, most writers, for instance, Suarez, understand this sanctification at the level of being, for Christ's work to have its effect, to require a supplemental habitual grace. Vasquez, by contrast, regards the grace of union as sufficient: he adduces a wealth of patristic texts. For Nazarius, similarly, the grace of union surpasses every ("accidental") habitual grace; and for John of St. Thomas, too, the personal holiness of the Logos sanctifies his humanity.

Usually the Scholastics hold fast to a twofold sanctification of Christ's humanity. The one takes place substantially (physically) through the union itself but, as it were, only *radicaliter*, so that Christ's humanity needs a further (accidental) endowment of sanctifying grace for his work and suffering. The former is attributed to the divine Son himself (or, in the case of the hypostatic union, *in fieri* to the whole Trinity),[32] the latter to the Holy Spirit.[33] Scheeben essentially repeats the Thomist

---

[32] "Incarnationem quoque huius Filii tota Trinitas operasse credenda est, quia inseparabilia sunt opera Trinitatis. Solus tamen Filius formam servi accepit" (*Concil. Tolet.* XI, DS 535). There will be some reflection on the application of the principle of "inseparabilia opera Trinitatis" at the conclusion of this section.

[33] Examples: P. Galtier, *De Incarnatione et Redemptione* (Paris, 1926): The three Persons effect the union in concert (144); the work of the Incarnation is only *attributed* to the Holy Spirit. By the power of union, *vi unionis*, a *sanctitas substantialis* is effected; by the *plenitudo gratiae sanctificantis*, a *sanctitas accidentalis* (*Theses* 21–22, 255ff.). Similarly in Pohle-Gierens II, 8th ed. (1937), a distinction is drawn (falsely appealing to Thomas) between the substantial and accidental holiness of Christ's humanity; again it is the whole Trinity that operates, and the "overshadowing" is only *attributed* to the Holy Spirit. Hales first raised the question whether, in the case of Christ's humanity, habitual grace is the precondition for union or its result; here (as is often the case) the latter alternative is chosen. Diekamp und

view once more by first stressing the holiness that belongs to God's essence, which not only "consecrates" the Son's human nature, but permeates it through the Word of God united to the divine essence. Thus no *gratia creata* is necessary, for this permeation (the Fathers say "anointing") of the human nature by the Logos is far deeper than any habitual grace would make it.[34] It includes the "consecration" of what is creaturely in Christ to the exclusive service of God.

Let us now take a look at the speculation we have outlined here. First, when the Son's *assumptio naturae humanae* is attributed to the entire Trinity, we must ask whether it is right to speak of an *opus ad extra* (which merely calls for appropriation) in a case like this, where *one* Person becomes man. Bonaventure asked whether the Incarnation should be termed more a work of the Father in sending the Son or of the Son in fulfilling this mission or of the Spirit, who, as Love-in-Person, realizes the plan of love of Father and Son. Ultimately he "appropriates" this one work to all three Persons—and this expression must refer to something real, something in the order of being.[35] Without wishing to follow Bonaventure in all details, one will have to agree with him in his fundamental intuition that the Son's Incarnation is a trinitarian work, in the sense that, in him, each divine Hypostasis participates according to its specific *tropos hyparxeōs*. The Father does this first and foremost by sending the Son and allowing him to go, thus setting the whole drama in motion; he not only permits it: he entrusts his own *sperma Theou* (1 Jn 3:9) to the

---

Jüssen, 11th-12th ed. (1959), emphasizes the unique, preeminent quality of the *gratia unionis* (over against all *gratia accidentalis*), but it is grace, "est ipsum esse personale gratis divinitus datus humanae naturae in persona Verbi". While the whole Trinity effects the Incarnation, the shaping of Christ's body in Mary is attributed to the Holy Spirit, because the Spirit (1) is the love between Father and Son; because (2) grace is attributed to him; and because (3) Jesus is to be holy and the Son of God, and all other men become such by the Spirit. It is specifically stressed that Christ is holy through his anointing with the Godhead, not through the Holy Spirit, whose mission follows after (!) that of the Son: "gratia habitualis consequitur unionem". Then, however, it is also said (in harmony with many passages in Scripture and the Fathers) that Jesus was anointed with the Holy Spirit; this refers to Jesus' accidental holiness.

[34] *Dogmatik* III, 160.

[35] 3, d. 4, a. 1, q. 1.

Spirit, so that he may implant it in the womb of the Virgin. For what the Spirit will fashion in her womb is, not a "natural son" of the Spirit or of the entire Trinity, but expressly the Son of the Father. But as we have demonstrated, the active operation of the Spirit is too well attested for us to limit it to the merely secondary production of accidental grace. Recalling the words of Basil and Gregory Nazianzen, the Spirit is the "Forerunner", in the sense of the primary agent. This being so, the work of the Son can only be understood as a willingness to "let it happen". (We have often referred to the Son's "a priori obedience", cf. *Theo-Drama* III, 186f.; V, 247–48.) Of course, this must not be interpreted in a passive sense, but his whole action consists in obedience to the Father and—insofar as the Father commissions the Spirit to carry out the work—to the Spirit, too. What we said about the "trinitarian inversion" (*Theo-Drama* III, 183ff.) must be upheld here, together with all the consequences (and relativities) that become apparent during Jesus' earthly life as a result of the Spirit's being "in" him and "above" him. After all, for this period of time, the Spirit is the Spirit of the Father and, hence, the Spirit of instruction from heaven; while at the same time being the Spirit of the Son, that is, the Spirit of obedience in the Son. The "economic" inversion changes nothing with regard to the *taxis* of the Divine Persons. What it does do, in accord with the theme of this section, is to point to the simultaneity of the missions of Son and Spirit, whose mutual relations change according to the needs of the *oikonomia*: first, the Spirit is sent to incarnate the Son and to accompany the man Jesus to his death; then, the Risen One can resume charge of the Spirit and, together with the Father, send him upon the Church. These reflections lead, not to mere appropriations in the modern sense, but to three *propria* of the Persons acting in divine unity; for the Father, too (and particularly he), is at work "with his two hands".

To put it in another way: we are faced with an apparent dilemma. On the one hand, biblically, the act of Incarnation is attributed to the Holy Spirit. On the other hand, it is the Logos alone who becomes man; he cannot allow this Incarnation to take place by another Divine Person. Most often, recourse is had to the double action we have described: first that of the

Logos, who unites himself with human nature (in the *gratia unionis*), then that of the Spirit, who equips this human nature with the accidental graces it needs for its operation. H. Mühlen, who deals with this question thoroughly, adopts the latter view: "On the basis of what Scripture says about the anointing of Jesus, and from the entire context of the mysteries, we must conclude that Jesus' 'accidental' holiness, in which Christians share, is to be attributed to the Holy Spirit's activity in the man Jesus."[36] Why is it necessary to take this way out, which does not really correspond to the Lucan account of the Incarnation? Because of the strict refusal to make room for any kind of inversion in the transition from immanent to economic Trinity. The priority of the Son's action (at least at the logical level) must be upheld vis-à-vis that of the Spirit for reasons of trinitarian *taxis*, as Thomas himself insists.[37] If this veto is allowed to stand, the encyclical *Mystici Corporis* can adopt Cyril's formula (quoted above) and say that the Logos, at the first moment of his Incarnation, anointed himself with his own Spirit.[38] To overcome this dilemma one could first point out that the Holy Spirit is not only concerned with "sanctifying" (*pneuma hagiosynēs*, Rom 1:4), but is also the Creator Spirit. Nonetheless we must avoid saying that, in descending upon Mary, the Spirit "created" the union of the two natures of the Logos. The true answer could be found by reflecting on the essence of the Spirit insofar as he proceeds from Father and Son, and Cyril's text could form part of such reflection. At the same time one would have to renounce the idea of an exact correspondence of the immanent and economic *taxis*. The Spirit is the Spirit of the Father and of the Son; it is as the Spirit of the Father, clearly, that he is sent to the Virgin; at the same time (and not *per prius*), it is as the Spirit of the Son that he moves the latter, in accord with his filial willingness, to allow

---

[36] UMP 223.

[37] "Missio autem Filii, secundum ordinem naturae, *prior* est missione Spiritus Sancti, sicut ordine naturae Spiritus Sanctus procedit a Filio et a Patre dilectio. Unde et unio personalis, secundum quam intelligitur missio Filii est *prior*, ordine naturae, gratia habituali, secundum quam intelligit missio Spiritus Sancti" (*S. Th.* III, 7, 13c).

[38] "Primo incarnationis momento Aeterni Patris Filius humanam naturam sibi substantialiter unitam Spiritus Sancti plenitudine ornavit" (no. 31; cf. no. 56).

the hypostatic union to take place—in a priori, but not passive, obedience. Thus Incarnation and "anointing" simply coincide, just as the "anointing" of Christ's humanity coincides with the divine nature and the Holy Spirit (since God is just as "natural" as he is "personal"). "[As for] the things done in the dispensation of the coming of our Lord in the flesh . . . all is through the Spirit", says Basil;[39] but insofar as the Spirit is the agent, as Spirit of the Father, he bears "the seed of God" into the Virgin's womb, and insofar as he is the Spirit of the Son, the latter obediently accepts the Father's command (in other words, he obeys, even in the process of becoming man). Through both aspects of the Spirit, it is the Father who is the ultimate agent (acting through his "two hands"); so the passages in the Fathers that portray the Father anointing his Son in the Incarnation are by no means mistaken.[40] As we have said, the Incarnation is a trinitarian work, yet not by "appropriations" in the modern sense.

[39] *De Spiritu Sancto* 16 (PG 32, 140c).

[40] H. Mühlen (UMP 223) has assembled a number of impressive texts, beginning with Irenaeus' famous passage: "In Christi enim nomine subauditur qui unxit et ipse qui unctus est et ipsa unctio in qua unctus est. Et unxit quidem Pater, unctus est vero Filius, in Spiritu qui est unctio" (*Adv. Haer.* III, 18, 3). Similar passages in Ambrose, Basil, Chrysostom, Cyril, Damascene. For further texts, cf. L. Thomassin, *De Incarnatione* VI, 2.

3

THE DYAD OPERATES IN CONCERT

a. Divinization and Incorporation

The Father's two hands do not operate separately in juxtaposition or in sequence (as if the Spirit only arrives once Christ's work is completed): they operate in very distinct manners with and in one another, for (it must be remembered) the Spirit is always Christ's own Spirit. So the formula we initially used for trinitarian theology, "the Son reveals the Father; the Spirit reveals the Son",[1] needs to be restated in a more precise form. The Father shows himself in the Son, who, for his part, points to the Father; and the Spirit (who is of both) directs attention to this reciprocal "showing" that reveals God as love. Of course, by pointing to the reciprocal relationship of Father and Son, he simultaneously reveals the essence of the Persons.

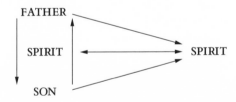

Therefore we must be on our guard against too simple a Spirit-Christology, such as many Antiochenes put forward, where the Spirit mediates the entire (divine) work of the man Jesus; such a teaching, strictly applied, leads to Nestorianism.[2]

---

[1] "Sicut Filius qui procedit a Patre, clarificat in suis operibus Patrem a quo est, sic et Spiritus Sanctus . . . enuntiat Filium a quo procedit" (Bonaventure, *In Joh.* 16 [Quar. VI, 459b]).

[2] According to Theodore of Mopsuestia the Spirit operates everything in Jesus (*De incarn.*; PG 66, 980; *Comm. in 1 Tim* 3:16; *In Rom* 13:14; *In Gal* 2:13f.). In Chrysostom, too, there is a perfect communion between Word and Spirit (*In Rom* 8; PG 69, 519). Nestorius seems to propose the same belief as we tried to show (above): the Spirit forms Jesus in the womb of the Virgin (in Cyril, *Adv. Nest.*,

The Spirit shows and interprets the twofold movement of the Father to the (incarnate) Son and that of the (risen) Son back to the Father as a single, indivisible movement; at the same time he interprets the definitive Incarnation of the Word (which reveals the Father and is not superseded even by the Resurrection), and the glory, divinity, and inner infinity of the Son (which is revealed in the Son's return to the Father), and, finally, the reciprocal love of Father and Son that all this implies. That is the theme of this entire part: first we shall deal explicitly with the unity of the (more Greek) concept of "divinization" and the (more Latin) concept of "incorporation into Christ". On closer inspection, the differences between these two concepts are almost entirely obliterated. The Greeks' "divinization" presupposes God's Incarnation and its continuation in the Eucharist; here, too, it follows that there is no other way to the Father than—in the Johannine and Pauline manner—through the Son and in the Spirit. For the Latins, incorporation into Christ is the only way of participating in the divine and triune life; Augustine himself will not reject the concept of "divinization".

It has rightly been said that the Greek theology of divinization began with Irenaeus;[3] in his battle against the Valentinians, who were defending the gnostics' "natural divinity", he shows that the man of body and soul is *phtartos*, corruptible, and can attain to the exclusively divine incorruptibility (*aphtharsia*) by grace alone and on the promise and achievement of the incarnate Son (II, 20, 3; V, 2, 2) and his heavenly Eucharist (IV, 18, 5). Man

---

PG 77, 176, 181); but more radical is his defense of the view that Jesus possessed unity with the divine Word only after receiving the Spirit at his Baptism. Cyril's ninth anathema counters this: If anyone shall say that Jesus performed miracles and drove out devils "using a power alien to him", "let him be anathema" (DS 260). At this, Theodoret rose up and refused to say that the Eternal Word was formed in the Virgin's womb and baptized with the Spirit (PG 76, 432).

[3] Michel Aubineau, "Incorruptibilité et divinisation selon S. Irénée", RSR, 1956, 25–52. On what follows, cf. the celebrated studies of J. Gross, *La divinisation du chrétien d'après les Pères grecs* (Paris, 1938); O. Faller, "Griechische Vergottung und christliche Vergöttlichung", *Gregorianum* 6 (1925): 405–38; M. Loth-Barodine, "La Doctrine de la déification dans l'Église grecque jusqu'au 11ᵉ siècle", *Rev. Hist. Rel.* 105 (1932): 1–43, 106, 525–72; 107 (1933): 8–55; also Y. Congar, "La Déification dans la tradition spirituelle", *Vie Spirituelle*, suppl. 43 (1935): 91–107, and the article "Déification" in DSp.

gradually wins "incorruptela gloria infecti" (IV, 38, 3) the pre-
rogatives of God by means of the slow growth in him of the
fruits of immortality (IV, 5, 1; V, 12, 4; V, 9, 1), whereby the
Spirit leads the baptized who have received him to the Son, "and
the Son, in turn, leads them to the Father, and the Father makes
them partakers of intransience. Thus it is impossible to know
the Word of God apart from the Spirit, and without the Son no
one can come to the Father. For the knowledge of the Father
is the Son, and one acquires knowledge of the Son of God by
the Holy Spirit" (*Epid.* 7). Knowledge, for Irenaeus, is identical
with (eternal) life (V, 3, 3; IV, 20, 7). He saw more clearly than
anyone else that the precondition of the Incarnation is the precondition of divinization (III, 19, 1; 18, 7; IV, 33, 4) and that
this comes about through the Spirit (IV, 4 and 6; V, 6, 1; 9, 1–
4; 12, 2).

It was Clement of Alexandria who coined the word *theopoiein*
(cf. *Protr.* 1, 8; *Paidag.* 1, 6, 26): divinization occurs through
baptism and the Word of God. Origen says the same: it is only
thanks to the incarnate Word that all attain sonship and union
with God (*In Joh.* 1, 16; 19, 4), "so that human nature may be
divinized, not only in Jesus, but in all who, having received the
faith, lead the life that Jesus led, which brings us to friendship
and fellowship with God" (*C. Cels.* 3, 28). So too in Hippolytus
(*Philos.* 10, 34). Athanasius places more emphasis on the image-
character of the man whom the Logos has created and, by becoming incarnate, restored (*Inc. Verbi* 3, 101c, and 13, 120b); but
he can also use the simple formula, God becomes man so that we
can become God (ibid., 54). Of course, man's image-character
is insufficient for this: the Incarnation is necessary as a bridge
between our flesh and the divine Spirit. Here, in the *Letters to
Serapion*, the Holy Spirit comes in, he who must be God if he
is to divinize us through the Logos (1, 24). Athanasius, however, understands divinization in a biblical sense, as becoming
God's children (*C. Ar.* III, 19, 24–25). For Basil, similarly, it
is created man's assimilation to the Son of God that divinizes
him (*De Spir. Sancto* 26). Gregory Nazianzen speaks much of
divinization: the fact that the Spirit effects it proves his divinity,
but the precondition is always the Incarnation (*Or.* 38, 11 and
13; 45, 9). For Gregory of Nyssa, too, the distance between God

and his creature is bridged only by the Incarnation (*Or. cat.* 21, 1f.), and here, for the first time, he mentions the role of the Eucharist as well as that of baptism (ibid., 37).

In the East, it would be true to say that the high point of this stereoscopy of incarnation and divinization is attained in Cyril of Alexandria, who not only repeats the traditional insight that incarnation is required as a precondition if men are to become divinized (*In Joh.* 1, 3–4); Christ must be God if he is to divinize men (*Thes. ass.* 1), but he must also be man (*In Joh.* 14, 33). In the context of divinization (and, later, against Nestorius) the role of Christ's "life-giving flesh" is strongly emphasized. This teaching is already contained in the commentary on St. John, quoting Colossians 2:9, which says that "in Christ the fullness of Godhead dwelt bodily" (*In Joh.* 4; PG 73, 601, 604); there is reference not only to Christ's God-forsakenness on the Cross on our behalf (*Quod unus sit Christus*, PG 75, 1325) but, most importantly, to the Eucharist. In it we see "the goal of the Son, to allow us to participate in him in a way that is both spiritual and bodily, thus elevating us above corruptibility" (*Adv. Nest.* 4; PG 76, 197). The Eucharist is the means "devised by the Son's wisdom to unite and fuse us with God and with one another, although in our bodies and souls we are individual beings" (*In Joh.* 11, 11; PG 74, 560). Together with the Eucharist, Cyril sees the Spirit at work: in his Oneness we are fused with God and with one another "into one Spirit". "As the virtue of the holy flesh unites those who receive it into a single body, the one Spirit who dwells in all brings all to a spiritual unity", and thus "the one Father of all, who will be God in all, will lead all who share in the Spirit into a unity with one another and with himself through his Son" (ibid., 561; cf. 564–65). Cyril is not afraid to say, on the basis of the union of the entire human nature with the incarnate Son, that the latter, as an individual man, is the Son of God by nature and is a Son by grace together with us, his brothers, so that we, in union with him and *in him* (alone), are sons of God by nature, whereas *in ourselves* we are sons "by participation and grace" (PG 76, 1177).

In view of this, we are no longer astonished by Maximus the Confessor's ultimate daring when he speaks of the divinization of man and the humanization of God as a single process in which each side heightens the other: the more man is divinized, the more God is humanized, and vice versa (*Amb.*; PG 91, 1113bc). John Damascene will repeat the customary teaching (*De fide orth.* IV, 9–13).

If we turn to the West, we find hardly any difference, even if Augustine uses the term "divinization" less often ("to divinize those who are men, he who was God has made himself a man": *Sermo* 192, 1; cf. *Sermo* 47, 12; *Ep.* 10, 2; *Sermo* 166, 4, and emphatically *In Ps.* 49, 2: "The one who divinizes is God of himself, and not by participation in another. The one who justifies also divinizes, for in justifying [men] he makes [them] children of God"). The core of this argument is that, because of Christ's Incarnation and Eucharist, we are incorporated into him, our Head, as his members. It is not necessary to cite the countless passages and formulas in which we are identified with him ("We are he", *In Ps.* 29, 2) and in which Christ the Head "loves himself" by loving his Body. More important in this context is the role that Augustine attributes to the Holy Spirit. Without the Spirit's operation, as J. Ratzinger has shown,[4] there would be no *communio* of the ecclesial Body of Christ. For Augustine the Spirit is *caritas* and *donum*, so much so that both can be regarded as his *opus proprium*. Thus he is the Initiator of salvation history (*De Trin.* XV, 18, 32), the Founder of the Church (not only as love, but also as institution and law),[5] although, within the Church, it is the victorious Christ who apportions the gifts of the Spirit: Christ, as Head, distributes them from above and simultaneously receives them below in the person of his members (*De Trin.* XV, 19, 34).[6] Augustine sees the inseparable collaboration of Son and Spirit (*Sermo* 71, 36; *Ench.* 22, 83), particularly

---

[4] "Der Heilige Geist als communio: Zum Verhältnis von Pneumatologie und Spiritualität bei Augustinus", in: HM 223–38. Cf. J. A. A. Stoof, *Die deificatio hominis in die sermones et epistulae von Augustinus* (Leyden, 1952).

[5] J. Ratzinger, in: HM 231, 234.

[6] G. Philips goes a little too far in his article "L'Influence du Christ-Chef sur son Corps mystique suivant S. Augustin", in *Augustinus Magister* II (Paris, 1954), 804–15: Christ's humanity as the Head of the Church is only the moral cause of salvation, the real source being the Spirit, who implies the presence of grace in Christ's Body. But, as the above passage says, the Spirit is distributed by Christ: "per donum quod est Spiritus Sanctus in commune omnibus membris Christi multa dona . . . dividuntur. . . . De his aedificatur domus Christi, quae domus appellatur Ecclesia."

in what concerns ecclesial office (*In Ps.* 67, 16; *C. Ep. Parm.* II,
11, 24).[7]

It would be superfluous to present all the texts in the other
Latin Fathers that speak of the unity of incarnation and divinization; Ambrose and Hilary were well versed in Greek theology;
the former emphasizes the "exchange" between God and man
(*De myst.* 7, 37–42), the latter, like Cyril, puts the accent strongly
on the *caro vivificans* of Christ.[8] The monks of the twelfth century
offer a rich harvest in the same tradition;[9] it is continued in the
Scholastics in the wake of Gilbert, Lombard, and Alexander, and
up to Bonaventure, Albert, and Thomas. As we know, Lombard's
unacceptable teaching—that the Holy Spirit is directly the act
of love in us—was remedied by the idea of a *gratia creata*; Albert,
who often uses the word *deiformis*, assures us that such grace is
not a *medium* between us and God. Thomas, for his part, wres-
tles to establish the nature of the divinizing grace of the Holy
Spirit, which, according to him, leads to the glory of a direct
participation in the divine nature (*S. Th.* I/II, 2, 3), yet which
even in this life "esse quoddam divinum . . . animae confert"
(2 *Sent.* 26, 1, 4), "homo . . . per gratiam infusam constituitur
in esse divino" (2 *Sent.* 27, 1, 5 ad 3).[10]

b. Theoria and Praxis

A second aspect of the interwoven activity of Son and Spirit is
the inseparability, in the field of revelation, of *theoria* and *praxis*,

[7] For details, cf. Felix Genn, *Trinität und Amt nach Augustinus* (Einsiedeln: Johannesverlag, 1986).—Man's salvation is wrought by the Trinity: the Father achieves
in man a likeness to Christ through the Holy Spirit: *In Joh.*, tr. 18, 10; *De Trin.*
XV 11, 20.

[8] Texts in E. Mersch, *Corps Mystique* I (1936), 410–37. Cf. *In Ps* 91, 9 (PL
9, 499): Reborn by the Spirit in baptism, we are "justified by the body of his
[Christ's] flesh", so much so that Christians, purified by baptism, "should be
aware that they no longer have any other flesh but Christ's". Furthermore, we
shall be raised up in Christ's flesh and "rise up to his glorious Body, reposing in
him in the greatness of God." We remain united to Christ's flesh even when our
being is in God. Cf. again *De Trin.* 9, 8 (PL 10, 287).

[9] A wealth of texts in DSp III, 1399–1413.

[10] For the influence of Greek theology on Thomas: I. Backes, *Die Christologie
des hl. Thomas von Aquin und die griechischen Kirchenväter* (Paderborn, 1931).

or, in more contemporary terms, of orthodoxy and orthopraxy.
This interplay cannot be reduced, however, to a simple formula:
it must be unfolded in its entire complexity. We see this inseparability in the Father, working with his "two hands": "My Father
is working still", says Jesus (Jn 5:17), looking to the Father and
imitating him, and at the same time the Father, in sending Son
and Spirit, causes them both to work—under his gaze. Thus the
Father appears beyond all beholding and doing: both have their
origin in him and return to him.

1. First of all the Spirit directs our attention to the Son, for he
lives by the pure act of revealing the Father. He opens our eyes
to a preliminary theoria in which we discern the Son's praxis,
living, dying, and returning to the Father. This theoria is only
possible because we have received the "salve to anoint your eyes"
(Rev 3:18), the salve of faith that, as we showed in *The Glory
of the Lord*, is necessary if we are to discern the truth of Christ.
This truth consists in his "adequate translation" (*Theo-Logic* II)
of the Father and his trinitarian life into the terms of human
existence. If man wanted to begin with orthopraxy without first
opening himself to the sight of the truth, his praxis could never
be right (*orthos*) in God's sense. The fact remains, however: even
if faith is a pure gift of the Holy Spirit, it is necessary for man
to "buy" it (Rev 3:18), that is, he must bestir himself to accept
this gift and make it his own act. Some say that this decision on
man's part is not some second thing in addition to, or beside,
the gift: this is only a half-truth; it must be insisted that man
has been given freedom, by the Holy Spirit, to make the act of
faith within this freedom. Of course, he can also refuse, within
the freedom with which he has been endowed, to make the act
of faith. As for the act of theoria, of discerning the Son (an act
that continues in the form of contemplation of him whom he
has seen), it is experienced by the believer himself as a unity: it
is both a gift and a decision, both something unhoped for that
captures his astonished gaze *and* something he has fought for. It
is a primal reality: act embedded in theoria.

However, the Spirit does not simply point to the Son and his
work, as it were, with an outstretched finger: he is also Interpreter and Guide. Again, these two activities cannot be separated. For the beholder's benefit he interprets the Son's act as

the opening up of the realm of love between Father and Son, and he could not do this (as it were, from outside) without leading the beholder into this realm, where it is not a matter of mere "words", but where it is a matter of acting and loving "in deed and in truth" (1 Jn 3:18). Thus, in a new way, the believer's theoria cannot stand still at some abstract spectacle: it must immediately turn into a challenge and into readiness for discipleship. This challenge is issued by both the Spirit and the Son, who cannot afford us any insight into the act of his existence unless we travel with him: "Come and see" (Jn 1:39). Only if we come to him and go with him shall we really "see"; nor is this something followed from outside, like an aircraft's flight path: we ourselves must walk with him along the road. This will lead us very much farther than Nathanael realizes, overpowered as he is by faith and falling down before the Lord: "You shall see greater things than these" (Jn 1:50). Right from the beginning, the Spirit leads us into the *whole* phenomenon of Jesus Christ: into his life, death, and Resurrection. That is why, as Paul and John teach, we shall not attain real vision unless we live, die, and rise *with* Christ; only in this way are we guaranteed admission into that place where interpretation of the Son is given.

Here, too, however, the Spirit does not interpret, does not initiate us from outside, as it were. He does not point away from himself and toward the Son. For he himself is in the Son as the Agent of the Son's Incarnation and of his entire, subsequent work of interpreting the Father. He is *in* the Son (he is the Spirit of the Son) and *above* the Son (he is the Spirit of the Father, sent by the Father) and, as such, helps to facilitate the Son's obedience; this obedience leads to the fulfillment of his filial mission, right up to the witness of Spirit, water, and blood that comes from his opened side. "He who saw it" (theoria) is the same person who walked (praxis) along the path with Jesus from the beginning (no doubt the unnamed disciple in John 1:39, who "came and saw where he was staying; and . . . stayed with him"), and "his testimony is true, and he knows that he tells the truth—that you also may believe" (Jn 19:35). He is the best authority for the statement that theoria is perfected by walking with the Son right to the end and, in this way (and only thus), participates in the theological truth of the Son. Preeminently, however, the one who walks with the Son is the Spirit in-and-above Jesus. As a result, he is also the most experienced Interpreter and Guide, initiating us into the work that has been transacted between Father and Son for the Church, together with the disciples who "continued with [him] in his trials" (Lk 22:28), who had been "with [him] from the beginning" and so could "bear witness" together with the "Spirit of truth" (Jn 15:27).

2. On this basis, Maximus the Confessor's dictum (quoted above) that the more man is divinized, the more God is humanized, seems less of a paradox. For it was the Spirit in Jesus who accompanied his Incarnation from its earliest moment to its final consequences, so that we can say that the Incarnation of the divine Word is perfected in nakedness and in the inarticulate cry of death on the Cross; John sees in this the ultimate glorification of the Father, but also, without any break (*euthys*, "at once" Jn 13:32), the glorification of the Son. This implies that the peak of Incarnation coincides with the perfect "pneumatization" of the Son: "breathing out" the Spirit, he becomes the Lord of the Spirit, whom he subsequently "breathed on" his apostles (Jn 20:22). Furthermore, since his obedience is perfected, he does this as commissioned by the Father and together with him (cf. Acts 2:33); he has both "become flesh" and "become Spirit", justifying the expression, "the Lord is the Spirit" insofar as the latter is "the Spirit of the Lord" (2 Cor 3:17).

This paradox can be seen in the lives of the Church's saints: they become fully incarnate, fully persons, to the extent that their spiritual mission becomes transparent in them. This is super-evident in Paul; it is equally visible in the greatest charismatic Francis of Assisi, who receives the bodily wounds from a *seraph* (a Spirit-Christ); we see it in John of the Cross, who attains to the purest faith through the deepest, hellish night and who knows that "he who seeks not the cross of Christ seeks not the glory of Christ."[11]

Now we can take a preliminary look at the paradoxes of Christian prayer, which will occupy us more later. Prayer—adoration,

[11] "*Maxims on Love*", no. 23, in *The Collected Works of St. John of the Cross*, trans. Kieran Kavanaugh and Otilio Rodriguez (Washington, D.C.: ICS Publications, 1979), 675.

praise, thanksgiving, intercession—always presupposes a certain distance between the believer and God, even if it is only the distance between a child (with his *timor filialis*) and his heavenly Father. And at the same time there is a fundamental familiarity that invites the believer to take the risk of prayer. We cannot pray to God on the basis of an imaginary elevation, but only from real, ground-level creaturehood, for it is in the truth of this creaturehood that the Spirit sets us down—in a place where we do not know what we should pray (Rom 8:26); but it is precisely here that the Spirit, with "sighs too deep for words", acts as our Advocate, so that the Father understands these sighs as man's prayer and infallibly hears it according to the Spirit's travail in us. Just as the Son, in his prayer that is pure obedience, is "always heard" (Jn 11:22, 42), so it is with the Spirit who prays in us. He always prays in us in the Son's humility, so that anyone who asks, in the Spirit, "in the name" of the Son (Jn 14:13) is infallibly heard, and not only subsequently, but in the act of petition itself (Mk 11:24; 1 Jn 5:15).

3. Lastly we must include in this context of theoria-praxis what is called—a much-misused term—Christian "experience". The scope of this term is vast, for it is rooted in everyday human life and exhibits many facets, both in the generally religious dimension and in Christianity.[12] What follows will be based, not on (philosophical) experience of transcendence, but, more modestly, on a purely theological fact. The word "experience" [in German, *Erfahrung*] means a getting to know through making a journey. We only need to recall what we described at the beginning, that is, that the Spirit leads us (into a theoria that has been opened up for us) *and* that we make the decision ourselves to set out in faith, as believers, to follow Christ's path; this shows us that man, journeying in experience, always experiences more than his own decision and his own setting out: he also experiences that he has become the recipient of a gift, that he has

---

[12] Cf. the survey in Christian Schütz, *Einführung in die Pneumatologie* (Darmstadt, 1985), 211–26; K. Lehmann, "Erfahrung", in *Sacramentum Mundi* I (1968), 1117–23; K. Rahner, "Erfahrung des Heiligen Geistes", in *Schriften* 13 (1978), 226–51 [English trans., *Theological Investigations* 16 (London and Baltimore, 1979)].

been empowered, that he has been accompanied (and perhaps also pushed along!) on this path.

Once this experience of being "driven" by the Spirit is behind him, so to speak, he has ahead of him the experience of the path that opens up before him as he walks along it. Since the Spirit, as we have shown, essentially leads us into the realm between Father and Son, the believer who walks along this path in all seriousness is necessarily brought into this divine realm, which opens up for him. It all comes from the incarnate Son, his word and his actions, his suffering and Resurrection, but it has a depth dimension that expands more and more beyond what is purely human. Thus, for instance, the words of Jesus, in themselves so clearly circumscribed, open up to give the believer a view of the eternal Word that they interpret: the Super-Word that was in the beginning with God and was God. The word found in the letter of Scripture is heard or read, but the depths of this word are not to be found crammed into the letter (which, in itself, "kills"); it is the Spirit, who is in the word itself ("[my] words . . . are spirit and life", Jn 6:63), who leads us into this depth dimension. Here—and not in the letter—the word is truth; here, when we allow ourselves to be shown and when we make personal efforts to reach these depths, is Christian theoria, contemplation, in the proper sense—or, since it is a question of a divine word speaking to us, Christian "hearing". It is precisely in this paradox that we find the difference between Christian contemplation and any other religious contemplation, since the incarnate Word always remains the starting point and the abiding substratum of the upward movement toward the "Word [who is] with God", however this may transcend human speech and utterance. It is this very depth dimension of the Gospel events that is meant when the Ignatian Spiritual Exercises lead us to an "inner feeling and tasting of the things" (no. 2) and to "smell the indescribable fragrance" and "taste the boundless sweetness of the Divinity" (no. 124)—expressions that have a thousand-year-old tradition behind them.

By all means, this being drawn into the "deep things of God" can be attributed to the gifts of the Holy Spirit, as Thomas Aquinas does (S. Th. I/II, 68); it is not, however, an isolated experience of the Spirit, but a penetration into God's triune "mansions"—and the interrelating divine Hypostases exercise an equal participation in it. And while, in this process, particular earthly aspects of the Church's organism disappear from view, what *never* disappears is the pneumatically transfigured humanity of the Son, the "Lamb standing as though it had been slain" (Rev 5:6) that stands, alive, on the Father's throne.

c. Concrete and Universal

With this topic, which we have discussed on many occasions,[13] we have arrived at the point where we feel most tangibly both Christianity's unique opportunity and its abiding stumbling block. It is an opportunity, because man is a historical person, and every religion that does not take account of this must inevitably bypass the real human being, if it does not actually question his whole existence or (like the doctrines of rebirth) dissolve it. But how can a historical person aspire to universal validity? There are only two ways of doing this: either the essence of the person is located in the purely spiritual realm, in which case the body becomes a "grave"; or else the Incarnation is understood as just one avatar among others, which would mean surrendering the concrete uniqueness of this person. This dilemma is the crux of all non-Christian religions; it can only be solved along trinitarian or, more precisely, pneumatological lines. The Father works, not with one hand, but with both. This is nowhere so clear as in this perspective.

1. During his mortal life, Jesus' claim was doubtless a universal one. His mission is not one among others but the final mission that includes and surpasses all the others. Nor is this true only after his Resurrection ("All authority is given unto me . . . I am with you always, to the close of the age"); rather, it is true most definitely in the midst of his mortal life, which is where we find the "But I say to you" sayings. He can speak and act thus because

---

[13] Cf. *Theology of History* (reprint, San Francisco: Ignatius Press, 1994), 81ff.; *Das Ganze im Fragment* (Benziger, 1963), 201ff.; *Neue Klarstellungen* (Einsiedeln: Johannesverlag, 1979), 52ff. [English trans., *New Elucidations* (Ignatius Press, 1986)]; *Katholisch* (Einsiedeln: Johannesverlag, 1975) passim [English trans., *In the Fullness of Faith* (Ignatius Press, 1988)].

the Spirit of God rests upon him, "inspiriting" him, so much so that he can rejoice "in the Holy Spirit" (Lk 10:21) at the fact that the Father desires to implement this very paradox, which will forever remain an insoluble riddle to the wise and clever. As the Spirit-Bearer, therefore, he already claims universality. Not only this, he actually lays the foundation for this universality in his mortal existence, not only in the validity of his words and deeds ("Heaven and earth will pass away, but my words will not pass away"), but primarily in the power given to him to take universal sin upon himself, thereby reconciling the world in its totality to God (2 Cor 5:15-21). More than this, he anticipates his Passion in the institution of the Eucharist, declaring in advance that his bodily dimension is available, indeed indispensable, "for many" ("He who does not eat my flesh and drink my blood has not life in him").

There is an obvious objection: If the historical Jesus was able to do all this, doubtless in the Holy Spirit, why did he not implement this universality himself (for it was already planned and a present reality) instead of apparently handing it over to the Holy Spirit ("The Spirit will guide you into all the truth")? There is a twofold answer to this entirely justified question. In the first place, the Son's primary task, in his Incarnation, was to carry out the trinitarian work of salvation within the temporal limits of one human life, including dying and being dead. This task included "the world's hatred", his not being accepted by most people, his pro-existent living, suffering, and dying. All this had to take place within these limits and had to end in this particular ruinous fate; the consummation ("consummatum est") lay precisely in the form of this death, which, while it included the universal ("I will draw all men unto me"), could not bring it into effect. This gives us the second part of the answer: What Jesus achieved was taken over and universalized by the Holy Spirit from Easter and Pentecost on; but, since the Spirit was already present in the universal words and deeds of Jesus, this could not take place without the Son's active (and not purely passive) presence and operation. This is abundantly clear from the ending of the Gospel according to Matthew, with its fourfold "all"—all authority, all nations, all things, all the days to the close of the age.

It is correct, of course, that just as Jesus did not incarnate himself, he did not raise himself from the dead, either; Scripture clearly emphasizes that it is God the Father who resurrects the Son "through [the Holy] Spirit" (Rom 8:11).[14] Insofar as he is a dead body, he cannot reanimate himself; on the other hand, his assertion, "I lay down my life . . . of my own accord . . . and I have power to take it again" (Jn 10:17f.) must not be assigned one-sidedly to the Son's divine nature;[15] he says this as the God-man, and the Spirit who raises him is also his Spirit. The Resurrection is primarily attributed to the Father's "superabundant power" because of the traditional concept of God (Yahweh), "who gives life to the dead and calls into existence the things that do not exist" (Rom 4:17). This event, which is trinitarian in a complex way, inaugurates the time of the Spirit (that Jesus assuredly announced), that Spirit who is our Interpreter, guiding us into all the truth. From now on he will always be the Spirit who was breathed out by Jesus and whom Jesus breathed upon the disciples—which, as we have already said, shows that his presence is active, not only passive. Even when Jesus' earthly mission in the dimension of time is complete, he does not look on passively while it is universalized (as we might conclude from a premature interpretation of Hebrews 10:13: "then to wait until his enemies . . ."), but "he must reign until he has put all his enemies under his feet" (1 Cor 15:25), and the Book of Revelation portrays the Lamb sallying forth "to make war" (19:11; 17:14).

Yet this "reigning" is, essentially, allowing the Spirit to do what he is charged to do: to unfold God's "hidden treasures",

---

[14] As Schlier points out, it does not matter whether *dia* takes the genitive here (as the Greek Fathers assumed) or the accusative (as, predominantly, but not exclusively, the Latin Fathers did, cf. Aland's commentary). In connection with this verse, see the lengthy excursus on the Holy Spirit in Paul in the commentary by Otto Kuß, *Römerbrief* (1959), 540–95. On the Holy Spirit's raising of Christ (albeit in a more indefinite sense, i.e., as the Spirit of God, compared to the mortal human flesh), cf. 1 Pet 3:18; 4:6 ("by God's power in the Spirit") and Rom 1:4. Elsewhere this "power of God" is attributed in the first place to the Father who sends: Eph 1:19f., Rom 4:24.

[15] As Thomas does in the question "Whether Christ was the cause of his own resurrection?" (*S. Th.* III, 53, 4), although he does add (ad 2) that the Son "merits" his glorification through his humiliation on the Cross and accordingly asks his Father (cf. Ps 40:11) for it: "Christus orando petiit et meruit suam resurrectionem inquantum homo, non autem inquantum Deus."

which are all found in Christ, down the centuries of the world, by his own freedom and power and according to his own plan and good pleasure (and not man's). The revelation of Christ may be "concluded with the death of the last apostle" (the last historical witness); but the Spirit's revelation is never concluded. And if the Spirit never withholds anything of Christ's fullness from any generation, but always opens up the entire treasure of truth (the interpretation of the divine love in Jesus Christ), yet he remains free to throw new light on this totality and in particular on its center, so that not only does this totality, as such, *preserve* its newness: through this ever-new illumination it is actually always *receiving* its newness. We shall have to return to this theme.

It is in the mystery of the Eucharist that we can best see that "the Father's two hands" do not cease working in concert. However important the epiclesis of the Holy Spirit may be, the latter does not effect the miracle of the presence of the bodily Christ on his own (which we cannot imagine, in any case); rather, he does so in an ineffably intimate cooperation with the Son, who promised his disciples that he would return together with the Father: "I go away, and I will come to you" (Jn 14:28); "If a man loves me, he will keep my word, and my Father will love him, and we will come to him and make our home with him" (Jn 14:23). The fact that Christ dwells in us spiritually (and we would surely expect the Spirit to make this possible) is already a great gift; but that he comes to us *sōmatikōs*, bodily, is far more, as the Greeks insist.[16] Furthermore, this bodily coming is actually essential if, together with the Holy Spirit, he is to make his Church both "his Body" and a "temple of his Spirit". What is made present by the Spirit's operation is the bodily human nature of Christ (of which the Spirit has always been the Agent), but it is now completely permeated by him [the Spirit]; *he*, the bodily Christ, becomes a "life-giving spirit" (1 Cor 15:45), and yet the words of consecration do not utter a lie when they speak of the "body given up" and the "blood shed"—which is, not a mere historical reminiscence, but a present reality.

---

[16] "Le 'sōmatikōs' de Cyrille (*In Joh.* 1, 10; PG 94, 341–44) ne se situe pas en deçà, mais en quelque sorte au-delà de son 'pneumatikōs'", H. de Lubac, *Corpus mysticum*, 2d ed. (Paris: Aubier, 1949), 363.

It is meaningless, in the context both of his humiliation and of his exaltation (and both of these have been demonstrated by what we have said so far), to ask "Cannot Christ do it on his own?"; only his "status" has changed and, with it, his relationship to the Spirit, who is always present to him.

2. A second perspective shows this even more clearly. When Christ identifies himself with truth, both in the presence of his disciples and before his judge, he does so most definitely in a trinitarian sense. In this affirmation he includes not only his relation to the "true" God (the Old Covenant's favorite expression), whom he has interpreted in a definitive and adequate way, but also, equally, the Holy Spirit. For it is in the Holy Spirit that he has begun his authoritative interpretation of the Father, and it is the Holy Spirit who will declare this definitive and unsurpassable interpretation to be a universal norm and, as an Advocate, will defend it against all the other claims to truth that the world may make. Here again it is clear that the Spirit does not play a supplementary role, let alone a subordinate one, in this process: he is the Spirit of the Father, handing on the Father's will to the Son; and he is the Spirit of the Son, carrying out this same will in the obedience of the "Suffering Servant". This shows that the universality that, as Paraclete, he manifests is absolutely his own or, rather, that it is *trinitarian*. Nor is this contradicted by the fact that he performs his work within the framework of a mission, a ministry.

Once more we must recall that the Spirit was together with the God who speaks, and with his divine Word, when genesis first resounded; similarly, that the Old Covenant spoke simultaneously of the "word" and the "breath" of God, on which all living things in the world depend. (Indeed, this provides the Fathers with a comparison: no word can issue forth from the mouth of man or God apart from the breath.) Here we must remember that God's truthfulness implies two things: his truth and his faithfulness and goodness. This means that whenever, in the context of the "economy", interpretation of the Father takes place (if it takes place at all), both aspects of this truthfulness are brought out, both in the Son and in the Spirit. This is quite evident in the case of the Son's life and destiny. In the case of the

Spirit's operation, further reflection is required: when the Spirit operates as Interpreter, infusing divine love and knowledge into our hearts, he is also "guiding us into" God's truth and, hence, into his love, faithfulness, and goodness, which is "poured into our hearts through the Holy Spirit" (Rom 5:5). While not forgetting the inseparable aspects of the divine *emeth*,[17] we can say, with Augustine: "For the Son, who is Truth, the Father is the true source, and the Son is the Truth (*veritas*) who is born of the true Father; the Holy Spirit is that goodness (*bonitas*) that proceeds from the good Father and the good Son; from all this neither the divinity (*divinitas*) is to be distinguished, nor is the unity (*unitas*) to be separated."[18]

The Spirit, who is Love, is the fruit of the trinitarian relations; in economic terms he interprets and impresses upon us that God's very essence is love; revealing himself, the Spirit also *interprets himself*, so that we can say, with Anselm, "indeed, if this love is actually designated by the name Spirit, as by its own name, since this name equally describes the Father and the Son: it will be useful to this effect also, that through this name it shall be signified that this love is identical with Father and Son, although it has its being from them."[19] These quotations should remind us that the Spirit, though an "advocate", does not carry out his work of "universalizing" as a task that is external to him; rather, he leads the hearts of those who do not resist him into the truth of absolute love.

That this is possible without compulsion we can see from the biblical teaching that man is created in God's image and likeness: that is, in his being he possesses an image not only of the Son but of the whole Trinity, including the Holy Spirit; the latter can take this image as his starting point. Furthermore, since the divine *oikonomia* manifests an inseparable inner unity, it puts into the world not only *logoi spermatikoi* but also *spermata pneumatika*; and, just as the Son's domain extends over the entire creation, that of the Spirit is coextensive. All this is implicit, for instance, in the Church's theology of the *baptismus in voto* (with all its

---

[17] Cf. *The Glory of the Lord* VI, *Theology: The Old Covenant* (San Francisco: Ignatius Press, 1991), 173f.

[18] *Sermo* 71, 11, 18 (PL 38, 454).

[19] *Monologium* 57 (Schmitt I, 69).

consequences) and of "spiritual communion"[20]—which is always to be understood in connection with, and leading to, sacramental communion. From the very first, therefore, there are
analogies at the natural level (and then, since the Cross has universal meaning and effect, analogies at the level of grace) to what,
subsequently, we shall describe as "Church": a *concretum* that has
to be—in its own, missionary, way—*universal*.

At this point we need to supplement something that was said
in the third volume of *Theo-Drama* regarding the theological concept of the "person". What we dealt with in that volume was
"Christ's Mission and Person",[21] and so we saw and portrayed
the human conscious subject as it is deepened to become a person, primarily through participation in Christ's mission that he
received from the Father.[22] John 20:21, too, clearly brings out
this aspect. But Jesus was "anointed" by God "with the Holy
Spirit and with power [*dynamis*]" (Acts 10:38) for his mission;
it follows, then, that some form of endowment of the Spirit indwells every concept of mission and person that comes from
Christ. The Acts of the Apostles shows how manifold this gift
of the Spirit can be; it is noteworthy, however, that it always
relates to a christological mission: either it aims at it (when the
reception of the Spirit precedes baptism: Acts 10:44-48) or—
more normally—it accompanies baptism in the name of Jesus
(cf. 10:17-18; 2:38).[23] In Paul's view, any charismatic manifestation that does not either refer or lead to Jesus is a priori inauthen-
tic, even demonic (1 Cor 12:2-3); for him, genuine charisma
is identical with a mission within the "Body of Christ". So he
speaks of all ecclesial roles in trinitarian terms: they are of the
Father, of Christ, of the Spirit (1 Cor 12:4-7). Not only are "the

---

[20] H. R. Schlette, *Die Lehre von der geistlichen Kommunion bei Bonaventura, Albert dem Großen und Thomas von Aquin* (Munich, 1959). See also his *Kommunikation und Sakrament: Theologische Deutung der geistlichen Kommunion*, QD 8 (Herder, 1960). Schlette refers to the Council of Trent and the Roman Catechism and to the development of spiritual communion as a form of devotion.

[21] *Theo-Drama* III (San Francisco: Ignatius Press, 1992), 149-229.

[22] Cf. esp. 207-8; 220: "*In Christo*, however, every man can cherish the hope of not remaining a merely individual conscious subject but of receiving personhood from God, becoming a person, with a mission that is likewise defined *in Christo*."

[23] E. Schweizer, art. "Pneuma", in ThW VI, 410f.

Father's two hands" at work: the Father himself works, sending both Son and Spirit.

3. A third consideration brings us back to the origin of this entire trilogy. Christ is present to faith as an indivisible and hence believable figure or form [*Gestalt*] (including the formlessness [*Gestaltlosigkeit*] of the Cross); yet it is the Spirit who gives believers eyes to discern God's revelation as a integral, organically differentiated form [*Gestalt*]. Not from the remote standpoint of a dispassionate observer, but by being drawn into the form itself; for it is only from within it that we can experience and evaluate its rightness. Initially it seemed paradoxical that the Cross— which represents the "smashing of the form"—belongs at the very center of this planned and sustained form, but now the paradox is resolved: if the form of Jesus is contemplated from within, and in-formed in the beholder, the latter clearly sees that the figure or form of Jesus must remain unintelligible, and even meaningless, apart from the *pro nobis* of the Cross; for Jesus lives for this hour, was born for it, and the whole significance of his Resurrection comes from it. At first, Pauline theology seemed peripheral with regard to "seeing the form" [cf. *The Glory of the Lord* I], but when we come to consider that interior beholding which is mediated by the Spirit, this same theology moves into the center. This is because the "aesthetic" view is now complemented by the "theodramatic", which inserts itself into the total Christian experience. The battle on the stage of world history between infinite freedom, which is the Good, and finite freedom that can choose between good and evil is concentrated in the Cross and its "other side"—the descent to hell. It is in this concentration, finally, that we discern the third dimension: "logic"; it is due to this "logic" that the figure of Jesus can be designated as "the truth".

We can also see why an inversion had to take place in the economic Trinity vis-à-vis the immanent Trinity: simply so that the Lord could become the Servant. It is not for the Spirit of the obedient Servant to act as Lord over the Spirit; the Son "lays up" his "form of God" with the Father, "emptying himself and taking on the form of a slave", demonstrating that readiness to perform the Father's will which is eternally present in his loving response to him. This attitude of readiness is fitting for the pure creature, but its prototype is and was always found in the eternal Son, so that, without alteration to his Godhead, he could be "born in the likeness of [or equality with] men. And being found in human form he humbled himself and became obedient unto death, even death on a cross" (Phil 2:7-8). This Spirit, of whom he has always been the possessor and dispenser, now becomes the Spirit of perfect obedience to the Father *in* him and, simultaneously, the Spirit of the Father, instructing him and inserting him into human form, hovering *over* him ever since his Baptism, and making him—the greatest of the prophets—the recipient of the Father's commands all his life long. In and through all this, the Spirit does not need to undergo any change. He becomes as man what he has always been as God, namely, the One who receives his own self as the Father's Word, the One who testifies to what he has seen and heard (see Jn 3:11), displaying the sovereignty of the eternal Word, uttered by the Father: he receives his self (as gift) and so has self-being.

When the eternal Son becomes man, the immutable Son of God takes on the "alien", "mutable" form that is man's. Necessarily, therefore, this also involves a mutation in his (immutable) relation to the Holy Spirit, who has always been the Spirit of his loving response to the Father. This loving response brings out in man—and particularly in the one who represents sinners —the readiness to go to the very limit in obeying the Father's commands. So we can say, again, that the "inversion" to which we have referred, which is based on the Son's "becoming obedient to death on a Cross", causes the Holy Spirit to have a share, as it were, in the experience of what it means to be a creature vis-à-vis God. The Spirit is not merely an "external" witness of what Jesus does and suffers on earth (—he is that, too): but as the "Spirit of Christ" (Rom 8:9) he also acquires an inner experience of the latter's deeds and sufferings. He is not only the Spirit who "searches even the depths of God": now, as the Spirit of the Son, who plumbs the "depths of the world" right down to the *katōtera tēs gēs*, he is the terminus of all human existence: Death followed by Hades (see Rev 6:8).

This is the Spirit of Jesus who will be breathed upon the Church, not a Spirit who is at a loss in the face of human destiny, but the Spirit who, in Jesus, has inner knowledge of what, henceforth, the Church's witness (*martyrion*) to Jesus will entail: "He will bear witness to me; and you also are witnesses" (Jn 15:26–27). From now on, these two can form a single, integrated witness.

At this point the subject of the next main part of this volume opens out before us, namely, the Spirit and the Church, with its confusing multiplicity of aspects. Before this, however, another theme interposes itself; it is one that can no longer be avoided, and, particularly in view of what we have just been saying, it is urgent: To what extent can the Holy Spirit be called the Spirit of Jesus in the sense we have described? This is the question of the *filioque*.

4

ON THE FILIOQUE

We have developed Irenaeus' metaphor of "the Father's two hands" with regard to the economy of salvation. The question arises: Does it not favor the theology of the Father's *monarchia*, which subsequently became a sticking point for the Greeks, according to which the other two Divine Persons proceed solely from the Father? How can one of the "hands", the Son, be a joint cause—or at least have some role—in the coming to be of the other "hand"? This brings us to the tiresome issue of the *filioque*. We have no intention, after a thousand years of dispute, to set forth the whole problem in detail yet again; we will simply situate it, as briefly as possible, in the context elaborated so far.

The history is well known. First there was a long period of peaceful coexistence between two different theologoumena on the dogma of the Trinity, which was shared by both traditions. In the West there was the view, transmitted by Tertullian, Novatian, Hilary, Ambrose, and Victorinus, and developed by Augustine,[1] that the Spirit proceeded from Father and Son (*filioque*); this was formulated by Leo I (d. 461) in a letter to the bishop of Astorga, taken up by a Spanish synod and declared binding at the Third Council of Toledo in 589. The East complained about it for the first time during the reign of Pope Martin (649–653), but Maximus the Confessor declared that the Eastern view was reconcilable with the views of this pope; it was promoted by Charlemagne, and Pope Leo III was under pressure to introduce it into the Roman Creed, but he refused for the sake of peace with the

[1] A clear, short summary of the Latin development can be found in J.-M. Garrigues, *L'Esprit qui dit "Père!" et le problème du filioque* (Paris: Téqui, 1981), 57–84. "St. Augustin, qu'on a souvent présenté comme l'inventeur du *Filioque* . . . n'a pratiquement pas fait oeuvre de novateur en cette matière. Il a surtout synthésisé les divers éléments qu'il trouvait dans la tradition latine antérieure" (ibid., 70). As far as he could, however, Augustine did try to take account of the Greek tradition, in particular the Cappadocians: G. Bardy, "Saint Augustin et la pensée orientale", *Irénikon* 1948, 249–73. The numerous articles by B. Altaner on Augustine's relationship to particular Greek Fathers are presented in C. Andresen, *Zum Augustin-Gespräch der Gegenwart* (Darmstadt, 1962), 532.

East. It was only introduced after Photius, in 867, had sharpened
the difference of approach into a decisive doctrinal split, saying
that the Spirit proceeded from the Father "alone". The break between the Churches took place only after this period, in 1054,
under Patriarch Michael Cerularius. It was the Latins' introduction of this term—to which the East subsequently took exception—into the Nicene-Constantinopolitan Creed that triggered
the theological dispute, which has been constantly rekindled,
ever since, by one-sided attacks by the Greeks against the Latins.
On the Latin side, following the failed attempts at reconciliation
at the Councils of Lyons (1274) and Florence (1439ff.), further
overtures were made as time went on: there was the suggestion
that the recitation of the *filioque* in the liturgy should be dropped
(Clement VIII, 1592–1605; Benedict XIV, 1740–1758);[2] per-
mission was granted for the Greek Uniate Church to omit it;[3]
its omission was agreed between the Orthodox, Old Catholics,
and Anglicans, with increasing Catholic support. Thus Scheeben
praises the "organic" Greek formula;[4] Paul Henry, S.J., writes a
peremptory article "Against the *Filioque*";[5] Garrigues,[6] Bouyer,[7]
and Congar[8] call for it to be dropped for the sake of peace in
the Church, emphasizing that the Greeks should have the right
to adopt the contrary view, that is, the right to acknowledge the
filioque as a possible theological interpretation of the trinitarian

---

[2] Pius XI, celebrating Mass in St. Peter's in 1925 according to the Greek Rite,
omitted the *filioque*, as did John Paul II on the occasion of the 1500th anniversary
of the Council of Constantinople.

[3] The important text is at the beginning of Garrigues' work (*L'Esprit*, 117–25).
He mentions Maximus the Confessor's significant attempt at reconciliation (PG
11, 133–36) and the disputation between Anselm von Havelsberg and Metropoli-
tan Nicetas. The text of this disputation (in PL 188, 1163–1210) is translated in
its entirety and introduced by P. Le Guillou in *Istina* (1972), 375–424.

[4] Scheeben (*Dogmatik* I, 1874) describes the Greek formula (which he completely ties down to the *dia hyion*) as "organic" (820–21). At the same time he
points out the danger associated with it, i.e., that, if the Son is seen as the image
of the Father, and the Spirit as the image of the Son, "instead of an organic link
of the two processions, there is only a loose succession along the lines of the
reproductive relationship of human persons."

[5] In *Irénikon*, 1975, 170–77.

[6] *L'Esprit*, 94f.; also in ÖKÜ 128.

[7] C 299–307 (stressing the dubious nature of both solutions).

[8] ES III (1980), 278.

dogma shared by both sides, just as the Latins can allow the Greek interpretation to stand. This attempt to bridge the difference by maintaining a common dogmatic faith in the Trinity, but allowing several possible formulations, is echoed by Reformed scholars like Moltmann,[9] but also by Orthodox writers such as Bobrinskoy.[10] Behind this suggestion stand Bolotov's celebrated theses; the last of them says this: "It is not the question of the *filioque* that caused the split in the Church. Consequently the *filioque*, as a private theological opinion, cannot be regarded as a diriment impediment" between the Churches.[11]

The West's charges against the East are, however, at least as serious. Neither the pope nor his legates nor any Western bishop was invited to the second council to describe itself as "ecumenical", the Council of Constantinople (381) summoned by Theodosius. (At the same time a Latin council was meeting in Rome under Ambrose, who had already proclaimed the *filioque* in the sense in which Tertullian used it.) The Council of Ephesus (431) did not result in acceptance of the Council of Constantinople; it was only recognized as ecumenical by Greeks and Latins thirty years later, at Chalcedon. By that time, however, Augustine's systematic teaching had already been set forth, and Pope Leo, as we have mentioned, had already proclaimed the *filioque*. The Latins were bound to recognize the definition of 381 according to their own understanding of it, which the Greeks did not contradict.[12]

---

[9] *Trinität und Reich Gottes* (Munich: Kaiser, 1980), 194–206. [English trans., *The Trinity and the Kingdom of God* (London, SCM Press)].

[10] "Das Filioque gestern und heute", in ÖKÜ 107–19. He stresses that "the whole Orthodox Church must commit herself to a radical renewal of her theological task" (119).

[11] The theses first appeared anonymously ("par un théologien russe") in *Rev. internat. de Théologie* VI (1898), 681–712; they are reproduced under his own name in *Istina*, 1972, 261–89.

[12] Great importance must be attributed to the period in which a common faith coexisted with diverse theological interpretations. This fact speaks more authoritatively than the assembling of individual passages from the Fathers, "which are always questionable, since texts cannot be artificially isolated from their context" (A. de Halleux, in ÖKÜ 72). "It was on the basis of one and the same Creed, which the East regarded as excluding the *filioque* . . . and the West regarded as including it, that the pneumatological development was to proceed along two

After this brief recital of the historical facts we proceed to the theology, and the first thing we find is that in many instances, strangely, the opponents accuse each other of the same transgressions.

1. First there is the importing of purely economic considerations into questions of the immanent Trinity. The Latins are accused of arguing from the power of the resurrected Lord in distributing the Spirit to his power within the Trinity, together with the Father, to breathe him forth. Conversely, the Greeks can be accused of taking the fact that, at the Baptism of Jesus, the Spirit descends upon him and "rests" on him and applying it to the immanent Trinity—with the result that the Spirit proceeds only from the Father in order to "rest" on the Son (as Damascene, following others, says; a line of thought continued by Gregory Palamas). The fundamental point to be made in the face of these arguments is that we have no access whatsoever to the *immanent* Trinity except as a result of the Trinity's *economic* self-manifestation. It can only be maintained as axiomatic that the two are equal unless and until the economic form (that is, the Son's obedience to death by taking upon himself the world's sin) demands a change in the picture here presented: this was thoroughly dealt with in the thesis of the "trinitarian inversion" in *Theo-Drama* III, 183ff., and in the explanation of it given in this volume (pp. 182–83 above). In concrete terms we must say that the image given in Jesus' Baptism is "economically" conditioned and does not permit us to extrapolate it into the inner realm of the Trinity; the same applies to the two phases of redemption: in the first, Jesus the "Suffering Servant" lets himself be led by the Spirit, whereas in the second, the risen Lord has power to send and breathe the Spirit upon those he wishes.

initially parallel lines" (Garrigues, in ÖKÜ 122). Garrigues succeeds in finding a major authority on both sides, Greek and Latin, namely, Hilary of Poitiers and Gregory of Nyssa, who both achieved a synthesis of East and West (PL 10, 251A and PG 45, 464), anticipating the later synthesis of Maximus. Cf. Bolotov's theses 19 and 20: "At that time the Oriental Church raised no protest against Augustine's Western solution. Many Western thinkers, preaching the *filioque* to their faithful, lived and died in communion with the Eastern Church without the latter presenting any objection."

Thus the attacks made by both sides fail to address the issue. Nor do we need to repeat that it is inadmissible, as we have shown, to try to overcome the difference between *economia* and *theologia* by projecting the *economia* into heaven and distinguishing (as Palamas does) between a "higher Godhead" in which the Spirit proceeds solely from the Father and a "lower Godhead"—the sphere of the "energies" radiating from the divine essence—in which the Son mediates the Spirit. Such a construction obscures the trinitarian God's transparent self-revelation to the world, as the Gospel presents it, by interposing an opaque layer between them; and in doing so, it does not preserve God's ineffability (as in apophatic theology) but prevents him from truly giving himself. Palamas may give the impression that he has diminished the Father's autocracy and reinstated a kind of "trinitarian joint decision", but he does this at the cost of blurring the hypostatic distinctions.

2. A second element requires no less attention—a theological problem arising from a philological one. We recall the difficulty Eastern theology had, initially, in finding a term for the procession of the Spirit. Gregory Nazianzen held fast to the Johannine *ekporeuesthai* (15:26), which he regarded as unsatisfactory, "what, after all, *is* this procession?": seeking to understand it would drive one mad (*Or. Theol.* V, 8; PG 36, 141B). Inevitably, this word became a shibboleth far beyond the Latin translation *procedere*, which was understood to mean only some kind of proceeding, whereas "*ekporeusis*" (cf. Athanasius, *Ad Serap.* 4, 3, 1; PG 26, 625; Basil, *C. Eun.* 2, 28; PG 29, 637) referred specifically to what proceeds from a primal cause (*aitia*)—and so could not be applied to the Son, who "caused" himself (*aitiaton*). Garrigues has been at great pains to exhibit a credible etymological distinction between *ekporeuomai* and *pro-cedere* (which actually means "to retreat forward", the Greek *pro-chōrein*). But this whole enterprise on the part of Greek theology collapses in the face of the view of modern exegetes, who say that John 15:26 refers, not to the Spirit's eternal procession from the Father, but to an economic proceeding; anything else would be outside the Johannine purview.[13] Moreover, a New Testament concordance

[13] R. Schnackenburg, *Johannes* III (1975), 136 [English trans., *St. John's Gospel*,

shows how frequently the Greek term is used for any and every "going out"; using it for the mysterious "going out" of the Spirit is therefore just as "risky" as using the secular *gennāsthai* (does this mean "begotten" or "born"?) for the mysterious origin of the Son in the Father. We know just as little about this latter procession; it is simply that our ignorance is veiled by the words "Father" and "Son".

If we look back at the genesis of the Greek version, we can identify in history the existence of two (in themselves entirely correct) "binities": the first is that of the "two hands", that is, the inseparable missions of Son and Spirit, their reciprocal priority and reciprocal interpenetration. The second is the achievement of the Nicene Creed: consubstantial unity of Son and Father, with (as yet) no mention of the Spirit. The resultant diagram

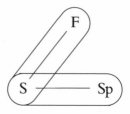

needs to be complemented by adding the Father/Spirit relation; this is provided by "simul adoratur" of the Constantinopolitan Creed, which, naturally enough, Athanasius explains thus: "The Spirit is inseparable from the Son, as the Son is inseparable from the Father" (PG 26, 608A), which seems to assure that the Spirit is *homoousios*. "Athanasius seems never to have considered that this could imply a relation of origin."[14] Similarly Basil: "If the Spirit is united to the Son, and the Son to the Father, it follows that the Spirit is equally united to the Father" (PG 32, 148A). The attempt to establish the Spirit's mode of unity with the Father (as Gregory Nazianzen will formulate it) thus results in

---

vol. 3 (Burns and Oates)]. I. de la Potterie, *La Vérité chez Saint Jean* I (Rome, 1977), 385ff., adduces several reasons for the "procession temporelle de l'Esprit" in this passage.

[14] M.-J. Le Guillou, *Réflexions sur la procession du Saint-Esprit*, in EE 206.

the following twofold assertion: the Spirit proceeds from the
Father (because the Spirit is God), and this takes place somehow "through" (*dia*) the Son. The Son is already there, since
otherwise the Father could not be called Father. In the Greek
perspective the interpretation of this *dia* is thus an open question;
Bulgakov rightly observes that the word is far too vague to substantiate any particular argument.[15] A minimalist interpretation
would be simply that the Spirit comes forth from the Father
(since the latter *is* Father), or, more positively, that the Spirit
"receives"[16] something from the Son. A maximalist interpretation would be that, when the Spirit "receives", the Son is a real
cooperator; a certain few but indisputable passages suggest this,
using *ek* ("out of") instead of *dia* ("through").[17] As is appropriate in the *economia*, it is always possible to draw a distinction between a Spirit who "rests" on the Son at his Baptism
or "radiates" from him (as on Tabor) or goes out from him (as
after the Resurrection); and all these aspects are found in the
Greeks.

Before objecting that this is an impermissible importation of
economia into *theologia*, we should give a hearing to Wolfgang Marcus,[18] who substantiates the view that the ante-Nicene Fathers
largely held an "orthodox subordinationism" (particularly in the
case of Tertullian, but also Justin, Irenaeus, Hippolytus, and the
Alexandrians right up to Dionysius) that was by no means an
embryonic stage of the Arian and heterodox subordinationism
based on Greek philosophy: rather, it wanted simply to portray
the Divine Persons' relationship of origin as the prototype of
their relationship in salvation history; later this was termed their

[15] *Le Paraclet* (Paris: Aubier, 1946), 93; the *dia* cannot be part of dogma, it is a
"question mark handed on to some future Pneumatology" (94). In Bulgakov's
view, it cannot be used to substantiate Photius' "from the Father alone".

[16] Cf. passages in Epiphanius (*Ancoratus*, nos. 8, 9, 11), and particularly Basil
(the whole section in PG 29, 653–80), Gregory of Nyssa (PG 45, 364BC), and
Cyril (PG 71, 377B).

[17] Cf. the passages just quoted from Epiphanius; Athanasius: "With the Father
is the Son, who is the source of the Holy Spirit" (PG 26, 1000A, cf. 998B). Cyril,
Thes. ass. 34 (PG 75, 585): "ex Patre et Filio . . . procedens". On this whole issue:
Petavius, *De Trin.* VII, 5; Pohle and Gierens, 9th ed. (1936), I, 366–76.

[18] *Der Subordinatianismus als historiologisches Phänomen* (Munich: Max Hueber,
1963).

taxis within the Godhead and was deduced quite straightforwardly from Scripture.[19] This would justify later Greek teaching on the Trinity insofar as designating the Father alone as *aitia* ("cause")[20] and would not call into question the Son's (unspecified) role in the procession of the Spirit. The Latins never doubted the priority of the Father in this procession, and Augustine's phrase "principaliter (a Patre)" was retained right up to Thomas Aquinas.[21]

However, when Photius and his followers insist on "from the Father alone", the very thing of which they accuse the Latins becomes a danger to the Greeks: by introducing the *filioque*, they say, power over the Spirit is attributed to the Son, which leads not only to a Western "Christomonism" (allegedly contrasted with an eastern "Pneumatism") but, by an inner logic, to a papalist system of oppression and legalism—accusations that were still being repeated by the Slavophiles[22] and the strange philosopher Karzavin. Karzavin was influenced by Soloviev; initially he was a Hegelian but gradually found his way to a Christian doctrine of the Trinity and finally died as a Catholic in a concentration camp in 1922. He had two followers who went in opposite directions, namely, Vladimir Lossky, who, as a Neo-Photian, continued to

[19] Early Christian subordinationism "can only be understood in its dialogical position or in its apologetic situation, that is, in its relation to anti-trinitarian and heterodox teaching like Sabellianism or Marcionism" (ibid., 85). "The Logos and the Spirit are subordinated to the Father in that they proceed from him. This means, however, that the suprahistorical idea grounding the historical process (including the process of creation and salvation history) is to be sought in connection with the Son's and the Spirit's relation to the Father, which is one of being generated and brought forth" (ibid., 172). Marcus also refers to L. Atzberger, *Die Logoslehre des hl. Athanasius* (Munich, 1880), calling into question the latter's substantial dependence on Plotinus, etc., as against the influence of Greek philosophy on Arius (ibid., 96).

[20] On the "inadequacy" of the ("unavoidable") concept, cf. the studies by Urs Küry in K. Stalder, "Das Filioque in den altkatholischen Kirchen", in ÖKÜ 93. The same result is found in Bolotov.

[21] "De Patre principaliter" (*De Trin.* XV, 26, 47 [PL 42, 1095]).

[22] Alexei Chomiakov accuses the Roman Church of "fratricide" within the unanimous body of the whole Church by having imposed new dogmas. The slavophile *sobornost* imitates the trinitarian "communion" by "creating a deep inner unity in love, in contrast to the Latin and Germanic West, which was incapable of reconciling the enforced unity of Roman Catholicism with the individualistic freedom of Protestantism" (quoted in A. de Halleux, in ÖKÜ 67).

make the old attacks on Rome, and Bulgakov, who, through
him (in the spirit of Soloviev), pressed for a reconciliation with
the West.[23] Compared with these insinuations, however, what
shall we say of the tyranny, in the Eastern Church, of the purely
monarchical Father, whose "two hands" have nothing to do but
carry out his commands! And does the lack of certain ecclesial
structures automatically produce a Pneumatology?

3. At this point a further reciprocal accusation can be neutralized. Is the West totally unjustified in seeing, in the Eastern
monarchia, after all, a residue of that Hellenistic philosophy according to which the absolutely One is the truly Divine, whereas
what is "caused" by him—which includes the Son and the Spirit
—is subordinate, having its existence by participation,[24] and
where the Trinity becomes a monad expanding to its own full
extent?[25] Gregory Nazianzen can take up this terminology of the
"*monas* that, having from all eternity arrived by motion at a *dyas*,
finally came to rest in the *trias*"[26]—which Maximus the Confessor felt it necessary to provide with a soothingly orthodox commentary.[27] If, for the Cappadocians also, the fullness of the Godhead seems to be preserved from all taint of subordinationism,

---

[23] M.-J. Le Guillou, "La Critique du Filioque de L. P. Karsavine", *Istina*, 1972,
293–310.

[24] Thus we have Origen's dangerous formulation that the Son is "divinized by
participation" and "cannot be called *ho theos*, but only *theos*" (*In Joh.* II, 2). Later he
abandons this formulation and says, "The Redeemer is not God by participation:
he is God by nature" (*In Ps.* 135, 2).

[25] As Dionysius says, "Thus, without dividing the Unity, we expand it into
a Trinity; conversely, without diminishing the Trinity, we hold it together as
a Unity": A. Bienert, *Dionysius von Alexandrien: Das erhaltene Werk* (Stuttgart:
Hiersemann, 1972), 81.

[26] *Or. Theol.* III, 2 (PG 36, 76B), albeit more clearly in *Or.* 32, 8: "The perfect
Three was complete when the Unity, through its own inner abundance, moved,
surpassing the Two (because the Godhead lies above the opposition of matter
and form, of which bodies consist), and perfected itself within the bounds of the
Three . . . so that the Godhead should not remain in restriction or pour itself out
boundlessly (*apeiron*)" (PG 35, 1160C).

[27] *Ambigua* (PG 91, 933–1066). G. L. Prestige, *God in Patristic Thought* (London,
1936, new ed., 1952) is at pains to show that this "organic monotheism" becomes
increasingly clear in the patristic period. Thus he quotes Tertullian: "quando unitas, ex semetipsa derivans trinitatem, non destruatur ab illa, sed administratur"
(= translation of *oikonomeō*, 102); in Basil he discovers a new meaning of *monarchia*, since here Son and Spirit are no longer derived from the Father, but the three

the central mystery remains, for them, in God the Father, who "is simultaneously *anarchos* and *archē* of the Godhead",[28] so that "divinity and personal relations coincide in the first Person of the Trinity."[29] Given this "glass house", there is not much point in the East throwing stones at the West, particularly at Augustine, accusing him of "essentialism", that is, of regarding the processions as coming from the one divine essence; in his writings, after all (and just like Gregory), he does nothing but expound the inner riches of this unity in its Trinity. How could a theologian, thinking in the biblical perspective, do other than start with the one God, particularly if he had come through Manichaean dualism and the triads of Plotinus? He would have to do this in order to contemplate God's threeness within the unity, however inadequate his creaturely metaphors for it might be. Indeed, Augustine clearly recognized the limits of these metaphors; nor did they hinder Thomas from developing his doctrine of the Hypostases in the context of the one God.

4. The *reductio in mysterium* is unmistakably clear in both approaches; it is clearest, no doubt, in the embarrassment experienced when it comes to giving a credible account of the procession of the Holy Spirit. This is increasingly evident in the Greek model, the more the Son's *dia*, which began by being active participation, dissolves in pure passivity. For in this case—to say nothing of all the other aspects that can hardly be reconciled with the New Testament revelation—we end up with a picture of God that no longer has an inner "form". What kind of Father-God would he be, with two distinct Hypostases emanating from him: on the one hand, the Son and, on the other hand, a Spirit (without a personal name), whose reciprocal relations cannot be put forward convincingly in terms of the "immanent" Trinity—

Persons result from the one, concrete *ousia* (233). Accordingly, he is obliged to regret the excessive abstraction of the notion of *ousia* occasioned in Chalcedonian Christology (because human and divine *ousia* somehow have the same meaning in Christ: 270ff.); this he regards as the triumph of old Greek "formalism" (265–81). Prestige sees the authentic concept of God's concrete triune essence restored in Cyril and Damascene, in the notion of *perichōrēsis* (282–301).

[28] Garrigues, *L'Esprit*, 33.

[29] J. Moltmann, "Dogmatische Vorschläge zur Lösung des Filioque-Streites", in ÖKÜ 150.

unless one has recourse to "economic" situations? Can this kind of immanent structure still be given the name "Love", which the New Testament attributes to the triune God?

The Achilles' heel of the Western model lies in the notion, which reflection cannot reduce to comprehension, that the Spirit "proceeds in wondrous manner", "from both" Father and Son, "who ineffably breathe forth the Spirit" (Anselm).[30] As Augustine put it, "Father and Son are the principle of the Spirit; not two principles", but "relative ad Spiritum Sanctum unum principium",[31] a view that enters into the tradition through decrees of popes and councils. Ultimately Thomas will find himself asking whether, in this process in which there is no relative opposition of the Persons, it is the common nature that effects the Spirit rather than (primarily) the two Persons. The "unum in virtute spirativa" implies "quodammodo (!) naturam cum proprietate". There is no objection, he says, to two *supposita* having a common attribute, since they possess a like nature. On the other hand, if one considers the spirating *supposita*, the Holy Spirit proceeds from Father and Son, who are plural: "He proceeds from them as the unitive love of both."[32] This is where Photius announced his objections, albeit of a very formal kind. Either, assuming that the Son co-spirates the Spirit, it means that the Son shares in the Hypostasis of the Father; or, if the Father causes the Spirit to proceed on the basis of his essence, it means not only that the Son had a part in the Spirit's procession, but that the Spirit himself was involved in the coming to be of his own mode of existence.[33]

No doubt the only way to disarm such formalistic objections is to advert to two truths: first, the impossibility (demonstrated above) of using the concept "person" univocally for the divine Hypostases, however much this may cut across every creaturely idea of the mystery of the Trinity; and second, the name of "Love", given to God by John (1 Jn 4:8, 16), a name that must presuppose, not numerical, but transcendental plurality, if it is to go beyond mere self-love (*dilectio*) and become *caritas*—the highest of the perfections created by God and which is found

---

[30] *Monolog.* 57.

[31] *De Trin.* V, 14, 15 (PL 42, 921).

[32] *S. Th.* I, 36, 4 ad 1.

[33] *De S. Spiritus Mystagogia* 16–17 (PG 102, 293AB, 325A).

supereminently in him. The Eastern theology of the Trinity does not speak much of this; only in one passage does Palamas adopt an Augustinian formulation to this effect. Ever since Augustine, by contrast, the Western doctrine constantly circles around this central thought. And as for the Spirit being both epitome and fruit of the eternal love, the New Testament is full of it. It is this induction from the unity of Son and Spirit, in the *oikonomia*, and specifically in terms of love, that causes Karl Barth to insist convincingly that this unity must be anchored in the immanent Trinity,[34] a view he maintains in the face of those who would suspect him of speaking (at least in *Church Dogmatics* I/I) in a way that approaches modalism.[35] Catholic theology has taken similar paths all along.[36] At the same time, each divine Hypostasis retains its own, irreducible mystery; the Father, in that he is able to be both utter self-giving (*relatio*) and yet One who gives himself; the Son, the answering Word, in that, while giving himself to the Father, he is able to share in the latter's originating power in such a way that, in union with this power, he can not only *be* love, but *produce* it; and the Spirit, in that he is both the highest divine, sovereign freedom *and* perfect selflessness, only existing for Father and Son. In Jesus Christ all these mysteries are not only visible, but given so that we may imitate them and they may dwell in us. This is quite sufficiently "apophatic"; and it is a theology that is also, as it must be, doxology.

---

[34] *Church Dogmatics* I/I, section 12.

[35] George S. Hendry, *The Holy Spirit in Christian Theology* (London, 1965).

[36] E.g., J. Auer, *Kleine Kath. Dogmatik* II (Regensburg, 1978): "Love in the Christian sense is most profoundly the destiny of all personal being in its fulfillment, because God, the primal Super-Person, is 'Love'" (343). L. Scheffczyk, "Der Sinn des Filioque", in *Internat. Kath. Zft. Communio* 15 (1986): 23–34: "The Filioque . . . makes it clear that the Son's begetting as the Word of the Father (to which the answering Word corresponds) brings about an assimilation and a fellowship between Father and Son, fulfilled in reciprocal love. That is why, from the very first, the Holy Spirit has been described as the bond of love between Father and Son" (33f.).

IV. THE ROLE OF THE SPIRIT IN THE WORK OF SALVATION

I

DEFINING THE QUESTION

Two things were involved in speaking of "the Father's two hands". In the first place, it was taken for granted that the Spirit is involved alongside the Logos in the divine work of salvation; for Irenaeus this was so evident that no demonstration was necessary. Secondly, however, the Spirit's work must be distinguished from the work of the Son. This, too, was accepted as given in Scripture, so that the question of whether the Son sufficed to complete the work, or was able to complete it, simply did not arise. There was never a question of the Son's operating on his own at any stage of salvation history, whether in the Old Covenant, in the Incarnation, in his public life, or in his Passion and Resurrection. Not even when the Spirit seems to take over from the Son's completed work and begins to work in the Church in diverse ways; for in this epoch, too, the Spirit acts, not alone, but always in the context of the Son's presence, who, for his part, makes the Father present.

Thus the question of distinguishing the functions of Son and Spirit (granted their de facto inseparability) is a pressing one, for we are moving toward the next chapter, which will deal with the relationship between the Spirit and the Church. The question cannot simply be approached on the basis of the multiplicity of the Spirit's utterances in salvation history and, in particular, in the Church; this would lead to a fragmentation that could hardly be brought to a synthesis. The path from the multiplicity of functions or charismata to the unity of the One who gives them presupposes that we already have a knowledge of this unity. Such knowledge, however, can only come from seeing the Spirit's position within the *taxis* of the Trinity. This means, of course, that we shall have to decide in advance what model of the Trinity to adopt: the Eastern or Western model. In practical terms we have already taken this decision in the preceding pages, where we endeavoured to show that, ultimately, only the *Filioque* enables us to call God "love" in the way Scripture does—and here we must preserve the Augustinian *principaliter* (*a Patre*) just as much as the form of the *per* (*Filium*), which depends upon it. Nonetheless, this modification cannot go so far as to limit, in any way, the gift of Godhead (with its sovereign generative power) that the Father makes to the Son in generating him.

At first sight, however, the Son does seem more clearly apt for the work of creation and salvation than the Spirit. For, in bringing forth the Son, the Father not only utters his own, infinitely powerful essence but also, in that essence, everything that divine power could create. Thus the Son, the eternal Word, directly becomes the exemplary cause of all possible worlds and of the world that is actually to be created. It was Bonaventure, preeminently, who set this forth on a broad canvas in the first *collatio* of his commentary on the seven days of creation.[1] In the Son's generation Augustine sees primarily the world as it will really be created,[2] including the task the Father lays upon the Son, namely, to stand as guarantor for this world right up to the Cross, and the latter's filial readiness to fulfill the Father's every wish. Thomas includes all possible worlds, all worlds that could freely be created, in this generative act: the only Son, indubitably, would be the primal Idea of these worlds, too.[3] As for the Father's self-utterance in the Son, there is most assuredly nothing indifferent about it: it must be loving and affirming in the highest degree. According to Augustine, however, love is found in the very *generatio Verbi*, and this generation is *cum amore notitia*, so that this first procession in God seems to contain the entire *circumincessio* of knowledge and love.[4] It is in this way that the Son's mission to the world from the Father takes place in love and is carried out in love by the Son—which could make it seem, initially, as though the Spirit's role were superfluous. The truth that abides in the Son is already loved as such. If the Spirit's function in God's work with the world is to be identified, we must look for it beyond the Father's love for the Son

[1] *Coll. in Hexaem.*, ed. F. Delorme (Quaracchi, 1934), 1–18.

[2] "Nihil dixit Deus, quod non dixit in Filio; dicendo enim in Filio quod facturus erat per Filium, ipsum Filium genuit, per quem faceret omnia" (*In Joh.*, tr. 21, 4).

[3] "Pater enim intelligendo se et Filium et Spiritum Sanctum et omnia alia, quae in ejus scientia continentur, concipit Verbum, ut sic tota Trinitas Verbo dicatur, et etiam omnis creatura" (including all possible creatures S. *Th.* I, 34, 1 ad 3).

[4] "Cum itaque se mens novit et amat, jungitur ei amore Verbum ejus. Et quoniam amat notitiam, et novit amorem, et verbum in omne est, et amor in verbo, et utrumque in amante et dicente" (*De Trin.* IX, 15 [PL 42, 909]).

as we have described it here, even beyond the fact that the Son is the world's exemplary cause. Perhaps it may be even beyond the words of John 3:16: "God so loved the world that he gave his only-begotten Son."

A second difficulty, although of a quite different kind, is cast up by the classical patristic treatises on the Spirit (Athanasius, Didymus, the Cappadocians). For their central concern is, not to establish the Spirit's specific operation in the work of salvation, but to prove his divinity. Their emphasis, therefore, is on showing that the Spirit's operation demonstrates his equality of essence with Father and Son: the Spirit could not make us holy if he were not holiness itself, and he could not divinize us unless he were God, and so on. The goal of these writings is essentially attained in the definition of the First Council of Constantinople. Our concern here is different: assuming the divinity of the Spirit, we wish to know what are his specific attributes (*idiotētes, priorietates*). The roots of the latter must lie in the concept of "procession" (*ekporeusis*)—a somewhat pale concept in terms of inner-trinitarian life, which only acquires color through the "economic" characteristics (*notiones*) attributed to the Spirit in Scripture (*notiones sunt, quibus divinarum personarum distinctio innotescit*).[5] In what follows, therefore, the Spirit's position within the Trinity must not be neglected, since it is only on the basis of this position that his role in God's work of salvation can be understood; on the contrary, we shall attempt, on the basis of the economy, to make concrete what *ekporeusis* positively means.

Three key words suggest themselves when we consider the ways in which the living God manifests himself in his mode of being as Holy Spirit: gift, freedom, and inward and outward testimony.

Gift, in the highest sense, means what God hands over to man and puts within him: "God's love has been poured into our hearts through the Holy Spirit who has been given to us" (Rom 5:5). God has "given us his Spirit in our hearts as a guarantee" (2 Cor 1:22; 5:5); "by this we know that he abides in us, by the Spirit which he has given us" (1 Jn 3:24; 4:13); "for it is not by measure that he gives the Spirit" (Jn 3:34). *Freedom*, likewise in the broadest possible sense: "Where the Spirit of the Lord is, there

---

[5] Thomas, *Compendium Theologiae*, c. 59.

is freedom" (2 Cor 3:17). "The law of the Spirit of life in Christ Jesus has set me free" (Rom 8:2). "The wind blows where it wills, and you hear the sound of it, but you do not know where it comes from or where it goes; so it is with every one who is born of the Spirit" (Jn 3:8). "We have received . . . the Spirit which is from God. . . . The spiritual man judges all things, but is himself to be judged by no one" (1 Cor 2:12, 15). *Testimony* is given by the Spirit both inwardly and outwardly: as "the Spirit of truth" he "bears witness" to Jesus (Jn 15:26). Outwardly he bears witness before the world, by convincing/convicting it (Jn 16:8ff.). Inwardly "the Spirit himself [bears] witness with our spirit that we are children of God" (Rom 8:16); "the Spirit is the witness, because the Spirit is the truth" (1 Jn 5:7). All three concepts, particularly the third, but the second and first as well, refer equally to the operation of Father and Son; while specifically mentioning the Spirit, they always refer to the Son's salvific work,[6] in which the Father's eternal "working" is manifested to the world (Jn 5:17). Nonetheless these three terms have a particular reference to the Spirit; we shall see that the terms are inseparable: they interpenetrate. We now have to elucidate this on the basis of the Spirit's position within the Trinity. Much of what belongs here has been anticipated in previous chapters; it will be our task here to show how the various aspects belong together.

---

[6] Didymus shows this convincingly in his treatise on the Holy Spirit (PG 39, 1033–86). Thus he adduces Ephesians 3:16–17, where God strengthens us by his Spirit, so that Christ may dwell in the hearts of believers (1055A). "Where the Holy Spirit is, the Son too is immediately to be found" (1058C). "Just as the Son can do nothing of himself, since he cannot be separated from the Father, the Holy Spirit cannot in any way be separated from the Son" (1065B). "What is God's cannot be known except by the Spirit of God." Then he says, "The man who does not have the Spirit of God does not belong to him", and further, "whereas if Christ is in you. . . ." This shows most clearly that the Holy Spirit is inseparable from Christ, for wherever the Holy Spirit dwells, Christ is there too; and wherever the Spirit of Christ withdraws, Christ too withdraws. "For if a man has not the Spirit of Christ, he does not belong to him." So it is possible to say, "If a man belongs to Christ in such a way that Christ is in him, the Spirit of Christ is in such a man" (1069AB). Finally this is applied to divine sonship: "All who are driven by the Spirit of God are children of God; and it is the Spirit in us who makes us sons of God together with Christ, crying 'Abba, Pater' " (1070C).

2

THE KEY WORDS OF THE SPIRIT

a. Gift

1. A gift that is not given *gratis* is not a gift but a business transaction. Similarly, a gift that is not intended to express and give the giver remains at the level of a prospective deal. In a genuine gift, the giver wishes to give himself by means of a transparent token. This brings us once more to the paradox expressed by the Fourth Lateran Council, namely, that the eternal Father gives his entire Godhead, without holding anything back, to his Son (that is, the Father does not merely give the Son some divine essence distinct from, and excluding, the Father's Person), yet without losing his Godhead in this act of self-surrender (DS 805). In this perfect gift, which in this case is the inscrutable source and origin of God and of all being, we discern something that will subsequently come about in all love, however imperfectly realized, namely, the distinction (taught so insistently by Ferdinand Ulrich) between giver and gift, so that the giver can be really present in the gift—understood as a "giving-away".[1] The Father is and remains Father as he renounces any (Arian) being-for-himself-alone; but since the Son receives from the

---

[1] F. Ulrich, *Leben in der Einheit von Leben und Tod* (Frankfurt am Main: Knecht, 1973). "The gift would not express the giver . . . if it remained trapped in its original unity with him. . . . The umbilical cord must be cut so that the blood system of the receiver can become independent and he can pursue his path; for this is the purpose of being's Yes, which empowers and liberates." For the giver, this means that "the Other's otherness is not a sting of death, piercing him in the flesh of his 'I = I'; it is not an 'objective provocation' that has to be overcome! Rather, he accepts the Other's otherness, which arises from their separation, in such a way that, inwardly, it actually facilitates his self-communication. Only in this way can he verify that his gift has separated itself from him, that his being is lived as gift, that is, has been received. Only through separation from the thou can the I appropriate itself and, in this act, affirm the origin of its own being (together with the Other)" (79–81). Accordingly, however, "the more deeply and pristinely a gift comes from the heart, from the inwardness of the giver, the more clearly is his figure inscribed upon it, the more the origin of his gift is present and the more intimate is the primal unity of giver and gift. To see the gift of someone who thus shares his own life is to see, in it, its origin, that is, the giver" (79).

Father not merely "something" (for example, the divine essence), but the self-giving Father himself, he receives the "giving" in the "gift". In receiving, therefore, the Son is not only thanksgiving (*eucharistia*); he is also gift in return, offering himself for all that the Father's self-giving may require; his willingness is absolute. Nor does this imply any subordination, as between "master and servant": the Son shares the same, native, divine sovereignty and freedom that the Father *is*, so that the Father does not issue a "command" to the Son (as the eternal misreading of Anselm's doctrine of the Incarnation would suggest), but, as Adrienne von Speyr says, with profound insight: "Thus the Father is the first to ask, and he asks the Son, in order to give him the joy of granting his request. . . . Even before the Son asks him, the Father wants to make his request, as if to give the Son precedence in the delight of granting." The Father does this, seeing the Son's willingness, seeing "how spontaneously love answers him in the Son"; so he asks him "to help promote the fatherly purposes. . . . The Father's intentions, now committed to the Son, are like preludes, beginnings taken up by the Son to be realized. Here we have a parallel to the Son's words, 'Into your hands, Father, I commend my spirit.' For here the Father gives his Spirit (his purposes, his work, his creation) into the Son's hands."[2] We have yet to discover, however, what the Spirit is.

First of all, it is clear from the words of Jesus about his relationship with the Father that they interpenetrate in their reciprocal loving self-surrender. Both renounce being a mere "I" without a "thou": this allows us to glimpse the identity of poverty and wealth in the divine love; for wealth and fullness are found in the self-surrendering Other (this also applies to the Father, since without the Son he could not be Father). Since this wealth—with its implicit renunciation—is experienced by both as a single gift, and neither keeps account of the renunciation it demanded, the wealth of both (which in each case is a *received* wealth) coincides in a oneness. For both, the event of this oneness is a gift: the *bonum* of a mutual love is a *donum* for the lovers. Thus both, the loving Father and the loving Son, receive this mutuality as a gift. This gift, however, is not the calculable total of their love, nor is it the resultant identity of their love: it is an unfathomable

---

[2] *The World of Prayer* (San Francisco: Ignatius Press, 1985), 64, 63.

more, a fruit (as the child is the fruit of the "one-flesh" relationship of man and wife); for even divine love, and every love that reflects it, is (as we have already said) an "overflowing", because, in it, the pure, unmotivated nature of goodness comes to light, as the ultimate face, *prosōpon*, of the Divinity. It is something that over-takes, sur-prises (*über-rascht*)[3] us (and, since we are in the timelessness of eternity, it does so in ways that are ever new), because we can never plumb the fathomless love of Father and Son. Thus the resultant unity and fruit is the unfathomable Spirit who, as such, brings to light and "searches" (1 Cor 2:10) the ever-deeper abysses of the renunciatory love of Father and Son. "Although everything is given in the Word, who owes his being absolutely to the Father in an eternal obedience unto death, yet the uttering Father and the Word the Father hears are eternally surprising one another with life that is eternally new and ever-young."—He is

> Spirit of the Word, by whom the Word conceals himself in silence in the Father and the truth of the divine love, which utters and unveils him as Word; he is Spirit of the Father, in whom the Utterer sets his Word free, separating from him in the separation of death; thus God communicates himself. He is the "Spirit" who proceeds from Father and Son, but he is not the Utterer as such, nor is he the Word as such. Rather, he is the positive fullness of his silence, the Father's breath in the Word.[4]

"Despite his omniscience, God loves in such a way that he always lets himself be surpassed and surprised by the beloved . . . , since the central thing in eternal fellowship is love, which even knowledge serves."[5] There is more to be said, however. The pure fruit of a love that renounces self-sufficiency does not, as such, rest on a self-emptying but is the pure positivity of the Good. "There is no self-emptying (*exinanitio*) in the case of the Holy Spirit." From the philosophical standpoint of the real distinction (of which the Trinity is the unsurpassable primal image) it can

---

[3] These expressions, whether in English, French, or German, all come from the context of combat: one "overtakes" one's opponent [in German, one runs "faster than"]. Obviously this original context disappears when we "surprise" someone with a gift.

[4] F. Ulrich, *Leben in der Einheit von Leben und Tod*. On the "breath" by which the Word is uttered, cf. p. 55 above.

[5] Von Speyr, *World of Prayer*, 49f.

be said that "if the Good is prior to all self-emptying of being, there can be no *exinanitio* in the Good in the sense of a negating of being. If the Good were not superior to the self-emptying of being, it would lie entirely within being's responsibility for it-self, in which case the 'terminus' of the negation of being would be purely positive reality, . . . and being would dissolve into essence." Nonetheless the Good's place is "not 'juxtaposed' to self-emptying. The necessary meaning of being is manifested in being's self-emptying as the gift of love. In love, the meaning of being presents its credentials as the 'ether of self-emptying', its 'vital element' and dynamism. It is 'indistinguishable' from the crisis of being that it accompanies, without being identified with it."[6] "Precisely because the *bonitas* of all self-emptying is prior and does not empty itself", it is the "abiding origin-less-ness" that guarantees (in theological terms) both the Father's and the Son's self-emptying.[7]

This demonstrates the whole gift quality of the Holy Spirit in its full dimensions. Since he is gift first of all for Father and Son—in the twofold sense that each gives him to the other and each is overtaken by the utter "fruit" quality of the Spirit (that is, he is the unfathomability of divine love, lived out in personal terms, within the Trinity)—he can be the God who is given to the world, too, as utter gift. Of course this is not "in addition to" the *exinanitio* of the Son, in which the Father's fundamental self-renunciation is so superabundantly manifest (the Father "so loves" the world that, for its sake, he even "renounces" his Son, cf. Jn 3:16). We have already spoken of the Word concealing himself in silence in the Father in view of the ineffable miracle of the Spirit, so that the Spirit may be referred to as "The Un-known Lying beyond the Word";[8] accordingly, the Spirit takes up his endless interpretation of the Word—which has gone "to the end" (Jn 13:1)—at the very point where it falls silent in death ("he bowed his head and gave up his spirit": Jn 19:30) and, in doing so, utters the full extent of the Father's love. The

---

[6] F. Ulrich, *Homo Abyssus. Das Wagnis der Seinsfrage* (Einsiedeln: Johannesver-lag, 1961), 436f.

[7] Ibid., 437.

[8] In *Creator Spirit, Explorations in Theology* III, trans. Brian McNeil (San Fran-cisco: Ignatius Press, 1993), 105–116.

Spirit, who is absolute Gift, will "bear witness" to no other love than "mine", says the Son; for his love *is* his only because he possesses the whole love of the Father (Jn 16:13–15). Since he is the boundless liquefaction of the Father's love as gift, not only can he be "poured out" as "grace" into the hearts of believers (Rom 5:5), he can liquefy also the apparently solid flesh and blood of the Son and make it into a Eucharist to the Father that includes the whole world.

2. In terms of salvation history, therefore, we have here a considerable advance as we move from the Old to the New Testament. In the Old Covenant the Spirit of God permeates the whole of creation in power: God gives life to all living things through his own breath. The Spirit and the Word by whom things come to be are very closely allied: "By the word of the LORD the heavens were made, and all their host by the breath of his mouth" (Ps 33:6). Since the Word has not yet expressed himself as man, so, too, the Spirit has not yet been given as the self-giving God. The hiatus between God (in heaven) and man (on earth) is bridged by the covenant, which essentially rests on a free saving act on God's part. Therefore the sealing of the covenant is introduced by the explanatory words: "The LORD, a God merciful and gracious, slow to anger, and abounding in steadfast love and faithfulness" (Ex 34:6). Grace is God's undeserved favor to man, his graciousness and kingly condescension—a climate in which the covenant partner can live. But God's attitude is made clear in his saving deeds that accompany his people's journeyings; even his "jealousy" and his punishments do not indicate the limits of his favor but are its necessary expression. The distance between the gracious God and man only *seems* to be called into question when God equips men and women with his Spirit in order to give concrete form to his guidance of them within history: thus, from the judges to the kings and up to the prophets there are people equipped with sagacity, justice, and skill in battle; there are those endowed with kingly wisdom; there are even those entrusted with the word of God and miraculous power. All these are special organs of God's covenant providence. God's royal condescension to the wretched "worm", Israel, is revealed more and more, in the course of history, as the divine love that

flares up from God's innermost being (*rahamim*); it calls for more than just faithfulness to the precepts contained in the covenant: it calls for a response of love that challenges the whole man (Deut 6:5f.). God's graciousness in making the covenant was incomprehensible to Israel; when love breaks forth in God it seems incomprehensible even to him: "Is Ephraim my dear son? Is he my darling child? For as often as I speak against him, I do remember him still. Therefore my heart yearns for him; I will surely have mercy on him, says the LORD" (Jer 31:20). The answer to this question that God asks himself (Hos 11:8–9) is initially given only by way of promise: the external character of the covenant relationship, according to which God's gracious mercy (*hesed*) is shown in the laws he decrees from heaven or from the mountain and which are meant to make the people holy as God is holy, must be transcended; they must be interiorized in a way that is classically expressed by the eschatological promise of a deepened ("new") covenant: "I will put my law within them, and I will write it upon their hearts" (Jer 31:33). "A new heart I will give you, and a new spirit I will put within you; and I will take out of your flesh the heart of stone and give you a heart of flesh. And I will put my spirit within you" (Ezek 36:26–27). "I will pour out my spirit on all flesh" (Joel 3:1[2:28]). All this remains at the level of promise in the Old Covenant because it presupposes the *kenosis* and the Eucharist of the Son, however much the divine Spirit was already at work in the Old Covenant, "spoke through the prophets", and may have given valid responses (through the life of the God-fearers, the poor, and in the symbolical actions of spirit-filled men) to the fundamental instructions of the covenant God.

We have already mentioned the *donum doni* in connection with the "divinizing" of the creature;[9] this gift can only begin to be distributed when God, the author of the two-sided covenant, bestows upon it its two-sided fulfillment by crossing over to man's side in his divine Word (which unites both "natures" in his Person). Thus, once again, the miracle of the Spirit who does not empty himself can take place between the Father and

[9] See above p. 162. Cf. Cyril of Alexandria: "Christ did not receive the Spirit for his own Person but rather for us; for the good gifts (*bona*) come to us through him" (*In Joh.* V, 2 [PG 73, 754]).

the Son (who, as man, has emptied himself); this time, however, it involves the Father's total self-surrender to the incarnate
Son and the latter's (creaturely) obedience to the Father who
first lets him go and then finally abandons him. The miracle
now—*in Christo capite*—indwells man; henceforth, on the basis of Christ's unity with the rest of mankind, it can be called
"grace" in the specific sense, rather than the mere "favor" of
God that we find in the Old Testament. This grace must now
be called "Spirit of the Father" and "Spirit of Christ" (Rom
8:9, 11) without any distinction; as we have already said, this
Spirit has acquired the experience of being human through the
life and death of Christ and can henceforth "drive" man (Mk
1:12; Rom 8:14; Gal 5:18) in a more interior way than formerly.
The fact that "being driven" by the Spirit can be simultaneously
a conscious and deliberate "walking by the Spirit" (Gal 4:16)
is something that belongs to the next mark of the Spirit, that
is, that he is at the same time both freedom and setting free.[10]
Mention of this mystery leads us to make a brief assessment here
of the relationship between the Spirit as "uncreated" grace and
his inner operation in man (by the so-called "created" grace).

3. Theology should beware of trying to reduce to words this
mystery of the Spirit and of materializing it through endless distinctions that provide no illumination. Theology will proceed
on the basis of the given structures of man as creature, structures that already presuppose the mystery of the Trinity (as we
discussed in the second volume of *Theo-Logic*): only if, within
the Godhead, the Father hands over to his Son both his entire
divinity and the sovereign freedom that belongs to it can we understand that he is also able to endow man with self-subsistence
and freedom. This is already "grace" in a preliminary but valid
sense, as Fathers like Tertullian and Origen have emphasized
(while distinguishing this grace at the level of creation from divine grace as such).[11] True, what is highlighted in this preliminary
"setting free" is the apposition of God and man (who, unlike
Father and Son, do not share an identical concrete nature) and,

---

[10] "The Christian's action is always attributable both to a leading of the Spirit
and to a personal decision" (H. Schlier, *Römerbrief* [1977], 231).

[11] Tertullian, *Adv. Marc.* II, 5–10; Origen, *De Princ.* III, 1, 18f.

hence, their dialogical relationship; but once this dialogue becomes christological, the indestructible diastasis between God and the creature is overcome: the image is fashioned after its origin. Following Clement, Athanasius, Gregory Nazianzen, and Cyril, this transformation is called the "divinization" of the creature; and, as we saw above when comparing the Greek and Latin doctrines of grace, both traditions anchor this "divinization" in the Incarnation of the divine Word.[12] This raises the question of how the origin can impress itself on its image; or how the uncreated can draw the created into itself in such a way that the latter is elevated and not destroyed but rather is perfected beyond its natural endowments (*gratia non destruit, sed elevat et perficit naturam*). Insofar as grace, understood here as the handing over of the divine *donum*, does not destroy the "dialogical" relationship of Father and Son within the Godhead but rather brings it to superabundant perfection, there can be no question of this giving of the *donum* to the creature threatening the latter's dialogical position over against God. As the Gospel says, grace "elevates" the creature from a slave relationship to a child relationship in Christ the Son. The Son made himself a slave, humbling himself to accept even the alienation of sin; taking all that has been thus alienated and bringing it home to the status of the child within the Trinity requires that the whole process of mediation so comprehensively described by Augustine as "justification" and "sanctification" be carried out by an essentially "healing" grace (*gratia sanans*). It is important, however, that this grace's mediating function—though it be mediated by the Cross of Christ itself—should not be overlooked. Pelagius, of course, had got stuck by employing a concept of grace that lacked the requisite nuances (he understood natural freedom as grace): Augustine had forcefully to point out to him the necessity of this healing, which is at the same time a liberation of the will that is enslaved to sin (*gratia liberans*); he liked to do this by stressing that the divine gift of "God's love . . . poured into our hearts through the Holy Spirit" (Rom 5:5) is the goal of God's definitive covenant. What is perhaps his most beautiful work, *De Spiritu et littera* (412), presents a complete synthesis of this. Here the

[12] See above, chap. 3, section 3a.

Holy Spirit—beyond creaturely freedom and the *praecepta* of the
Old Testament—is called the divine love that is poured upon
us: "participating in this divine love, the rational soul is, as it
were, set aflame, so that it, too, may become a created light."[13]
Augustine sees very precisely the difference between the Spirit's
presence in the Old and in the New Testament;[14] but he also
sees that human freedom (of choice) can only attain its own, its
highest freedom as a result of the divine freedom that is given
to it in the Spirit.[15]

In principle, this insight establishes two aspects that will later
develop along different lines. First, the Spirit's work of justifying and sanctifying the sinner is a dynamic process (and not a
sudden or dialectical event, as the Reformers largely assumed),
so that one can rightly distinguish the grace that helps to initiate
the process (*gratia actualis praeveniens* and *subsequens*) from that of
the goal attained (*gratia gratum faciens, sanctificans*). Naturally, this
goal is not a situation of rest (as the expression *gratia habitualis*
could wrongly suggest) but, particularly given our pilgrim status
on earth, signifies a constant pressing on (Phil 3:12), so that the
grace accompanying the process remains constantly active and
effective (*gratia cooperans*). The whole process character of conversion was set forth in detail by the Council of Trent.[16]

The second aspect, which comes to the fore as early as Augustine, is that divine grace really operates in the creature. This
implies that a separation of Giver and gift must take place in the
identity of the Spirit given to the soul; otherwise the gift would
remain in the recipient like something not actually communicated, which Peter Lombard did not sufficiently consider when
equating the human act of love with the Holy Spirit. The immediate reaction against this short circuit, which did not meet the
case it was intended to prove, namely, the Spirit's immanence in

---

[13] *De Spiritu et littera* VII, 11 (PL 44, 206).

[14] Ibid., XXI, 36 (222).

[15] "Liberum ergo arbitrium evacuamus per gratiam? Absit: sed magis liberum
arbitrium statuimus, . . . quia gratia sanat voluntatem." His opponents fail to notice "in ipso nomine liberi arbitrii utique libertatem sonare. Ubi autem 'Spiritus
Domini, ibi libertas' " (ibid., XXX, 52 [233–34]). "Potestas datur, non necessitas", (ibid., XXXI, 54 [235]).

[16] DS 1524–31.

the human spirit, resulted in the somewhat infelicitous distinction between *gratia increata* (that is, the Holy Spirit) and *gratia
creata* (that is, its effects in man); the drawback here is that the
effects of the divine presence in the soul are expressed in the
categories of creation. This explains the attempts made in early
Scholasticism (and extending right up to Thomas) to express
the "separation of Giver and gift" on the analogy of the sun and
its radiance,[17] which the modern theology of grace endeavors
to express by avoiding the *causa efficiens* and replacing it with a
causa (quasi-)formalis. The intractable difficulty here is that, while
the otherness of God and the creature is refashioned and drawn
into the otherness of Father and Son, it is not destroyed. Look-

[17] Cf. above pp. 178–79. If grace can be understood as a "radiation" of the Holy
Spirit in this way, we should not overlook the element of truth in Peter Lombard's
theory. To do so would be to reify grace—a practice that the Reformers, in particular, strongly condemned. Rondet (see n. 28 below), partly basing himself on
Landgraf ("Caritas und Heiliger Geist", in *Dogmengeschichte der Frühscholastik* I/1
[1952], 220–37) has assembled a great number of texts tending in this direction.
Peter Lombard bases himself on Augustine, *De Trin.* XV, 17, 27. God himself
is caritas, and this love of his is poured into us *per Spiritum Sanctum* (Rom 5:5);
accordingly, this idea cannot be entirely discounted, even after Lombard's insuf-
ficiently considered thesis has been refuted, as the following show: Sedulius Scotus, Odo von St. Emmeran (PL 146, 63D); Paschasius Radbertus (PL 120, 1460:
"qui habet caritatem in se, Spiritum Sanctum habet, quia Spiritus Sanctus caritas
est"); William of St. Thierry (PL 184, 372, 375A); Gilbert Porreta, *Commentary on
St. Paul*, cod. Bamberg Bibl. 126 (cf. Landgraf, "Caritas", 222–23); Ruysbroeck
(Rondet 190). Cf. Bonaventure (I, d. 17, p. 1, a. and q. 1); Thomas (*S. Th.* II/II,
q. 23, a. 2; *De Car.* q. and a. 1; 1, d. 14, 2, 1 sol. 2: "per prius recipimus Spiritum
Sanctum quam dona ejus"). For a continuation of the Lombard's thesis in an
orthodox sense (which is also a precursor of the modern theory of a quasi-formal
causality of the Holy Spirit, as uncreated grace, in man's sanctification), cf. the
subtle remarks of Johannes a Ripa (Paul Vignaux, *De S. Anselme à Luther* [Vrin,
1976], 405–37). Thomas, too, however, can say that in Christ "gratia habitualis
intelligitur ut sequens hanc unionem (hypostaticam) sicut splendor solem" (*S.
Th.* III, 7, 13). The genuine continuation of this thesis is found in the famous
thesis of Petavius, namely, that the Holy Spirit sanctifies the soul "formae instar";
"solus Spiritus Sanctus quasi forma est sanctificans et adoptivum reddens . . . filium" (*Dogm. theol.* VIII, c. 6, n. 8). Scheeben cautiously repeats the idea of the
Spirit as formal cause in his *Die Mysterien des Christentums* (1865) [Eng. trans., *The
Mysteries of Christianity* (Herder, 1946)], sections 26 and 30, and in more detail in
Dogmatik II (1878), 169, where *gratia increata* is shown to be "the *forma constituens*
of the state of grace" (375). Further development and partially new arguments (on
the basis of the beatific vision) are given in Karl Rahner's celebrated essay "Zur
scholastischen Begrifflichkeit der ungeschaffenen Gnade", in *Schriften* 1 (1954),
347–75 [Eng. trans., *Theological Investigations* I (London and Baltimore, 1961)].

ing from below upward, as St. Thomas likes to do, we can say that human virtues and habits (*habitus*) are transformed, whereas, looking from above downward, it is more that the divine qualities express themselves in the created spiritual being. It is impossible to squeeze these two ways of viewing the mystery of God's indwelling in the creature into a single comprehensive system. Finally we should not forget that, while God can posit the creature as "the other", he himself never becomes "the Other"; he remains *Non Aliud*. *"To Pān estin autos"* (Sir 43:27).

Since God is essentially spirit, self-giving, receiving, and loving (that is, far beyond what Greek "substance" philosophy understands as "Being"), the relationship of this God to the creature whom he indwells should be located beyond the opposition between physico-ontic and purely personal concepts. Historically speaking, it should be located beyond the dispute between Thomists (*praemotio physica*) and Molinists (*gratia sufficiens* and *efficax*, the latter operating on the basis of man's consent). Neither Thomists nor Molinists really reflected upon the *Non Aliud* to which we have referred, which is why the dispute was doomed to be fruitless.

We should, however, reflect upon the fact that, within the Godhead, the *bonum* of the Spirit not only presupposes the twofold self-surrender (*exinanitio*) of Father and Son, but actually contains it. This being so, the "economic" question arises: What is the connection between the "reckoning of the merits" of the Crucified (or, at a deeper level, the economic *kenosis* of Father and Son) and the Spirit's love that is poured into man's heart? This, of course, is the question that was debated in late Scholasticism and the Reformation, right up to the Council of Trent, namely, the "double justification" of the *imputatio meriti Christi* and the *inhabitatio Spiritus* (Seripando). Here too, however, the mystery is not solved by drawing the distinction: whether we take Thomas' preference for the (already traditional) image of grace flowing from Christ the Head into his members or that in which Christ himself breathes his Spirit into the disciples in the *Triduum Mortis*, the indissoluble unity of both aspects is quite clear.[18]

---

[18] Further distinctions were drawn in the doctrine of grace; but since these depended on a questionable eschatology, they should be jettisoned along with the

b. Freedom

It was primarily Augustine who spoke of the Spirit in "economic" terms as "freedom" and "the Liberator". This usage has its roots in Scripture: "The Spirit blows where he will", that is, he cannot be tied down, and "where the Spirit is, there is freedom." Once again this mark is not exclusive to the Spirit: after all, the creation is the Father's free act, and redemption is the Son's free act ("no one takes [my life] from me, but I lay it down of my own accord", Jn 10:18); nonetheless, Jesus shows himself as the One who is preeminently obedient to the Father unto death, whereas there is no mention of the Spirit "emptying himself" of his freedom. True, he "will not speak on his own authority, but . . . he will take what is mine and declare it to you" (Jn 16:13–14)—showing that his indwelling origin is from the Son and hence from the Father; but his way of declaring and interpreting the hidden "treasures of wisdom and knowledge" in Christ (Col 2:3) is sovereignly manifest throughout world history: it cannot be encapsulated in any law and cannot be predicted. This means that we must look for the origin of the Spirit's freedom within the Trinity; the freedom of the Spirit must be just as divine as that of Father and Son, yet distinct from it.

Of course there is nothing arbitrary in the Son's generation by the Father. "In God necessity is not a blind necessity of nature, preliminary to his qualities of mind and personhood. It is a divine necessity which expresses his spiritual nature. It has no parallel among us creatures; we can only describe it as lying beyond all creaturely freedom and necessity."[19] We have already shown that the Son eternally consents to being begotten by the Father and freely makes himself available for the Father's purposes; that is, his freedom already has the contours of obedience, so that he may fulfill the Father's wishes, which count on his collaboration. The encounter of Father and Son, accordingly,

---

latter. The controversy between Baianism and Jansenism produced a distinction between a *gratia sufficiens* (which, however, was not in fact sufficient for salvation) and a *gratia efficax* (which really sufficed); this was supposed to explain "double predestination" (whether *ante* or *post praevisa merita*)—which is totally unknown to Scripture. Such unbiblical concepts do nothing to illuminate revelation.

[19] Von Speyr, *World of Prayer*, 58.

becomes the procession of the Spirit, understood as the unity of two interpenetrating consents. (Here we can speak of *duo spiratores* and *una spiratio*.) This results, not from an agreement at the intellectual level, but from that "surprise" wherein love shows itself to be more, and more fruitful, than had been envisaged, even if (in its reciprocal self-emptying) it was the most selfless of loves. It follows that the "condilectus" that, according to Richard of St. Victor, accompanies selfless love cannot be posited as some third entity outside the reciprocal love of the two lovers but must spring from the inner "logic" of selfless love itself. This "third" is the quintessence of divine love, its ultimate fruit, which represents the result of the Father's "necessary" will and the Son's will (which consists of divine necessity *and* freedom):[20] the concept of "necessity" cannot be applied in the case of this "third". Here we must speak of love's freedom; certainly, it is a freedom that owes its being to Father and Son and is ready to carry out their plans (which count on its collaboration), but it does so as a love that is free. It is free to choose, within the vast horizon of the divine imagination, the ways in which God's purposes are to be implemented; this is a new and, as it were, original synthesis. The Spirit blows where he will, even though he can and will blow only within God's infinite expanses. So this "freedom of the Spirit" is already rooted in its position between Father and Son; it is something within the Godhead, not something that arises in the wake of the creation.[21] The Spirit "can freely do whatever he can devise to promote the love of Father and Son".[22] In saying this we are not, of course, importing any temporal dimension into the divine processions, but the *taxis* of the processions, which is essential to divine freedom, is irreducible; thus we may say that the Father's experience is fulfilled in the Son, and the expectation of both is over-fulfilled (as it were) in the Spirit. No "becoming" is implied here, but rather the law of eternal love: it is "expectation which, though unsurpassable, is surpassed by the fulfillment"; God's nature is to be ever "more",[23] an insight we can find, perhaps, in Plato,

---

[20] Cf. ibid., 60–61.

[21] Ibid., 62.

[22] Ibid., 63.

[23] Ibid., 30.

where he places the Good above all things;[24] Gregory of Nyssa makes this the object of explicit reflection.[25] It is in virtue of this freedom that the Spirit, the innermost love of Father and Son, will also be their witness. (We shall have to discuss this.) But as a witness he will be free: that is, he is not chained to a given, binding truth; rather, he witnesses to it in a freedom that allows him infinite interpretation. This interpretation does not begin, however, only when the *consummatum est* is uttered on the Cross and Jesus' spirit is breathed forth: it must already be located within the Trinity itself, for this is where the divine plan for the world (namely, to set forth the highest possible representation of triune love) is ultimately sealed; and this is also where it attains full realization. Here it becomes clear that it is the Spirit in God (the will to love) who everywhere brings the divine plan into actuality—whereas the Son allows events to take place and follows the divine will. This is something we shall be able to experience directly, for instance, in the inspiration of Scripture, in the sacraments, in ecclesiastical office, and in tradition.

As we have indicated, the Spirit is the one who brings things into effect. This is already true of the work of the Son's Incarnation, that is, from that point in time when we begin to differentiate the Divine Persons (Lk 1:26–38), at the Annunciation: the Spirit brings the *sperma Theou* (of God the Father) into the womb of the Virgin, the Father entrusts this work to the Spirit, and the Son consents to being incarnated. The Spirit accompanies the entire work of incarnating the Son in such a way that the Son, in his humanity, can be the Father's word of love both *in* the Spirit who animates him and *through* the Spirit who brings the Father's will to him; these words, spoken and carried out, can only be understood if they are received as "spirit and life", for "it is the spirit that [in the divine sense] gives life, the flesh is of no avail" (Jn 6:63), not even the mere flesh and blood of Jesus, for the latter can only become real food and real drink when it has been transfigured by the Spirit, when the Risen One has become "a

[24] *The Republic* VI, 509.

[25] God is not only "beyond" all that can be thought and desired but "beyond the beyond": *hyper epekeina, In Eccl.*, hom. 7 (PG 44, 732C). On this issue see our *'Presence and Thought: Essay on the Religious Philosophy of Gregory of Nyssa'*, trans. Mark Sebanc (San Francisco: Ignatius Press, Communio, 1995), 57–69.

life-giving spirit" (1 Cor 15:45). Origen was right to distinguish the quality of the inspired word in the Old Covenant from that of the enfleshed Word in the New Covenant: whereas the former, however inspired, was predominantly a written code, the latter, since it is Love incarnate, is predominantly spirit.[26] The goal of this life is to bring about the worship of the Father "in Spirit and truth" (Jn 4:24); this goal will be realized, throughout the history of the Church and the world, in the inseparable unity of Christ—transfigured by the Spirit—and the Spirit himself. And it cannot too often be reiterated that what the Spirit will do is, not to produce imaginative variations on the basis of an ultimately limited, fixed (written) text, but to bring to light "treasures" that are "hidden" (Col 2:3) in the enfleshed figure of the Word, which is already permeated by the Spirit.

Christ, both as God and as man, is a priori obedient to the Father in the Spirit; accordingly, in his case, there is no problem about the way in which the Spirit, in him and above him, creates a seamless unity between the Father's will and his divine-human readiness to accept everything, including the agony on the Mount of Olives. It is only in the case of sinful man that there arises the problem—to which Paul devoted so much attention —of man's choice between "flesh" and "spirit", showing the renewed relevance of the questions of the doctrine of grace to which we have referred. However true it may be that the *ecclesia immaculata* (Eph 5:27), which Augustine calls the *columba,* manifests the same undivided obedience of love as Christ himself, it is also true that the question of the individual's decision cannot simply be traced back to the Church's mediation.[27] There can be no circumventing the encounter between the freedom of the divine Spirit and man's freedom, not even by means of the doctrine of grace worked out—on an Augustinian basis—by the Council of Orange (529) (see DS 370–97). In its first great canons there is constant mention of the Holy Spirit by whose *donum gratiae* we are actually granted the ability to make a free choice for or against God; but this grace of the Spirit will in no

---

[26] Cf. Henri de Lubac, *Histoire et Esprit* (Aubier, 1950), esp. chaps. 6 and 7.

[27] This is the basic tendency of L. Weimer's work, *Die Lust an Gott und seiner Sache* (Herder, 1981).

way compel our freedom to respond to it, as Jansenius' "caricature" of Augustine's thought[28] will suggest—as if the greater
delight (*delectatio*) in God's service, which the Holy Spirit offers
to us, will automatically carry the victory. As the Council of Orange puts it, closer to Augustine: Without the illumination and
inspiration of the Holy Spirit, who gives "suavitatem in consen-
tiendo et credendo veritatis" to all, fallen nature is unable freely
to choose the divine. The grace of the Spirit sets man free so
that he can freely choose, and "he becomes all the more free,
the more the Spirit brings him healing, so that he can abandon
himself to the divine and gracious mercy."[29] "His compassion
always precedes us, but whether we follow the divine call or
refuse it is a matter of our own will."[30] Thus, in Augustine,
the Spirit's work of "attraction" is not far removed from what
the Greeks, from Irenaeus to Origen, described in terms of advocacy, the activity of advising and seeking to convince: "The
light subjects no one to violent compulsion, nor does God force
anyone who refuses to allow his art to operate upon him."[31]
Augustine speaks of "suasio"; "potestas datur, non necessitas";
he speaks of "inspirata gratiae suavitas per Spiritum Sanctum";
"consensio autem utique volentis est".[32] If we leave aside those
manifestations of a certain rigidity that becomes apparent in his
last works, what we glean from the classical Augustine is this
wholly balanced doctrine: the Spirit, with his grace, frees man so
that he can grasp his genuine human freedom, which, however,
he only attains by consenting to that freedom of the divine love
that indwells him. Here again we must remember that God's
freedom cannot be created freedom's opposite "other"; created
freedom can only be perfected within the context of absolute
freedom, which is identical with love. At this point any theo-
logic encounters its own limits, and to go beyond them is to

---

[28] H. Rondet, *Gratia Christi: Essai d'histoire du dogme* (Paris: Beauchesne, 1948):
"La doctrine janséniste de la *delectatio victrix* n'est qu'une caricature de la pensée
d'Augustin" (104).

[29] "Voluntas libera tanto erit liberior quanto sanior, tanto autem sanior quanto
misericordiae gratiaeque subjectior" (Augustine, *Epist.* 157, 8 [PL 33, 676]).

[30] *De Spiritu et littera* XXXIV, 60 (249).

[31] Irenaeus, *Adv. Haer.* IV, 39, 3.

[32] *De Spiritu et littera*, passim.

incur the danger of betraying it. Here we see, definitively, that the christological obedience of love is wiser than all the wisdom that lacks obedience.[33]

This realization, bringing us back to the beginning of our presentation of the freedom of the Spirit, can introduce us to a deep mystery of freedom that is anchored in the very trinitarian being of God. The Spirit's perfect freedom to blow whither he will, to distribute gifts as he will, arises from the renunciation of both Father and Son: both refuse to be understood except in terms of self-emptying. Their bestowal of freedom presupposes this self-emptying, this *kenosis*, this *exinanitio*. Those who are reluctant to import such concepts into God (preferring to stay at the level of the equation *relatio* = *persona*) ought to remove these imperfect likenesses from the world. Hegel insisted on the inner connection between generation and death; this becomes clear once we take seriously both generation and birth (which is often so close to death). Feuerbach developed this whole aspect in his first book (*Todesgedanken*, 1830): Man must love, otherwise his mere existence as "I" will smother him to death; but his real death is when he goes out to a "thou", for "love would not be perfect without death"; the lover

> recognizes that natural death is, not the beginning of death, but its end, and that it is nothing other than an exhalation, a breathing out of the inner, hidden death. . . . Where could death come from, if not from your innermost being? It is only the manifestation of the act of that inner letting go which ratifies your love; it is the proclamation that, throughout your entire life, you have been silently making, namely, that, without the object of your love, you are nothing. . . . The higher always grounds the lower: it is from the highest that man summons death and pours it into the creation; . . . should not death have its prototype, its ground, in the deepest depths of things and beings? (*Werke* I, 20f.)

[33] "In God there is no dominance of knowledge over love, no possibility of increasing insight to a point where it no longer corresponds to love, no possibility of the Father seeing no longer the Son but himself when he looks at the Son. To try to substitute persons in this way is an abuse of love. For this is where worship has its place. An essential feature of worship is reverence" (Von Speyr, *World of Prayer*, 55).

The child awakes to genuine freedom only through his parents' sacrificial self-denial. We see this in Christian terms in the death of Christ, which is the fundamental act of his life; subsequently it is confirmed in every genuine prayer of self-giving for the liberation of a brother or sister: their freedom will be bestowed as a result of the sacrificed freedom of the one who prays to God for them. (Anyone who knows how to decipher the hieroglyphs of hidden Christian existence will find that the miracle of this birth of freedom is confirmed again and again.) Mary's perfect freedom, which is born of the Cross, must go and stand under that same Cross in order to help the Spirit of freedom to arise in the Church. Finally we must remember that the entire freedom of the creation rests upon the slaughter of the Lamb: "You know that you were ransomed . . . , not with perishable things such as silver and gold, but with the precious blood of Christ, like that of a lamb without blemish or spot. He was destined before the foundation of the world" (1 Pet 1:18–20). "He entered once for all into the Holy Place, taking . . . his own blood, thus securing an eternal redemption" (Heb 9:12), "for where a will is involved, the death of the one who made it must be established" (v. 16).

c. Testimony

It is true, of course, that Jesus calls first and foremost upon the testimony of the Father in support of the truth of his revelation, for it is the Father who is present in him in word and work. He is also aware of the testimony of the Old Testament (Jn 5:45–47) and of John the Baptist (Jn 5:33–36). But the testimony of the Spirit, whom he will send into the world upon his return to the Father, is crucial for the completion of his work of salvation. Here we see that the Spirit's function as testimony passes over seamlessly into his function as advocate of Jesus' life and work—which is that of the Father (Jn 15:26f.; 16:7–15). If we inquire as to the origin of this role of the Spirit within the Trinity, we encounter once again that twofold aspect of the one and inseparable Holy Spirit: that is, he is both the act of reciprocal love between Father and Son and the fruit of that act—an act that presupposes the distinction of Persons in the unity of the Godhead and guarantees that this distinction makes possible, through their loving union—and to their "surprise"—the unity of the loving Persons. This unity is more than could have been "expected", and so, while it is "bound" to those from whom it proceeds, it is endowed with the greatest possible freedom. Here it is most important to hold fast to the unity of both aspects of the one Hypostasis of the Spirit: considered as the innermost fire of love of Father and Son, he is absolute knowledge of love from within; but considered as the product, the fruit of this love, he is—as love—also the objective testimony to the effect that this love takes place eternally (which means that the image of the child as testimony to a past, temporal act of love on its parents' part is only a pale echo of it). Since the Spirit is both things simultaneously, he can be regarded as the one who eternally arouses the divine love; and this love, in turn, can never be exhausted (as human love, alas, can be) because the divine Lovers are constantly aware that their Fruit is always above and beyond.

We have already drawn the comparison between the twofold aspect of the Holy Spirit and Hegel's subjective and objective Spirit. We saw that there were important similarities—partly because of this philosopher's theological origins and partly because objective Spirit is indispensable for the Spirit's consummation in the Absolute—but the dissimilarities remained greater, because the procession/succession *of subjective-objective-absolute Spirit* was read off from a theory of "becoming" that does not correspond to the trinitarian *taxis*. While it is true that, ultimately, it is inappropriate to speak of "subjective" and "objective" in God,[34] it is possible, in the "logic of love", to distinguish the Spirit's two aspects; but, contrary to Hegel, they should be seen, not as moments in the self-realization of absolute Spirit, but precisely in his eternally realized being. If we see them in the context of their ultimate goal, we can distinguish (not separate) them within the economic work of the Trinity, not, as in Hegel, as moments of absolute Knowledge in its onward path, but as moments (to

---

[34] "There is nothing objective in him [God] outside love, and love itself is the most objective thing because it is absolute" (ibid., 54).

some extent, genuinely temporal moments) of absolute Love as it asserts itself in the world's becoming.[35]

With regard to the theological economy, the Incarnation of the Word in Mary is, certainly, a work of the Holy Spirit; yet the result, the hypostatic union of a humanity constituted of body and soul with the divine nature in the Person of the Logos, is so specific to the second Divine Person that the objective manifestation of the Son of Man among the rest of mankind is not identical with the objective aspect of the Holy Spirit. We have already given an adequate account of the Spirit's place in the events of the Incarnation: he mediates the Father's will to him "who became obedient unto death" (symbolized in the dove that hovers above him), and through this mediation he will play his part in the economy as the indestructible divine unity at the very point at which the distinction of Persons within the Godhead becomes manifest, in salvation history, in the form of a "separation" that goes to the length of abandonment.[36] He is that love which, even in the form of "separation" between the one who "commands" and the one who "obeys", holds fast, undiminished. Thus he shows the Son's economic relationship of obedience to the Father to be a form and a representation of absolute Love. True, the Holy Spirit is also a collaborator in the implementation of the enfleshment of the Word insofar as, even before the Resurrection, this flesh is penetrated by the Spirit (hence the eucharistic promise: "It is the spirit that gives life, the flesh is of no avail" Jn 6:63); this is proved by the fact that the flesh is not "suspended" by the Spirit (even if this is taken to mean "sublated" in the Hegelian sense), either at the Trans-

[35] It is important to bear in mind what we have already said: the Church has received from above (from the realm of absolute Spirit) the Holy Spirit, distinguishable as subjective and objective. The moments of "objective Spirit" are at the service of the soul (in the dimension of time) in its ecclesial becoming; eschatologically they dissolve in pure divine "objectivity". On the other hand, the soul, in its upward striving, needing the objective ecclesial Spirit in order to attain subjective fulfillment, will never be identical with the objective ecclesial Holy Spirit that comes down from above.

[36] "It is as if the Spirit is witness that the distance between them can never be separation because he constantly bridges the permanent, perpetual [and continually increasing] distance" (Von Speyr, *World of Prayer*, 48).

figuration on Mount Tabor or ultimately at the Resurrection. The Spirit will impart an infinite fluidity to the flesh, yet it will not dissolve it into Spirit: "It is sown a physical body, it is raised a spiritual [pneumatic] body. If there is a physical body, there is [will be] also a spiritual [pneumatic] body" (1 Cor 15:44). Every Adam bears a physical body, but only in this sense can the "second Adam" be called "a life-giving spirit [*pneuma*]" (v. 45): a *pneuma* who will bear his scars and stand on the Father's throne as the "lamb as though it had been slain".

The two-in-one quality of the Spirit's work shows itself more variedly in the Church's structure. This is first and foremost because her subjective and objective aspect must be understood in reference to both Christ and the Holy Spirit. The Church that comes from Christ and that is his "Body" and "Bride" must have both a physical, visible aspect and a spiritual, invisible aspect; a Church that was purely spiritual in a subjective sense could in no way be the representation of his abiding presence through history. All the Church's objective features, not only Scripture and the sacraments, but also office, tradition, and law, come directly from the fleshly form of the Word, insofar as the earthly life of Jesus remains the norm for the Church that follows him on earth. Nonetheless, while it can be shown that Jesus laid the foundations for all these objective, visible aspects of the Church community, he left it to the Holy Spirit to fashion and equip it, with the result that the Spirit's twofold form will imprint itself on the Church's organism.

Here again we see the Spirit's twofold form as love, even at the level of the Spirit's procession within the Godhead—that is, not only as the act of love between Father and Son, but equally as the highest fruit of this love. Therefore, in all the Church's objective institutions that the Spirit builds, we must recognize the work and expression of divine and holy love, just as much as in the subjective holiness that the institutions make possible. It is only man's imperfect view of things that sees a tension between *pneuma* and institution: from the perspective of the Spirit they belong together; indeed, they are one, just as he himself, within the Godhead, is one, both act and fruit, event and result, conditioned (by origin) and unconditioned (in freedom).[37] Not only is the Church's objective, institutional aspect, as it were, a "trellis" up which personal love can climb; "the more down-to-earth, formal objectivity that the Church adopts in her official and sacramental functions . . . is nothing other than the utmost concrete form of the Church's personal encounter with the individual subject. At the same time it must quite definitely share in the personal character of the all-embracing ecclesial institutions if obedience offered to the Church is to become an appropriate form of ecclesial love and freedom."[38] Thus the objective and ecclesial Spirit points to "the 'institution' character of the Holy Spirit himself".[39]

The concept of "institution" may seem somewhat premature here, however, since we have not reflected sufficiently on the connection between the Spirit's testimony and the object of his testimony. "He will take of what is mine", and "mine" is "all that belongs to the Father": this means that the object of the Spirit's testimony is the love between Father and Son that has appeared in "economic" form, that is, in the Incarnation of the Word. By testifying to the meaning of the Incarnation, the Spirit is "the Spirit of truth" (in the sense in which "truth" was defined theologically in the second volume of *Theo-Logic*), for only here does truth become tangible for us: this is the teaching of the entire First Letter of John. "No one who denies the Son has the Father. He who confesses the Son has the Father also" (1 Jn 2:23). "By this you know the Spirit of God: every spirit which confesses that Jesus Christ has come in the flesh is of God, and every spirit which does not confess Jesus is not of God. This is the spirit of antichrist" (1 Jn 4:2–3). "And the Spirit is the witness, because the Spirit is the truth. There are three witnesses, the Spirit, the water, and the blood; and these three agree" (1 Jn 5:7–8). So the Spirit's testimony is always incarnational; everything that would disincarnate, spiritualizing in the direction of

[37] Cf. our *Spirit and Institution, Explorations in Theology* IV (San Francisco: Ignatius Press), esp. 209–43; also Medard Kehl, *Kirche als Institution* (Frankfurt am Main: Knecht, 1976), 239–311.

[38] Kehl, *Kirche*, 262.

[39] Ibid., 275, also 276–83 and 299–303.

idealism, is anti-Christian. Otherwise the Spirit of truth would be self-contradictory; for he is one with the "witness" that God bears to his Son. Anyone who does not believe God "has made him a liar, because he has not believed in the testimony that God has borne to his Son" (1 Jn 5:10). This unmasks all philosophy, theology, and mysticism that is hostile to the body; it is shown to be anti-Christian. However, before the Body of Christ, which is the Church, animated by the Holy Spirit, can be spoken of as "institution", we must find a concept that is closer to the body and portray it in terms of "organism", in the literal, not metaphorical sense. The "Spirit of truth" promised by Jesus "will bear witness to *me*" (Jn 15:26); even if he "blows where he will", since he is the Spirit of the truth of the Father in the Son, his freedom can only blow in the saving work of Father and Son. This work is directed to "all flesh" with the aim of imparting "eternal life" to it (Jn 17:2).

Here again we see that the work of the exalted Lord who has become spirit is inseparable from the work of the Holy Spirit breathed into the Church by her Lord. Similarly, the equipping of the Church with all the necessary organs is attributed to the Lord who is exalted far above all the heavens (Eph 4:10ff.) but also to the Spirit who apportions ministries or charisms, "to each one individually as he wills" (1 Cor 12:11).

Two facts emerge from this community of operation. The first is that anyone called to discipleship is set upon the path of obedience to the Cross; this is clearly shown by the context in which the discourse on the Spirit is situated (Jn 15:20–16:4). According to Jesus, this obedient faith liberates us to follow the Spirit (Jn 8:31f.). Paul draws the strict consequence from this: the one who has been liberated by Christ to follow the Spirit must "serve . . . in the new life of the Spirit" and "bear fruit for God" (Rom 7:6, 4); he must "fulfil the law of Christ" (Gal 6:2) and bring forth "the fruit of the Spirit" (Gal 5:22). When Christ liberates a man to embrace the freedom of the Spirit, he also initiates this liberated man into the obedient discipleship of Christ; this paradox is resolved once we consider that Christ's own obedience to the Father, in the Spirit, is an expression of his freely given love (Jn 10:18). Thus anyone who follows him and surrenders to his "law" of free obedience in love has shattered the prison of his own self-will: "It is no longer I who live, but Christ who lives in me . . . who loved me and gave himself for me" (Gal 2:20). And the more freedom, the more persecution there will be: "Blessed are you when men revile you and persecute you . . . on my account. Rejoice and be glad" (Mt 5:11f.).

The second fact is a harder paradox, located within the Church, which is directly drawn into the Spirit's bearing of testimony: the Spirit "will bear witness to me; and you also are witnesses, because you have been with me from the beginning" (Jn 15:26–27). This concrete unity is also illustrated by Jesus' word: "And when they bring you to trial and deliver you up, do not be anxious beforehand what you are to say; but say whatever is given you in that hour, for it is not you who speak, but the Holy Spirit" (Mk 13:11; Lk 12:11). In his freedom, the Spirit is both in and above order in the Church; right from the beginning (ever since the election of the Twelve and their being given *exousia*) there has been a certain tension between official ministerial order and community charisms. Of course the Spirit is in and above both; he is "in" insofar as he completes and ratifies the official ministerial orders that Christ began; he is "above" insofar as his divine order (which is beyond our grasp) is continually shattering our purely human order that tends to ossify, in order to refashion it after his own free vision. But the Spirit is also in and above the community charisms; he is "in" them insofar as he genuinely bestows them upon individuals for their use, giving them the spiritual qualities necessary; he is "above" them insofar as no member of the Body of Christ can stubbornly insist on his own charisma and try to wield it against the comprehensive ecclesial order of the Body. This results in the delicate relationship between the charism of office and the personal charism within the community. This tension-filled dialogue can only be maintained if, on the one hand, there is respect for the Spirit-given charism of one's dialogue-partner and if, on the other hand, there is a joint attention by both partners to the divine, free blowing of the Spirit over the whole Church. (The Church's office-bearers, without compromising themselves, should respect the community charisms, and the latter should in turn respect the charism of office.) The Spirit's testimony and the Church's testimony are not simply identical, nor are they of equal rank, as the third Spirit discourse makes clear: "The Spirit . . . will bear witness to me; and *you also* are witnesses" (Jn 15:26–27 [emphasis added]). The Church's main task is to bear witness "to the end of the earth" (Acts 1:8), to bear witness "to all nations" concerning "repentance and forgiveness of sins" (Lk 24:47); in short, it is to teach mankind everything that Jesus was and taught (Mt 28:19–20): and she cannot address this task before, in prayer, she has received "power from on high" (Lk 24:49), the baptism of the Holy Spirit (Acts 1:5). It is the "power" of the Holy Spirit (Acts 1:8) that will make the disciples into witnesses and inspire them with the necessary words on whatever occasion they have to give testimony (this is the meaning of John 16:13: "he will declare to you the things that are to come"); for the task of being a witness will replace that knowledge of "times and seasons" that the disciples begged of the departing Lord.

The hallmarks of the Holy Spirit we have indicated here remain mere outlines. Our aim was to show that the three circles (gift, freedom, testimony) overlap and also that the concept "testimony" must include the notions of "interpreter" and "defender" (advocate). According to Paul, the Spirit of the exalted Lord is identically the Spirit of Christ and the Spirit of the Father: he is the Spirit of their reciprocal love in the latter's personal freedom. Thus the Spirit has "all truth" at his disposal: he administers it in divine sovereignty, yet in such a way that there is no truth outside the truth of the love between Father and Son.

V. THE SPIRIT AND THE CHURCH

A preliminary word is necessary as we proceed to the following section. Under this heading we are entering a vast field containing a great number of individual questions, each of which would require a substantial treatment. None of these questions can be given such treatment. We can only talk in general terms and in a fragmentary way. But since the present volume is also the final one and attempts a synthetic view, no essential aspect can be omitted. If, despite the fact that the whole work has a deliberately intended inner structure, it leaves the reader with the impression of uncontrolled, straggling growth, no harm will be done. Not only because we are operating at the center of the mystery, and while human reason has intimations of the *nexus mysteriorum*, this same reason "never becomes capable of apprehending mysteries as it does those truths that constitute its proper object" (Vat. I, c. 4; DS 3016); but also because the Holy Spirit, for the sake of his own "systematics"—impenetrable to us—is continually upsetting all the artificially constructed systems that man makes.

It is unavoidable, as a result, that much of what we shall say will refer back to things already discussed. After all, the "economic" revelation of the triune God is a single revelation, but it is infinitely rich in aspects. Thus this single revelation is seen as in a kaleidoscope (if the metaphor is not too childish), showing itself in ever new constellations formed from the same elements. Finally, the following section should not be thought of as a tightly structured totality: it should be seen to be open to all that has been presented so far and also open to the remaining sections, as the introduction clearly shows.

THE CHURCH BECOMES WORLD;
THE WORLD BECOMES CHURCH

a. God's Goal: The Salvation of the World

Scripture nowhere says that God's plan is to redeem the Church; it is always a case of redeeming the world: "God so loved the world" (Jn 3:16) that he entrusted "all flesh" (17:2) to the Son whom he sent into the world and whose intention, now that he is exalted above the earth, is to "draw all men to himself" (12:32). Furthermore, there are "other sheep that are not of this fold; I must bring them also" (10:16). To say that Jesus died only for a band of chosen ones is heresy (DS 1880, 2428ff.). The exalted Lord continues to make all his enemies submit to him, so that he may lay the perfected kingdom before the Father's feet, so that God may be all in all (1 Cor 15:24).

This universality of the Son's work corresponds to that of the Spirit, who, according to the prophecy fulfilled at Pentecost, is to be poured out "upon all flesh" (Joel 3:1f. = Acts 2:17). It is probable that the Old Testament text meant only Israel,[1] but in Acts 2:7ff., where all the foreign peoples are listed, the entire world is clearly meant. In the area of Judaism there are already transitions between the two interpretations from the national to the cosmological, particularly in the apocalypses.[2] It is well

[1] "It is certain that the prophecy does not mean 'all the world', . . . but everyone in Israel, for, according to the introduction, 2:19, this word is addressed to the People of Yahweh. A few verses earlier Yahweh has promised to manifest himself 'in the midst of Israel' (2:27). What he says regarding the other countries is entirely different (4:1ff.). Furthermore, Joel interprets the promise made to the 'house of Israel' in Ezekiel 39:29 ('I will pour out my spirit upon the house of Israel') . . . as being addressed to 'your sons and your daughters', and concerning 'your old men' and 'your young men' " (H. W. Wolff, *Dodekapropheton 2, Joel und Amos*, Biblischer Kommentar zum AT 14/2 [Neukirchen, 1967], 80).

[2] Cf. Allan D. Galloway, *The Cosmic Christ* (London: Nisbet, n.d.): "It was against this (apocalyptic) background that the work of Jesus as the Christ was interpreted in the Synoptic Gospels and in Christian Apocalyptic. This is the basis of the cosmic eschatology of Christianity" (122).

known that Paul, in parallel with the all-embracing cosmic aspect of Christ's reconciliation and rule, had to insist on the ecclesiological aspect (cf. Col 1:18; Eph 1:22f.). He is always able to unite the two aspects. Of the Christ who is exalted above all cosmic powers as their Ruler, Paul says, in the second passage, "[God] has put all things [ta panta] under his feet and has made him the head over all things [ta panta] for the church, which is his body, the fulness of him who fills all [ta panta] in all." Schlier comments: "He who is Lord of the Church is also the Lord of the powers. In the presence of the Lord of the powers all the world stands in the presence of the Lord of the Church."[3] Paul does not forget that the unity of Christ's cosmic rule is mediated through the unity of the Church, who, on her part, owes her being to the crucified body of Christ, which includes the whole cosmos: "Here we see clearly how the one body of Christ on the Cross, by the power of the Holy Spirit, continually upbuilds itself into the body of the Church. It does this through that 'representation' that is effected by the Holy Spirit, in the sacramental Body, in the bread of the Lord's Supper, which is this Body."[4] Insofar as the Church is, and should be, "one body and one spirit", she is "called to the one hope" (Eph 4:4), a hope that embraces the entire cosmos (Rom 8:19–39; 1 Cor 8:6).

In coming to discern the universal position of the Spirit,[5] equally universal as that of the cosmic Christ, it does not seem particularly profitable to examine the cosmic function of the Spirit of Yahweh in the Old Covenant. Rather, it is more promising to reflect on the Nicodemus discourse in John 3, where Jesus speaks of a "birth from above" (see v. 3), a being "born of . . . the Spirit" (v. 5), for "that which is born of the Spirit is spirit" (v. 6). I. de la Potterie has shown it to be probable that the

[3] *Epheser* (1957), 89.

[4] H. Schlier, "Die Einheit im Denken des Apostel Paulus", in *Die Zeit der Kirche* (Herder, 1956), 289.

[5] There can be no doubt that, from the beginning of Genesis right up to the Psalms, the Spirit's role is that of God's creative power. Cf. E. Schweizer, *Heiliger Geist* (Stuttgart and Berlin: Kreuzverlag, 1978), 25ff., 41, 52ff. (Sir 24:3; Wis 11:20). Hendrik Berkhof, *Theologie des Heiligen Geistes* (Neukirchen, 1968), chap. 5: "Geist-Welt-Vollendung", 107–24. A. M. Henry, *L'Esprit-Saint* (Paris: Fayard, 1959), 11f.

reference to the "water" along with the Spirit is a later interpolation, perhaps made by the Evangelist himself.[6] Jesus cannot
have spoken to Nicodemus of Christian baptism; this mention
of it must have been later, perhaps a post-Easter addition. One
wonders whether the reference to being born again (as a way of
entering the "kingdom of God"—a *hapax legomenon* in John) is
connected with Matthew 18:3 parr. on the necessity of becoming a child in spirit in order to be received into the kingdom. In
John this "becoming" becomes a "rebirth from above" (in the
prologue it is "of God": 1:13; here it is "by the spirit"). This
rebirth, in turn, coincides with a coming to "faith" (so 1 Jn 3:9;
5:1; 5:4). True, our present text juxtaposes water and spirit, yet
we should not tie the Spirit down to the water, since faith is a
precondition for baptism; the Fathers are of one voice in this.
New birth is not solely the sacrament, but faith. And this faith,
as at least modern theology emphasizes, can bring justification
even "outside the Church", on the basis of a "baptism of desire". "The Spirit blows where he will."

If the distinction between the visible Church and the world
has already been overcome in Christ and his Holy Spirit, this
means that the Church, in her innermost being (including sacraments and organic structures) is orientated to the world in a missionary manner. The Acts of the Apostles shows this in an exemplary way and the concluding passages of Matthew and Luke
express it in words. It would be wrong, therefore, to adumbrate
a pneumatic ecclesiology exclusively concerned with the question of how the Holy Spirit is related to Christ and the Church[7]

[6] "Naître de l'eau et de l'esprit" (included in I. de la Potterie and S. Lyonnet,
La Vie selon l'Esprit, Unam Sanctam 55 [Paris: Cerf, 1965], 31–63). Those who
consider this "water" to have been interpolated by a later hand are Wellhausen,
Bultmann, Lohse; those who regard it as coming from the hand of the Evangelist
are Wendt, Bernard, Flemington, Léon Dufour, van der Bussche, A. Feuillet (ibid.,
39). On the history of interpretation: 32–38. For an objection to the view that
"water" represents an interpolation, cf. H. Schlier, "Zum Begriff des Geistes im
Johannesevangelium", in *Besinnung auf das Neue Testament* (Herder, 1964), 270,
which includes reference to O. Cullmann's demonstration of the sacramental features in the Gospel of John (*Urchristentum und Gottesdienst*, 2d ed. [1950]).

[7] This objection could be made against the great and profound work of Heribert Mühlen, *Una Mystica Persona* (= UMP) (1964; 2d ed., Paderborn: Schöningh,
1967). We shall return to it.—For H. de Lubac, the Church's existence and
mission constitutes a single, identical, primal given: "L'Église n'a pris conscience

without including the cosmic dimension of the Spirit and the missionary dimension of the Church (which is, so to speak, her embryonically cosmic dimension). From this perspective, many of the Fathers' views will have to be revised: that of Origen, for instance, who allotted the realm of the whole creation to the Father, that of the merely rational creatures to the Son, and that of the saints (in the Church) to the Spirit: "It seems to me that the Holy Spirit only operates in those who have repented, turned to a better way, and walk 'on the path of Jesus Christ'."[8] This applies to Augustine, too: he acknowledges that the Donatists have a genuinely sacramental baptism, but he denies that they have received the Holy Spirit. This narrowness contradicts the Acts of the Apostles, which affirms that the gift of the Spirit, or faith at least, precedes baptism. This is clearly the case with the conversion of Cornelius, the "God-fearer" (see 10:2), whose prayers and sacrifice ascend to God and who is taught by the angel that his longing for the truth will be satisfied. "While Peter was still saying this, the Holy Spirit fell on all who heard the word", so that the Jewish believers were amazed "because the gift of the Holy Spirit had been poured out even on the Gentiles. For they heard them speaking in tongues and extolling God." Thus Peter came to understand that he could not "forbid water for baptizing these people who have received the Holy Spirit just as we have" (10:44–47). It may be that Luke has clothed a theological point in narrative form; but what is vital here is precisely this theological core, which is expressed as a general conclusion in Acts 11:18 and 15:8. Even Paul receives his mission before being given the Holy Spirit by the imposition of hands and, subsequently, baptism (9:15f.), and the eunuch comes to full faith before Philip baptizes him (8:36f.).

The Church's mission to the world is evident, furthermore, through two facts. First, there is the existence, today, of innumerable Christian communities whose baptism cannot be regarded as invalid. While this kind of "ecumenical" splintering of the Church's unity is not foreseen in Scripture, it is nonetheless

---

d'elle-même qu'en s'éveillant au devoir missionnaire que lui avait tracé son Fondateur, et c'est d'abord par ce devoir qu'elle s'est expliquée à elle-même" (*Le Fondement théologique des missions* [Seuil, 1946], 18).

[8] *Peri Archon* I, 3, 5.

a fact that makes it impossible to think in terms of a direct opposition between Church and "world". The second fact, which
can rarely be established in exact or statistical terms, is that of
the radiation of Christian faith and ideas beyond the boundaries
of the Church. Nowadays there is a kind of anonymous leavening of all cultures with Christian (or, more generally, biblical) substance, whether their attitude to Christianity is friendly,
indifferent, or hostile. Islam is unthinkable without the Bible;
so is Marxism; and Gandhi's influence on Hinduism, as well as
certain social emphases in Zen Buddhism, cannot be explained
apart from this Christian leavening. It does not need to be attributed to the influence of historical Christian missionary activity; the Holy Spirit is present and operative throughout the
whole world.

b. The Church's Twofold Movement

"Go therefore and make disciples of all nations, baptizing them
. . . , teaching them to observe all that I have commanded you"
(Mt 28:19–20). Here we have the Church's twofold movement
and twofold task; until the end of the world it will be impossible
cleanly to distinguish these two directions. On the one hand,
the Church must go outward to the nations and teach them
the Christian truth in such a way that they can understand and
accept it ("inculturation"); and, on the other hand, she must
take care that, with all its plurality, the truth does not become
splintered: she must embrace it within her own "pleromatic"
unity. All questions of apologetics, of the "point of contact",
of fundamental theology, and of theological "pluralism" come
together here. This means that both the aspects referred to at the
end of the previous section can occur separately or intertwined:
elements of non-Christian cultures, philosophies, and religions
can provide "points of contact" (perhaps prepared by the Spirit),
which, of course, will need to be "baptized" if they are to become Christian; one is reminded of the way Arius' Greek theology was reinterpreted by Athanasius and Nicaea. Alternatively,
genuinely Christian elements that have been distorted into positively anti-Christian forms can be brought home again; for instance, no one can seriously doubt (and Hegel demonstrated it

at a crucial point)[9] that the Declaration of Human Rights can be traced back to Christian insights concerning the dignity and freedom of persons, who participate equally in the image of God and hence are all brothers. The consequences of this were explicitly drawn in England and then in America (the Virginia Declaration, Jefferson), while the French "Déclaration des droits de l'homme et du citoyen" (1789) rejected the divine Lawgiver and deduced everything from the "expression de la volonté générale". Péguy, no doubt, was the first to discern the Christian meaning underneath this disguise, and the more recent popes have not been slow to follow him in this view. Paul VI said in a sermon: "There were points of agreement between Christianity and the great ideas of the Revolution; after all, the Revolution only appropriated some of Christianity's ideas and made them its own: brotherhood, freedom, equality, progress, the striving to raise the condition of the oppressed masses, and so on. All this, we know, is Christian, only it took an anti-Christian direction."[10] John Paul II said the same thing, but even more openly, on his first journey to France.[11]

We must be very clear, however, that the existence of *pneumata spermatika* in the ideas of the nations and the latent or patent radiation of Christian ideas and Christian living out into the world does not mean, in practice, that it will be easy to embrace everything within the unity of the Church. Foreign cultures, even in accepting the seeds of the Christian life, can sometimes show a growing resistance to what is Christian as they assimilate it into their own modes of thought; for her part the Church has to wrestle with almost insoluble questions of inculturation. These facts show that the difficulties are not only technical but actually theological in kind. The twofold movement—to all nations, yet with a message that must not be abridged—puts those who

[9] Society and the state are ultimately based on the reciprocal recognition of personal dignity and rights. This idea entered history with Christianity. The entire structure of Hegel's philosophy of law rests on this insight.

[10] Many similar utterances are collected in K. W. Kraemer, ed., *Papst Paul VI. an die Welt* (Osnabrück: Fromm, 1970), under the heading "Menschenrechte" (277).

[11] Jean-Marie Cardinal Lustiger, Archbishop of Paris: *Osez croire, osez vivre* (Centurion-Gallimard, 1986), 431.

bear the message of Christ in the situation of Christ himself. For his claim, though rooted in the Father's original plan of creation, brought him the "world's hatred" and meant that he had nowhere to lay his head (Mt 8:20) and was a "wanted man" (see Jn 11:57), and it ultimately led to betrayal, condemnation, and execution. The same fate is emphatically promised to the disciples as they go out on their missionary work (Jn 15:20–16:4): it is a necessary and "blessed" feature of discipleship (Mt 5:11f.). This persecution, in turn, renders the Church's mission fruitful, as Paul is aware (2 Cor 1:4ff.). The Lord's own prediction of this, on several occasions, serves to strengthen the Church through the knowledge that, if she is persecuted, she is on the right path, the path of discipleship (Jn 15:20–16:4).

According to Thomas, the Church's missionary activity can address both the natural law in all men and the "superadded grace" in them.[12] Thomas calls this "superadded grace"—which must be presupposed to exist everywhere—*gratia fidei*, which is inwardly given to those who "believe explicitly or implicitly" and thus belong to the New Testament.[13] Compared with this, "certain deeds, moral and sacramental", are secondary, for "the New Law does not consist chiefly in these latter things, as did the Old Law."[14] From this vantage point the Church's mission has two opportunities: either to transpose what is given in natural law into Christian terms or to make explicit what is implicitly Christian outside the Church. Both these approaches are

[12] "Dupliciter est aliquid inditum homini. Uno modo pertinens ad naturam humanam: et sic lex naturalis est lex indita homini. Alio modo est aliquid inditum homini quasi naturae superadditum per gratiae donum. Et hoc modo lex nova est indita homini, non solum indicans quid sit faciendum, sed etiam adjuvans ad adimplendum" (*S. Th.* I/II, 106, 1 ad 2).

[13] *S. Th.* I/II, 106, ad 3.

[14] *S. Th.* I/II, 107, 1 ad 3. Accordingly, many who lived in the time of the Old Covenant are accounted as belonging to the New, whereas many in the Church of Christ "live according to the flesh" and belong to the Old (107 ad 2). Thomas' view is confirmed by what Origen says, namely, that while sacramental baptism is associated with the Holy Spirit, the Spirit must have already brought a man to faith even beforehand; after baptism the believer will have to show whether, in fact, he knows how to live and act according to the Christian faith. Thus Wolf-Dieter Hauschild, *Gottes Geist und der Mensch, Studien zur frühchristlichen Pneumatologie* (Munich: Kaiser, 1972), 99f., can speak on p. 95 of an "ethical tri-chotomy" (see n. 15 below).

combined in the Pauline *Haustafeln*, or ethical exhortations, and where he urges the Philippians to strive for "whatever is true, honorable, just, pure, lovely, gracious, excellent, and worthy of praise"—and in this matter he gives his own life as an example of such Christian transposition (see Phil 4:8–9).

This anthropology, which also applied to those outside the Church, characterized the reflections of the Church Fathers. Taking up Paul's threefold distinction in 1 Thessalonians 5:23 (*pneuma-psychē-sōma*), they developed a broad doctrine of man that extends from the first theologians (Ignatius, Tatian, and especially Irenaeus), via Clement and Origen, to Augustine in the Middle Ages, to the Renaissance and the Reformation, and hence to modern times;[15] here, essentially, the "soul" is seen as hovering between the body and what is (supernaturally) pneumatic, that is, in a perpetual dramatic situation of decision.[16] Of course, this notion can only be regarded as a starting point and an encouragement for the Church's mission: it cannot serve as binding doctrine; the Church will always be having to come to grips with the persistent distinction between the concrete and personal form of her "doctrine" of Christ as the revealer of the Father and of the Spirit as the revealer of their reciprocal love—and the ideas and ideologies that have been adopted by ethics and religion among non-Christians. And it seems to be a law that, the more sophisticated a non-Christian ideological superstructure is (perhaps having been polished over thousands of years), the harder dialogue becomes. Perhaps, however, once all the other disputed issues have been solved, the final and apparently most difficult (and yet most promising) battle will consist in the attempt to reach agreement on the mystery of the Holy Spirit.

There can be no doubt that proclaiming the Gospel to non-Christians will have to begin with some kind of "Christology

---

[15] This is illustrated by H. de Lubac in his "Anthropologia tripartita", in *Mistica e Mistero Cristiano*, vol. 6 of his *Opera omnia* (Milan: Jaca Book, 1979), 59–117 (available only in Italian translation to date).

[16] Some material also in H. Crouzel's article on the Spirit in RAC 9 (1976), 491–545 (with bibliography). Serious attention must be paid, in this context, to Karl Barth's great section on "The Spirit as Basis of Soul and Body" in chapter 10, "The Creature", *Church Dogmatics* III/2 (Edinburgh, 1960), 344–66.

from below". This is utterly indispensable, as Karl Rahner so strongly insisted, and it will have to embrace the cosmic Christology of Teilhard de Chardin as well as all forms of "transcendence awareness" in the face of the existential and ethical questions concerning the meaning of life. However, while this program must be pushed as far as possible, we must be aware that it can never, of itself, turn into a "Christology from above"; indeed, it cannot ever be reconciled with the latter within a single system.[17] This is necessarily so, otherwise there would be no room for the genuine act of repentance and faith, as it is presented (somewhat dramatically) in Augustine's *Confessions* in terms of a turning away from the docetic Christology of Neoplatonism to an ecclesial Christology that calls for the humility of the Cross. Here, too, in spite of Teilhard's principle of ascending "personalization" within an evolutionary cosmos, the commitment to the particular, individual person of Christ requires an indispensable leap, an "option"; Blondel, in his *L'Action*, can envisage and call for this option, but it is only in the grace of Christ that he can actually perform it.

The whole problem of ethics in the situation of missionary dialogue can be regarded as a mediation between that of dogmatics and that of Pneumatology (which remains to be discussed). Ultimately it is a question of deciding between an (individual and social) ethics on the basis of autonomous freedom and an ethics (again individual and social) on the basis of "theonomous" freedom. There is no contradiction in this. A "theonomous" ethics would somehow see man's moral decision making as enabled by, and hence in harmony with, an absolute freedom. The Stoics could provide an example of this. In the absence of an absolute Good, human freedom would be incapable of weighing up relative values and preferring the "objectively" better (that is, that which is more consonant with the absolute Good). Where this norm is missing, some relative value (the advantage of the party, the will-to-power) is posited as absolute, and ethics is trampled

---

[17] We are indebted to J. M. Dermott, "The Christologies of Karl Rahner", *Gregorianum* 67 (1986): 87–123, 297–327, for having demonstrated this following a detailed analysis of Rahner's Christology. "His Christologies from above and from below do not ultimately coalesce. . . . His bifocular vision was incapable of attaining a true unity" (325).

upon. It is both possible and necessary to maintain a Christian dialogue with non-Christian ethics, for, often enough, the path to orthodoxy can be found via orthopraxy. It is relatively easy to agree that, for ethical conduct, some transcendence beyond the ego is necessary; what is contentious is *which* is the highest value to which the ego must surrender.

Ultimately it brings us to the question of the nature of true "selflessness". If we exclude the Marxist and positivist (Comte) solutions as too myopic, we are left with the extreme alternatives of Buddhist (including other Far-Eastern forms) and Christian "selflessness"; in other words, on the one hand, trinitarian love and, on the other hand, a compassion that regards the creature's suffering as essentially intractable. The Buddhist view sees the "being for itself" of the individual I as an embodiment of its fatal egoism; it calls for the elimination of this individual I. The Christian view sees the individual I as an *imago Trinitatis* in which each hypostasis exists solely for the sake of the others and can only understand itself in that context. A religion of *nirvana* and the equally void *samsara* (which can be equated with one another in their nothingness) cannot grasp what *kenosis* means in Christian terms, although it is so close as to touch it. In the area of Pneumatology it could be fruitful to conduct a dialogue between these two views—which, given God's Incarnation, on the one hand, and the avatar, on the other, could not be more diverse.[18]

One difficulty of all missionary work is the fact that the truth of the Christian revelation cannot be embraced in its fullness apart from its prehistory, that is, the experience of Israel. Every "inculturation" that attempts to replace Christianity's prehistory with the history of a particular culture will necessarily fail to attain the catholicity of Christian culture and introduce some kind of nationalization of Christianity. Hitler's "German Christians" should be a constant warning for us here.

Finally we can have recourse to the Church's "social teaching", particularly in the form it has adopted in the philosophy

---

[18] For an initial sketch of this kind of dialogue, cf. the writings of Masao Abe, which are discussed in H. Waldenfels, *Absolutes Nichts* (Herder, 1980), 92f., 25f., 210f. On this whole topic: Maurus Heinrichs, *Christliche Offenbarung und religiöse Erfahrung im Dialog* (Paderborn, 1984).

and theology of John Paul II, which sees things simultaneously at the level of a "philosophical" anthropology and at the level of their "theological", Christian fulfillment—a fundamentally dialogical mode of proceeding. To do this is not to cover over the yawning gulf that separates the two levels: there remains the distinction between the "peace that the world gives" and the peace of Christ, "which the world cannot give", but the latter has, of itself, an anthropological content without which genuine peace is unthinkable in the world. Christianity does have its political and economic consequences (on which "liberation theology" stakes its whole program), but it is impossible, on the basis of the world's categories and ignoring the eschatological dimension, to construct any synthesis.

It is precisely at this point that that charisma of the Holy Spirit intervenes which Paul designates the discernment of spirits (1 Cor 12:10).

In his book *Der heilige und der unheilige Geist*,[19] Wilhelm Dantine has set forth the issues here on a wide canvas.[20] The Spirit, he says, has the function of "unveiling all the crucifying powers in their macabre godlessness and inhumanity": the Spirit, in the midst of history's riddles, possesses "the clarity of the Spirit". While Dantine, a Protestant, targets "the alleged possession of the Spirit by the institutional church",[21] he sees its prophetic ministry to the world functioning primarily, and authentically, wherever the chosen individual participates in a "hard" critical dialogue, which is new at each time in history; nonetheless, such dialogue must include the presentation of a genuinely trinitarian dogma,[22] even if this can only claim to be an anticipatory adumbration of some future state of mankind, in which true freedom will reign at last. Let us put it more simply: the final criterion by which a "discernment of spirits" is vindicated is this: whether secular power devotes itself to the pure service of Christian, powerless love or whether Christian love uses secular power in order (allegedly) to attain its purposes and goals. This

[19] *Über die Erneuerung der Urteilsfähigkeit* (Stuttgart: Radiusverlag, 1973).

[20] Although "resolutely turning away from the traditional Pneumatology of the Church hitherto" (115).

[21] Ibid., 175.

[22] Ibid., 249.

has been a problem ever since the "Constantinian shift",[23] and we see it in the Crusades, in the Inquisition, in the liquidation of the Jesuit missions (Paraguay and Peking), and in the various instances of political "restoration"; it is a problem today where mission is confused with propaganda in many "movements" that loudly advertise their Church credentials. Discernment of spirits must be active above all wherever "Satan disguises himself as an angel of light" (2 Cor 11:14), wherever a well-meaning Peter needs to be reprimanded and unmasked as a "Satan", that is, a tempter, because he is "not on the side of God, but of men" (Mt 16:22–23). Church institutions as such are no more satanic than any secular power administered with a sense of Christian responsibility;[24] but the tendency toward power, the tendency, in all personal and social areas, to slip out of the umbrella of the greater love and seek autonomy, calls for constant vigilance in the pneumatic discernment of spirits. And by "love", here, we do not mean a virtue to be wielded by human beings; rather, we mean that grace which needs constantly to be asked anew of the *Pater pauperum*, a grace that can only be received by those who are "poor in spirit" and can only be poured into hearts by God himself, as his own love in the Holy Spirit (Rom 5:5).[25]

c. Justification, Sanctification, Freedom

It may seem strange to allot these three themes to this first chapter, partly because justification is mostly treated as a primarily christological topic (and so it is inseparable from sanctification,

[23] Cf. Hernegger's distortedly one-sided, yet thought-provoking book *Macht ohne Auftrag* (Olten, 1963).

[24] Reinhold Schneider ceaselessly both affirmed this insight and called it into question, e.g., by regarding as irreducibly tragic the relationship between the one who wields power and the powerless saint.

[25] Again, this does not prevent a "Pneumatology from below" being constructed and offered to non-Christians, as we have already seen in our discussion of what constitutes true "selflessness". Hermann Bertrams tried to do something of this sort in his celebrated work (largely shunned nowadays) *Das Wesen des Geistes nach der Anschauung des Apostels Paulus* (Münster: Aschendorff, 1913). In it, he discusses pneuma as part of the natural man, pneuma and psyche, pneuma as a supernatural power, as the power of the Christian life, pneuma in the recipient of grace, pneuma as divine nature, pneuma as a Divine Person. This ascending path should not be dismissed as illegitimate from the very outset.

a task attributed particularly to the Holy Spirit) but also because freedom, in the New Testament, is regarded as primarily an ec-clesiological topic (and at the same time, in Paul and John, it is intimately connected with the Holy Spirit).

Nonetheless, as we stressed at the beginning, it must be re-membered that God's work of reconciling the world to himself in Christ applies to the cosmos as a whole, even if this work is particularly manifest and fruitful in the Church, Christians being necessarily the "heralds" of this universal reconciliation with the task of urging men to reconcile themselves with the God who is already reconciled (2 Cor 5:20; cf. the "much more" of Romans 5:10). Here again we can see the Church's twofold thrust.

The three themes will not be treated exhaustively here, but only insofar as they relate to the Spirit's role—which is insep-arable from the work of reconciliation and liberation that the Father performs in the Son. Although, as we have shown, Paul was at pains to interpret Christ's function as the hinge of the en-tire creation (Col 1:15–17) on the basis of his Cross (Col 1:20) and of his being the "head of the . . . church" (Col 1:18; Eph 2:22f.), he also says in Colossians 2:10 that Christ is the "head of all rule and authority" in the cosmos. The context shows that he has subjected all cosmic powers to his own authority —in fact, they were subject to him in principle ever since the creation (Col 1:17)—and he has stripped them of their indepen-dent power as a result of his act of reconciliation (Col 2:15). On the one hand, this means that "in the body of the Redeemer" (who has consummated the reconciliation of the universe in his own body: Eph 2:14) "we experience the 'body' of the creation" (Schlier);[26] on the other hand, though with the same meaning, it can be said that "it is not cosmic powers that form the body of Christ but the Church alone" (Gnilka).[27] The purpose of this in the context of Colossians is to reassure the community: even the powers, which Christ controls, cannot prevent them from

[26] Article "Kephale", in ThW III, 680.

[27] Kolosserbrief (Herder, 1980), 131. Schlier adds, "when the Church, as his Body, endeavors to draw the world into herself, she is only trying to embrace what is her own. That is why the Church concerns us, individually and all together" (ThW III, 680). This underlines once again the Church's profoundly missionary function.

having a share in the fullness of the Godhead that dwells in Christ (2:11–15).

It does not matter whether the main accent of Christ's reconciling act is placed on his Incarnation (Irenaeus), on his "redemption" of mankind from the powers (Origen), or on the satisfaction he has made for sins (from Cyprian, via Augustine, to Anselm and Thomas): in terms of Spirit-Christology it will always be the ever-present Spirit who operates in the being and work of the Son. This is quite evident in the case of his conception in Mary and his entire ministry in the wake of his Baptism, so it must apply equally, in redemption and atonement theology, to his Passion. For it cannot be denied that Jesus was accompanied by the Spirit; hence "the Holy Spirit has entered into New Testament salvation history."[28] Thus Hebrews 9:14 —which could seem somewhat isolated—should be interpreted as referring to the Holy Spirit,[29] as Thomas Aquinas does,[30] following Peter Lombard: "How much more [than the blood of animals] shall the blood of Christ, who through the eternal Spirit offered himself without blemish to God, purify your conscience from dead works to serve the living God."[31] Jesus' surrendering of the Spirit (of his mission) to the Father at the end of his earthly mission (Lk 23:46) points in the same direction, as does his breathing forth of the Spirit to the world and the Church (*inclinato capite emisit spiritum*, Jn 19:30). Hebrews 9:14 mentions blood and Spirit in the same verse: this can be understood in connection with the Johannine threesome of the witness of the Spirit, the water, and the blood (1 Jn 5:8), that is also entirely consonant with the Pauline view.

It follows that the Spirit has a substantial share in the reconciliation between God and the world and between heaven and

---

[28] Mühlen, UMP 242, who goes on to sketch a "history of the Holy Spirit" in the life of Jesus and later in the Church (247ff., 257ff.).

[29] And not, as C. Spicq suggests (*Hébreux* II [1953]), to the divine nature ("esprit d'éternité").

[30] "Causa quare Christus sanguinem suum fudit . . . fuit Spiritus Sanctus, cujus motu et instinctu, scilicet caritate Dei et proximi hoc fecit" (*In Hebr.* 9, lect. 3).

[31] "Spirit is short for the Holy Spirit. . . . In this sacrificial act, too, Christ is governed by the objectivity of the Holy Spirit; the Holy Spirit is . . . the power that supports his office and sacrifice" (O. Michel, *Hebräer*, 12th ed. [Göttingen, 1966], 344. UMP 274ff.).

earth (Col 1:20) that is effected in *acto primo* by the body of Jesus on the Cross (2 Cor 5:19). This act of God, which is prior to all human decision, must be seen as the antecedent and precondition for all instances of the justification of individuals; as a principle, it is initially universal and (in the narrower sense) socio-ecclesiological, and on this basis the justification of each individual person is already part of an interpersonal context. Personal justification is never private. If the *pro nobis* of Christ's reconciling deed is taken seriously, we must say that even in this very first deed a burden of sin is lifted from mankind, although mankind is not in a position to see this objective deliverance for what it is (and hence take this new opportunity to seize hold of personal freedom). Initially it is only accessible to faith, as is its dialectical opposite, "original sin". That inherent compulsion in the sinner, insofar as he is really turned away from God, that makes him incapable of turning back to God by his own strength is fundamentally taken away from him—which does not at all mean that he can actually turn toward God by his own strength of will (in the Pelagian sense). Just as, in principle, what we call the "wrath of God" (Jn 3:36) is lifted when the Crucified One ("by the eternal Spirit") transforms the alienation, making it the form of his uttermost love for the Father; now God's offer of love to the sinner, whereby he invites him to join in his reconciliation with the world, effects a real change in the sinner's relationship with God.[32] The Church's task is to proclaim this invitation, the proffered gift of the Spirit of freedom, *gratia liberatrix*: ". . . God making his appeal through us. We beg you on behalf of Christ, be reconciled to God" (2 Cor 5:20).

At this point, however, between the initial offer and its acceptance in the act of faith that justifies, we must interpose some clarification concerning human freedom by briefly recapitulating *Theo-Drama* II, 189–316. There we showed that genuine creaturely freedom (*autoexousion*, what Thomas calls *sui causa*), which is finite—because it had a beginning and has yet to reach its fulfillment—can only understand itself in the context of some Infinite toward which, in self-transcendence, it tends. Plato calls this Infinite the Good; the Bible calls it God in his absolute

---

[32] K. Rahner, article "Rechtfertigung", in *Sacr. Mundi* IV (1969), 46.

freedom. Creation itself is mysterious in that God's absolute freedom is so free that it can create genuine, albeit relative, freedom; but it is heightened by the covenant, for here God's absolute freedom is surrendered as a gift, both looking for and facilitating the partner's free response of love without exerting the least compulsion.[33] Israel could turn away to its idols, or it could take possession of God's loving commandments and try to fulfill them (as "Law") in its own strength, even though theoretically, in the "Shema", it already knew the only true response, the response of love. The Psalms plead for this loving self-giving, and it was actually attempted in an inchoate manner by the "poor of Yahweh"; but the full response that transformed the temporal covenant into the "eternal covenant" was given on the Cross of Christ. This changes man's relationship with God: God's Spirit is offered to man in a new way,[34] as we see from the fact that henceforth both the Spirit *and* Christ's "blood" are "poured out" in the Church. Only in this way can the Spirit be present in the cosmos. In respect of the world, the Spirit is now the "Spirit of truth"; thus offered to mankind, he reveals the loving relationship between Father and Son.

Now we can discern the structure of the second and final form of justification: God's liberating freedom personally accepts whatever may be entailed by it, and the Spirit lets himself be poured into our hearts, simultaneously incorporating us into the (now fluid) Body of Christ. Thus each of us is given an utterly personal mission (charisma) for the sake of the unlimited totality of this "Body". "Freedom from" (our egoistic drives and passions) is only the springboard for a "freedom for" that issues from the innermost center of our freedom and our personal endowments—and here the Pauline concept of freedom shows itself to be identical with a readiness to minister to the universal—so that that we can say, with Hegel, that all genuine

[33] In *Theo-Drama*, II, 227, we quoted Pico della Mirandola: "The divine, moving Spirit constantly urges your spirit forward. . . . If you let him have his way, you will be brought to God. . . . This is real blessedness, being one spirit together with God and thus possessing God in God and not in us; it is knowing as we are known."

[34] Texts in W. Warnach, article "Freiheit" in *Hist. Wörterbuch der Philosophie* II (1972), 1071f.

personal freedom seeks and acknowledges the freedom of all, yours no less than mine. This is the basis of the freedom of the Church (from the world) and also of the state (from all kinds of despotism) insofar as the state is subject to the rule of law. However, the most interior mode of receiving our freedom from the Holy Spirit remains that open readiness which is the effect of the Spirit's grace. This is also (by reciprocal causation) what makes it possible for human freedom to be in-formed by divine freedom: it is a readiness in the all-embracing Pauline and Johannine sense, that is, it is that *faith* which allows the truth of God's love to be true for us and in us (Gal 2:20; 1 Jn 5:1–4, 10–12). And since God's freedom is not formless but has a particular profile and is "for us" (in the covenant fulfilled by Christ), our free readiness to enter his freedom also implies that we are ready to embrace a particular mission. Carrying out this mission is part and parcel of the gift of freedom: it is a duty and privilege; and thereby the gift of our personal freedom is both proved and perfected. What looks like dependence on God's particular will is in reality a being drawn into divine freedom.

This sheds light on the riddle of why creaturely freedom (if it is genuine freedom!) cannot liberate itself vis-à-vis God. Augustine and even Luther admit that the creature can take decisions in temporal matters; but it cannot perform that fundamental conversion or turnaround (*epistrophē*) and bring about reconciliation with God by its own volition. Many of the ancient Greeks had an inkling that this was impossible. Thus Plotinus, for example, links conversion with the insight that, in order to be free, we must be descended from the One who is his own cause and being (*autoousia*); Proclus defines freedom as man's free readiness to serve God (*ethelodouleia*) and Iamblichus defines freedom as the release (*lysis*) from the necessities of nature: "This takes place decisively through the act of surrender to the sole Divinity, whereby the divinizing power gains the upper hand in man's soul." The Bible consummates this insight: Created freedom is dependent: it is a gift, in which the Origin of this created freedom becomes operative in it, freeing it from its obstinate attempts to "absolutize" itself. This can be seen most easily in the concept of sanctification: God alone is holy; no creature could or would attribute substantial holiness to itself (nor could it do so on the basis of a self-produced conversion) in order to acquire a share in the divine holiness. That is why the divine Spirit of holiness is required, for he alone, as the ancient anti-Arian treatises so conclusively stressed, can "anoint" the finite spirit with divine holiness. And, as the Second Council of Orange tirelessly insists, even the yearning for such a conversion cannot come about except through the prevenient "inspiration of the Holy Spirit", which "turns our will from disloyalty to faith and trust".

> Anyone who says that we obtain mercy from God without his grace but by believing, willing, yearning, endeavoring, laboring, praying, watching, striving, pleading, seeking, and knocking, and fails to confess that all this takes place through the infusion and inspiration of the Holy Spirit; and who makes the assistance of grace depend on man's humility and docility instead of acknowledging that our obedience and humility is a pure gift of grace—such a person contradicts the word of the Apostle, who says, "What have you that you did not receive?" and "by the grace of God I am what I am." (DS 375, 376)

This also shows that justification both has a history and runs toward a goal. Often enough, within his striving for the goal, the individual, while he is in principle liberated, can lag behind the task he has been given and hence fail to reach his personal full development. In other and better words: he can lag behind full participation in God's holiness. Thus he can be *simul justus et peccator* in a truly Catholic sense: not in the sense of a dialectic of contradiction (*Theo-Logic* II, 335–45), but in failing to produce the "fruits of the Spirit" that the justified (and hence sanctified) man should yield; this results from some kind of return to his own "I", whereas Jesus teaches that he should utterly lose this "I" (by exercising love) and so "gain" himself. The history of grace, understood as the Spirit's grace entering us, has not only levels of penetration but also—and the Council of Trent puts great value on this—preliminary stages: here the sinner is helped by the proffered "actual" grace to open himself to that faith or consent whereby the Spirit (by dispensing his "sanctifying grace") inwardly heals the free human being and so makes him a "child of God" by being reborn "of God".

No man, and no Christian, can say that he has "obtained this" (Phil 3:12); he knows that he is only on the way toward it.

While he has indeed been overtaken by God's grace (ibid.), he himself has not caught up with grace. In what way, then, is the New Covenant, the Church, qualitatively different from the Old Covenant, which was also "on the way toward" the fulfillment? The New Covenant, the Church, must differ from the Old in that it is based on a perfect act of faith; this was necessary so that God's Word could take flesh in her unrestricted and willing consent. In Mary the Church is the *immaculata* (Eph 5:27); she must be immaculate, not only for the sake of the Incarnation, but also for the sake of him who is to be received into his "Body", which is the Church. The Church must be perfect at some point if the Church is to be the "Body" of the "Head" and the "Bride" of the "Bridegroom": this is what makes it possible for all other believers, inwardly linked together as members, "to attain to . . . mature manhood, to the measure of the stature of the fulness of Christ. . . . We are to grow up in every way into him who is the head, Christ" (Eph 4:13–15).[35] All this, however, takes place *en heni pneumati*, in the one Spirit (Eph 2:18).

We have not mentioned one central problem of justification, namely, how the unjust man, a sinner, who is turned away from God, can become "the justice of God" (2 Cor 5:21)—not merely forensically, that is, by being declared just, but by acquiring justice as something that is his own—without denying and overthrowing everything we understand of justice in the world. Can divine love go beyond the sphere of justice without at the same time "sublating" (in the positive sense) and absorbing it?[36] This raises the question of the ethical foundations of forgiveness, which will be treated separately elsewhere.

---

[35] Following the translation and interpretation of H. Schlier (*Epheser*, 190). "The final goal is Christ, the Head of the universe. This goal is irrevocably linked to the growth of the Church. The edification of the universe always implies the edification of the Church, and vice versa" (206). Despite F. Mußner's critique of Schlier (*Christus, das All und die Kirche*, 2d ed. [Trier, 1968]), he acknowledges the crucial point here: "What the universe and the Church have in common is the exalted Christ" (168).

[36] How are we to understand the Council of Trent's statement that Christ is the "causa meritoria" of our justification, while "misericors Deo gratuito abluit et sanctificat" (DS 1329)?

2

FROM THE *CIVITAS DEI*
TO THE CHURCH

This section can be seen as a corollary to the foregoing one. As we saw, the universality of the salvation that God offers the world in Christ has as its consequence the twofold movement of the Church to the world and from the world to the Church. From the point of view of the Holy Spirit, this consequence was necessary, since he both blows where he wills, that is, wherever God wishes to extend his work in Christ, but also wherever the Risen One breathes his Spirit and thus entrusts his Church with a mission "to all nations". This dynamic unity of the Church, which to the world seems purely particular and yet itself claims catholicity, addresses a multifaceted question to Christians and to mankind; many attempts at an answer have been made, and here we shall examine three of them.

a. *Augustine's* Civitas Dei

Augustine's world-embracing synthesis has rightly been called the first Christian theology of history.[1] Its whole concept is so universal that the *civitas Dei* that pursues its "pilgrim" path on earth is only a (middle) segment of its totality that is found in heaven; in the ancient world, by contrast, both *civitas* and polity were certainly religious but (both in Athens and Rome) were also particular in their juridical basis.[2] There were, of course, several universalizing tendencies before Augustine. The first was doubtless the Platonic *politeia*, which, while Plato conceived it as an ideal state, he himself endeavored to make a reality. Then there were the great political enterprises of Alexander (which Plutarch interpreted as an attempt at a universal state) and

---

[1] É. Gilson, *Les Métamorphoses de la Cité de Dieu* (Louvain/Paris, 1952), 68–69.

[2] On these two fundamental qualities, the religious and the juridical, cf. J. Ratzinger, *Volk und Haus Gottes in Augustins Lehre von der Kirche* (Munich, 1954), 255ff.

Augustus, whose universal *pax* had a new religious character (Virgil). On an entirely different track there was the Jewish universalism in God's world-embracing covenant with Noah and in the covenant with Abraham, from whom, somehow or other, all the (surrounding) nations were descended and in whom they were to "bless" themselves. In Christianity, in accordance with the universal visions of the Kingdom of Christ (1 Cor 15:25: Christ "must reign until he has put all his enemies under his feet"), there were the universal claims of Tertullian and the *Epistle to Diognetus*. The former links up with the universal vision of the Stoics (which is no longer an earthly and political vision), in which the *civitas* and homeland was no longer the *oikumene* but the cosmos in its entirety (thus Marcus Aurelius: men are "members of that supreme City in which all other cities are as households": III, 11) and cries out: "Unam omnium rem publicam agnoscimus: mundum."[3] The latter sees Christians as the soul of the earthly and political world:

> They cannot be distinguished from the other men whose *poleis* they inhabit and whose language they speak . . . , and yet they manifest a strange and paradoxical behavior in their *politaiai*. They are at home everywhere, and every home is an exile to them. They obey the established laws, and yet, by their manner of life, they outstrip what is purely legal. They love all men and are persecuted by all. In short: what the soul is to the body, Christians are to the world. The Christians are held in the prison of the world, yet it is they who hold the world together.[4]

Scholz rightly comments: "It is a cosmopolitanism on an a-cosmic basis."[5] We can discern two elements in this universalism: the immanence of the transcendent "Kingdom of God" in the earthly kingdom (which thus gives it ultimate meaning and form) but, at the same time, the conflict and persecution it suffers.

The second source is, of course, as Augustine himself says, the Holy Scriptures of the Old and New Covenants (from the

---

[3] *Apologeticum* 38.

[4] *Epistle to Diognetus* V–VI.

[5] *Glaube und Unglaube in der Weltgeschichte: Ein Kommentar zu Augustins De Civitate Dei* (Leipzig, 1911), 95.

"Gloriosa dicta sunt de te, civitas Dei" [Ps 87:3], to the descent of the holy *civitas* Jerusalem from God at the end of the Apocalypse [Rev 21:2]).[6] Scripture sets the pattern by setting the two *civitates* against one another in the symbolism of Jerusalem and Babylon.

Then we come to the amazing passage in the commentary on the Apocalypse (of which only fragments have survived) written by Tyconius, to whom Augustine owed many a crucial inspiration: "There are two *civitates*: God's and the devil's. . . . The one wishes to serve the world, the other to serve Christ. The one wishes to serve the world, the other wishes to flee from it. . . . The one kills, and the other is killed. . . . Both *civitates* show the same zeal, one in the pursuit of damnation, the other in the pursuit of salvation."[7] This gives the basic outline of Augustine's work in a nutshell. (Tyconius died in 390; Augustine began his work in 412 at the age of fifty-eight.)

It can be asked whether Augustine, during his ministry, changed his idea of the *civitas* by moving from the notion (based on Cicero) of a society founded on justice[8] to a definition on the model of reciprocal love;[9] at any rate we can leave this question open here. More important is the question, "How universal is the *civitas* he envisions?"—and it must be regretted that the possibility of any such universality is vitiated by his a priori system of predestination. However earnestly he may urge the citizens of the City of God to put a Christian shape on the secular state, and however positive a description he can sometimes give of a Christian emperor, his system of predestination compels him—

---

[6] A wealth of references in ibid., 71.

[7] On Revelation 3:12 and 21:2. In G. Bardy, article "Tyconius", in DTC XV/2 (1946), 1934. The expression *duae civitates* already exists in the Pseudo-Clementine literature, where God appoints kings who are mutually antagonistic: one is faithful, the other is transitory; one is King of the coming Kingdom, the other the king of this present age (*Recogn.* II, 2; *Hom.* VIII, 21; *Hom.* XX, 2).

[8] Which (as in the case of Sallust) involves saying that the latter-day Rome does not possess true justice and hence is no longer the true *civitas*; true justice is henceforth to be found in the *Civitas Christi* (*Civ. Dei* II, 21, 4; PL 41, 68). Cf. the Ciceronian definition: "Populum esse . . . coetum multitudinis, *juris* consensu et utilitatis communione sociatum" (ibid., XIX, 21, 1 [648]).

[9] "Populus est coetus multitudinis rationalis, rerum quas *diligit* ratione sociatus" (ibid., XIX, 24 [655]).

given the divergent orientations of the two *civitates* (namely, *caritas* and *cupiditas*)—to conclude that these two orientations are bound for opposite ultimate destinies. As a result, the *civitas terrena* must constitute at least a shadowy anticipation of the *civitas diaboli*.[10] This constitutes a considerable handicap for those who, with Augustine[11] and in opposition to Protestant scholars (who like to make the greatest possible separation between the *civitas Dei* and the visible Catholic Church), endeavor practically to equate these two realities.[12] Even in the Church, as Augustine well knows, there are many who are citizens of the "worldly state", for the Church is a *societas permixta*. Edgar Salin was right in saying that "it would be a serious misunderstanding simply to equate the Kingdom of God and the Church. . . . The *civitas* is represented on earth, and that manifestation, that 'representation', is the Church of Christ." As we know, it was in order to defend this *civitas* (after the scandal of Rome's collapse in the face of Attila) that "the great drama" was written; "thus, in certain places in Augustine's work, and at certain times in history, *civitas Dei* can and must mean 'Church'." "Church" here must be understood in Christian terms, "Christian in the strict sense of the divine *life* of Christ. That is why, ever since the foundation of the Church, there is no access to the Kingdom of God except through the Church."[13]

[10] Ibid., XXI, 1; XVII, 20, 2.

[11] "Civitas Dei quae est sancta ecclesia" (*In Ps.* 98:4).

[12] F. Hoffmann, *Der Kirchenbegriff des Hl. Augustinus* (Munich, 1933), 485–516. J. Ratzinger, *Volk und Haus Gottes*, 279, 294f., with the necessary qualifications, 296ff. Many interpreters put forward the view that Augustine equated the *civitas Dei* and the Church in *Civ. Dei* XX, 9: W. Kamlah, together with Karl Müller (*Kirche und Reich Gottes bei Augustin* [1928]) produced a thorough and convincing refutation of this view, relocating this passage in the whole context of Augustine's eschatological teaching: "Ecclesia und regnum Dei bei Augustin", *Philologus*, 1938, 248–64.

[13] E. Salin, *Civitas Dei* (Tübingen, 1926), 180. É. Gilson, in his article "Église et Cité de Dieu chez Saint Augustin", *Archives d'Histoire doctrinale et littéraire du moyen âge* 1953 (Vrin, 1954), 5–23, showed irrefutably that, against the background of Augustine's teaching on predestination, the *civitas Dei* and the earthly Church cannot be identical, since the latter is expressly *permixta*, i.e., she has elements that are destined to perish, whereas this is impossible in the case of the former. So when, on several occasions, Augustine equates or at least seems to equate the two, he must be referring only to those of the Church's members who are predestined

However, can the universality of the *civitas Dei*—understood as an attitude of love that unites heaven and earth—be substantiated on the basis of the universal saving act of Christ, as is the case with Augustine's other works? Hardly. And can the history of the covenant be seen as pointing to Christ if the Old Testament is primarily associated with the *civitas terrena*? It is true that Augustine is aware of individual pagans—but only from the time before Christ—who, on account of their attitude, are to be reckoned as belonging to the City of God, but they remain exceptions; Augustine is very far from allowing the City of God to have the same extension as the objective scope of Christ's saving act.

The two opposing states are present in potentiality in Adam as we see him in paradise: they diverge in the figures of Cain and Abel. So we see the emergence, in Augustine, of the theologoumenon of an *Ecclesia ab Abel*,[14] although he does not explicitly treat it as such.[15] In the framework of the *civitas Dei*, the Church of the Old and New Testaments remains an episode. This all finds its genuine center in the magnificent concept of sacrifice found in *Civitas Dei* X, 6, where love is understood as surrender to God and thus everything gathers around the central sacrifice of Christ, "ut tota ipsa redempta Civitas, hoc est congregatio societasque sanctorum, universale sacrificium offeratur Deo per sacerdotem magnum." Since love is here interpreted as sacrifice,[16] and there is a focus on the Church (and, in particular, the Holy Spirit), we can discern the connection between the *civitas Dei* and Augustine's doctrine of the Church and of

---

to blessedness, who live "according to the Spirit", not "according to the flesh"— even if, on occasion, he speaks of Christ as the "King and Founder of the Christian religion, the *civitas Dei* itself" (*Civ. Dei* XVII, 4, 2). Even those predestined for perdition can have received baptism. Of course it is the earthly Church's task to promote the Kingdom of God or the city of God, but the "Church from below" does this only partially, whereas the "Church from above" actually corresponds with the *civitas Dei*. The two concepts never attain a "true identity" (21).

[14] Y. Congar, "Ecclesia ab Abel", in *Abhandlungen über Theologie und Kirche*, Festschrift Karl Adam (1952), 79–108.

[15] Texts from Augustine are given in Congar, ibid., 84. Augustine's writings subsequently found great resonance in Leo I and Gregory the Great.

[16] J. Ratzinger, *Volk und Haus Gottes*, 197–215.

ecclesial office;[17] but here the unity is something more than a convergence of individual themes, as is usually the case with Augustine.

b. Paul's Parable of the Cultivated Olive Tree

Paul takes us in an entirely different direction when he sees Christ's universal position and act ("in him all things hold together" Col 1:17) as grounding the totality of the "Body of Christ"—a unity consisting of the Abrahamic covenant and the covenant fulfilled in Christ; the latter, by uniting Jews and Gentiles, constitutes the "Pleroma" of Christ who fills all in all.

Both the theology of history presented in Romans 9–11 and the letters Paul wrote from prison insist on Israel's prerogative. Israel is the "holy root" (see Rom 11:16), the nation that was first made an "heir" (cf. Eph 1:11–14). The faith of Abraham, it is insisted, plays a foundational role for both Jews and Gentiles, for Abraham was granted justification even as a Jew, albeit "before circumcision": "the purpose was to make him the father of all who believe without being circumcised and who thus have righteousness reckoned to them" (Rom 4:11). Abraham's fatherhood antedates the accession of the Gentiles by a lengthy interval; it puts the seal of universality, so to speak, on the Abrahamic covenant, which is reaffirmed by the image of the olive tree: the Gentile branches cut from "from a wild olive tree" are only "grafted" onto the cultivated olive, and so they must remember that "it is not you that support the root, but the root that supports you" (Rom 11:18). If the cutting off of the Jewish branches demonstrates "the severity of God", the branches that have been grafted on should, with profound humility, consider "the goodness of God", who is perfectly able to graft the natural branches "back into their own olive tree" (11:24).

Pursuing this metaphor one can ask (with Jewish theologians, but also with Karl Barth): Does not speaking of an "Old" and a "New" Covenant suggest that there are two different covenants with God—and if this is the case, does it not obscure the unity

---

[17] F. Genn, *Trinität und Amt nach Augustinus* (Einsiedeln: Johannesverlag, 1986), 227ff., 237ff. On the topic of "Christ, the Spirit, and the Church": 254–55.

of election of the People of God? And is there not, in the "Old" Covenant, a succession of new covenants, which find their fulfillment with the advent of the promised Messiah, the "heir" promised to Abraham (Gal 3:16) and whose day Abraham longed to see? "He saw it and was glad" (Jn 8:56).[18] No one has laid greater stress on Israel's abiding substance in the Church than Cardinal Lustiger, Archbishop of Paris, a man who in no way considers that, in becoming a Christian, he has stopped being a Jew. He sees his Jewishness fulfilled in the conception of Jesus as the Messiah. "In God's eyes the totality of humanity is Israel and the nations; ultimately they are to be united into one single nation."[19] As he goes on to say, this is an eschatological affirmation. However, "the New Testament cannot be understood unless it is seen to be grounded on the call of the Jews, the call of Israel, the call of Christ with regard to the Gentiles. This is the basic fact of the Christian faith."[20] With regard to Isaiah 53, "the term 'son' has both a collective and a personal meaning."[21]

All this is undeniable. "Salvation is from the Jews" (Jn 4:22). But this "totality", which envelops the fullness of the nations entering the covenant, has an express forward direction ("sense" means "direction"): all biblical texts agree that Israel will only find its fulfillment if its river flows toward Christ; and this river will grow deeper and broader than what Israel, through its multiplicity of irreconcilable images, is expecting. For Israel's whole meaning is to be found exclusively in the Messiah who fulfills. This becomes clear from two facts: first, the fact that there is an irreversible relationship between Abraham (the root) and Christ (the cornerstone on which all else rests and of whom Moses wrote, [cf. Jn 5:46], considering "abuse suffered for the Christ greater wealth than the treasures of Egypt" [Heb 11:26]).

---

[18] S. Talmon, "Der Gesalbte Jahwes", in *Jesus-Messias? Heilserwartungen bei Juden und Christen* (Regensburg: Pustet, 1982), 27–68. K. Barth, *Church Dogmatics* II/2 (Edinburgh, 1957), 233–62: If and when "Israel becomes obedient to its election by rising to life in the Church", its identity will be maintained, i.e., its identity as the Church's secret source, as the hidden substance that makes the Church the community of God.

[19] "Nos racines juives", in *Osez croire, osez vivre* (Gallimard: Centurion, 1986), 70.

[20] "Antisémitisme: l'irrationel", ibid., 107.

[21] Ibid., 113.

It will never be right to say that Christ is grafted onto Abraham, since everything, including Abraham, exists through him.
Second, there is the fact that the promise of the Holy Spirit
is only fulfilled once Jesus has accomplished his earthly work.
Lustiger is well aware of this: "The disciples only understand
from that moment when they receive what they are to communicate to mankind of the Passion and Resurrection of Christ.
The promised gift is the Holy Spirit, who changes men's hearts.
The Spirit causes hearts to 'burn' and changes stony hearts into
hearts of flesh according to Ezekiel's prophecy."[22]

There is a lively fellowship between the *ecclesia ex gentibus* and
the *ecclesia ex circumcisione*, as we can see most clearly from the
symbolism of the Apocalypse, where we find the twenty-four elders of the twelve tribes of the Old Covenant and the twelve disciples of the New; the twelve gates of the heavenly Jerusalem bear
the names of the twelve tribes of Israel, whereas on the twelve
foundation stones "the twelve names of the twelve apostles of
the Lamb" were inscribed (Rev 21:12–14). Moreover, heaven
reveals the Temple and the altar of incense, but the whole book
of world history is nonetheless only opened and deciphered by
"the Lamb standing, as though it had been slain", and who sends
out the "seven spirits . . . into all the earth" (Rev 5:6). The number seven, the number of the Holy Spirit, runs throughout the
entire final book of the Bible, and the Spirit, in unity with the
Bride of the Lamb, utters together with her the eschatological
"Come!" (22:17). The heavenly Jerusalem is trinitarian.

Despite what we have said here under (a) and (b), the question can be raised: When does "Church"—in the full sense of
the word—come into being? In the covenant with Abraham?
Or in the Sinai covenant, when Israel is chosen to be a "nation
of priests" and called to be holy "because I am holy"? Does she
originate in the gift of the Spirit to the prophets or in the Spirit's
descent upon Mary or in Jesus' election of the disciples or when
he consecrates them to celebrate the Eucharist and (at Easter,
breathing upon them) gives them official authority to forgive
sins? Or should the Church's birthday be celebrated at Pente-

---

[22] Ibid., 119.

cost, when the apostles are finally empowered to go out into the whole world in virtue of "power from on high"? Should we imagine the Church developing slowly and gradually, parallel to the diverse and ever-more intensive forms of the Holy Spirit's presence and immanence? Such an idea, which would not need a particular point in time, must be rejected on the word of the fourth evangelist, for in John 7:37–39 he says that the Spirit, which is to come forth from the human and crucified body of Jesus as "rivers of living water", has not yet been given. According to this view, as S. Tromp has endeavored to show, the Church would have originated on the Cross, where "the Spirit, the water, and the blood" form a single witness; so that what, in John, is given in principle to the disciples at Easter would have been communicated experientially and fully to all at Pentecost. The existence of the pre-Easter Jesus, who alone is filled with the Spirit (and, as Head, bears within himself the whole fullness that is to be poured out on the Church), will "give birth" to the Church in his act of total self-giving in the *Triduum Paschale* —and not until then.

It is true, of course, that what we mean by "Church" (in its distinctive sense) is present, in principle, as a result of the Incarnation of the Word, accomplished by the Spirit. We can say that the Church is perfected on the Cross (and on Holy Saturday), when, on our behalf, Jesus undergoes the entire reality of sinful human existence right up to the dereliction of Sheol. Nonetheless, the event of the Incarnation itself—in which the "lowly" Maid, putting herself at heaven's disposal, is overshadowed by the Holy Spirit—is the precondition for all that follows. Mary's Yes on behalf of the whole human race, truly and archetypically representing mankind, has far-reaching effects: it is the first act in which God's covenant with mankind is fulfilled, and as such it remains unsurpassed. It remains present as a *Realsymbol* and is not eclipsed by the "creation", out of Christ, of the Church (as Christ's "Bride" and "Body"). The scene we find in John 19:25–27 is full of significance: it is "the mother of Jesus" standing beneath the Cross who, entrusted to the disciple, becomes the prototype and the personal center of the "bridal" Church. In other words, her motherhood (by the Holy Spirit)

bears the Church within herself potentially, just as Jesus (in the
Holy Spirit), as "Head" and endowed with all the *gratia capitis*,
bears the "Body" in himself potentially.[23]

This unity between the Spirit's overshadowing and the Word's
becoming flesh sheds light on the more distant relationship between the Old Covenant and the Church. In spite of the oft-
repeated statement of the Fathers (including Augustine) that the
genuinely just men of the Old Covenant (and individual pagans)[24] were already true members of the New Covenant and
hence of the Church, the "Synagogue" as such cannot be described as an inchoate Church. The Creed's "qui locutus est
per prophetas" shows that God's Word and God's Spirit were
present in the Synagogue. But it is clear from two complementary passages in the Epistles of Peter that this prophetic utterance
in its totality remained prospective (even when it spoke of Israel's present): 2 Peter 1:20f. insists, along with the entire New
Testament (Mk 12:36; Acts 3:21; 2 Tim 3:16), that "men moved
by the Holy Spirit spoke from God". First Peter 1:10–12, however, completes the picture in two ways: this Spirit at work in the
prophets is referred to as the "Spirit of Christ"; and, further, the
prophetic utterances were an initially obscure searching after the
ultimate future, that is, "the sufferings of Christ and subsequent
glory"—in other words, the prophecies were not primarily for

[23] Accordingly I would distance myself from the remarks of H. Mühlen (UMP),
who rejects (445f.) the view I expressed earlier. He makes frequent reference to
the need "to reintegrate Mary dogmatically into the Church" (461ff.) and to the
"progressive relegation of statements on Mary's mediatorship" in the compilation
of *Lumen Gentium* VIII (468ff.). He asserts that one "cannot say that the Church,
'as subject', is in Mary in an inchoate manner and is only 'perfected' subsequently
by the Holy Spirit." Nor can one say "that the Church that streams forth from
Christ has her 'personal center' in Mary" (460). There is insufficient reflection
here on the fact that Christ is indebted not only to the Old Covenant (G. Kokša,
*Die Lehre der Scholastiker des 16. und 17. Jahrhunderts von der Gnade und dem Verdienst
der alttestamentlichen Gerechten*, [Rome: Herder, 1955]) but also, supereminently, to
the Virgin's New Covenant Yes. Revelation 12 makes it clear that there is a unity
between the Old Covenant, Mary, and the Church. No doubt *Lumen Gentium* has
not uttered the last word on Mary's position in the unfolding of the Church. Note
that, in *Lumen Gentium* 2, the Church is "prepared" in the Old Testament and
"established" in the New, and here the "making manifest" (Pentecost) is distinct
from its "establishing".

[24] J. Daniélou, *Les Saints Païens de l'Ancien Testament* (Paris: Seuil, 1955).

their own time but for Christians and "for the preaching of the gospel in the power of the Holy (Pentecostal) Spirit that was sent from heaven". The Spirit in the Old Testament, like the Word in the Old Testament, is authentic Spirit but looks forward to that Holy Spirit who will be given definitively as the Interpreter of the gospel of the incarnate God. Thus the phrase "Ecclesia ab Abel" must be understood in a thoroughly dynamic and prospective sense.

However, just as the Old Covenant looks forward to the New, and Abraham looks forward to his "one" seed, Christ (Gal 3:16), there is a looking-forward to the Redeemer of all humanity— irrespective of any particular covenant. Thus in the "One" (and his concrete Church) we can also look back behind the Old Covenant that begins with Abraham to that covenant which God made, in Noah, with all humanity—and, indeed, with all creation, as we see in Christ (Col 1:15–20; Heb 1:1–3). In Jesus every particular covenant is "exploded" and opened up to the universality of creation, which is why his "Mystical Body", the Church (as we have already shown), has a universal scope in her mission to all nations, even if in world-time this universal scope is only manifest in particular, inchoate steps and stages. At the consummation the Church will not dissolve into the totality of (redeemed) creation: on the contrary, redeemed creation will be taken up into *her*, for she is and has always been *de jure* universal and Catholic. "By its light shall the nations walk; and the kings of the earth shall bring their glory into it, . . . they shall bring into it the glory and the honor of the nations" (Rev 21:24–26). Then it will be possible to say, "*Spiritus Domini replet orbem terrarum*; and that which holds all things together knows what is said" (Wis 1:7).

c. The Problem of "Corporate Personality"

It is questionable whether the concept of the "I-writ-large" (H. Mühlen) and of what is called "corporate personality" (H. Wheeler Robinson, J. de Fraine) has anything to contribute to the present issue. For there can be no doubt that its primary locus is a particular situation rooted in the history of civilization,

namely, the "extended family" that we see as a clear sociological feature in the Old Testament and that has echoes in subsequent periods. Here those who belong to this family, under the
leadership of its head, feel themselves to be a real unit vis-à-vis
isolated individuals or outcasts from the clan. (Of course the
family members *are* individual human beings; indeed, it may be
that they become full human beings only in such a context.)
Scholars continually point to a certain fluidity in this clan experience: the individual is not *only* an expression of the head who
holds the whole together; he is also a person in his own right;
but he is not *for himself*; he is in and with the other members.
Such a concept (prior to any notion of the democratic state) is
doubtless correctly described as an "early" or even a "primitive"
stage of civilization[25]—even if God's promise to the banished
Cain (Gen 4:15) should be a warning to us not to regard it as
absolute—but it is clear that the Old Testament elevates this
sociological reality into the religious sphere: ultimately, Israel's
"I-writ-large" is Yahweh himself, by whose "vital power" (A. R.
Johnson) the chosen people exists in grace.

However, once this category is cut loose from its sociological basis and applied to the New Testament and to Christ's relationship to his "Body", the Church, it must be considered
doubtful.[26] De Fraine justifies his view mainly with reference to
what he sees as reminiscences of the Old Covenant in the New.[27]
H. Mühlen, basing himself on Schnackenburg, thinks that Paul,

---

[25] "Primitive man's 'I' only exists as part of, or in identity with, the 'I-writ-large'
of society. The outcast thus succumbs to moral, psychic, and physical dissolution
and, hence, ruin. He no longer has an 'I'. He has lost a firm grasp on life". (S.
Mowinckel, *Psalmenstudien* I [Kristiania, 1921], 3).

[26] "Die alttestamentliche Vorstellung des 'Groß-ich' in der neutestamentlichen
Ekklesiologie": Mühlen, UMP 92–136.

[27] There may be similar social structures in the patriarchal realm: a man is converted and "believes, and all his house" (J. de Fraine, *Adam und seine Nachkommen*,
[Cologne, 1962], 202); or there may be concepts such as the "progenitor", the
capital city as "Mother", etc.; or the Mystical Body may be understood as the
"effulgence of Christ" (210); or "Christ" may be used to designate "sometimes
the individual person, Christ, and sometimes the totality of the faithful joined
together with Christ" (cf. 1 Cor 12:12) (215). This would exhibit the same "os-
cillation between two poles" as was observed in the religious sociology of the
Old Covenant (218).

"the learned Pharisee", would "at all events have been familiar" with the "I-writ-large", a "fundamental category of Pauline
thought";[28] Mühlen wants to show "that both metaphors, that
of the 'Body of Christ' and that of the 'People of God', are dependent on the Old Testament view of the 'I-writ-large' ".[29] This
being so, Christ (by analogy with Adam in the New Testament
view) would be a "universal personality": "Christ, the 'primal-I',
extends himself in the Church and so, as it were, attains his own
fullness."[30] This, however, seems to be over-stretching the faint
analogy between the "I-writ-large" in the Old Testament and the
"Christus totus" (Augustine) found in the New Testament. According to O. Cullmann, salvation history is like an hourglass,
getting narrower and more personalized as the Old Covenant
moves toward Christ, until God's covenant in Noah, Abraham,
and Moses, embracing all nations, is concentrated in the one person of Jesus; then—but issuing from him alone—it once again
spreads out to embrace the whole universe. Though chosen by
God, the "I-writ-large" in the Old Testament was only the representative of the people, and it was the people that was God's
partner. (The people, inchoately, was aware of this and knew
that it prefigured the one person of the Messiah.) By contrast,
when Jesus says "I", he is by no means the representative of a
group; it is by his own authority that he calls individuals to him,
and it is according to the Father's will that he acts as the representative of and bears responsibility "for many"; these "many"
are incorporated into the "one" (Gal 3:16, 28) in an entirely
different way, on his own free initiative.[31]

Mühlen, while he is aware of all this, passes it by, intent on
his own theological panorama; for he is writing, not a Christology, but a Pneumatology. Accordingly, he continually turns aside
from the idea of the individual believer's incorporation into the
Body of Christ insofar as by "the Body we mean the historical,
individual Christ",[32] since we are by no means incorporated into

---

[28] UMP 98.
[29] UMP 102.
[30] UMP 111 (according to Oepke).
[31] O. Cullmann, *Christus und die Zeit* (1946), 107ff.
[32] UMP 123, hence the warning against ecclesiological "monophysitism" (417)
and against a *communicatio idiomatum* between the Person of Christ and our persons.

the hypostatic union;[33] and he sees the "corporate" union between Christ and the Church (what Paul's prison epistles speak of as the union between "Head" and "Bride/Body") mediated primarily by the Holy Spirit. For, within the Trinity, the Holy Spirit—this is Mühlen's fundamental thesis—is already a Person in two Persons (Father and Son), and hence, in economic terms, he can be *one* Spirit in the Person of Christ and in the many persons of the faithful (who already exist as persons because they are creatures). "Within the 'I-writ-large'" the Spirit has "a mediating function between Christ and us . . . and is the principle of unity of the Body of Christ".[34] As we have already said, Mühlen rejects everything we have called "trinitarian inversion" with regard to the economy; in fact he goes so far as to give priority, within the Trinity, to "Sonship" over the Spirit's "spiration", which explains, in his view, the ultimate distinction between the Incarnation and the Church.[35] It follows that Christ, in the Holy Spirit, carries out his redemptive work on earth before (as the Exalted One) breathing forth the uncreated Spirit to fashion his Church; this Spirit will be the same uncreated Spirit in the Church as in him, "whereas created grace is by no means one and the same in Christ and in us, as was wrongly maintained by the so-called Panchristism".[36]

The significant question for us, however, is this: What is the relationship between the exalted Christ who rules over the entire cosmos and the Church articulated by his Spirit? It seems to be important here that Mühlen (in connection with *Unitatis Redintegratio* of Vatican II) tries to go beyond the structures of the Catholic Church and speak of an indwelling of the one Spirit of Christ in the "separated churches" also, seeing in them, not merely individual elements that actually belong to Catholic fullness, but an "anticipatory understanding" of what it means to

---

This is a frequent concern, esp. in section 7: "Die Differenz und der Zusammenhang zwischen Inkarnation und Kirche" (173–216).

[33] UMP 169, 168.

[34] UMP 195; accordingly, the Incarnation is logically prior to the Anointing (244).

[35] UMP 211.

[36] UMP 506.

be "Church".[37] Just as the totality of the divine reality is manifest "always only in a fragmentary way" even in the Catholic
Church,[38] we can assume that "the unity of the one Church
of Christ is primarily the continuation of that unity which the
Church had right from the start, a priori, in the one Pneuma
of the historical Jesus: it is not merely the subsequent unification of those churches that are now distinct bodies."[39] Thus the
Pneuma descends into the history of (sinful) human freedom
"in order to link men, existing in separated confessional bodies,
with Christ and with one another".[40]

On the basis of the foregoing discussion there are two questions to be put to the position roughly outlined here. One concerns the relationship of the universal, exalted Christ, Lord over
heaven, earth, and underworld (Phil 2:10), to the particularity
of his Spirit-articulated Church, which (in the second edition of
Una Mystica Persona) was subsequently expanded to the Church's
ecumenical arena. The question is this: Does this Pneumatology give sufficient thought to the relationship of the enspirited
Christ (who as such is the "life-giving Spirit": 1 Cor 15:45) to
the Spirit-dispensing Church? Has enough attention been paid to
the fundamentally missionary structure of the Catholic Church
and the other churches? This is part of the problem of the relationship between the Holy Spirit and the universal *Weltgeist*,
with which we shall deal later.[41]

[37] UMP 526.

[38] UMP 513-14.

[39] UMP 538. Mühlen is well aware that the integration of the question of sacramental office is central to the ecumenical dialogue, but he also rightly emphasizes
—and Catholics will take heart from this—that sacramental office cannot be separated from the Spirit (and from the handing on of the Spirit).

[40] UMP 475, 536-50.

[41] W. Kasper emphatically insists that the Spirit can blow outside the institutional Church: "Kirche als Sakrament des Geistes" in Kasper and Sauter, *Kirche—
Ort des Geistes* (Herder, 1976), 46ff. He sees this as a substantial corrective to that
ecclesiology which equated the Church and the Mystical Body of Christ (from
Augustine to *Mystici Corporis* [43]). It is only since Christ (through the Spirit)
becomes the *concretum universale* that meaningful dialogue is possible between the
Church and the world (36).—This topic is at least considered by Thomas, when
he speaks of different grades of belonging to the Church and says that Christ is the
Head of all men (*S. Th.* III, 8, 3), even of the angels (III, 8, 4), even if many men
belong to the Church only "potentia", "quae tamen est ad actum reducenda" (3c),

The second question arises from 1 Corinthians 10: Has enough attention been paid to the exalted, pneumatic Christ in his eucharistic self-surrender? Or, out of a distaste for "ecclesiological mysticism", has the eucharistic mystery been over-spiritualized? "The cup of blessing which we bless, is it not a participation in the blood of Christ? The bread which we break, is it not a participation in the body of Christ?" There may be a justified fear of entertaining a condemned doctrine here,[42] and it is clear that a naturalism of this kind would dissolve the eucharistic mystery. Nonetheless, the question remains and leads us on immediately to the next section.

"quae quidem potentia . . . fundatur principaliter in virtute Christi" (3 ad 1). Of course this "potentia" lacks that visibility which belongs to the Church *in actu*. Here (as will become clear in what follows) it is not a question of a mere "incarnational Christology" that would envisage all human natures incorporated in the one human nature of Jesus: what is being aimed at is a soteriological (and hence pneumatological) doctrine of the relationship between Christ and the Church.

[42] Cf. K. Pelz's book *Der Christ als Christus* (Berlin, n.d. [1939]) indexed under 1940; its fundamental thesis is "Christ and Christians constitute one single Person" (137). UMP 48.

3

SON AND SPIRIT IN THE CHURCH

a. "The Lord Is the Spirit"

The question posed in the foregoing section concerned the co-extensive relationship of the work of Christ and of the Spirit in the work of world redemption. The answer given was twofold: first came the work of the Passion of the Son through his bloody self-sacrifice "in the eternal Spirit" (Heb 9:14). This was then followed by the handing over of the Spirit by the Son, whereby he gave this Spirit, from the Father, to a Church speaking in a language that all peoples could understand, a Church that is sent out to all nations, to the ends of the earth. This sending, this mission, is itself a work of the Son, who promised that he would be with the Church all the days, to the end of the world; in other words, he explained that his departure would be characterized by a constant "coming". This same mission, however, was equally a result of the imparting of a Spirit who would not speak on his own authority but who would constantly refer back to the Son (and hence to the Father), ultimately uttering the Son's fundamental cry, "Abba, Father", in the hearts of believers.

The first question raised by the collaboration of Son and Spirit in the wake of the Passion—a collaboration that admits of no absolute distinction (nor can the two be simply equated)—is this: What is the relationship between the incarnate Son, now glorified, and the Holy Spirit? In the Pauline affirmation "the Lord is the Spirit" (2 Cor 3:17a), "the Lord" is certainly Christ, and "the Spirit" is certainly the Holy Spirit.[1] The two are in the closest possible proximity, but the context, as well as many

---

[1] The context clearly shows that "the Spirit" cannot be the subject and "the Lord" cannot be in apposition, for this whole passage concerns the transfigured Christ; he, namely, who abolishes the literal interpretation of the Old Covenant by removing the "veil". "The Apostle is here alluding to the ancient Christian teaching that we can only grasp the meaning of Scripture if Christ gives us the necessary insight" (Cerfaux, *Le Christ dans la théologie de S. Paul*, 10th ed. [Paris: Cerf, 1954], 221).

other passages in Paul, expresses the distinction equally clearly. The proximity is most credible where, on the one hand, the Eucharist is portrayed as the ground of our being "one body in Christ" (Rom 12:5).[2] (In 1 Corinthians 10:16–17 the word *sōma* is used twice, first to mean "participation" in the real Body of Christ; second it refers to the community as "body".) On the other hand, it is the Spirit who is regarded as the one who fashions the body of the Church: "For by one Spirit we were all baptized into one body, . . . and all were made to drink of one Spirit" (1 Cor 12:13). We should note that this last metaphor points to the Johannine image of spirit/water, which believers are to drink from the *koilia*, the physical being, of Jesus. This gives us the correct approach to what is a difficult problem.

What is excluded, of course, is any suggestion that believers, who are, after all, created spiritual subjects, are brought into the hypostatic union of the God-man. Excluded too, therefore, is any form of eucharistic union that would be understood as an incorporation into what the encyclical *Mystici Corporis* calls Christ's "physical body".[3] But has there been adequate reflection on what Ephesians 2:13–17 says about Christ's crucified body: "in his flesh destroying the hostility; . . . reconciling both to God in *one* body through the Cross, . . . bringing the hostility to an end"? This is speaking about Christ acting on behalf of sinners and taking *hamartia* upon himself, which has been described as the "center of Pauline theology".[4] "Flesh" and "body" (like "flesh" and "blood" in 1 Corinthians 10) signifies the whole humanity of Christ, but it is a humanity by which, joined hypostatically to the divinity, he was empowered to take the world's sin (2 Cor 5:21) on himself, that sin which killed him and so was killed by him. We shall grasp nothing of the *admirabile com-*

---

[2] Here, too, it is clear from the context ("members one of another") that this expression is only a more accurate description of the "Body of Christ" in 1 Corinthians 12:12ff.

[3] That is, the body that, "born of the Virgin Mother of God, now sits at the right hand of the Father and is hidden under the eucharistic veils" (no. 58). However, the question is whether sufficient reflection has been devoted to this definition of Christ's personal body. It can be taken as a reaction against a "mysticism" that would undermine the subject's possession of his own personality (no. 59).

[4] E. Percy, *Der Leib Christi* (Lund und Leipzig, 1943), 43; cf. O. Cullmann: "Der Gedanke der Stellvertretung . . . als das Prinzip aller neutestamentlichen Heilsgeschichte" (*Die Christologie des Neuen Testaments* [Tübingen, 1957], 290).

mercium, which takes place concretely in the Eucharist, unless we go back to this mystery: what the crucified Lord has taken from us into his "body of the Cross" he gives back to us in the form of his transfigured Body. Thus 1 Corinthians 10, despite all misgivings and objections, remains the "key" to the Pauline understanding of the Church as the "Body of Christ".[5] However, we must draw the appropriate conclusions from this. The first is that the death of Jesus, which is the "consummation" of his mission of self-sacrifice, is both the cause and the prototype of that participation in it which will be made possible in the Church. *Mystici Corporis* is right when it says that Christ "offers to the heavenly Father not only himself as Head of the Church, but in himself his mystical members also" (no. 82). So the forms and features of life he subsequently dispenses, in the Church (Paul calls them "charisms"), are so many forms and features of his surrendered life, since no one possesses such a charism for himself but only for the "benefit" and "upbuilding" of the other members of the body (cf. Eph 4:12, 16). Having a charism means not only being sacrificed, passively, through Christ: it is necessarily an active offering of oneself together with him. No one has pursued and expressed this line of thought more consistently than J. Ratzinger, who, in connection with Augustine (*De civ. Dei* X, 6: "Hoc est sacrificium christianorum: multi unum corpus in Christo"), has again and again stressed that the Church's true nature is seen where Christians "participate in the Lord's Body and so are themselves 'Body' ".[6] "Jesus' sacrifice of his life, consequently, is the source of the life of the Mystical Body."[7]

---

[5] For authors who take this view, cf. F. Malmberg, *Ein Leib—Ein Geist* (Herder, 1960), 73. On the Church's emergence from the dying and crucified Savior, cf. the various writings of S. Tromp prior to and after the encyclical *Mystici Corporis* —which he helped to prepare (*Corpus Christi quod est Ecclesia* I, 2d ed. [1946]; his edition of the encyclical in *Documenta subsidiaria*, 3d ed. [1958]; *De Spiritu Sancto Christi Anima Corporis Mystici* [Rome, 1960]).

[6] "Herkunft und Sinn der Civitas-Lehre Augustins", in *Augustinus Magister* II (Paris, 1954), 978; also his *Volk und Haus Gottes in Augustinus' Lehre von der Kirche* (Munich, 1954), 205–18; see also (on what follows) his "Der Heilige Geist als communio", in HM (1974), 223–38.

[7] Malmberg, *Ein Leib*, 165. Malmberg, who is attacked by H. Mühlen (UMP 184–87), does not erect his doctrine on the Incarnation as the foundation stone of the Church's unity, as is suggested. He does discuss this theory, but the

The second conclusion to be drawn is that Christ, sacrificing himself in the eternal Spirit for us and on our behalf, breathes forth this Spirit at his death: he breathes forth the Spirit both to the Father (Lk 23:46) and to the world (Jn 19:30). It is the Spirit of the *Son*—that Spirit who sustained the Son through the economy of our salvation—whom the Son gives back to the Father along with his completed mission; it is that same Spirit he received from the Father (visibly at his Baptism). Thus the twofold nature of the Spirit's role in the economy (that is, he is both the Father's *mandatum* and the Son's obedience) is once again dissolved—along with the "inversion"—but in a way that benefits the world: the Son gives the Spirit to the world both as "his" Spirit (the Spirit of obedience out of love for the Church, crying "Abba, Father", as the Spirit of the *Son*) and as the *trinitarian* gift that, henceforth, will be indistinguishably the Spirit of Father and Son and, hence, can become the Church's unifying power. Of course this presupposes a third element: the raising of the Son by the *power* of the Father's Spirit (Rom 8:11; cf. Col 2:12; Eph 2:20; Rom 1:3). The Son, as man, cannot raise himself from the dead; so it is for the Father to show the Son's human death to be the consummation of the Father's eternal love manifest in the world and to exalt him (in that "glorification" which is the Johannine unity of Cross and Resurrection) into the pneumatic mode of being. Here the economic distinction of roles (or "inversion") no longer has any meaning: what the exalted Son gives to the Church is the trinitarian Spirit, who is both the (subjective) epitome of the love between Father and Son and the (objective) witness, the fruit, the *donum* that "does not empty itself" (that is, is not kenotic).[8] Later we shall examine in more detail the way in which this formative presence of the

---

ultimate foundation, as the quotation shows, is the sacrifice of the Cross. Accordingly, Malmberg (by contrast with Congar's understanding of the Church) sees the most intimate connection between "external" sacramental fellowship and the inner bond of love (95–100).

[8] It would be better, therefore, to dispense with H. Mühlen's reiterated assertion that the Spirit's kenotic descent into man's sinful will is even more profound than the kenosis of the Son (UMP 406). On the other hand, we can agree with him when he calls the "we-consciousness" of believers unique "because the Spirit of Christ is present at the deepest ontological root of the human person" (UMP 327, 450).

Spirit is expressed both subjectively (and personally) and objectively (sacramentally and hierarchically): the latter applies to our life on earth and is designed to deepen the former, which is why the Church's entire structure exhibits an "anagogic" movement toward the perfected *communio* of those who will enjoy Resurrection.[9] In this connection Schmaus was right to draw attention to Hengstenberg's distinction[10] between corporality [*Körperlichkeit*] and embodiment [*Leiblichkeit*]: the former, an agglomeration of material masses, will be discarded at the Resurrection, for "what is material has been transformed, that is, it has come under the sovereign law of the Spirit, who is filled with the glory of God." Thus Christ can "penetrate our human nature, just as he suddenly stood in the room (in the presence of the disciples). We can be *joined* to him in a most intimate manner, because his body does not hold us back like an impenetrable wall."[11] In such statements, however, two things must be borne in mind: first, the universalization of the Body of Christ on the Cross has already begun, essentially, at the moment when he takes the world's sin upon himself; and second, the fact that the risen Christ becomes "pneumatized" and completely "fluidized" is a direct consequence of this universalization.

The mystery is that the risen Son, in giving the gift of the Holy Spirit, also gives himself as Son; conversely we can see that the Giver is perfectly present in the Spirit as Gift. That is why the Spirit in the Church will continually be pressing on toward perfect embodiment and will be alien to all Idealist spiritualization. This is another reason why the Catholic Church (with her unity of sacramental office, with the Petrine guarantee of unity, with the sacraments, with Scripture and tradition) will always be recognizable over against the "separated churches" through her embodied form, which is the center of all Church unity. This universalizing of the Son's work is the precondition so that the Spirit may testify that God (the Father) cannot be found anywhere else but in the incarnate Son who has died for the

[9] On this whole issue, cf. H. de Lubac, *Corpus Mysticum* (Aubier, 1949), in particular where he speaks of the unity of Christ's "threefold body" (in particular in Paschasius Radbertus), 34ff. On the Eucharist as an anticipation of the ultimate *communio*: 79–83.

[10] *Tod und Vollendung* (Regensburg, 1938).

[11] *Kath. Dogmatik* III/1 (Munich, 1940), 56f.

world (1 Jn) and that the world is being convicted/convinced that God's righteousness is demonstrated in the Son who will act as Judge over the sin (of unbelief) (Jn 16:8ff.).[12] The Spirit given to the Church, the indivisible *donum Dei*, is the gift equally of Father and Son; in his tendency to embodiment he manifests the Son, but with equal power he proclaims the love of the Father, whose love for the world was revealed precisely in surrendering his Son (Jn 3:16). So the Son's Eucharist, effected by the Spirit, is an eternal thanksgiving to the Father—something the Church clearly acknowledges and implements in her Eucharistic Prayers.

It should be plain from what we have said that the Spirit is clearly the definitive Interpreter of the divine "logic". As the love between Father and Son, he is their reciprocal gift to each other, but he is also their fruit, enabling this love to be freely given away. In this twofold aspect the Spirit is, as it were, the Interpreter of himself, but only insofar as he interprets himself as the reciprocal love and full revelation of the first two Persons, manifested in the Father's sending of the Son, even unto the Cross. And although we use words like "teaching", "instructing", "guiding", "testifying", and "convicting" in the context of the Spirit's work of interpretation, he does this, not by words (unlike the Logos), but by communicating insight informed by love, through his "anointing" (1 Jn 2:27), which imparts a *gnōsis* that cannot be communicated by any teaching in words.[13] We shall return to this in more detail when we come to speak of the relationship between the Spirit and theology.

Jesus, however, the "last Adam [who] became a life-giving spirit" (1 Cor 15:45), henceforth utters Spirit-words to the Church, as the circular letters in the Apocalypse show. He commands the seer to write and also speaks in person (Rev 2:1, 8, 12, and so on); but he speaks in the Spirit (2:7, 11, 17, and so on) and leaves the final prophecy to the Holy Spirit. Here, as throughout the whole of the Church's history, the Spirit-Interpreter only

---

[12] Cf. part two of John Paul II's encyclical *Dominum et Vivificantem* (Easter 1986), nos. 27–48.

[13] Thus it is inappropriate to see the Johannine Paraclete as the mere power of the preaching of Jesus as Redeemer (as E. Schweizer maintains in his article "Pneuma" in ThW VI, 442). To do this is simply to adopt the Jewish *pneuma* of prophecy and to see it as present in the preaching to the community.

interprets the spiritual content that is already there in the Son's words; since he "does not speak on his own account", he is only universalizing whatever is already present—what is universal but as yet undeveloped—in the particular words of Jesus. And although Jesus himself is a "life-giving spirit", he does not, for all that, override the Holy Spirit's function. Just as, in earthly terms, the Crucified One left his work uncompleted and expressly entrusted it to the promised Spirit (since his earthly mission was "accomplished" with his death), the now exalted Lord who "sends" the Spirit will not give the latter any instructions about how he is to carry out his work. Indeed, though he is Lord and Head of the Church, he allows himself to be inserted into the Spirit's work (as once he did while on earth), as we can see from the familiar interpretation of the epiclesis in the celebration of the Eucharist.

We must be quite clear that the freedom of the exalted Logos can never be opposed or subordinated to the freedom of the Holy Spirit. Thus we read both that the Lord, exalted over all, dispenses the Church's gifts and ministries from the heaven of heavens (Eph 4:9ff.; 1 Cor 12:5) *and* that the Spirit apportions the charisms (1 Cor 12:4) "as he wills" (12:11). This shows us that the Spirit is both *Pneuma Christi* and a distinct, free Hypostasis in God.

b. Withdrawal as a Precondition of the Gift of the Spirit

Nonetheless we must consider a feature that is clearly stressed twice in the Farewell Discourses. While it is true that the exalted Lord and the Holy Spirit are inseparable in their unity, it is also true that the earthly Jesus proclaims an indispensable distinction between his tangible form and his pneumatic mode of being: this is the precondition, if he is to send the Spirit and if he himself is to return in a spiritual manner. The gap between these two presences is essential so that the universality latent in the particularity of Jesus' earthly existence can be made manifest.

"Nevertheless I tell you the truth: it is to your advantage that I go away, for if I do not go away, the Counselor will not come to you; but if I go, I will send him to you" (Jn 16:7).

This seems to imply that while Jesus remains on earth he cannot send the Spirit, since the disciples cannot have both *his* presence and that of the Spirit at the same time. This assertion has an absolute ring about it and seems not to take into account those other statements where Jesus says that, after having gone away, he will return during the Spirit's reign (Jn 14:3; 14:28). This return, however, will be different in kind; it will be in the Spirit. Thus the Risen One who appears to the disciples will be a *"pneuma zōopoioun"* (1 Cor 15:45), able to appear and disappear, to go through closed doors—which are not characteristics of the mortal body. But even this risen Lord, who has authority to give the Spirit as he wishes (Jn 20:22), wishes to withdraw from visibility, as the Resurrection accounts, in different ways, make very plain. The scene with Magdalen at the tomb shows that it is wrong to grasp and hold on to Jesus' bodily form, for the Risen One is about to ascend to the Father. The scene involving Thomas—the concluding scene in the first version of the end of John's Gospel—gives a general application of the instruction, "Blessed are those who have not seen (and do not desire to touch) and yet believe." The disciples cannot follow Jesus directly when he goes away. "Where I am going you cannot follow me now; but you shall follow afterward" (Jn 13:33, 36). When Jesus disappears before the eyes of the Emmaus disciples, leaving them with his Eucharist, he presents us with a kind of commentary on the promise, "It is the spirit that gives life, the flesh is of no avail" (Jn 6:63). Thomas Aquinas rightly comments, in connection with a passage in Augustine: "Christ did not wish to give his disciples the Spirit during his lifetime because they were as yet unprepared; for, since the Holy Spirit is a spiritual love, it is opposed to fleshly love. The disciples clung with a certain fleshly love to Christ's humanity and had not yet attained a spiritual love of his divinity. . . . For as long as he dwelled among the disciples, he seemed to be a man like them."[14] Of course there is the consoling promise of his return, but for the duration of world time it will be a spiritual and internal coming, and the indwelling of Christ and the Father in

<hr/>

[14] *Super Evang. Joh.* (Marietti, no. 2087). Similarly Bonaventure, *In Joh.* (Quar. VI, 460a).

the disciples, as well as their "seeing" the Lord (Jn 14:19, 21, 23), will be mediated by the Spirit: it will be spiritual.

So a real and irrevocable withdrawal of Jesus is announced; moreover, he demands that the disciples be glad about it—at least for the sake of their love for him—although it seems a kind of death to them. "If you loved me, you would have rejoiced, because I go to the Father; for the Father is greater than I" (Jn 14:28). In calling for this selfless love, Jesus is actually assuming that they have already received the Holy Spirit of perfect selflessness that will be given as the fruit of his disappearance. At the same time this demand is the very quintessence of every demand (and promise) contained in the earthly Lord's entire teaching: "He who wants to acquire[15] his life will lose it, and he who loses his life for my sake will find it" (Mt 10:39); or, "whoever would save his life will lose it" (Mk 8:35); this is in connection with the necessity of denying oneself and taking up one's cross in discipleship of Jesus. Again, selflessness is called for: "for my sake and the gospel's" he demands that self-surrender which leads to "saving" one's life. "Whoever seeks to gain his life will lose it" (Lk 17:33; also Mt 16:25). The words "for my sake" show that it is not the case of a general ethic of "dying in order to grow" [Stirb und werde]; rather, we must be drawn into the way of the Cross of Jesus, who desires to lose his life "for many". Here the "saving" of his life is not part of his mission: it is something reserved for the Father and his Spirit.

It is only by a radical renunciation—not of a thing, but of one's own self, and in this context this means a renunciation of the possession of the tangible, visible, experiential Jesus—that we can hope to receive God's highest gift, the Holy Spirit. It follows that there must be a renunciation of any grasp of "times and seasons" in the establishment of the Kingdom, of any autonomous planning on the Church's part (Acts 1:7). The whole of the Acts of the Apostles shows that the decisive planning is that undertaken by the Holy Spirit himself, whether in pushing things forward or obstructing plans or revealing in advance things that men would never have planned (Acts 26:22ff.) and that, nonetheless, they have to carry out at the risk of their own

---

[15] Cf. H. Preisker, ThW II, 767f.

lives (26:24). The post-Easter community, instructed to plead
for the expected gift of the Holy Spirit, is drawn into discipleship of its Lord (who is in process of withdrawing); he is well
aware that the saving gift he will bequeath to them flows from
his mortal wound: "If any one thirst, let him come to me, and let
him who believes drink" (Jn 7:37). The Evangelist here rightly
interprets what "flows" from the Lord as the Spirit, who is "not
yet there" because he presupposes the death of Jesus; thus "the
Spirit, the water, and the blood" constitute a single witness (1 Jn
5:8) to the fact that, by surrendering his Son, God has gone "to
the limit", "to the end" (Jn 13:1). Jesus had already promised
the Samaritan woman (Jn 4:14) that this life of God, flowing
from death, would be implanted in the soul of those who thirst
for it and would there become a "spring of water welling up to
eternal life".

Here we clearly see the Son's "economic" death as the revelation, in terms of the world, of the *kenosis* (or selflessness) of
the love of Father and Son at the heart of the Trinity. As we
have shown, this is the precondition for the procession of God's
absolute, non-kenotic Spirit of love. This self-surrender on the
part of the economic Trinity is the foundation of all Christian
existence. As Theo Kobusch rightly says, "the doctrine of *kenosis*
is what is specifically Christian."[16] Paul described baptism, entry
into this existence, as being "baptized into his death" (Rom 6:4);
the early Church took this meaning of baptism most seriously.[17]
According to 1 Corinthians 10:2 the passage through the Red
Sea is an image of baptism; according to 1 Peter 3:21 it is the
escape from the Flood; both texts speak of a life that is gained
through death, a life that is won as a result of a *descensus* into
the milieu of death.[18] The Fathers interpret the sacramental act
of death, documented in the Gospel, as an attitude that governs

---

[16] "Freiheit und Tod: Die Tradition der mors mystica und ihre Vollendung in
Hegels Philosophie", ThQ, 1984, 185–203, here 187.

[17] K. H. Schelkle, "Taufe und Tod", in *Wort und Schrift* (Düsseldorf, 1966),
216–26; also the same author's *Theologie des Neuen Testaments* 4/2: *Jüngergemeinde
und Kirche* (Düsseldorf, 1976), 130–35.

[18] Per Lundberg, "La Typologie baptismale dans l'ancienne Église", Acta Sem.
neotest. Upsaliensis X (Leipzig and Uppsala, 1942).

a person's entire Christian existence: it is a "dying with Christ" and a hidden life with him in God (cf. Col 3:3).[19]

What is crucially important in the Acts of the Apostles, with regard to the expectation and reception of the Spirit, is that the gift of Pentecost (with a view to the developing Church's self-renunciation unto death) points in two directions: toward the Church's missionary openness to the world and toward discipleship of Christ in persecution and death (understood as *martyrion*).

c. The Church's Head and Soul?

Theological metaphors—of which there are so many that they imply a mutual critique of each other[20]—can tempt us to restrict the coextensive operation of the exalted Christ and the Holy Spirit in the Church, suggesting that Christ operates "only" as "Head", and the Spirit "only" as "Soul", of the Church and that each of them unites the Church in a different way.[21] First of all, we must observe that the term "head", as applied to Christ, only occurs in the Letters from prison, whereas those writings that are certainly genuinely Pauline only speak of the "body of Christ". The term "soul" for the Holy Spirit is often used as a

[19] The tradition of the Christian era is broader than Kobusch (note 16) indicates. For the Middle Ages he cites only the *mors mystica* of the mystics. Cf. the wealth of illustrations in Alois M. Haas, *Mors mystica—Thanatologie der Mystik* (1976), reprinted in *Sermo mysticus* (Fribourg, Switzerland, 1979), 392–480. He convincingly shows that Hegel builds on the Christian idea of selfless love—deliberately alluding to Christianity and showing a knowledge of Eckhart—but only as far as personal attitude is concerned, not as regards the ultimate purpose (i.e., the state, which Hegel considers absolute). This reading should be complemented by the following: "Augustins Rede vom christlichen Leben als eines 'quasi cotidianus baptismus' " (S. Guelf. 1, 19; Morin 449) and Ekkhart Sauer's study of it in *Zeichen des Glaubens*, Festschrift Balthasar Fischer (Benziger and Herder, 1972), 23ff.; Wilhelm Breuning, "Die Bedeutung der Taufe für die Einübung ins Christentum"; Emmanuel v. Severus, *Taufe und geistliches Leben* (ibid., 155ff.; 207ff.).

[20] A radical critique of these metaphors can be found in M. D. Koster, O.P., *Ekklesiologie im Werden* (Paderborn, 1940).

[21] What follows is a brief response to the great study of S. Tromp, *De Spiritu Christi Anima*, which to a large extent corrects itself as a result of the vast number of approaches and witnesses to tradition that it presents.

"metaphor"[22] (alongside other images)[23] in the Fathers, Scholastics, and in the modern encyclicals, but it has no literal foundation in Scripture, although of course the Spirit is described
as "animating, unifying, and fructifying" the Church. But does
this not also apply to the Son's Eucharist?[24] Is it right to say,
on this basis, that the operation of the "Head" and that of the
Spirit can be "set against" one another?[25] Can one say that the
earthly Jesus initially creates a "socio-legal" entity and forms his
disciples into a company of "teachers, leaders, and prophets"
and that, on the other hand, we have the Spirit, exhaled on the
Cross and breathed into the Church at Easter and Pentecost,
animating the disciples in the same way that Adam, in paradise,
was first fashioned out of clay and subsequently had life breathed
into him?[26]

Before proceeding, let us briefly address the great trinitarian passage in Ephesians 3:14–19, where Paul solemnly puts a
threefold request to God the Father: that the community may
"be strengthened with might through his [the Father's] Spirit in
the inner man", that "Christ may dwell in your hearts through
faith" and that (through both) the community, rooted in love,
may know all the dimensions of the superabundant love of Christ
and be filled with the whole fullness of the (triune) God. The
strengthening that comes from the Spirit of the Father is intended
to lead to Christ's indwelling in their hearts by faith (which, as
always in Paul, is one with love); both together lead to the Christian *gnōsis* of that fullness which is beyond all knowledge. Justi-
fiably, this led to the view that the growth of the "inner man"
is ultimately identical with Christ's indwelling in the heart, in
accordance with the Pauline "spiritual anthropology".[27] The fact
is, Christ does not appear here (as elsewhere in the same letter)

[22] Ibid., 23, 107, 207.

[23] Ibid., 43–48; on "heart", cf. 33f.

[24] There is no treatment of this topic as such in Tromp's entire work.

[25] "Spiritus Sanctus-Anima proprie opponitur Christo-Capiti" (ibid., 113).

[26] Ibid., 120–22.

[27] Markus Barth, *Ephesians* I, Anchor Bible (New York, 1974), 392: "The 'inner
man' of Ephesians 3:16 is Jesus Christ himself." Galatians 2:20 ("It is no longer I
who live, but Christ who lives in me") shows that the anthropology of Ephesians
is genuinely Pauline.

as the "Head" of the Church but as her innermost principle of life—inseparable from the Holy Spirit. Thus many Fathers (like Origen) speak of Christ as the Soul of the Church, and others (like Suarez) ascribe this role (according to the Ephesians passage) to faith.[28] Cyril of Alexandria, in many places, sees Christ and the Holy Spirit carrying out this task together and inseparably.[29]

At all events, therefore, we must get beyond the dualism outlined at the beginning. The glorified Christ's union with his Church (whether she is termed "Body" or "Bride") doubtless takes place in a communication of his Holy Spirit[30] but no less through Christ's self-surrender in his sacraments and particularly in the Eucharist. If the comparison is drawn between the man who cleaves to a prostitute and becomes one flesh with her and the man who cleaves to (*kollōmenos*: "sticks to") Christ and is "one spirit with him" (1 Cor 6:16–17), this "one spirit", in context, means a "spiritual body".[31] Thus the next passage urges us to keep the body holy (vv. 19–20). In fact, as Clement of Alexandria stresses, it is a question of a union in a "pneumatic body".[32] This union fulfills Christ's prophetic assertion that when he is lifted up he will draw all men to himself (Jn 12:32). This means that we must look for an interpenetration of the two images of "head" and "soul",[33] and in doing so it is not enough to consider, first, Christ's hypostatic union and his endowment with the gifts of the Spirit (*gratia capitis*) and, then, go on to leave the animation and articulation of the Church (solely) to his Spirit;[34] this would fail to account for (what is alleged to be) the pre-Easter Jesus' purely juridical establishment of the Church's structure, whereas this entire preparation is

[28] Tromp, *De Spiritu Christi Anima*, 36–46.

[29] Texts in ibid., 115–16, 127–28, 231.

[30] Ibid., 217–70, although he does not give sufficient emphasis to the fact that the Spirit of Christ is also the Spirit of the Father (cf. 247).

[31] "One actually expects to read . . . 'one body'. This is, in fact, what lies behind this passage. *Hen pneuma* only tells us what kind of body this one body is" (H. Conzelmann, *Der 1. Brief an die Korinther* [1969], 135).

[32] *Strom.* VII, 14 (PG 9, 522).

[33] Tromp, *De Spiritu Christi Anima*, 263ff.

[34] As Tromp does in practice (without any mention of the Eucharist) in his great treatise on ministries and charisms, ibid., 271–395.

perfected by him (and not only by his Spirit as his *vicarius*)[35] through the sending of his Spirit.[36]

The structure of the Church as she pursues her pilgrim path on earth only becomes intelligible in the unity of what the pre-Easter Jesus has founded (including the celebration of the visible Last Supper and the express handing over of this celebration to the disciples, that is, to those officially "consecrated" as priests) and what he, as the resurrected Lord, gives his Church in the Spirit. For our sake, since we dwell here in the flesh, all that is spiritual and charismatic must be put into visible structures, but these structures are inwardly filled with the goods dispensed by the risen and now pneumatic Christ. When we say this, we mean more than merely that the Church is both visible and invisible; we must put it more concretely and say that, for as long as the Church dwells on earth, she is both pre- and post-Easter. The point at which both spheres intersect is the death of Jesus, for he concludes his earthly life with the highest possible act of sacrifice, simultaneously loosing the Holy Spirit upon the Church. This implies that the Church's Eucharist, which is a "proclaiming of the death" of Jesus (see 1 Cor 11:26), is drawn into his perfect sacrifice: the whole Church (she who is the first to receive the Eucharist) is summoned to enter the sacrifice: "It belongs to the Church's very being, as she celebrates the eucharistic sacrifice, to become a sacrifice herself, a sacrifice for her own sins and for the sins of the world. In this world there is no redemption without sacrifice, and there is no redeemed existence in this world that is not, at the same time, a sacrificial existence."[37] We have already shown how crucially all the Spirit's charisms presuppose this sacrificial existence. But if it is true that all charisms proceed from this point and all the sacraments are aimed at it (and in the case of

[35] Ibid., 258ff.

[36] This is acknowledged to some extent when Tromp observes that, while the Spirit is united to the Church in a non-appropriative way, he is united to the Father and the Son *titulo specialis* insofar as they send forth the Spirit for that purpose; "ratione specialissima haec vivificatio adscribitur Christo, who sends *his* Spirit into the Church" (267). Nonetheless, what is lacking here is an ultimate synthesis.

[37] J. Auer, "Das Mysterium der Eucharistie", in *Kleine Kath. Dogmatik* VI, 2d ed. (Regensburg, 1974), 279.

baptism it is Paul who shows this most emphatically in Romans 6:3), it is particularly true in the case of the priesthood: in the context of Jesus' life it is an "institution"; in the context of the Risen One it is the charism of an abiding ministry; but since it looks toward the Cross (Jesus says, "For their sake I consecrate myself, that they also may be consecrated in truth"—Jn 17:19)[38] the priest is bound to live out "the unity of existential and institutional holiness".[39] He has a mediating function between a "religious system" and Christ's unique self-sacrifice, and so he "no longer has a private life" but must provide a living example of that "bodiliness under rule" that comes from God-made-man, of that "objectification of the inner Spirit"; thus he "can represent Christ's sacrifice in space and time, here and now". "So the merely objectivist, merely anti-Donatist priest of the *opus operatum*, the priest who fails to fill this *opus* inwardly with the whole strength of his person, is not the priest he should be."[40]

This brings us to the topic of the next section.

---

[38] A. Feuillet, *Le Sacerdoce du Christ et de ses ministres* (Éditions de Paris, 1972).

[39] K. Rahner, *Einübung in die priesterliche Existenz* (Herder, 1970), 113–27. "Le Prêtre est un homme donné": A. Chapelle, *Pour la vie du monde: Le Sacrement de l'ordre* (Brussels, 1978), 374.

[40] On Augustine: F. Genn, *Trinität und Amt nach Augustinus* (Einsiedeln, 1986), 237ff.

4

SPIRIT: SUBJECTIVE AND OBJECTIVE

a. The Meaning and Limits of the Distinction

We have just introduced a distinction between the objective, in-stitutional element and the subjective, existential element in the Church, arising out of the christological tension between the pre- and post-Easter existence of Jesus. However, on the basis of all we have said so far, this tension also has a pneumatological origin. We now turn to the latter's theological specification and seek to contrast it with philosophical distinctions of subjective and objective Spirit (Hegel). As we have already shown, this tension is rooted, not (as in Idealism) in the necessity of Spirit to objectify itself (as the not-I or as an objective moral norm) in order to achieve its full, absolute subjectivity, but in the twofold aspect of the eternal Holy Spirit in God: the Holy Spirit is both the innermost crucible of the movement of love between Father and Son and its product and fruit—the objective testimony to that fire of love.

J. A. Dorner, the great Protestant dogmatician, deduced this tension of the Holy Spirit in the "economic" realm from his place within the Trinity:

> The Holy Spirit only exercises the same office in the economic Trinity that he exercises in the immanent Trinity, where he is equally the principle maintaining the distinctions and the prin-ciple uniting them. His office in the world is to glorify Christ, and he does this by making the world into the Kingdom of God with the Church at its center and by making both of them into a graphic representation of the indissoluble *unio* of the inner, or merely subjective, and the external and objective; or of the ideal and the historical; or of the divine and the fully human; this *unio* is achieved prototypically in Christ.[1]

[1] "Das Prinzip unserer Kirche nach dem innern Verhältnis der materiellen und formalen Seite desselben zueinander" (184), in *Gesammelte Schriften* (1883), 99. Quoted in K. Barth, *Die Protestantische Theologie im 19. Jahrhundert* (Zollikon, 1947), 531.

Within the Trinity, however, both aspects of the Holy Spirit (that is, union and distinction, love and testimony) are simply identical. The one Spirit is identically the Spirit of the Father and the Spirit of the Son, so that Mühlen's formula for the Spirit ("one Person in two Persons") is adequate.

If we ask why this identity is manifest as a distinction in the ecumenical field, the initial answer is, because of the Son's kenotic becoming-man: within the Godhead, his readiness to do the Father's will causes him to take on the form of human obedience, which brings about what we have called "inversion": the Spirit from the Father comes as *mandatum*, and the Spirit from the Son says "not my will". It is crucial, however, in pondering this distinction, to keep in mind the abiding identity: each is the (economic) form of a single love, which takes on a twofold form only because God and man cannot constitute an identity. Insofar as Jesus is God, he obeys the Father in the same Spirit-love that the Father offers him. Insofar as Jesus is man, this love takes the form of *mandatum* and *oboedientia*. And once we become aware of Jesus' life as the prototypical form of human and creaturely being, we also begin to see that every instance of creaturely obedience toward God would have to be the primary form of creaturely love. It was to restore this that Jesus came with his redemptive work, overcoming the disobedience of "Adam".

This must be seen in conjunction with the aforementioned distinction between mortal (pre-Easter) and immortal existence. Two things follow. First, the ecclesial form of existence coined by Jesus, corresponding to his and our mortal and transitory existence, must exhibit the distinction between objective and subjective structure. On the other hand, this twofold structure will continually transcend itself insofar as ecclesial man, in his discipleship of Christ, understands the *mandatum Patris* as the economic form of the Father's love and so recognizes creaturely obedience as an invitation (addressed to a man who is as yet sinful and reluctant) to enter into love.

Once this has been grasped, it will become immediately apparent that it is quite impossible to make a clean separation between "objective" and "subjective" in the Holy Spirit's structuring and sanctifying of the Church.[2] In fact, where there is

²Cf. UMP 412.

consistent discipleship of Christ, tension will be subjectively most tangible where objectively it is closest to dissolving. Christ, on the Mount of Olives and on the Cross, feels the burden of his task weighing on him most heavily just when it is nearest its consummation; accordingly, that pure and holy Church which Augustine habitually calls the "*columba*" will find it hardest to bear witness (*martyrion*) at the very point where her love is most purified. Thus Paul was "so utterly, unbearably crushed" and so "despaired of life itself" that he was made to "rely . . . on God who raises the dead" (2 Cor 1:8–9). In this way the Church, institutionally constituted, goes over to being the pure *communio sanctorum*.

Theologically speaking, therefore, we can only speak of one or the other aspect of the Holy Spirit being prevalent: what is objectivistic about the Church is an expression of the divine subjectivity. Nor is it something incidental: for man, in his earthly striving, it is a norm of love, constantly hovering above him, subjectively beyond his reach (cf. Phil 3:12–14). Subjectively, of course, this same man can feel that he is near to God, but since the objectivity of absolute love (incarnate in Scripture, sacraments, tradition, and ecclesiastical office) is always beyond him, he can never settle down complacently with his loving experiences. However fervent we may be at Communion, we know that we cannot receive the sacrament in an adequate manner or respond to it adequately; and, in all probability, the closer we get to a reception and response that *is* adequate, the more we shall be aware of this.

Office, tradition, sacrament, Scripture, and preaching—this is a Spirit-filled totality, a path to love; and the Christian should be well aware that "the whole juridical element is at the service of the pneumatic",[3] that the transmission of ministerial office, for instance, does not merely hand on rights and duties but, along with them, gives the Spirit's charisma;[4] he must know that, in New Testament terms, Scripture is not a letter that kills but is full of the Spirit (2 Cor 3:6) and that tradition is something quite different from a handing on of dead formulae: nor is it only a

---

[3] J. Mouroux, *L'Expérience chrétienne: Introduction à une théologie* (Paris: Aubier, 1952), 202–3.

[4] UMP 373, 530.

drawing from living sources but rather is *itself* a living source. This must be shown to be the case even with canon law, which is profoundly different from secular law since it is a law of grace and sacraments.

In the New Covenant there is no longer any official cult that is not also personal, leading people into the personal *communio sanctorum*. If it is possible to distinguish between "sanctification" of the individual and "consecration" (for service to others), the fact is that both forms of sanctification are intertwined: all personal sanctification is for the sake of service to the Kingdom of God; and ministerial sanctification does not terminate in this service but, as we saw, demands a life in accordance with it. A mere *opus operatum* without an *opus operantis*, while it remains a minimal concept necessary as a result of sin, is, from the perspective of God's redemptive plan, a nothing, something that ought not to be. It *does* exist, in an anti-Donatist sense, for the benefit of those who receive grace through it; but it remains fruitless for the unprepared sinner who distributes or receives it.

b. The Church: Two in One

1. We must now undertake a thorough examination of the "two in one" of the Church's subjective and objective holiness, keeping in mind its foundation, that is, its christological-pneumatological preconditions. In christological terms, Tertullian's *caro cardo salutis* remains irreducible: true, the flesh itself is of no avail (Jn 6:63), but that unity which is constituted by the enfleshed Word for the world's salvation must under no circumstances be "dissolved" (1 Jn 4:3, Vulgate). That is why the post-Easter Spirit, if he is to be authentic, must resolutely point back to the fact "that Jesus Christ has come in the flesh" (1 Jn 4:2)—a flesh that goes to the Cross, a flesh that carries its Cross daily. In pneumatological terms, however, the identical trinitarian Spirit (who is both subjective love and objective fruit) steps forward as the Interpreter of the economic love of Father and Son for the world, in the service of the christological distinction between the mortal, tangible Son and the exalted, untouchable Son. The Spirit makes both the Son's earthly glory and his risen glory (since he

is the Servant of God and the Lord "above all heavens") a reality in the Church, in accordance with his own twofold aspect: he is both objective holiness, which cannot be subjectively attained, and subjective holiness, which is only holy if it "nobly strives"* within the horizon of objective holiness and is guided by it, that is, if it serves as the path and goal of this objective holiness. With its *sola scriptura* Protestantism acknowledges the existence of such an objective norm that gives direction to all that is subjective in the Church: as for the Catholic Church, as the constitution *Dei Verbum* has clearly shown, she sees the *circumincessio* of Scripture (*norma normans*)—tradition—office (*normae normatae*) as the full form of objective holiness, which even guarantees the normative character of Scripture itself.[5] It should be noted how often this constitution speaks of the operation of the Holy Spirit in connection with these three interrelated aspects of the Church's objective holiness: it is in the Spirit that Scripture is inspired, and it is in the Spirit that Scripture is interpreted, through all time, in doctrine, life, and culture, so that this "Tradition that comes from the apostles makes progress in the Church, with the help of the Holy Spirit" through a pondering on the meaning of the Scriptures, through the "sense of spiritual realities" that believers "experience", but also through "the sure charism of truth" in those who have received the episcopate, who, "enlightened by the Spirit of truth, . . . faithfully preserve, expound and spread it abroad by their preaching".[6] It is the objective Holy Spirit in the Church (and to the three elements we have mentioned we must add the sacraments and canon law) that guarantees the triune God's utter sovereignty—far from all manipulation on our part—even in the most personal encounter with him. Thus, in the great hymns to the Holy Spirit, we constantly implore this

---

* Goethe, *Faust*, p. 2, act 5: "strebend sich bemüht".—TRANS.

[5] *Dei Verbum* 10: "It is clear, therefore, that, in the supremely wise arrangement of God, sacred Tradition, sacred Scripture and the Magisterium of the Church are so connected and associated that one of them cannot stand without the others. Working together, each in its own way under the action of the one Holy Spirit, they all contribute effectively to the salvation of souls" (ed. Flannery, *Vatican Council II* [Dublin: Talbot Press, 1975]).

[6] *Dei Verbum* 8, 9 (ed. Flannery). The Holy Spirit is mentioned thirty-three times in this constitution.

"Spirit of holiness" to come down anew upon the Church and her members. Just as no one can give himself any ecclesiastical office and no one can take a sacrament for himself, the Church's unity is ultimately not created by men—however much they ought to be at pains to preserve it—but by the objective Holy Spirit, who, as Holy Spirit, is always the self-surrender of the Church's Lord, who has become pneumatic. This is why the Church is clearly more than the sum of the empirical local and partial Churches; the latter are only what they are in virtue of a unity that is given to them all from above, a unity that comes from the Trinity-in-unity. Here all the objectivity of ecclesial holiness ministers to the incorporation of believers, with their subjective love, into the Body of Christ; in turn, these believers are kept safe in a unity that transcends all interpersonal love and unity.[7] The various aspects of objective holiness can be given the "title" "holy", but this must not be interpreted as referring to them subjectively. We speak of "Holy Scripture" and the "holy sacraments", and the Orthodox synod and the Catholic council are called "holy", and by a similar usage the pope is called "Holy Father": this appellation refers to the office, not to the person who bears the office.[8]

2. The distinction between the Church's subjective and objective holiness, and their reciprocal relationship, is clearly seen in the two representative figures of the Church, that is, Mary and Peter. Both are omnipresent in the Church, to the extent that we see the Church in her response to Christ: "The entire Church is priestly; the entire Church is Marian."[9] It follows

[7] "Koinōnia tou hagiou pneumatos" in 2 Corinthians 13:13 means primarily the objective participation in the Holy Spirit (as does Philippians 2:1) and only secondarily the effect, namely, the fellowship that the Spirit creates among believers.

[8] On this topic: Hendrik Berkhof, *Theologie des Heiligen Geistes* (Neukirchen-Vluyn, 1968), esp. 46–105.

[9] R. Laurentin, *Marie, L'Église et le sacerdoce*, 2 vols. (Paris: Lethielleux, 1953), II, 34. Laurentin's thesis is the most thorough historical and systematic treatment of the topic and, hence, indirectly, of the question of the priesthood of the woman. A full but less precise treatment is in Scheeben's *Dogmatik* III, sections 1763–1812; he speaks of a "chief sacrifice" and a "contributory sacrifice", but he rejects any suggestion that Mary is a "priestess" (section 1812), allowing only the expression "diaconia" (section 1800).

that both can be distinguished from the general priesthood of believers while at the same time being connected to it. Tradition shows a remarkable reluctance to bring them closer together.[10] If Mary's function is elevated high above that of the (Dionysian) choirs of angels, it is tacitly elevated also above the ministerial priesthood.[11] And if she is regarded as "offering" something in her compassionate suffering at the Cross, this is first, because what she is offering to the Father is her own flesh and blood and, second, because she does this "on behalf of" the whole of mankind.[12] From the standpoint of tradition the requirement is only that the hierarchical priest should try to acquire the subjective attitude of Mary beneath the Cross; or that vocation to the priesthood comes through Mary's sacrifice.[13] "Spirituals" (like Olier) are the exception, mistakenly trying almost to equate the hierarchical priesthood with subjective holiness.[14]

According to Scripture, the disciples, at the outset, are radically challenged to leave everything so that they can be entrusted with an objective Christian mission. Thus, right from the start (Jn 1:42), Peter is designated "the rock" on whose faith the Church will be built (Mt 16:18); Peter's faith is as yet very imperfect, and he can become a "hindrance" to Jesus (Mt 16:23), attaining his office only after having betrayed the Lord (which is strongly underlined by all four Gospels). For his office to become a reality, for him to be allowed to pasture the flock of the "Good

---

[10] Laurentin, *Marie*, the whole of vol. I (5, 40f., 73, 93).

[11] Ibid., I, 73. In the Pseudo-Albertine "Mariale" we read: "Habet convenientiam cum Papa beatissima Virgo: omnium ecclesiarum sollicitudinem, potestatis spiritualis plenitudinem, privilegiatorum actuum universalitatem" (Borgnet 37, 87; this is taken over from Antoninus, Bernardino, and others: 104, 124). These points of comparison, however, do not touch the real priestly office. Only metaphorically can Mary be called "quaedam sacerdotissa" (II, 44, 4)—an expression that subsequently found no echo.

[12] Primarily in the school of St. Bernard (Laurentin, *Marie*, I, 140ff.).

[13] "The more I am sacrificed, the more they will be priests" (ibid., II, 51).

[14] Olier regards the priesthood as a kind of religious state of life, and the latter gets dragged into the sphere of the spiritual priesthood of all believers. It is not surprising, therefore, that Mary is presented—without any differentiation—as the model of the priest (II, 32; cf. 78). There is an analogous danger in Scheeben: he understands the hierarchical priesthood as one of the Church's maternal functions (*Dogmatik* III, sections 1790–1794).

Shepherd", he must first profess his "greater love" (Jn 21:15) and then receive the promise that he will indeed follow Jesus to a cross (v. 19). His consciousness of his official role is evident both before Easter (cf. Jn 6:68f.; Mt 14:29f.; 17:24ff.; Jn 18:16) and after Easter (Jn 21:7, 11; Acts 1:15ff., and so on). It is of the essence of the office given to him (objective holiness) that he should profess his love for Christ and receive (and personally strive for) the grace of discipleship unto death on a cross. This is similar to the call of Paul, who is primarily seized by Christ and taken into his service and secondarily has to endeavor to respond subjectively to this call ("I press on to make it my own, because Christ Jesus has made me his own": Phil 3:12). Ministerial office tends toward subjective holiness.

By contrast, Mary's perfect subjective holiness does not in any way tend toward ministerial office. It is of a qualitatively different kind. She only has to unfold this perfect holiness—which she has always possessed, in the Immaculate Conception—to its ultimate extent (to the piercing of her heart: Lk 2:35). By her unconditional Yes she has always given herself unreservedly; this means that, as she stands beneath the Cross, it is less a question of self-sacrifice than of giving away the fruit of her body and her soul, her Child. For it is the Child who sacrifices and gives himself and asks of his Mother what is hardest and most painful for her: her consent to his self-surrender. "The consent hidden in her first *fiat* unfolds its ultimate consequences on Calvary. Here her unconditional Yes becomes an offering of the sacrifice of the Cross (of the Son) in union with Christ."[15] In utter love Mary surrenders what is most her own, her offspring, in his self-sacrifice for the world's sin: only in this way does her perfect subjective holiness become a precondition enabling Christ's sacrifice and his Eucharist to become a single, perfect sacrifice in the exercise of the hierarchical priesthood. The Son performs the sacrifice, and the Mother-Ecclesia, in perfect love, allows it to happen.[16] Mary not only utters her Yes here in a neutral sense

---

[15] Laurentin, *Marie* II, 116. Scheeben, too, recognizes that the "consensus" aspect is central (Dogmatik III, section 1796). Georg Bätzing, in connection with two of my works, has shed light on the loving consent of Mary (as representing the *Ecclesia immaculata*) in his book *Die Eucharistie als Opfer der Kirche* (Einsiedeln: Johannesverlag, 1986).

[16] "Mary represents the Church, but in a particular sense she is more than the

"loco totius generis humani": "at the same moment she must become, effectively, the Mother of all those who are responsible for this death."[17]

It is important to see, not just *that*, but *how* the two aspects of the Church tend toward each other in order to become the one Church of Christ, both Body and Bride. This movement is not symmetrical, since all objective holiness exists for the sake of the subjective movement of the Church's members toward the holiness of Christ in the Holy Spirit, whereas perfect subjective holiness (in Mary), on the one hand, is the precondition for the existence of Christ himself and, on the other hand, acts as "Mother" (cf. Rev 12:17) to the entire subjective-objective Church—including the ecclesial office and the sacraments instituted by Christ. In virtue of what she is, she can "fill out" the deficiencies in people's subjective reception of the sacraments and in their response to office exercised within the Church. This reciprocal movement—to emphasize it once more—manifests the identity of the one Holy Spirit in his twofold aspect.

3. However, this two-in-one reality brought about by the Spirit in the Church is exhibited under a further heading: it is the twofold effect of the one Spirit who brings forth both office and charism. From the very outset, in Paul and even in the Gospels, the two are almost confusingly one: the permanent offices head the list of charisms (1 Cor 12:29), and Timothy's ordination by the laying on of hands is designated a "gift [charism] of God" (2 Tim 1:6). Then again, the charisms give their recipients a semi-official function in the community—and yet the two are clearly distinguished. Thus Paul's apostolate cannot be allotted

---

Church. Whereas priests are imperfect copies of Christ, Mary is the prototype of the Church. Whereas priests continue Christ, she is prior to the Church. The priest is in some manner the impersonal representative of Christ, but Mary is the personal representation of the Church. When the priest says, 'This is my Body' or 'I absolve you', these words only have meaning insofar as he disregards his human person and lends his words and gestures as a servant of Christ. Mary says, 'I *am* the handmaid of the Lord'; she really engages her own person."—"In the Mass the priest makes Christ's sacrifice present, whereas Mary *is* present in it."—"Mary's sacrificing activity is superior to that of the sacramental priest. But it is less priestly, in the proper sense, than his" (Laurentin, *Marie* II, 121–23).

[17] Ibid., 153.

to the charisms (even if others who do not belong to the primitive apostles may perhaps be called "apostles" in a charismatic
sense: Barnabas in Acts 14:4, Andronicus and Junias in Romans
16:7), nor can the ministry of those he appointed as his representatives and assistants [like "auxiliary bishops"]. The position of
Timothy and Titus in the Pastoral Epistles shows this clearly. But
if the non-hierarchical charisms are distinct from the charisms
that confer office, the latter must definitely exhibit charismatic
features: their bearers must be prophets, teachers, men of wisdom and knowledge, able to distinguish spirits, and so on.

However, the Spirit-wrought unity of the two goes even farther. In 1 Corinthians 13 Christian love is portrayed as the "more
excellent way" without which even the highest charisms are use-
less (1 Cor 13:1-3). Charisms without love are (theoretically)
possible, but to be effective they need to be lived in love and
in the infused theological and cardinal virtues.[18] For Paul, as we
know, every genuine Christian life is a life in the Holy Spirit, in
a lively faith, hope, and love (both of God and of man), so that
the ordinary Christian life is charismatic per se, even anterior to
the distinction between "office" and "charism" in the narrower
sense. Titus is a "true child in a common faith" (Tit 1:4), and
we read that the entire Body of Christ and all its members grows
into maturity through reciprocal acts of service "and upbuilds
itself in love" (Eph 4:16). In this way all are "called to the one
hope" (Eph 4:4). Thus both office and particular charisms are
subsumed under the general charismatic dimension of Christian
existence.

Comparing the lists of charisms found in Paul's Epistles (especially Romans 12 with 1 Corinthians 12), we see how accidental and situational they are. Nor can they be clearly divided
off from one another; some may be regarded as having a distinct
profile (for example, the gift of healing or the giving of alms,
mercy, hospitality), while others interpenetrate: "exhortation"
(Rom 12:8, which elsewhere is a duty laid on everyone), "faith"

---

[18] Cf. my commentary on the treatise on the charisms in the *Summa Theolog-
ica* of St. Thomas, II/II, 171-82 ("Besondere Gnadengaben und die zwei Wege
menschlichen Lebens", in the Latin-German edition of St. Thomas, vol. XXIII
[1954]), esp. 284ff.: "According to Thomas, the giving of a charism in the full
sense of the word, while it does not presuppose holiness in the recipient, calls for
it, because apart from grace the recipient cannot be *idoneus susceptor*" (288).

(1 Cor 12:9), which must be only a particular intensity of the general Christian attribute, and, above all, "prophecy", which overlaps with the gifts of wisdom and knowledge (v. 8) and signifies the ability to communicate to the Church whatever God's will is here and now. Prophecy can persist in the Church in various gifts of the Spirit that do not appear by name in the Pauline catalogue: for instance, in genuine theology that is pursued in the Holy Spirit; and in the "mysticism" we find eminently in Paul himself, though as yet it is not called by that name. There are also the charisms of famous founders (such as the world vision of St. Benedict, the all-embracing vision of salvation in St. Ignatius of Loyola and the experiences of St. John of the Cross and St. Teresa) which are commonly called "mystical" but which are just as charismatic, being given "for the common good" (1 Cor 12:7) of the whole Church and in particular for the benefit of the particular Church family being equipped. The same applies to other charisms such as, for example, the profound intuitions of great Church Fathers (to mention only Origen, Basil, and Augustine) or great "mystics" like St. Hildegard, the two Mechthilds, or Lady Julian of Norwich. It is fruitless to try to distinguish the "charismatic" from the "mystical".

It must be insisted, however, that the Holy Spirit is also responsible for the distinct existence, in Church office, of charismatic elements, on the one hand, and non-charismatic ecclesial charisms, on the other. Accordingly, the tensions which may arise between them are to be endured patiently, in the same Holy Spirit, in a spirit of ecclesial peace. Church office is responsible in a special way for testing the spirits (though, according to 1 John 4:1 and 1 Thessalonians 5:21, this testing should be exercised by the whole community), and it is quite possible for a charismatic "spirit" to be found to be genuine even when it criticizes situations in the Church or when it is charged with introducing something new into the Church in response to the contemporary situation, that is, something that is not immediately obvious to the Church's office-bearers and is perhaps ahead of its time. One thinks of the tragedy of Mary Ward or of the tension between Ignatius and Pope Paul IV (Caraffa)—Ignatius did not live to see its resolution. Tensions such as these can be anguished and extreme, but they must be endured in that ecclesial and divine obedience to which we can apply the last of the Beatitudes; patience here attracts a special blessing and fruitfulness from the Holy Spirit.

The hierarchy, especially entrusted with the task of discerning spirits, must always remember that it is rarely the originator of those new departures in the Church that are willed and executed by the Spirit. Generally they come from the ranks of the nonofficial believers, such as Francis of Assisi, Ignatius, Teresa of Avila, and many others; or are called into being by priests afire with the Spirit, such as Francis de Sales, Vincent de Paul, Philip Neri, or Bérulle, who, like Newman, was late in being made a cardinal. The charism of great popes and bishops extends to the reanimation (*anazōpyrein*, 2 Tim 1:6)[19] of the Church or the diocese as a whole, and for this task they are equipped with the relevant charisms, such as "wisdom", "knowledge", "exhortation", "leadership", and "prophecy". It is mostly not their business to found special "families"; yet there are famous instances where Spirit-inspired communities have been used by them for the great sanctifying and missionary work of the whole Church.

Finally, it should not be forgotten that no hard and fast borderlines can be ascertained between the reception of the sacraments that confer the Spirit in a special way (baptism, confirmation) by all believers and the by no means "extraordinary" charisms, such as "showing mercy", "hospitality", and "almsgiving". Every Christian has his vocation and, thus, his "gift [charism] from God" (1 Cor 7:7), and he is to live according to it,[20] even if he should also "earnestly desire the higher gifts [charisms]" (1 Cor 12:31). Such aspiration, as the context shows, will always set him on, and point him toward, the "still more excellent way", the way of love.

---

[19] On the history and occurrence of this word, cf. the many references in C. Spicq, *Les Épîtres Pastorales*, 4th ed. (1969), II, 707f.

[20] On the correct interpretation of this passage, cf. N. Baumert, *Ehelosigkeit und Ehe im Herrn: Eine Neuinterpretation von 1 Kor 7* (Würzburg: Echter, 1984), 48–63.

5

OBJECTIVE SPIRIT

a. Tradition-Scripture-Church Office

Just as Yahweh's covenant was more than all the oral or written traditions that existed about it in Israel, the New Testament fulfillment of this covenant is more than all objective testimonies and instruments of Christ's presence and of his Spirit in the Church. On the other hand, these testimonies go far beyond the individual's relationship with Christ; the individual attains a true and divinely intended access to Christ only within the Church's all-embracing communion. For her part, the Church (as Christ's Body and Bride) shows herself to be "greater than" by the inner interweaving of tradition-Scripture-office, but also through her sacraments (to be discussed in what follows), her liturgy, her canonical order, and the theology that expounds these. This interwoven reality is objective for the individual: only through it is he introduced into the fullness of subjectivity of Christ and his Spirit.

This topic is vast. It can only be approached in summary form, our gaze fixed on its center, the Holy Spirit. For the Spirit—never separated from Christ—is the sovereign Lord of tradition (both of its content and of the act of communicating it), just as he is Lord of Scripture (which remains a dead letter apart from him) and most definitely Lord of ecclesial office, which we have just described as a prominent form of charism.

We begin with God's act of entrusting himself (*traditio*). In the Old Covenant he entrusts himself to Abraham and Moses, where all is sealed with words that are in the form of deeds; Scripture, with its work of capturing and fixing, comes only much later. Israel's traditions of mighty deeds are never recollections of a dead past, as is shown most clearly by the feasts that made these deeds present and the constant "relectures" of the words of the prophets, by which they were applied to current situations. The writing up of God's words/deeds takes place at a late stage; even when gathered together in the corpus of Scripture, it remains the testimony, not so much of new prophetic words from God, but of the certainty of his here-and-now covenant faithfulness in a period of spiritual desolation (Dan 9:1–19). It is highly significant that, since the covenant was two-sided right from its inception, God required Israel to give its consent, and Israel's appropriate response to God (for example, the Psalms) was adopted into the "inspired" word of God.[1]

Jesus, who is both the completion of God's word/deed, addressed to the world, and the world's answer to God, knows that he himself is not only the final speaker and actor of the Father's word to the world, but also the earth's fully valid answer to heaven. So his exegesis of the Father not only descends vertically from heaven: it is also a critical clarification and heightening of all the words of God addressed to Israel. He extracts the Father's original meaning and will (Mt 19:4–6) out of human falsification and overpainting (Mk 7:1–23). He knows that Moses' deeds and words have him as their goal (Jn 5:15ff.); accordingly, when he has risen, "beginning with Moses and all the prophets, he interpreted to them in all the scriptures the things concerning himself" "in the law of Moses and the prophets and the psalms" (Lk 24:27, 44), showing how they refer to himself, his death and Resurrection. In this way he established the pattern for the entire apostolic age: "interpretation of Scripture" is an unveiling (literally so in 2 Corinthians 3) of the meaning of the whole ("Old") Covenant, which is Christ. Ephesians 2:20 tells us that this was a new form of "prophecy" (by the apostles or others) that was foundational for the Church of Christ. Here we can begin to see the significance of apostolic office as a continuation of the authority of Christ.[2] The interpretation of the entire "Old Testament" with a view to the fullness that has come in Christ is the true meaning of "allegory" or "typology".[3] However, this living wealth of meaning was far

---

[1] G. von Rad, *Theologie des Alten Testaments* I (Munich, 1957), 333f.

[2] "The Church (of the first decades), which existed without apostolic writings, was a Church that possessed the prophetic writings and was animated and guided by the apostles" (Y. Congar, *La Tradition et les traditions*, 2 vols. [Paris: Fayard, 1960, 1963], a work that is practically inexhaustible on this subject, in terms of objectivity and bibliographical material). Cf. II, 171.

[3] H. de Lubac, *Histoire et Esprit: L'Intelligence de l'Écriture d'après Origène* (Paris: Aubier, 1956), 166ff., 206ff.

greater than could be put into words, so that it was impossible
for Christ, the Fulfiller, to write it down. Christianity is not
the religion of a book: the Bible cannot be compared with the
Book of Qumran or the Book of Mormon. Thomas gives three
reasons why Christ could not bequeath any written document to
us: first, because of his sublime dignity, which directly imprinted
words into the hearts of his listeners; second, "on account of
the excellence of Christ's doctrine, which cannot be expressed
in writing. . . . And if Christ had committed his doctrine to
writing, men would have had no deeper thought of his doctrine
than that which appears on the surface of the writing"; and third,
because he wished to give his disciples the task of handing on
his teaching, in part orally and in part in written form: this living mediation (written and oral) would serve the propagation
of his revelation—and here we see the dimension of ecclesial
office.[4] In Luke and John the interpretation and transmission of
Christ's existence is explicitly left to the Holy Spirit, who will
inspire both preaching and the apostolic writings. But again we
must say that the Spirit will "take what is mine and declare it
to you" (Jn 16:14): that is, not something of past history, but
something that makes present the hidden fullness of the Lord
who is present in the Spirit. Here we need to preserve a living
balance: the Spirit, who is the animator of the whole Church,
will be simultaneously the Spirit of tradition, of Scripture, and
of Church office.

The Gospel is none other than Christ himself. He is the source
(*fons*) whence we receive everything, by word of mouth or by
written letter (but mediated to us by the Church's preaching).[5]
If the Spirit is the Lord of the whole work of interpretation,
he does this by drawing upon the source, the living Christ. Irenaeus sees everything in the right context: "Those who do not
have the Spirit do not draw their life's nourishment from the
bosom of their Mother (the Church); they have nothing of that

---

[4] *S. Th.* III, 42, 4c.

[5] At the Council of Trent many theologians (following C. Schatzgeyer and N.
Herborn) accused the Protestants of equating Scripture and the Word of God.
"But Scripture is only a sign of the gospel, a document that attests it. The gospel
is not primarily a written text but the divine power that effects salvation." Claude
Lejay stressed that the canonical Scriptures were secondary to the gospel, which
alone possesses absolute authority. Cf. Congar, ES II, 46.

which comes from the purest source, the Body of Christ."[6] All that comes from him—word, sacrament, authority, all that we mean by "Church"—is "love": it is the fulfillment of what, in the Old Covenant, was only *figura*.[7] So Origen could construct a doctrine of the "threefold Body of Christ": his physical Body, his eucharistic and mystical Body, and his scriptural Body:[8] this gives a clear exposition of "sacramentality", that is, everything that comes from Christ, most definitely including his word.[9] What this picture fails to show is the sublime height of both Christ and the Holy Spirit above all these "embodiments". The latter can never fully contain God's inner self-surrender as act, for what we have here is, not something automatic or magical, but something that depends on the believing and loving receptivity of the receiving or transmitting subject. If the exegete treats Scripture like any other text, the "spirit and life" will not be revealed in the dead letter; if one receives Holy Communion without faith, one will receive nothing of the inner grace; one can "hand on" statements of the Fathers as if they were bricks, but this has nothing to do with God's primal "handing over" of himself. Even the bearer of office in the Church can go about his business in a "purely official" way, in which case his actions will have practically no claim on the authority imparted by such office. Christ's Holy Spirit, who guarantees what we mean by "Church", must indwell the act or entire process if his spark is to be transmitted to the recipient. The Church, as the sacrament of Christ, is guaranteed this contact because, at her core, she is the *immaculata* (Eph 5:27): she is ordained effectively to proclaim God's self-revelation and the unveiling of his mystery (Eph 3) down through the ages.

[6] *Adv. Haer.* III, 24, 1. In Hippolytus, the Body of Christ is paradise, from which four streams flow (cf. Jn 7:38): *In Dan.* I, 17 (Sources Chrétiennes 14 [1947]), 103–5.

[7] The topic goes right through the patristic era (cf. de Lubac, *Exégèse médiévale* "Omnia in figura" II/2 [1964], 60–84). It constitutes the main argument of Pascal's apologetics in his *Pensées*; cf. my [German] translation in *Schriften zur Religion*, Christliche Meister 17 (Einsiedeln: Johannesverlag, 1982), 256–328.

[8] For the texts and an evaluation of them, cf. H. de Lubac, *Histoire et Esprit*, "Les Incorporations du Logos" (336–73); there may be oriental influences here. H. de Lubac, "Textes alexandrins et bouddhiques", RSR, 1939, 336–52. There is an echo of this in Ambrose, *In Luc.* 6, 33 (PL 15, 1763).

[9] H. de Lubac, *Exégèse médiévale* I/2 (1959), 523f.

It is crucial, therefore, that God's gift of love be handed on through the believing and loving Church through all the ages of the world. That is her mission. This explains the primacy of tradition, the act of handing on the divine gift she has perfectly received. This is what Christ was charged to do in his preliminary mission and, subsequently, in his definitive mission once the Holy Spirit had come. This *traditio* is meant to be full and exhaustive: "Make disciples of all nations, baptizing them . . . , teaching them to observe all that I have commanded you" (Mt 28:19-20). While such tradition, of course, was essentially based on the fulfillment of the old Scriptures (according to Christ's explanation and example), the fulfillment consisted in God's superabundant love made visible; so, according to Thomas, "that which is preponderant in the law of the New Testament", the Gospel, "is the grace of the Holy Ghost, which is given through faith in Christ". The written "New Testament" that comes later is "secondary" and "dispositive".[10] What Christ's commissioned messengers say (and Baptism and Eucharist give the ultimate seal to their message) is primarily addressed to hearts and is written upon hearts (2 Cor 3:3),[11] and only the Holy Spirit can transform the external sound into an inner understanding. It will be the same once the Church possesses a New Testament "Holy Scripture", for

> Scripture is nothing other than the witness of the Church herself, written by the Holy Spirit, for it is he who speaks and testifies here. . . . The Holy Scriptures are not to be understood by everyone working out his own meaning: they are interpreted according to the meaning the Holy Spirit has taught, and continues to teach, through the Church down to the present time. Thus, on the basis of the Spirit who dwells in her, the Church can teach things that were hidden heretofore, showing that they are part of the truth of faith, either found in the Holy Scriptures already revealed or from the apostolic traditions that have come down to us or have been otherwise revealed by God.[12]

In the earliest period, however, "Holy Scripture" means the interpretation of the ancient writings with a view to Christ. There

---

[10] *S. Th.* I/II, 106, 1.

[11] Cf. Y. Congar, "L'Évangile écrit dans les coeurs", ES II, 245-53.

[12] J. Driedo, *De Eccles. Scripturis et dogmatibus* (1933), in *Opera* (Louvain, 1556), I, fol. 61v.

was, in this apostolic preaching, an organic norm separating what was central from what was peripheral, as we can see from the concept of the *regula fidei* or *veritatis*, evident in the baptismal formula, in the accompanying questions to the candidate, in the professions of faith that arose from this, and, finally, in the common teaching of all the Churches.[13]

> If it is true that, in the New Testament, Scripture has undergone a growth, it can no longer have that final and exclusive meaning which, according to Paul, it had in the Old Testament. Rather, it is an instrument whereby the old is opened up to the new context of the mystery of Christ. It is, as it were, the halted process of the new interpretation of Scripture centered on Christ. It does not wish to be autonomous in any way; it does not wish to be closed in on itself by exegesis of the letter: it can only exist within the spiritual reality of Jesus Christ, who, . . . in the Holy Spirit, discloses to the disciples what at one stage they were not able to bear.[14]

Indeed, we can say that, in its strangely fragmentary form (reminiscences of Jesus, more or less accidental letters, and a book of visions in which the Seer is commanded to write them down) and from a purely human point of view, Scripture was an indispensable help given by the Spirit—considering the rapid process of corruption of the memory of Jesus (in Gnosticism, but even in Papias). Scripture is given to the Church as a special charism, to serve as a sure standard for her authoritative tradition. "So this written testimony is not something extrinsic to tradition and its authoritative representatives; rather, it is an aspect of (and in) tradition, so that unity and constantly operative diversity (that is, the constant reality of Scripture's normative function) are both ultimately guaranteed, and guaranteed solely, by the ever-victorious power of the Spirit. . . . Thus there can be Holy

[13] In Irenaeus, the *regula fidei* is the "rule of faith that has come down from the apostles and is preserved in the Church through the succession of elders" (*Adv. Haer.* III, 2, 2; 3, 2). In Origen the first norm is not Scripture but the teaching that comes down from the apostles (in unbroken succession), whether it is called "word of God", "word of the Church", "ecclesial canon", or something else. (*In Jer.*, hom. 15, 14; cf. *In Matt.*, comm. 46 [PG 3, 1667D]).

[14] J. Ratzinger, "Ein Versuch zur Frage des Traditionsbegriffs", in K. Rahner and J. Ratzinger, *Offenbarung und Überlieferung*, QD 25 (1965), 38.

Scripture only within authoritative tradition."[15] In this sense, the New Testament Scriptures are "interstitial".[16] Nicholas of Cusa emphasizes that Christ built his Church "sine littera",[17] and even Irenaeus had pointed to the "barbarian nations" who "have salvation without paper and ink but, rather, through the Holy Spirit written in their hearts and who carefully and faithfully maintain the ancient traditions".[18] Blondel sees the Church as "the guardian of the original gift, which was not fully formulated as such or fully understood, but which she had always possessed in its entirety. The Church sets us free from the Scriptures themselves, while she constantly bends over them in reverence; she wishes to lead us, not solely through the Scriptures, to the real Christ, who cannot be exhaustively depicted or replaced by any literary portrait."[19] Hence the constantly repeated argument that Scripture must be interpreted and grasped under the influence of that same Spirit who dictated it,[20] for what is taking place is the Holy Spirit's delivery of testimony concerning Christ to someone who desires to accept it in faith.

So we can grant that Scripture has a *sufficientia*, provided that it has its place within the Church (herself endowed with the Spirit and with the guardianship of ecclesial office) and is preached, read, and interpreted within the Church. This is how the Fathers and the Middle Ages generally understood the sufficiency of Scripture.[21] But this understanding must be clearly separated from the *sola scriptura* principle of the Reformers, who—in a nutshell—lifted Scripture out of the "sacrament" that the Church is and set it up as a norm over against the Church. Revelation of God's love in Christ is "concluded" with the Cross and Resurrection, and the Spirit can interpret it in a new, different, and

---

[15] K. Rahner, "Zur Theologie der Heiligen Schrift", in *Sacramentum Mundi* IV (1969), 428f. See also his "Schrift und Tradition", *Sacramentum Mundi* IV, 443–51.

[16] A. v. Harnack, *Dogmengeschichte* II, 87, no. 3.

[17] *Ep.* 7 (*Werke* [Paris, 1514], II, fol. XX): "Non est igitur littera, quae per tyrannum penitus deteri posset, de essentia ecclesiae, sed Spiritus est qui vivificat."

[18] *Adv. Haer.* III, 4, 1–2.

[19] *Histoire et dogme*, 2d ed. (1956), 204–5.

[20] Examples in ES I, 169–70.

[21] Ibid., 139–50. Exhaustively presented in seven theses: ES II, 140–60.

deeper way until the end of the world, always starting from the testimony given by the Spirit in Scripture. The letter of this testimony, however, is so filled with the Spirit that its "forward-orientated"[22] interpretation can never come to an end.

The mission to preach and interpret the mystery cannot be divorced from ecclesial office, which comes explicitly from Christ's command. This much is clear from the time of Clement of Rome, Ignatius, and Irenaeus; but it is the pastoral office (more than the "teaching" office of recent centuries) that as such has the task of guaranteeing the genuineness of the interpreting tradition. Of course, the councils are part of this, aware that they are directed by the Holy Spirit. Here we need to make a special study of why there has been a gradual and increasing concentration on the hierarchy's more juridical functions (in medieval times it was first and foremost a court of law), strengthened by the Reformation critique and in the wake of definitions (Vatican I, where Magisterium and tradition come very close together).[23] What is important here is to notice that, right from the start, tradition (*paradosis*) was unthinkable apart from this secure anchor.

We have said enough to convince the reader that Christ alone (with his antecedents under the Old Covenant) can be designated the sole source of revelation, interpreted by the Holy Spirit in the tradition and in the Scripture (equipped with a special authority) that it contains. But

> tradition and Scripture do not constitute two sources that are merely externally complementary and independent. . . . Ancient Christians could not separate Scripture and tradition, for the former was an essential part of the latter—its core, so to speak. On the other hand, if the Bible is wrenched from the living totality of the multifarious elements of tradition that the self-consciousness of the ever-vigilant and ever-active Church preserves and transmits, it becomes unintelligible. For the Catholic, therefore, the Bible and tradition means, not the Bible *plus* some alien element without which it would be incomplete, but the Bible within its own native

[22] R. Asting, *Die Verkündigung des Wortes um Urchristentum dargestellt an den Begriffen 'Wort Gottes', 'Evangelium' und 'Zeugnis'* (Stuttgart, 1939).
[23] Cf. ES I, 271–78: "Limites mises au pouvoir ecclésiastique ou à son exercice".

atmosphere, its own vital sphere, its own original light. The Bible, yes, but the whole Bible, together with the guiding Spirit who dictated it and never ceases to inspire those who read it.[24]

If the Bible is not situated in this context, then, as Shakespeare says, the devil himself can quote Scripture for his own ends. Jerome had already observed that "we could all take the letter and use it to promote some new doctrine."[25] Taken in isolation, as in Protestant orthodoxy, it changes Christianity into the religion of a book. The great Reformers prepared a path for this development by cutting the Bible loose from tradition and office and then linking it with the Holy Spirit in such a way that the Spirit rendered the Bible "self-evident". Nowadays, however, this "principle of Scripture" is largely relativized; "proclamation" (Bultmann's *kerygma*) has moved into first place, or (as a way of avoiding biblical criticism) some spiritual experience mediated by Scripture or an intellectual grasp of the course of history, documented in the transition from Old to New Testament.[26]

The Spirit's role in office-Scripture-tradition overcomes any one-sided attachment to the past. Just as, in ecclesiastical office, the presence of Christ is continually brought about in the sacraments, so too, through Scripture's constant interpretation in the Spirit, it is continually rendered contemporary, relevant, and pointing toward the future. In a similar way, too, the elements of tradition—the saints, the Fathers, Doctors of the Church, and so on—maintain a kind of presence and currency that abolishes much of the historical distance between us and them, thanks to the supratemporal understanding of all true Christians in the *communio sanctorum*. There is no essential difference in the way Irenaeus understood the relationship between tradition, Scripture, and office and the way we understand it; in the eternal

---

[24] L. Bouyer, *La Bible et l'Évangile*, Lectio divina 8 (Paris, 1951), 11–12.

[25] *Ad Luciferianos* 28 (PL 23, 182A).

[26] See the article "Schriftprinzip" (G. Gloege in RGG, 3d ed. [1961] V, 1540–43). Gloege rightly sees that the watchword "sola scriptura" is much older than the Reformation but that the new understanding was prepared for by separating Scripture from office and tradition, as we have said.

Spirit we experience something of our sharing in the eternity of Christ's Church.[27]

Of course this does not mean that the individual believer could not receive direct illumination from the Spirit concerning a piece of Scripture or of tradition without the intervention of the external "teaching office". Ever since the Fathers we know that the *magisterium internum* in the hearts of believers is not bound to the official *magisterium externum*; the former must not be isolated from the latter. In the mystery of the Church, where everything that concerns our salvation has to be *received*, the *magister interior* speaks to the individual, never in a purely "private" capacity, but with a view to his Christian vocation, which is always related to the Church of today and of all time. It is Möhler and Newman who disclose the most profound insights here.

b. Proclamation and Liturgy

Karl Barth's bitter complaints to the effect that Catholic dogmatics proceed from the doctrine of grace and the Church and go straight to the sacraments, maintaining a *silentium altissimum* on proclamation and preaching ("the Mass may be complete without it"),[28] were largely obsolete when they appeared (in 1932). One only has to read all that the Second Vatican Council said on proclamation, preaching, and the homily and note what importance the sermon has acquired in today's celebration of the Eucharist. Nonetheless, we have to face the question of whether there has been enough theoretical and practical reflection on the way in which this primary ecclesial task is related to the Holy Spirit.

It is true that, in the Gospel, the task of proclaiming the good news is entrusted by Christ, first in a provisional way (Mt 10; Lk 9:1–6; 10:1–20) and then definitively (Mt 28:16–20); but the disciples have to wait to be finally "clothed with power from

[27] Very illuminating here is J. Ratzinger's interpretation of Trent's decree on tradition, "Versuch", 50–69.

[28] *Church Dogmatics* I/1 (Edinburgh, 1936–1975), 66. "In sharp distinction from the sacrament, preaching is not a constitutive element in the Roman Catholic concept of the priesthood" (67).

on high" (Lk 24:49): "You shall receive power when the Holy
Spirit has come upon you; and you shall be my witnesses . . .
to the end of the earth" (Acts 1:8). What is most striking in the
account of Pentecost is the conjunction of the Spirit, who comes
upon the apostles as a stormy wind, and the beginning of their
preaching to all the assembled nations (Acts 2). Only after the
most objective of all witnesses to God's work of salvation has
been given to the disciples can they become what Jesus wants
them to be: not merely people who report what they have experienced (however stupendous this may be), but "ambassadors"
through whom "God [makes] his appeal", who speak "on behalf of Christ" (2 Cor 5:20; 1 Tim 2:7), uttering not their own
word, but, through this word, proclaiming God's word to the
world. If the Spirit spoke of old through the prophets ("I have
put my words in your mouth": Jer 1:9) and empowered Jesus
to proclaim his message (Lk 4:18), and if Jesus entrusted his
Spirit-word to the disciples ("He who hears you, hears me": Lk
10:16), it follows that the word of God cannot be uttered by
the mouth of man unless the latter is empowered by the Holy
Spirit.

Paul[29] is profoundly aware of this: "Our gospel came to you
not only in word, but also in power and in the Holy Spirit and
with full conviction" (1 Thess 1:5). "My speech and my message
were not in plausible words of wisdom, but in demonstration of
the Spirit and power, that your faith might not rest in the wisdom
of men but in the power of God" (1 Cor 2:4–5). True, he speaks
as one claiming authority, because he has been sent in order to
preach ("And how can men preach unless they are sent?" Rom
10:15), but he can do this only because the power of what he has
to say is in emphatic contrast to his own weakness (2 Cor 12:9),
fear, and hesitancy (2 Cor 11:6); ultimately he preaches as a fol-
lower of Christ, who "was crucified in weakness, but lives by
the power of God" (2 Cor 13:4). God the Father's loudest word
of salvation was the Cross and his own silence; and so the Apostle, preaching "for the sake of Christ", in "weaknesses, insults,
hardships, persecutions, and calamities" (2 Cor 12:10) is certain

---

[29] Cf. Max-Alain Chevallier, *Esprit de Dieu, paroles d'hommes: Le Rôle de l'Esprit
dans les ministères de la Parole selon l'apôtre Paul* (Neuchâtel, 1966).

of the power of what he is communicating. Thus, in uttering his proclamation to the community and the world, he can call for the obedience of faith, not for himself, but for Christ (Rom 1:5; 16:26). Since he fights with "the sword of the Spirit, which is the word of God" (Eph 6:17), his proclamation can make present the Lord who speaks through him. Preaching Christ, he is not pointing to the past but to things that are utterly present and future for his hearers, for the Holy Spirit is essentially the One who makes the Son present and, in him, the Father. And this making present by the Spirit is not only a continuation of things in the past but also their fulfillment (Rom 15:19; cf. Col 1:25). In this way the Spirit renders the proclamation into an "event", not unlike the way he makes the mysteries of the Son's Incarnation into present events in the sacraments, administered ever anew. Insofar as this proclamation is a divine event, it is far greater than the human element in the sermon: "And we also thank God constantly for this, that when you received the word of God which you heard from us, you accepted it not as the word of men but as what it really is, the word of God, which is at work in you believers" (1 Thess 2:13).

Proclamation has this task of making salvation present, as "event", both in the community's worship and in its mission to those who do not yet believe. Each activity points to the other. And as for the one who is sent to proclaim this message, he is not some neutral instrument of the Spirit who only has to hand on information he himself has heard; he himself is summoned to collaborate in this making present by responsibly taking into account his hearers' intellectual constitution and cultural situation; he must take pains to make subjectively present what is objectively so. God's word and Gospel is rich and living: it is adequate for all historical times. The messenger does not have to engage in an artificial tour-de-force; prayer and meditation will be enough to throw a bridge between the inner fullness of the Gospel and the needs of his hearers.

So far we have been speaking primarily of the official mission to preach. However, the last council and the new codex have taught us that every Christian, whether priest or layman, is empowered and obligated, without having received any special *missio*, to proclaim the content of faith through what he says and how he lives. This follows from his baptism and confirmation. So far we have considered preaching primarily in the context of the objective Holy Spirit in the Church; but it is so intimately connected with the subjective holiness of the preacher that the Letter of Peter can speak of the influence of a wordless Christian life (1 Pet 3:1); in fact, the preacher's way of life has a decisive effect on the impact of his words.[30] If we reflect on what we have said about Christ as the Father's Word, it becomes clear, furthermore, that what the believer has to proclaim is to be found in the living existence of the God-man and not in the formulations of Holy Scripture: the content of the proclamation is the fact of "God's Word in the flesh", not the (doubtless normative) Bible. The fixed word of scripture points beyond itself to an ever-living mystery, which can announce itself even through the changing forms of living language[31]—and we say this without wishing to downgrade Scripture. On the one hand, Scripture gives the impression of immobility, yet we must not forget that it is the same Spirit (even in the Old Testament) who guided the Son,

[30] Pie Duployé, O.P., in his little work *Rhétorique et Parole de Dieu* (Cerf, 1955), quotes the following words of François Mauriac: "What I ask of the priest is that he give God to me, not merely talk about God. I am not undervaluing the preaching office, but, for me, the most effective preaching was the priest's own life. A good priest does not need to say anything to me: I just look at him, and that is enough." Duployé criticizes Mauriac severely (and it is true that the latter is given to exaggeration), but these words should nonetheless make the preacher think.

[31] At this point we can refer to the insights of Wilhelm von Humboldt in the area of the philosophy of language: "Language is objectively effective and independent insofar as it is subjectively effected and dependent. For it has no abiding city, not even in written form. Its dead limbs, as it were, must be continually recreated in the intellect, brought to life in speech and understanding, and thus they must transcend entirely into the subject. It belongs to this act of recreation, however, to objectify language; and on each occasion language thus experiences the whole influence of the individual. Again, this influence is in turn bound by what it creates and has created" (*Natur und Beschaffenheit der Sprache*, in *Werke*, 5 vols. [Darmstadt, 1963], III, 438). The preservation of language "through writing is always an imperfect, mummifying process, which needs to be brought before our senses through living speech. In itself it is not a work (*ergon*) but an activity (*energeia*)" (*Sprachbau und Entwicklung des Menschengeschlects*, in ibid., III, 418). Here Humboldt is speaking of ordinary human writing and is not concerned with the "pneumatic" character of holy Scripture; nonetheless the Bible also has this human side that he is describing.

inspired Scripture, and animates the Church's constant preaching. The Spirit, who is above history, lives in all three forms in the milieu of history. He does this in an explicitly eschatological manner, since, in the Church, all preaching and proclamation always addresses man as a traveller on the way to his eternal goal. We can make decisions that are correct for today if, in making them, we keep our eye on the personal and historical Omega.

So all proclamation in the Church, all Christian proclamation, is always transcending itself. First, because the historical past of the Son's theophany, even as made present by the Spirit, is ever greater and more mysterious than what the preached word can encompass. And second, because, at this stage, the pneumatic, eschatological Lord can only be embraced in hope, not by sight. This does not mean, however, that the preacher can only speak with a hesitant stammering; like the apostles, he is acting as the appointed servant in a precisely defined task: his mission is to proclaim the good news, *euangelion*, here and now, with his faith and his intellect, with his whole person.

Of course, the apostle acts as someone with a unique commission. After all, he is the original "builder" and "planter" of the communities; or rather, God is, using the apostle as his preferred instrument.[32] But the apostle himself takes it for granted that it is the same Spirit who both inspires his proclamation and shares in the delivery of it to the community, inspiring the latter by his word and by baptism. Not only has everyone his particular charism, through the Spirit's operation, for the benefit of the others; not only is there in the community both prophecy and didascalia; but the community as a whole is "a letter from Christ . . . written . . . with the Spirit of the living God . . . on tablets of human hearts" (2 Cor 3:3). Since, in the New Covenant, the Spirit is indissolubly linked to proclamation, this letter, written by the Spirit, must needs proclaim something to the world. And it does so, not only in the community's individual members, but as a totality, whenever it celebrates the Lord's Supper in liturgical form: "As often as you eat this bread and drink the chalice, you *proclaim* the Lord's death until he comes" (1 Cor 11:26).[33]

---

[32] Chevallier, *Esprit de Dieu*, 21–63.

[33] It is a matter of controversy whether the liturgical celebration as such is "pro-

The Supper is a doxology to God, but, as the apologists show, it contains nothing esoteric in itself: Justin can describe it in detail for the benefit of the public. The blessing of this Supper is not for the Church alone but for the world, since it is a participation of the Body and Blood of Christ, who died expressly for the world in its totality and into whom the community is incorporated. Why should there not be "supplications, prayers, intercessions, and thanksgivings . . . for all men" (1 Tim 2:1) during the eucharistic celebration? The Church continues to do this today, praying in her Eucharistic Prayers for "all your children wherever they may be",[34] for "all who seek you with a sincere heart",[35] for "all who sleep in Christ";[36] "He chose to die that he might free all men from dying. He gave his life that we might live to you alone for ever."[37] The Church knows, too, that this gathering of believers on behalf of the world takes place through the Holy Spirit: "ut a Spiritu Sancto congregemur in unum",[38] "in unum corpus a Spiritu Sancto congregati".[39] Paul had spoken of his open proclamation of the Spirit, in contrast to the Synagogue service in which "a veil lies over [the] minds" of those who hear the reading of the law (2 Cor 3:15). This being so, we can also apply to the liturgy the statement that Christians who celebrate together (*pantes*: 2 Cor 3:18) in the "Spirit of the Lord" behold his glory "with unveiled faces" and are "transformed" into it. And since, in the eucharistic liturgy, there is an explicit "proclamation" of Christ's sacrificial death on behalf of all men, we can go on to interpret Romans 12:1-2 on the same basis: "I urge you, brothers, by the mercy of God [shown on the Cross] to present your bodies [your entire existence in

---

clamation" or whether what is meant is a sermon on the death of the Lord, delivered within the framework of such a celebration. This controversy is summed up by J. Schniewind, ThW I, 70-71. I find the second hypothesis unlikely; first, because it would tie the preacher down to a single theme and, second, because the celebration of the Supper precisely manifests its content.

[34] Third Eucharistic Prayer.

[35] Fourth Eucharistic Prayer.

[36] First Eucharistic Prayer.

[37] Second Preface for the Dead.

[38] Second Eucharistic Prayer.

[39] Third Eucharistic Prayer.

the body] as a living, holy sacrifice acceptable to God; let this be your liturgy, full of meaning". Immediately afterward, as in 2 Corinthians, he speaks of being "transformed" into the will of God. What is liturgy? "Bodily sacrifice, which means, not self-interiorization and moral self-affirmation, but a life that, in its concrete realization in the world, is extraordinary, eschatological, and therefore to be understood in cultic terms".[40]

If we look back, from this liturgy that concerns mankind as a whole—Christ on the Cross, in the community's Eucharist, and in the self-sacrifice of the individual Christian—to the apostolic preaching, it is Paul himself who interprets the latter in the liturgy's total context: ". . . because of the grace given to me by God to be a minister [*leitourgos*] of Christ Jesus to the Gentiles in the priestly service [*hierourgōn*] of the gospel of God, so that the offering of the Gentiles may be acceptable, sanctified by the Holy Spirit" (Rom 15:15–16). This liturgy is made possible by the presence of the Holy Spirit, as is shown by its four dimensions (set forth by H. Schlier),[41] which are expressly New Testament in character: Paul's "priestly sacrifice" is "a worldwide service of worship" in which he distinguishes himself from "all religious propaganda", for this service is "public and official, by no means a 'personal, charismatic undertaking', but an authorized, legitimized and delegated mandate, although it must be fulfilled in terms of charism and life." Thirdly, it is an "eschatological service" and, hence, fourthly, a "universal" one. The sacrifice is offered, no longer in the Jerusalem Temple by the carrying out of a ritual, but among the Gentiles, who are themselves the offered sacrifice; and it is the Holy Spirit who imparts this universal dimension (which is not merely geographically, but essentially universal) to the particular, ancient liturgy. All these dimensions, which are opened up by the Spirit and inwardly saturated by him (because man himself is drawn into the sacrifice), are ultimately grounded in Christ's self-sacrifice "in the eternal Spirit". Thus, by grace, the Christian—be he apostle

[40] Schlier, *Römerbrief*, 358.

[41] H. Schlier, *Martyria, Leiturgia, Diakonia, Festschrift Volk* (1968), 242–49, reprinted in *Das Ende der Zeit* (Herder, 1971): "Liturgie des apostolischen Evangeliums", 169–83.

or individual—is given space within this all-sufficient sacrifice to "complete what is lacking in Christ's afflictions" (Col 1:24).

c. Sacraments

While it is true that the sacraments belong to the dimension of the objective, ecclesial Holy Spirit, we have strongly emphasized that the work performed by God's Spirit (the *opus operatum*) in the (always) two-sided covenant action can never dispense with the cooperation of the human partner (the *opus operantis*)—even if, in borderline situations, this cooperation has to be supplied by a proxy member of Christ's Mystical Body (as in the baptism of infants). The prototype here is the Incarnation of the Logos, which is the freest grace possible yet does not take place without the perfect receptivity of Mary. A particularly eloquent reflection of this is the Church's offering of bread and wine (the *prosphora*) and the faith by which the worshippers entreat the descent of the Spirit (the *epiklēsis*); in this case, however, faith can and must lean on the sacrament's institution by Jesus and on his command to repeat the action—and in this it goes beyond Mary's mere, perfect acceptance. Or, too, quite simply, it depends on the questions asked of the candidate by the one administering the Church's sacrament: Do you believe? Alternatively it is based on the presence of contrition, without which the sinner cannot be granted valid absolution.[42] God alone is responsible for the act, but he inserts it into the required potency. Here, however, we are concerned, not with a general doctrine of the sacraments, but with their inner relationship with the Holy Spirit. But again, we are not dealing with a Holy Spirit separate from the Trinity, an isolated Holy Spirit given to the recipient, for instance, in baptism and confirmation. Rather, the Spirit plays his part in

[42] Without this two-sidedness that is of the essence of the covenant, sacraments descend to the level of magic. Cf. G. Söhngen's corrective (in *Symbol und Wirklichkeit im Kultmysterium* [1937], and *Der Wesensaufbau des Mysteriums* [1938]) to Odo Casel's pioneering studies on the objective real presence of Christ's redemptive mystery in the Eucharist. Söhngen insists that this "inner sacrament" must be complemented by the "outer sacrament" of our personal involvement. On this issue, cf. John Gordon Davies, *The Spirit, the Church and the Sacrament* (London: Forth Press, 1954).

the sacramental event as the one who brings about the trinitarian and ecclesial dimension: the Spirit draws the individual subject (who, if he is to desire a sacrament and prepare to receive it, must already possess something of the subjective Spirit—that is, the sinner must be contrite and want to be liberated from his sin) into the ecclesial realm with its objective holiness, which fills out any inadequacies of all that is subjective.

This is the basic shape of the sacramental event. We should not allow ourselves to be distracted from this by any borderline considerations, for they can never provide material for a valid sacramental doctrine. For example, the fact that there can be a baptism of desire (or of martyrdom) does not call the sacrament of baptism into question; the fact that the baptized infant cannot perform any act of faith says nothing against the requirement that a person who has reached the age of reason must make such an act in order to receive baptism; and the fact that a person who dispenses a sacrament can do so validly, and hence can mediate salvation, even if in the state of grave sin constitutes no objection, either. Emergency situations that render licit such things as lay confession, general absolution, and marriage without a priest present cannot create rules for normal situations. On the one hand, the basic shape points to the finite nature of the Church's horizon of knowing, beyond which God's merciful dealings cannot be discerned ("What is that to you? Follow me!": Jn 21:22); on the other hand, it is not based on some unquestionable, divine arbitrariness that—without any intelligible reason—has appointed an area of visible ecclesial reality, but on the positive finiteness of Christ's incarnational structure. The Church, as his "Body", participates in this and, as such, is endowed with his Spirit and given a mission. The Church's social dimension can no more be relativized than Christ's humanity can (and the latter remains even in the Resurrection), particularly since he himself expressly gave it this relation to himself, furnishing it with the appropriate plenary powers and teachings. The borderline instances, then, all depend on the vital center: there can only be baptism of desire because there is the sacrament of baptism, which a person would receive if he had adequate insight into God's saving plan, and so on. The individual sacramental forms can change, but the Church's intention to follow her Lord's intention cannot. His intention is to enable man, at the decisive points of his life—whether they are once for all and unrepeatable (baptism-confirmation, ordination, matrimony, at least for the lifetime of the spouse) or repeatable—to participate in God's objective holiness in his Church, in order to promote his subjective efforts to follow Christ in his situation or his state of life (that is, in penance or matrimony) or to declare him qualified (in the sacrament of orders). It is in this sense—that is, seeing the sacrament as a participation, through the guiding, operant Spirit, in the objective, ecclesial holiness that is superior to all personal holiness—that we shall now make a brief examination of the sacraments.

Baptism-confirmation. It is well known how indissolubly the two aspects of this sacrament of initiation into the Church are linked, both in Scripture and in tradition. It would serve no purpose to try to distinguish them in detail here. We must simply hold fast to the fact that "even baptism on its own endows us with the Holy Spirit at a fundamental level, so that the anointing (*chrismatio*), a symbol of the imparting of the Spirit, does not contradict the supernatural reality of baptism." There is "a fundamental participation in Christ's priestly and royal dignity through baptism and a more intensive one through confirmation".[43] As early as the Acts of the Apostles, where Christian baptism (unlike the baptism of John) imparts the Holy Spirit in principle, there are the diverse and irreducible variants: normally baptism with the giving of the Holy Spirit (Acts 1:5; 2:38; 19:2–5), which can be followed by the laying on of hands (particularly where the giving of charisms of the Spirit is concerned, 19:6); but it can also happen that it is not at baptism but at the (later) apostles' imposition of hands that the Holy Spirit is given (8:17). It is also possible for the Holy Spirit to descend even before baptism, with baptism being administered subsequently (10:44–48; cf. 9:17–19). In the early Church, when the imposition of hands was accompanied by an anointing, it is possible to see that water-baptism was directed more to the washing away of sins (later, following Romans 6, in

---

[43] H. Elfers, "Gehört die Salbung mit Chrisma zum ältesten abendländischen Initiationsritus zur Taufe oder zur Firmung?" in *Theologie und Glaube* 34 (1942): 336, 341.

the context of dying with Christ),[44] whereas the imposition of
hands with anointing was directed more to the imparting of the
Spirit. Here, as we have already said, a first imposition of hands
and anointing belonged to baptism, while a second sometimes
belonged to what later became confirmation.[45] The growing significance of the consecration and anointing of Myros in the East
made the distinction clear, whereas in the West the imposition
of hands predominates and anointing is added later. There can be
no doubt that the idea was latent in the ancient Church—to become explicit later on—that "confirmation completes and confirms what has already been established in baptism."[46] In Paul,
who certainly was familiar with the imposition of hands as well,
the entire saving event of entrance into the Church—which is
both Christ's Body and the Temple of the Spirit—is understood
to be baptism. Baptism here means (christologically) dying with
and into Christ and (pneumatologically) being "reborn through
the Holy Spirit", both of which are a gift of the Father's mercy
(cf. Tit 3, 5–7). As we saw, John speaks both of "being born
. . . of God" (Jn 1:13, where there is a markedly christological
tone; in Paul we are said to be sons together with Christ) and
"being born of the Spirit", with a reference to the "water" (3:5:
here we have a pneumatological realization of our being born
of God, which is both trinitarian and ecclesial; the latter is clear
from 1 John 2:20ff.). In baptism-confirmation the Spirit is the
One who introduces us to the objective mystery of salvation.
Thus (and only thus) do we acquire a share in him.

Penance. Baptism brings the forgiveness of sins; yet baptism can
only take place once (since it is our entrance into the Church).
The question then arises of how this forgiveness of sins can be

---

[44] There are only a few isolated instances in which it is said that water-baptism
lacks the imparting of the Holy Spirit, which must be given by the imposition
of hands: Tertullian, *De baptismo* 6, where, in fact, an angel of baptism "prepares
the way for the coming Holy Spirit by washing away transgressions". Similarly
in *De resurr. mort.* 8: "It is by imposition of hands that the soul is illumined by the
Spirit."

[45] The first clear traces of this are in Cyril of Jerusalem (3d *Myst. Catechesis*) and
Ambrose, with antecedents. Cf. B. Neunheuser, *Taufe und Firmung: Handbuch der
Dogmengeschichte* IV/2, 2d ed. (1983), 135.

[46] Neunheuser, *Taufe und Firmung*, 137.

repeated. So penance, regarded as the "second plank of salvation", to be used once only, at most, came to be located very close to baptism. However, there was Jesus' Easter commission: "Receive the Holy Spirit. Whose sins you forgive. . . ." And even before the rigorism of the first centuries there was a variety of "forms of penance" as practiced by Paul, including a total exclusion from the Church for "medicinal" reasons and for a limited period of time (1 Cor 5:5; 2 Cor 2:5–11).[47] The Holy Spirit given at Easter is initially the objective Spirit of the Church's power (and obligation) to forgive; however, arising out of the triune Father's forgiveness, which is the fruit of the Cross (understood as penance undertaken on behalf of all), the Spirit empowers [the Church] to grant the ecclesial Spirit, and hence the subjective Spirit, to those separated from the communion of saints. This official authorization to bring back, by the Holy Spirit's power, those who are separated from the Church is the ultimate intensification of something that is given to every Christian within the Church, namely, to forgive his debtor if he himself wishes to ask forgiveness from God (Mt 6:12, 14f.). But how is the excluded sinner to confess his sin and repent of it, except by measuring himself against the norm that, not he, but the Holy Spirit holds up to him and unless he "looks into the perfect law, the law of liberty, and perseveres" (Jas 1:25)?—bearing in mind that this law is only fulfilled in Christ and is held up to us—as a "mirror for penance"—by the Holy Spirit. Only such a man can appreciate the distance between himself and the norm; only he can enter the process of penance with the grace of contrition, confession, and resolution and so be received once again into the subjective communion of saints by the Church's objective authority.

Eucharist. This sacrament, which is central—though what takes place in the eucharistic action is even more than a sacrament—concerns the Body of Christ, which has become a "life-giving Spirit". It follows that the question of the role of the Holy Spirit

---

[47] Cf. the counterpart within the Church's communion: "If anyone will not obey our priestly instructions, take note of him and avoid fellowship with him. But do not treat him as an enemy; rather, point out the right path to him as a brother." Cf. Jude 23.

in making this Body present for and through the Church will be an especially burning one. And since the assembled community consists of baptized believers who share the life and unity of Christ and his Spirit, there will be an unsurpassable intensity and urgency when, offering themselves, they ask God for Christ's bodily presence. The first question we encounter here is the much-debated question of the epiclesis, the center and high point of the offering (*anaphora*) of what the Church is commanded to offer—bread and wine—symbols of her self-offering to God.[48] Early eucharistic liturgy presupposes that the Logos, who has incarnated himself in the Virgin, will "incarnate" himself, in an analogous manner, in bread and wine; hence the epiclesis addressed to the Logos himself, asking him to "eucharistize" himself in the two species.[49] The request can also be addressed to the Father, asking him to cause his Logos to descend into the sacramental forms.[50] Moreover, one must remember that, in early times, the divinity of the Logos was often designated as *pneuma* (in contrast to *sarx*); this means that many early "epicleses of the Spirit" were in fact epicleses of the Logos. The most well-known example is found in the "Church Order" of Hippolytus, where the Father is entreated "to send his Holy Spirit upon the offered gifts of the Holy Church"; this comes from a time when the subsistence of the third Divine Person was not yet realized in conscious reflection; hence, "there is no factual distinction, but only a terminological distinction, between Hippolytus' epiclesis of the Spirit and the epiclesis of the Logos found elsewhere."[51] This can be shown to be the case in Ignatius, Justin, Irenaeus, Clement and Origen, Methodius,

---

[48] In this tangled question of the epiclesis we are following the helpful clarifications of Johannes Betz, *Die Eucharistie in der Zeit der griechischen Väter* I/1 (Herder, 1955). Astonishingly, his exposition of the development fits in with the basic lines of the Spirit Christology we have outlined above, without getting embroiled in the one-sided polemics of the late (fourteenth-century) Orthodox quarrels concerning the Spirit's epiclesis.

[49] First elucidated by F. J. Dölger, *Ichthys* I (1910), 68–87; II (1920), 54ff. Cf. J. J. von Allmen, *Essai sur le Repas du Seigneur* (1966), 23–36.

[50] Irenaeus, *Adv. Haer.* IV, 18, 5. Also in the *Euchologium* of Serapion: "God of truth, let your holy Logos come down upon this bread" (13, 15). Further examples in Betz, *Eucharistie*, 335, n. 350.

[51] Betz, *Eucharistie*, 339–40.

Eusebius, and even in Athanasius, the Cappadocians, Cyril of Jerusalem, and the Antiochenes.[52] Nonetheless, a change takes place in Athanasius: from now on the Holy Spirit, a Person, is inseparable from the Logos; and this applies in particular to the Incarnation.[53] This formula, which we already saw clearly set forth in Cyril of Alexandria, needs only to be followed through theologically in a twofold direction to become the epiclesis of the Spirit as understood (in a purely personal sense) by Orthodoxy: a certain passivity comes into focus with Jesus' self-surrender at the Last Supper, since to give himself as food presupposes his slaying (Gregory of Nyssa).[54] (At this point one should examine Hartmut Gese's distinctive teaching in "Die Herkunft des Herrenmahls",[55] where he draws attention to a particular form of thank offering called *Toda*, in which there is a recalling of the situation of death and deliverance from it, found most of all in the Psalms: when Jesus gives himself away at the Supper, he is thinking primarily of his being offered up to death—Psalm 22 —and of being rescued from it; that is why Paul describes the reception of the Eucharist as a proclamation of the death.) In this absolute self-abandonment Christ allows the Spirit to have charge of "all that is mine", including his Body—which provides a profound justification for an epiclesis addressed to the Spirit in particular. But this epiclesis of the Spirit must not be isolated, for polemical reasons, from the Eucharistic Canon, which is formulated in a trinitarian manner.[56] Jesus' "passivity" in self-surrender is his most fruitful deed, which, at a new and higher

---

[52] Ibid., 267–300.

[53] "Where the Logos is, there is also the Spirit; and what is created out of the Logos has the power of being from the Spirit from the Logos" (*Adv. Serap.* 3, 5). "When the Logos descended into the holy Virgin, the Holy Spirit also immediately entered her together with him, and the Logos formed and fashioned a Body for himself in the Holy Spirit" (*Adv. Serap.* 1, 31).

[54] *In Christi Resurr.*, or. 1 (PG 46, 612A–613B). Analogous expressions in Betz, *Eucharistie*, 92–105.

[55] In his *Zur biblischen Theologie: Alttestamentliche Vorträge* (Kaiser, 1977), 107–27.

[56] As happens, for instance, in Nikos A. Nissiotis, "Pneumatologie orthodoxe", in LSE 85–106; the author knows well that the "Father's two hands" always operate together (93, 100), and so he also knows that Western theology cannot be accused of "Christomonism" (102).

level, has active effects through all that he allows the Spirit to do. What deed is mightier than self-surrender? In 1 Corinthians 10:14ff. it is clear "how the one Body of Christ on the Cross, by the power of the Holy Spirit, is continually built up into the one Body of the Church. . . . The one Body of Christ on the Cross is present, by the power of the Holy Spirit, in the bread of the Lord's Supper. There is also present, together with him, the gift that he gives: the new dimension that is opened up in him, the new life." In those who receive him there is formed "that open existence, the blueprint of which is given by Christ's Body on the Cross". Pouring himself out, he pours himself forth, and "in the power of the Holy Spirit" he give his gifts "from above", namely, "apostles, prophets, evangelists, pastors and teachers" (Eph 4:11), who are all "instruments in the power of the Holy Spirit" for the upbuilding of the ecclesial Body of Christ.[57] Such is the vitality of him who is given up without reserve, whose self-surrender—which is finally entirely free—is the personal Spirit of himself and of the Father. The entire work is trinitarian: it is the Father who gives himself to the world in Son and Spirit; accordingly, as we find in the Roman Canon, the epiclesis also addresses him as the origin of all gifts: "munera, Domine, oblata sanctifica, ut tui nobis Unigeniti corpus et sanguis fiant."[58] Returning to what we said at the outset concerning the sacraments, we must recall that there can be no *opus operatum* without an *opus operantis*; the Church's *anaphora* and *epiklesis*, which are uttered in obedience to Christ's "Do this", are themselves part of the presence of the Crucified and Risen One that is actualized in the Holy Spirit. The Church offers (*offert*) by allowing herself to be drawn into the sacrifice of Christ through his Spirit and by giving her ("Marian") consent to it; but it is in virtue of his "Do *this*" and his implacable command to eat and drink "this" (as the prophets had to eat the sweet and bitter word of God)

---

[57] H. Schlier, "Die Einheit der Kirche im Denken des Apostels Paulus", in *Die Zeit der Kirche* (Herder, 1956), 289–99.

[58] For similar variants of this Latin epiclesis, cf. J. A. Jungmann, *Missarum Solemnia* II (Vienna: Herder, 1948), 231. "The formula is a plea for transubstantiation or . . . the transubstantiatory epiclesis of the Roman Mass" (232).

that she is granted a share, intimately, in his sacrifice.[59] While the *anaphora* and *epiklesis* suggest a movement of the Church toward the divine Father whereby this sacrifice is "offered" to him, the Communion shows the sacrifice being given back by him so that it can be incorporated into the Church. The "sacrifice of praise" and *logikē thysia* are not mere harmless spiritual truisms: they imply a self-consecration, a fulfillment of vows, a thanksgiving that summons one's whole life in response. The community gathered in the Holy Spirit must be ready and willing to be incorporated into Christ's sacrifice: here, subjective holiness is challenged to transcend itself, without reserve, in the direction of objective holiness; thus strengthened, the believer must return to face the demands of his everyday ethical decisions.[60] Since the two-sided nature of the covenant is fulfilled in the Eucharist, we can see here how, more emphatically than ever, it is in the same Holy Spirit that the "people" are not only drawn into God's activity but exist first of all by it. One should speak, not of an "increase of grace" through repeated participation in the cult, but of being drawn ever deeper in by the Spirit, who searches the unfathomable depths of the Godhead.[61]

Here follows a consideration of the two sacramental consecrations, for ecclesial office and for the state of matrimony.

Matrimony. We take matrimony first since, as a sacrament, it is a parable, elevated from human nature, of the eucharistic union of Christ the Bridegroom and the Church, his Bride (Eph 5). Since Christian marriage is measured by this highest union, it is more than what it was "in the beginning"—prior to the process of "hardening of hearts" (see Mt 19:8)—when it was already

---

[59] Cf. Helmut Moll, "Die Lehre von der Eucharistie als Opfer" in: *Theophania* 26 (Cologne, Bonn, and Hanstein, 1975; bibliography); Raphael Schulte, *Die Messe als Opfer der Kirche* (Aschendorff, 1959).

[60] Hans von Soden, *Sakrament und Ethik bei Paulus*, Marburger theologische Studien (Gotha, 1931); Paul Neuenzeit, *Das Herrenmahl*, Studien zum Alten und Neuen Testament 1 (Munich: Kösel, 1960), 229ff.

[61] For a more precise definition of what the Church's eucharistic offering consists in, cf. G. Bätzing, *Die Eucharistie also Opfer der Kirche* (Einsiedeln: Johannesverlag, 1986).

a personal, lifetime faithfulness. Now, however, the love that is demanded of the partners is so ultimate that it can only be attributed to the indwelling, in the spouses, of the Holy Spirit, who is able to transform the natural *eros* into an *agape* that has its origin in God. Again we see that subjective love, however intense and sacrificial it may be, is elevated beyond itself to become an objective love of the Holy Spirit; such is the love that is realized between Christ, giving himself for his Church (Eph 5:26), and the Bride he has purified so that she is holy and spotless (v. 27). This highest subjective love becomes, in the sacrament, the objective norm for the love of the human couple. Even in the unspoiled nature of human love one can see signs of a total self-expropriation in favor of the spouse[62] (1 Cor 7:4); this becomes binding in the norm presented by the sacrament. If conjugal love, which Thomas calls *maxima amicitia* (*C.G.* III, 123), is, even at the natural level, an ultimate achievement of the human spirit, it is right to speak more explicitly than we are accustomed to in Christian marriage of the indwelling of the Holy Spirit in all forms—both acts and renunciations—of true love. For *agape* is the Holy Spirit's proper name. And in the economy of salvation *agape* has no concrete being except in the fundamental sacrament, which is the love between Christ and the Church:[63] spouses must have a participation in this, however little they may be consciously aware of it. A full awareness of this participation grounds the Christian possibility—which can become a divine requirement—to renounce the use of marriage and live in a natural, unmarried state, nourished by the pneu-

---

[62] The Council of Trent asserts that when the first man, on seeing his wife, exclaimed that he had finally found his like (bone of his bones and flesh of his flesh), he did so "divini Spiritus instinctus" (DS 1797)—in other words, he was already elevated above the state of "pure nature". Thus there can be "no valid sacramental marriage without at least a minimum of faith". (W. Kasper, *Zur Theologie der christlichen Ehe* [Mainz, 1977], 94).

[63] There are "hierarchical steps", theologically substantiated, in this primal sacrament. This in turn provides a justification (theologically, and not in any other way!) for the reflection of these steps or gradations that we find in the theology and in the (old) liturgy of matrimony in the Church. Cf. Gertrude Reidick, *Die hierarchische Struktur der Ehe*, Münchener theologische Studien III, Kanonistische Abteilung 3 (Munich: Zink, 1953), 166–204.

matic (but by no means disembodied) love between Christ and his Church; this is in order to acquire a share in the Church's more than natural fruitfulness. Seeing himself as the father and mother of his community, the unmarried apostle is aware of this christological and ecclesiological fruitfulness that is above marriage. This is why Trent defines virginity as superior to the married state (DS 1810), at the same time countering the Reformation assertion that marriage is a purely "worldly thing" and defending it by insisting on its sacramentality. The Lutheran rejection of the way of life of the evangelical counsels has had a damaging effect on the dignity of Christian marriage; no one has exposed this more wrathfully than Søren Kierkegaard.[64]

Priestly ordination. Here again we shall be mentioning only those aspects pertaining to the present study. The Risen One's solemn utterance, "Receive the Holy Spirit", continues to echo throughout the Church's ordination liturgies. In the ordination of deacons there used to be a direct "Accipite Spiritum Sanctum", and in the concluding prayer there was a request: "Hear our prayer, O Lord, and send upon this your servant the Spirit of your blessing. . . ." Similarly, in episcopal consecrations, the bishops present lay hands on the candidate, expressly saying, "Accipite Spiritum Sanctum." In priestly ordinations the preface begins by asking God: "Hear us, O Lord our God, and pour upon these your servants the blessing of the Holy Spirit and the power of priestly grace"; at the anointing of hands the "Veni, Creator Spiritus" is sung; and after Holy Communion there are the words, "Receive the Holy Spirit, the Paraclete, whom the Father will send you"; and, finally, "Receive the Holy Spirit; those whose sins you forgive, they are forgiven them, and those sins you retain, they are retained." In the newly formulated rite of episcopal consecration, the bishops assisting the celebrant pray together: "Pour out, Father, upon these chosen ones, the power that comes from you, your ruling and guiding Spirit, which you gave to your beloved Son Jesus Christ and whom he handed on to his holy apostles, who founded your Church in all the

---

[64] Texts in H. Roos, *Kierkegaard nachkonziliar* (Einsiedeln: Johannesverlag, 1967).

different parts of the earth." The celebrant says, "May he receive
authority, through the power of your Spirit, the Spirit of high
priesthood, to forgive sins according to your command."[65]

In general the theologians do not have much to say about the
connection between priesthood and the Holy Spirit. They are
more concerned with the christological aspect: Christ chooses
his disciples and teaches them how to follow him in his ministry
of service: "He appointed twelve, to be with him, and to be sent
out to preach and have authority . . ." (Mk 3:14). These two
things, being interiorly with Christ and yet being sent away by
him, constitute "the trial and tension of the priest's calling for
all time", and yet, at a deeper level, these two are one: "Everyone who accepts this mission" is assimilated to Christ: "He
is expropriated for the sake of the One he trusts and for the
sake of those to whom he represents him." There is a decidedly
trinitarian significance here, since in God "person and relation
are identical."[66] Most of all, the "tension" expresses itself in ecclesiological terms: the priest, sent by God to be the leader of
the community, stands "over against" it, while at the same time
he is a member of the community. This results in an inseparably
twofold understanding of the priestly office: the priest "represents Christ" and "represents the Church"—which is nothing
other than his Mystical Body; two christological aspects comple-
ment each other here, too,[67] and once again the unifying concept
is service or mission. It must not be overlooked, however, that,
for this two-sided christological mission, ordination takes place
in the form of a "gift of the Holy Spirit": it is a charism, albeit
of a special kind, that "empowers the ordained to carry out their

[65] For the preconciliar consecrations (*Pontificale*, 1873), cf.: ordination of deacons, 34, 36; consecration of bishops, 60; ordination of priests, 40, 45f. In the
postconciliar *Liber de Ordinatione* (1971): Prayer for the Holy Spirit in the ordination of deacons, 22, 24; in the ordination of priests, 39 (in the concluding prayer
after the ordination: "Accipite spiritum Sanctum in vobis Paraclitum, ille est quem
mittet Pater vobis": 41). In episcopal consecrations all the consecrating bishops
pray together for the Holy Spirit to come upon the candidates: 69–70, 71.

[66] This is a brief summary of J. Ratzinger's stimulating essay "Zur Frage nach
dem Sinn des priesterlichen Dienstes", *Geist und Leben* 41 (1968): 347–76, here,
esp. 353, 371.

[67] P. Hünermann, "Mit dem Volk Gottes unterwegs", *Geist und Leben* 54 (1981):
178–87.

office and makes them 'instruments' of the Kyrios".[68] They do this in a twofold way, according to Thomas, since at Mass they pray *in persona ecclesiae* but consecrate *in persona Christi*.[69] G. Greshake (unlike J. Ratzinger) sees here the trinitarian connection of the priestly ministry: Christ's operation is inseparable from that of the Spirit: the priestly office stands at the point where the *auctoritas* (of Christ) intersects with the *communio* (of the Holy Spirit); in christological terms "the Church, the Bride of Christ, is integrated by him into a *congregatio fidelium* that takes its bearings from the figure of Christ and must allow this figure to be imprinted within it, constituting an external norm, as it were. In pneumatological terms, that is, within the context of the creative and unifying operation of the Holy Spirit, the Church is the 'Body of Christ'." "Thus the people of God is marked by the 'objective figure' of Christ and by the 'inner life' of the Spirit; by the 'external organic phenomenon' and 'spiritual power'."[70] He rightly sees that these aspects are mutually beneficial: "The external, objective, 'christological' form communicates and supports the Spirit's presence, and the Spirit is at pains to imprint Christ's form upon all living being. Form tends to become life, and life must find a form." "Wherever one starts from, it is a process of reciprocal mediation."[71] Nonetheless, we can inquire whether this mediation can be successful: Does it not need, perhaps, the distinction (not separation!) we have drawn between the two aspects of the Holy Spirit if it is to come to fruition? For, on the one hand, the priestly office that is imparted is not solely "christological" but (as the consecratory formulas express it) objective Holy Spirit; it is certainly a "charism", but of a special kind: it definitively confers authority in matters of Church leadership. In this way *communio* is not simply a work of the Spirit but also, as we have shown in some detail, the work of Christ who sacrifices himself by the Spirit. Only if we hold fast to the concept of a Spirit who is objectively holy shall we grasp what the older theology spoke of as the "ineradicable character" that is different from the personal holiness of the ordained person.

[68] G. Greshake, *Priestersein* (Herder, 1982), 57.

[69] Ibid., 87.

[70] Ibid., 91.

[71] Ibid., 91, 95.

There "remains a permanent distinction between the objective mission of the priestly office and its subjective realization".[72]

We must face this distinction if we are to speak of the absolute demand for subjective holiness that arises from the objective holiness residing in the office itself. If the latter implies an absolute and definitive appointment and authorization for service to Christ's flock, in discipleship of the Good Shepherd, it also contains an automatic and analytic requirement that this appointment and authorization should be carried out. Yet these two things cannot, nor do they need, to coincide—this was the Donatist error. This context helps us to understand the theologoumenon first broached by the Areopagite, but crystallized by Thomas, that the bishop, in virtue of his office, is in the "state of perfection", whereas the monk who does not have this office can only strive for this perfection. Perfection, according to Thomas, is love; and this office expropriates the bishop totally for the service of love to his flock, so that he has a duty to realize subjectively the objective expropriation that has taken place. It stands to reason that this realization is greatly assisted by the "evangelical counsels"; the convergence between these two forms of life[73] is the chief concern of H. Bouëssé.[74] It is essential here to hold the correct balance between equating objective and subjective holiness (as Tertullian and the Donatists did) and blithely separating them, which would lead to a purely functional or administrative priestly ministry. No consecrated person can avoid the urgency with which his objective office calls for subjective holiness. It follows from his discipleship of the Good Shepherd with his thrice reiterated question to Peter ("Do you love me more than these?"); and it follows from the truth of his words, which, if he were to fail to carry out himself what he preaches in Christ's name and demands of his community, would

---

[72] W. Kasper, "Die Funktion des Priesters in der Kirche", *Geist und Leben* 42 (1969): 102–16; here, 112.

[73] Cf. Greshake's excellent observations, *Priestersein*, 126–53.

[74] Humbert Bouëssé, *Le Sacerdoce chrétien* (Paris: DDB, 1957). He, too, gives all the relevant texts from Dionysius, Gregory I, and Thomas (esp. 197–201). It will not do, therefore, to associate the imparting of the Spirit at the various degrees of ordination with the subjective sanctification of the ordinand, as Raphael Molitor does, for instance, in his *Vom Sakrament der Weihe*, 2 vols. (Regensburg, 1938).

label him a Pharisee, "[binding] heavy burdens, hard to bear, and [laying] them on men's shoulders; but [not troubling to] move them with their finger" (Mt 23:4). All classical instruction on the priesthood—from Chrysostom to Olier, Möhler, Scheeben, Newman, and countless others—says the same thing here. It is more than a moral duty toward God and men: as we have shown, it is a question of the ineluctable logic of an indivisible unity, in God, between the objective and subjective aspect of the Holy Spirit. The priest must not lose sight of the fact that the same indivisible unity is also found in Christ, whose objective "high priesthood" is expressed, precisely, in his subjective, loving self-surrender "to the end"; but we also saw that in Jesus' life and suffering the two aspects of the Spirit have to diverge for the sake of his redemptive obedience. Thus Christology itself points those who are consecrated for the Church—bishop, priest, or deacon—in the direction of Pneumatology.

Anointing in the face of the approach of death. Every human being and every age of mankind has known that facing one's own death is a fundamental situation of human existence. Had there been no sacrament for the Christian in this situation, the Church would have had to invent one. Christ was well aware of the "baptism" that awaited him, and how he was "constrained" until it should take place! (Lk 12:50). He had to face this hour alone, forsaken by everyone except the Father (Jn 16:32)—and ultimately forsaken by him, too (Mk 15:34). During his lifetime he healed the seriously ill and raised the dead—under the Old Covenant sickness was a direct foreshadowing of death—in order to demonstrate his power over them both, seen as symbols of a spiritual dying to God and the embrace of God's grace; but he never entertained the idea of preserving men from sickness and death as some kind of miracle-working doctor ("Fool! this [very] night . . ." Lk 12:20). "The poor man died . . . the rich man also died" (Lk 16:22). First and foremost he wanted his disciples to follow him into his special and unique death (Jn 16:2). When he commissions his disciples to heal the sick by anointing them with healing oil (Mk 6:13) and to raise the dead (Mt 10:8), he sends them out with his own signs, as harbingers of his coming: he is the Resurrection and the Life now, eschatologically, and not only on the Last Day (Jn 11:25). In Acts the sick are healed and the dead raised in the name of Jesus (Acts 3:6); Paul makes no fuss about it (2 Cor 12:12).

James wrote that officials of the Church should pray over one who was seriously ill and anoint him with oil in the Lord's name so that the Lord should "raise him up" and, if he had committed any sins, they would be forgiven (Jas 5:14f.); it is certain that initially the Church interpreted this restrictively, to mean physical healing; it is equally certain that the Eastern Church has held on to this interpretation. Not until the Middle Ages was a deeper significance discerned here: then the realization grew that the Church was primarily intended, not to dispense supernatural medicines, but to care for man in the gravest situation of his life. G. Lohfink is probably right that it was initially baptism, seen as a genuine dying with Christ, that was the real eschatological Sacrament;[75] but, given the Pauline doctrine of baptism, which understands the Christian life as a true, existential dying with Christ (Rom 6) and a hidden resurrection with him (Col 3:3; Eph 2:6; Heb 12:22), this death does not seem to be as closely connected with the expectation of the imminent end of the world as Lohfink assumes. No doubt he is right, however, that "much of the fundamental eschatological orientation of baptism has been transferred, in the passage of time, to the sacrament of anointing of the sick"; "the gravely ill person is anointed and sealed with a view to the end." This was clearly seen in the Middle Ages, and theologians like K. Rahner[76] and A. Grillmeier[77] saw that it was necessary, at a time when the sacraments had been finally distinguished from other ecclesial blessings (sacramentals), to give consideration and definition to the sacramental aspect of man's existential position vis-à-vis his death. All this evidence has been assembled and expanded by G. Greshake in his irrefutable "plea for a sacrament of baptismal renewal in the face of death".[78] He rightly castigates the new

---

[75] G. Lohfink, "Der Ursprung der christlichen Taufe", ThQ 156 (1976): 35–54.

[76] K. Rahner, *Kirche und Sakramente*, 3d ed. (Freiburg, 1960), 55f.

[77] A. Grillmeier, "Das Sakrament der Auferstehung", *Geist und Leben* 34 (1961): 320.

[78] "Letzte Ölung oder Krankensalbung? Plädoyer für eine differenzierte Theorie und Praxis", *Geist und Leben* 56 (1983): 119–36. Paul VI's apostolic constitution

tendency to perform a (harmless) anointing of the sick upon the elderly or slightly ill as "merely going along with the social trend that seeks to banish death. Would we not serve modern people better by confronting them with the reality of dying and death",[79] rather than by jumping on the bandwagon of the charismatic healing boom?

We must ask where the Holy Spirit is in the context of this sacramental renewal of the existential baptism—which is a *death* —in the face of a life that is running to its close. The Spirit's significance comes from the fact that the imparting of the Spirit in baptism-confirmation acquires an ultimate urgency here. Many of the early Scholastics saw this explicitly,[80] and Thomas (with Bonaventure and Scotus) sees the desire to follow Christ, which is professed in baptism, being focused here in the readiness to hand oneself over completely to the divine Mercy;[81] anointing is indeed the "ultimum remedium quod Ecclesia potest conferre, immediate quasi disponens ad gloriam".[82] It is significant that

---

on the new order of Anointing of the Sick (November 13, 1972) and the German bishops' introduction to it (September 23, 1974) as well as the new Codex (1983, cann. 998, 1004 section 1), constantly speak, with regard to the point at which the anointing should be given, of a person who is "dangerously ill", whose health has been "dangerously undermined", i.e., of situations in which death is seriously in prospect. This can by no means be extended to the normal "infirmities of old age" or other curable sickness or accidents.

[79] Greshake, *Priestersein*, 130.

[80] B. Poschmann, *Buße und letzte Ölung*, Handbuch der Dogmengeschichte IV/3 (Herder, 1951), 135–36. Cf. also Trent: "Res enim haec gratia est Spiritus Sancti; cujus unctio delicta, si quae sint adhuc expianda, ac peccati reliquias abstergit, et aegroti animam alleviat et confirmat, magnam in eo divinae misericordiae fiduciam excitando" (DS 1696). Trent goes on to speak against the Reformers: the sacrament is not a now defunct charism of healing, inherited from the primitive Church and the Fathers (DS 1699). Rather, it is "totius christianae vitae . . . consummativum" (DS 1694). It is true that Vatican II yielded somewhat to the trend toward a mere Anointing of the Sick (*Sacrosanctam Concilium*, 73), yet *Lumen Gentium* (11) is quite traditional: "By the sacred anointing of the sick and the prayer of the priests the whole Church commends those who are ill to the suffering and glorified Lord that he may raise them up and save them. And indeed she exhorts them to contribute to the good of the People of God by freely uniting themselves to the passion and death of Christ."

[81] *S. Th.* III, 66, 9 c.

[82] *S. Th.* suppl. 32, 2 c, whence Thomas rightly concludes, "it ought to be given to those only who are so sick as to be in a state of departure from this life, through

Thomas, who, in the case of baptism, requires no awareness on the part of the child, does require such awareness here on the part of the sick person: where adults are concerned, sacraments do not work by magic and so *requiritur motus liberi arbitrii*.[83] This is entirely logical, even if the Church, in her mercy, has not followed it. The forgiveness of sins referred to by James is not, as in penance, a primary effect; rather, it occurs insofar as this "sacrament is the final one, as it were, rounding off the whole spiritual healing whereby man is prepared for glory".[84] We are not interested in the whole casuistics that has grown up around the various effects of the sacrament; the only relevant fact is that, often enough, the man wrestling with death is also facing fear and temptation and no longer knows how to pray as he should. It is at this point, more assuredly than ever, that "the Spirit himself intercedes for us with sighs too deep for words. And he who searches the hearts of men knows what is the mind of the Spirit, because the Spirit intercedes for the saints according to the will of God" (Rom 8:26–27).

d. Canon Law

"It was one of Liberalism's most dire errors to divorce Spirit and law. For Paul these two are complementary; this insight made it necessary to modify the whole of Pauline theology."[85] So wrote Ernst Käsemann, arguing against Sohm's distinction between one's duty in love and one's duty in law. He goes on:

> It is the Holy Spirit who issues decrees. Obedience is neither con-
> stituted nor limited by the views of the hearer. . . . The Spirit does
> not give free rein to arbitrariness but communicates a fixed order
> as a development and an essential component of sacred law. . . .
> [God] binds hearts far more severely than any lawgiver ever did.

---

their sickness being of such a nature as to cause death, the danger of which is to be feared."

[83] *S. Th.*, suppl. 32, 3 ad 2.

[84] *Contr. Gent.* IV, 73.

[85] "Sätze heiligen Rechts im Neuen Testament", in *Exegetische Versuche und Besinnungen*, vol. 2, 4th ed. (Göttingen, 1965), 75.

But he does not bind them to a program and a system, nor is he satisfied with purely external, physical obedience: he lays claim to our understanding and love in whatever he may command. It is his right to decree that those who are free make a total surrender of themselves; it is his right, his law, that lays all opposition under a curse. This law is also Spirit, insofar as it makes it possible for a man to obey with his eyes open. . . . Love, therefore, is, not a substitution for law, but its radical form.[86]

We can fully agree with this, even if the reason behind it, namely, "the eschatological expectation of the impending Last Judgment" is one-sided and inadequate.

Even in the Old Testament we can see that Sohm is wrong to set law against charismatic elements: the opposition he introduces is foreign to the core of the covenant as event. Israel's incorporation into the covenant results from God's incomprehensible choice, which rests on his utter freedom and mercy; it means that Israel is totally taken over by God—"be holy, for I am holy"—and therefore his exclusive demand upon man (which, to the sinner, seems to be an imposition) is in fact an ennobling prerogative. Here, originally, there is no place for the notion of "works": it is the sinner who twists this prerogative into such a notion, which both Jesus and Paul will have to condemn; what man does is simply the only appropriate response to grace. "Torah as grace".[87] Of course, the created man's *rectitudo* is not left behind: it is over-fulfilled, because the God who chooses is also the Creator who, right from the start, designed the creation with a view to this covenant—which will be fulfilled in Christ. In other words, creation has an inbuilt pre-understanding of grace, of love, and of the fact that it owes its being to God. In the Old Covenant, however, the chief commandment (Deut 6) is formulated as the highest duty because God has an absolute right to the loving response of his people (on the basis of his free election of them): not only because he loves, but because he, the God who is always in the right, loves them in this unfathomable way. So Israel condemns itself by scorning this love and turning away from it.

[86] Ibid., 76–77. On the connection between power and law, cf. Bernhard Welte, *Über den rechten Gebrauch der Macht* (Freiburg: Rombach, 1960).

[87] R. J. Zwi Werblowsky, "Torah as Gnade", *Kairos* 15 (1973): 156–73.

The fundamental structure documented in the Old Testament is fulfilled in a trinitarian manner in the New Covenant, where the "truth" of God's love in Jesus Christ goes to the ultimate limit and the "Spirit of truth" interprets—for the benefit of the Church and the world—the law that indwells God's loving action. All appearance of arbitrariness (the choosing of one nation rather than another) now disappears, since God freely manifests his own very being (as trinitarian love) in that freely given love that he shows to all in the extremity of the Cross of Jesus. What he does is what he *is*; which is why he now has a right (arising both from his nature and from his love) to the creature's unreserved, loving response. That is why, in the context of Jesus' preaching (cf. his condemning of the unbelieving towns in Matthew 11:20ff., as in Amos 1:9ff., Isaiah 23, Jeremiah 23:22, and so on) and of the apostles' preaching (cf. Heb 6 and 10), man's refusal of this offer of love constitutes a self-condemnation. Conversely the man Jesus who, in obedience to the Father, has followed the path of love for his brothers to its very end, has a "right" to be raised high and simultaneously earns a "right", for those of his brothers who accept him, to "be born of God" (Jn 1:12), a "right" that obliges believers to perform the loving surrender of their lives to God for their brothers (1 Jn 3:16).

This is the basis of law that applies in the community founded by Christ and equipped by the Holy Spirit. For the fundamental structure of this community is the unity of the love of God and brotherly love; consequently, it would contradict itself if it were to tolerate open rebellion, within its own ranks, against the very law of its being. The existence of "canon law", quite apart from any other considerations, arises simply from discipleship of Christ, in the same way that the Holy Spirit interprets the Spirit of Christ in the hearts of believers. He does this, insofar as they constitute a community, primarily through the perpetual making present of Christ in the Eucharist and the other sacraments, that is, by guaranteeing the "presence of the origin", which we have already encountered in the threefold interweaving of Word(Scripture)-tradition-office. If one abstracts from this structure of the Church—understood as a *communio* of the love of God and of one's neighbor—the element of law that permeates her, one can formulate a "canon law". The latter is only the guarantee that the Church cannot and must not be anything other than the community of that love which is shown to us in Christ and given to us in the Holy Spirit; sinners that we are, we must also be at pains to grow, through penance (which is both the sacrament and our daily following of the Cross) toward Christian, selfless love.

We are not concerned here to give an interpretation of the current canon law or criticize the theology on which it is based.[88] A few remarks must suffice. First we observe that all believers are equally indebted to Christ's Cross and his eucharistic presence, which creates a community in him that is primarily, not sociological, but ontological: "In virtue of their rebirth in Christ [and not merely on the basis of their human dignity] there exists among all the Christian faithful a true equality with regard to dignity and the activity whereby all cooperate in the building up of the Body of Christ in accord with each one's own condition and function. The Christian faithful are bound . . . always to maintain communion with the Church" (cann. 208–9). Those, therefore, who have been given ministerial office so that they may keep the Word and sacrament and preserve community order must keep in mind the maxim inculcated by Christ: Let the leader be as one who serves (for that is what he is, Lk 22:26). Or, as Paul says: "God has exhibited us apostles as last of all, like men sentenced to death" (1 Cor 4:9); "Bear one another's burdens" (Gal 6:2); "in humility count others better than yourselves" (Phil 2:3). Since there must be an order of penance in the Church, the one who has to submit to a penance for his correction should understand it as a privilege, not an imposition, bearing in mind the Church's meaning and goal; for the power to "bind", which Christ bequeaths to the Church's officers, is always given with a view to "loosing". Thus Paul knows that he has received authority from the Lord "for building . . . up, not for destroying" (2 Cor 10:8, 13:10). When he has to use excommunication, it is only the official recognition that a man has freely separated himself from the *communio*;[89] he is excluded

---

[88] On the unevenness of the ecclesiology that underlies the new Code, cf. E. Corecco, "Ekklesiologische Grundlagen des Codex Iuris Canonici", *Concilium* 22 (1986): 166–72 (with bibliography).

[89] L. Gerosa, "Strafrecht und kirchliche Wirklichkeit", *Concilium* 11 (1986):

"that his spirit may be saved in the day of the Lord Jesus" (1 Cor 5:5). Life in the *communio* that Christ gives with the Father and with one another is regulated by the unity between God's Word and sacrament, and it should be remembered, as we said earlier, that God's Word is incarnate in the whole humanity of Jesus: it is thus already sacramental, and he infuses his sacramentality into the Church. It is from this sacramental totality that the individual sacraments unfold;[90] this is also (no less) the source of the sacramental Word of God and the charism given to every individual Christian for building up the Body of Christ. This charism, too, since it is given by God, has a specific right to pursue its own task—once it has been tested by the appropriate Church authority. We see this in the great charisms of the religious orders and in the influence of particular saints in whom the Spirit shines forth. It shows how the Spirit's operation in the Church transcends the "legal" division into clergy and laity.

The Holy Spirit operates within the specific nature of all the ecclesial "states". Laypeople working in the secular realm are frequently urged to be "imbued with the spirit of the Gospel" (cann. 225, 2; 227); the bishop and his presbyterium have the obligation of gathering the faithful together in the Holy Spirit through gospel and Eucharist (can. 369), "discern[ing] new gifts of consecrated life granted to the Church by the Holy Spirit" (can. 605), and urging the institutes of consecrated life to "follow . . . Christ more closely under the action of the Holy Spirit"

198–204. There is a logical "connection between, on the one hand, the way in which the excommunicated person excludes himself from the Church community—that is what his excommunication is—and, on the other hand, his exclusion from the reception of the Eucharist because of the grave sin he has committed." But "the excommunicated person has only to give up his 'contumacia', his obstinacy, and he immediately has a so-called 'ius ad absolutionem'." "Even when the Church imposes sanctions, she never forgets that her correction is for healing. Thus the 'poenae expiatoriae' lead not only to a reconciliation, an 'expiatio' of the particular transgression; their retributory character remains within the framework of the total context of the Church's penitential discipline."

[90] Karl Rahner, *Kirche und Sakrament*, QD 10 (Herder, 1960): "It is where the Church, in absolute commitment, performs one of her fundamental acts, fully actualizing her nature as the primal sacrament of grace with regard to an individual, in situations that are decisive for his salvation, that we have a sacrament" (85).

(can. 573, 1). In all this the *successio apostolica*, too, constitutes one element in the imparting of the Holy Spirit to the newly consecrated bishop (can. 375, 1), which equally applies, of course, in the case of a papal election.

It is true, naturally, that the Church has her ever-new center and source in the holy Eucharist and in the community that, obedient to the Lord, meets around it. Fundamentally, therefore, we can describe canon law, as Karl Barth does, as "liturgical and confessional law";[91] it is in this context that the Church's official side performs its ministry, and so it should not be dismissed as a negative concept; all the faithful, and in particular the laity, are bound, in virtue of their baptism and confirmation, to take up a responsible mission in the world (cann. 211, 216).

If Church can be defined as *communio*, her "constitutive elements" must be "totally immanent in each other" in such a way that they "cannot be separated from one another. This is evident, for instance, in the reciprocal structural relationship between sacrament and Word, between the general priesthood of the faithful and the ministerial priesthood, between the faithful and the Church, between duty and law, between the whole Church and the local or national Church, between the pope and the college of bishops, between the bishop and the presbyterium."[92] It is this reciprocal immanence of elements, themselves structurally distinct and unconfused, that makes Christ's Church a reflection of the Trinity; thus, too, it renders the

[91] *Church Dogmatics* IV/2 (Edinburgh, 1958), section 67. Canon law is explained in some detail as liturgical law in H. Dombois, *Das Recht der Gnade*, 2d ed. (Witten, 1969), 280–438; on canon law and the confession of faith: 677–731. The title of Dombois' great book indicates the crucial distinction between secular and canon law: "Here we are not concerned with justifying men's claims against other men; we are concerned solely with God's claim on man . . . and only subsequently, on this basis, with the legal relationships between men" (*Recht der Gnade*, 211). "Grace demands no more than that we accept it and abide in it" (*Recht der Gnade*, 190). "To set forth the new state of the Christian life, the New Testament uses many legal concepts interchangeably: we are children of God and, as such, also fellow heirs; everything has been given and entrusted to us in Christ; we have a heavenly citizenship; we have a share in Christ's priestly and kingly office; and marriage can serve as a parable for Christ's relationship with the ecclesia", etc. (*Recht der Gnade*, 195).

[92] Corecco, "Ekklesiologische Grundlagen", 169a.

operation of the Holy Spirit in her a valid and salvific interpretation of the unity and distinction between the Father and
his incarnate Son, in which God shows his nature as love, and
love is manifested as the "law of grace".[93]

e. Theology

Man cannot attain to faith in Christ and the triune God without
having the gospel preached to him; nor can he do so without
justification. This being so, he cannot interpret this faith, either
to himself or to others, without faith. For this task, certainly, he
stands in great need of his spirit's interior illumination, that is,
of the grace of the subjective Holy Spirit; even more necessary,
however, is that objective light which the latter Spirit sheds on
faith's content: for it is this light that exhibits the content of
faith in its integrity and its divine profundity, compelling man
to fall on his knees in worship. So Markus Barth could say in
his valedictory lecture ("Theology Is a Prayer")[94] that "theology is the kind of thing that does not work without prayer."
If this is true, we can say that nothing is worthy of theological
reflection unless it can be the subject of prayer. This content
can never sink to the level of something hackneyed, something
already possessed, because the Spirit is in command, that Spirit
who "searches the deep things of God": "The Spirit not only
communicates the truth but also discloses it in a new way", for
"God's truth is only true in its fullness; either it is there completely, or it is not there at all."[95] Consequently, the theologian
is both confronted with a truth that is always greater than what
he thought he had understood and simultaneously forbidden to
adopt a merely apophatic stance vis-à-vis the God who is revealing himself to him in a new way.

---

[93] "Le droit de l'Église est le gardien de la communion" (Dupuy, in EE 326);
"On n'oublie que la loi de l'Église elle-même est sainte et qu'elle n'a pour fin que
de préserver la présence souveraine de l'Esprit" (ibid., 324). On this issue, see J.
Ratzinger, "Der Heilige Geist als Communio" in HM 223–38.

[94] In "Theologie—ein Gebet", *Theol. Zeitschrift* 41 (Basel, 1985): 330–48.

[95] Gerhard Sauter, ed., *Die Theologie und die neuere wissenschaftlich-theoretische
Diskussion: Materialen, Analysen, Entwürfe* (Kaiser, 1973), 254. Within our brief
compass we cannot enter into the subtle questions discussed here.

Here we must strike a shorter path toward the question before us.[96] There can be no question of doing without a philosophical anthropology: for one thing, the theologian has to make faith plausible to those who do not yet believe. It is also important for his own understanding of himself, for theology is a linguistic event—at one level it must utter words, and at a deeper level it knows that it has been addressed by the Word of God—and so we cannot avoid reflecting upon it. It would be wrong to regard the possibility of man's understanding and formulating God's Word as nothing but a miracle of grace that comes down from above.[97] We can concede that God can only be understood by God; yet that does not dispense us from reflecting on the fact that "understanding" is an act that is constitutive of man.

1. Human understanding begins with an encounter with a "thou", that is, with a freedom that is not my own and that engages my attention by indicating a particular state of affairs. The result, however, is not merely the realization of this state of affairs; this latter is flooded with light only within an open area or horizon within which things are illuminated, that is, shown to be meaningful, right, true. Language, which is always an indicative act, pointing to something, can only take place—and this applies to every conversation—within two areas: one is the common horizon of (pre-linguistic) intellection, and the other is the indemonstrable freedom of every speaker, whose utterance we must "believe", even if there is often empirical proof that he is right. In fact, the person thus addressed is always *indebted* to this free utterance. On the other hand, as we have said, the fact that we have been addressed can only be understood within a horizon of meaning, and this horizon of meaning is not above and

[96] We must therefore presuppose (and not repeat) what was said in TL II about the possibility of a bridge between divine logic and human logic as well as the brief remarks in the present volume on the Holy Spirit's interpretation of all that is pneumatic in Christ and on the Spirit's function as Illuminator (cf. Preludes, 2: "Is a Theology of the Spirit Possible?").

[97] For Karl Barth it is the Holy Spirit alone who can enable man fully to hear and understand God's word. That is why "the subjective reality of revelation as such can never be made an independent [Christian] theme. It is enclosed in its objective reality" (*Church Dogmatics* I/2 [Edinburgh, 1956], 240). The Holy Spirit alone is the subjective possibility of revelation (203–79).

sublimely indifferent to man's freedom; rather, it is the locus where man endeavors somehow to plot the meaning of his existence. This plotted meaning can be altered by objections, experiences of life (which, in their own way, "speak"), and the stereoscopy that unites things hitherto seen as separate, but such alteration can never go so far as to synthesize the open horizon piecemeal out of limited experiences of meaning or meaninglessness. Religions have the power simply to sweep away all that is piecemeal and hold on to the open realm that has been totally emptied out: they proclaim this void to be the all-embracing meaning and strive to attain it by ascesis. But they can also do something else, something more interesting: they can take things that are mutually contradictory in finite experience and project them onto this horizon, allowing them to melt into one another; thus paradoxes become reconciled. A single example will illustrate this, namely, the long final song in Mahler's *Das Lied von der Erde* (many passages in *Zarathustra* could serve just as well): all the sounds that make up the song of man's existence are here juxtaposed and interpenetrate; the earlier songs—of Dionysian rebellion, loneliness, conviviality, eroticism, ecstatic enebriation —have fallen silent, and now we have the farewell, separation without given reason, as the eternally restless heart has to "wander among the mountains"; yet at the same time we hear "I shall never roam to distant lands; my heart is quiet and awaits its hour. The dear earth blossoms in spring; forever blue and bright are the far horizons"; everything dies away with the word *ewig*, "forever". All the paradoxes of existence and the world are united in this "forever" which overarches them. No conceptual philosophical language (for example, crude words such as "pantheism") can approach this embrace of all life's contradictions within a totality that is posited, decreed, and experienced as ultimately open. We must not use the word "transcendental" here, for it is a question of mutually contradictory *existentiales*: sleeping and waking, life and death, possession and loss. Nonetheless a choice, a decision has been made: namely, to posit the Whole as valid (beyond my particular interests). This is to opt for a meaning that exceeds our ability to construct it,[98] to bear the insoluble con-

---

[98] Cf. Blondel's *L'Action* and H. Krings' *Transzendentale Logik* (Munich, 1964), 118, 186–88; H. Rombach, "Über Ursprung und Wesen der Frage", *Symposion*

tradictions in the world and in life by affirming an all-embracing meaning. Without this meaning, indeed, it would be impossible even to speak of the "meaning-lessness" of contradictions.

2. Only in Jesus Christ is it possible for the earthly dualism of language between a free "I" and "thou" to coincide with a prelinguistic or supralinguistic horizon encompassing both of them: namely, in a God who is simultaneously himself and his "Word"—where "Word" means belonging to his essence. The prototype of language is in God, but this does not mean that the freedom of one speaker is inaccessible to the freedom of another; in fact, they encounter one another in a single, common horizon of meaning within the Godhead, without the aspects of indebtedness, astonishment, surprise, and blessedness being (as it were) "smoothed out". So that, when God's Word "becomes flesh"—flesh understood as a whole human existence, not, one-sidedly, as just the finite word—it can endure the contradictions of human life because it remains united to God (the Father) within the single horizon (divine love) that embraces them: pain and death are identical to joy and life; tiredness and weariness are love just as much as zeal and inclination are; Jesus' being given and poured out (in the Eucharist) is love just as much as his personal integrity in Resurrection is. It may be that the creature has a certain pre-understanding of this, since, on the one hand, language can never be separated from interpersonal linguistic transactions[99] and, on the other hand, speaking involves man's entire bodily constitution and has man's "total existence" for its content. But this pre-understanding is not

---

II (1951): 135–236. K. Jaspers, *Von der Wahrheit* (Munich: Piper, 1947): "The man who penetrates the depths of being must have a very definite experience of the hiatuses to be found in the milieu that embraces us: he must be able to hold this embracing milieu together despite its abysses. . . . It is decisive, therefore, for the truth of my being, whether I keep hold of the totality of the modes of the embracing milieu or not" (163). "To philosophize about the modes of the embracing milieu requires a decision."—"The decision is whether, instead of being at ease with a satisfying knowledge of being, I am prepared to listen to whatever speaks to me in the boundless realm that embraces all horizons and itself has none; whether I am prepared to take note of the winking lights that indicate, warn, or entice—and which, maybe, make something known" (187–88, cf. 705–8).

[99] B. Casper, "Die Bedeutung der Lehre vom Verstehen für die Theologie", in his *Theologie als Wissenschaft*, QD 45 (1970), 24.

sufficient to grasp the most diverse aspects of Jesus' existence as the "language" of (what the creature sees as) the prelinguistic or supralinguistic horizon. The most a purely human understanding of the phenomenon of Jesus could attain would be an imparting of the meaning of all human boundary situations in a kind of silent supralanguage (for example, Heidegger's "revelations of being" or Bultmann's "understanding of existence"), where God is nothing more than one factor in human existence. Both of these represent the disintegration of a trinitarian "theo-logy", for in the latter the Holy Spirit is the indispensable Interpreter of that unity of "word" and "linguistic horizon" which is realized in Christ. Even a liberal theology in which Jesus is merely the herald and harbinger of the Father's love (in which scheme of things the Person of the Holy Spirit is superfluous) would never do justice to the totality of his utterance (for instance, his cry of dereliction on the Cross). Again, the Word-made-flesh that Jesus *is* points far beyond one "language game" among others (such as are played by the particular intellectual disciplines); right from the start it is an utterance of "total existence" and so enters into competition with the philosophical interpretations of existence. It remains a riddle and a stumbling block to them, since it proposes a single human existence as normative for the entire horizon. Nor can this phenomenon be challenged by the "symbol", for it "does not directly disclose what is symbolized but only indirectly through the transference of connotations, and so even the most illuminating symbol preserves the otherness and mystery of Being".[100] It is no different if we expand the notion of "symbol" to include related utterances such as myth, metaphor, and parable. All these modes of speech permit, indeed demand, a plurality of forms, whereas Jesus categorically claims to possess —uniquely—the identity of utterance and horizon.

3. This identity remains an unproven claim as long as men cannot discern it from the phenomenon itself. And they cannot

---

[100] As John Macquarrie insists: *God-Talk: An Examination of the Language and Logic of Theology* (London: SCM Press, 1967), 100. "Theology itself lives and has its meaning only in relation to the wider religious matrix from which it arises. When it strays too far from its source or when it gets separated from other modes of expression in worship and ethics, it degenerates into empty and arid disputes" (ibid., 19).

discern the identity if it does not reside primarily in the phenomenon itself, so that it can be read off from it. This means that, as far as faith is concerned (and that theology which expounds it conceptually), there is a prime need for the *objective* Holy Spirit, who produces and attests the unity of God (the Father) and of his Word (who, become flesh, is Jesus Christ); at a second stage this Holy Spirit (now *subjective* Holy Spirit) can disclose this objective unity to believers and commend it to their faith. He, and he alone, can show it to be objectively true that, in Jesus as a total phenomenon, the contradictions of existence— for example, Jesus' cry of dereliction, on the one hand, and the assurance that the Father never leaves him alone, on the other— are not made absolute: "paradox" and "dialectic" are not the last words concerning human existence, and the genuine contradictions in the world, such as love and sin, are united and dissolved —without contradiction—in the life of Jesus, which is a representation of absolute love. For us, "the word punishment indicates someone who punishes; but when God punishes, it is the implementing of a structural law of that person's existence as a result of his wrong action toward himself or others. By contrast, God's mercy is something *beyond* the intelligible and apparently contradictory data of kindness and punishment. Mercy is more than just kindness"—since it includes the Cross, which dissolves punishment in love; the man who recognizes this has the face of God unveiled to him, and he must live in accordance with this vision: "Be merciful, even as your Father is merciful" (Lk 6:36).[101] This image of God, which can only be unveiled to us by the Spirit, contains no paradox, let alone any contradiction, just as there is none in the Father of the Prodigal Son or in the Master of the Vineyard who pays each laborer the same wages. God deals with all that is anti-God, whether it be the alienation of sin or an earthly justice that is too narrow. This, however, is beyond man's understanding; he can only realize it if the Holy Spirit puts his objective light into man's subjective core in the form of conversion, faith, and the imitation of God. We would be involving ourselves in a further contradiction if we were to regard this light as a purely objective fact and treat it as such:

---

[101] Luigi Giussani, *Alla ricerca del volto umano* (Milan: Jaca Book, 1984), 30–31. Cf. John Paul II, *Dives in misericordia*.

there can be no "aesthetics" without a "dramatics". To comprehend apparent contradictions within a unified vision requires the art of simplifying the scattered elements, that "simplicity" which was so highly praised by the spiritual masters of the Middle Ages such as William of St. Thierry.[102] This is the wisdom of faith that is opposed to the "knowledge that puffs up", as Paul says; only this wisdom can open the "simple" (that is, "single") eye to God's truth. This simplicity can only unfold into a convincing theology through discipleship. And discipleship, in turn, means that we do not begin by reflecting on ourselves but by responding to the fact that we have been addressed and called by this divine miracle, namely, that the utterance and the horizon can be one and the same. "Thus God himself becomes the most self-evident reality [zum Selbstverständlichsten] because he underlies all self-understanding [das Selbstverständnis]; and at the same time he becomes the most un-self-evident reality [zum Unselbstverständlichsten] because his beginning, his presence, is a gift, not at all the result of other premises." For theology this means that "God begins with an answer, and this answer is a result that cannot be manipulated and produced by us." But does this not mean that human knowledge loses its sure foundation, that is, the ability to draw conclusions from its own evidence? Does this not mean that theology loses its entire philosophical foundation? Ultimately the answer will be the one we have already given: Among human beings all knowledge is itself based on a trust (in the other's freedom), and all sciences become preliminary stages toward the trust of faith. Not vice versa.[103] Just as a single word of a conversation can only be understood in context, Christian faith can only understand God's Word in its total context, that is, in the perfect unity of salvation history from Abraham right up to today, with its center in the unity of Jesus' life from his conception to his Ascension. And at the heart of this center stands the pro nobis of the Cross, without which it would never be possible to believe in the transcendence of God's mercy over both his kindness and his severity or in the commandment to take up one's cross daily. The "wise and un-

---

[102] Cf., among many other places, the Epistula aurea, ed. Déchanet (1956), 54.
[103] The best treatment is Klaus Hemmerle, Theologie als Nachfolge (Herder, 1975), 22f., 43f.

derstanding" will always try to get behind this *pro nobis*; only the "simple" see that this is what gathers all God's words into a unity and renders them intelligible. This alone is the point of intersection of the lowest abasement and the highest ascent (Phil 2:6–11), of God's prevenience and man's following ("where I am, there shall my servant be also", Jn 12:26). Here, in short, the two-sided nature of the covenant becomes a unity; here we have the realization of the *id quo majus cogitari nequit*. But all this is a work of the Holy Spirit, who takes the objective unity effected by him and enfleshes it in the subject: "No one can say 'Jesus is Lord' except by the Holy Spirit" (1 Cor 12:3).

4. So again we can say, "If theology is not prayer, if it does not come from prayer and lead to prayer, it is worthless."[104] There can be no doubt that it was prayer in the Fathers, in Augustine, Bede, and Anselm and in the flowering monastic theology of the twelfth century up to Bonaventure, and then again in the other great thinkers of modern times, Pascal, Kierkegaard, and Newman. For these writers it was always a "confessing theology". The "rational" theology, which did not begin with Thomas but always had to be put forward by the Fathers incidentally, so to speak, in order to defend the faith against heresy and which consists in illuminating and ordering faith's inner textural unity (*sapientis est ordinare*), can be nothing other than an indispensable preliminary to a praying and confessing theology; "this abstract discourse cannot, however, be elevated into a paradigm or norm" for theology.[105] Insofar as man is essentially a seeker (*fides quaerens intellectum*) and the God who finds me must continually be sought for (*ut inventus quaeratur immensus est*),[106] this rational endeavor is never to be excluded, even from the most prayerful theology (cf. Anselm). But it should take as its starting point, not man's *desiderium* as the creature's core *existentiale*,[107] but the fire that the divine Word has fanned into flame in it.[108]

---

[104] M. Barth, "Theologie—ein Gebet", 348.

[105] J. Macquarrie, *God-Talk*.

[106] Augustine, *Tr. in Joh.* 63, 1 (PL 35, 1802).

[107] Cf. my first essay in *Homo creatus est*, Skizzen zur Theologie V (Einsiedeln: Johannesverlag, 1986).

[108] This represents a certain limitation of the monastic theology of the twelfth century, inspired by Augustine and Gregory and their *desiderium*. Jean Leclercq

This theology understood itself throughout as *doctrina spiritus*, and Bernard can utter his lapidary "no theology without prayer" even if he knows that this praying theology involves the ascetic task, *inquirendi difficultas*. This task, however, is to grasp what the Holy Spirit has already presented to the theologian. For the Spirit is the bond of life between Father and Son, or, in the terms we have been using, between the horizon and the Word. The Son reveals the Father through the loving kiss that "dando revelat et revelando dat"; but "the illumination of this revelation that is carried out by the Holy Spirit is not only to give us knowledge but also to ignite our love. . . . The Spirit's doctrine does not provoke our curiosity but fans our love into flame."[109]

This theology is most intimately bound up with the liturgy. Indeed, some of it was composed in the form of theological hymnody, specifically designed for the liturgy. (We should remember that, in the Eastern Church, the catechesis of the faithful takes place almost entirely through the liturgy.) Just as in Plato the most sublime and arcane things are uttered in the form of myth, in Christian theology they are uttered in the hymn of adoration. Even in the case of Jesus, his last and most profound instruction runs into his high priestly prayer, the epitome of his "theology". Man's response to God's total revelation of this ultimate love seeks to go beyond a verbal theology, to the widest possible realm of comprehensive glorification. Liturgy calls for the assistance of all human modes of expression: music and the appropriate architecture for the whole event; the "total work of art" is portrayed and examined in the depiction by Suger of St. Denis of the construction and consecration of the church he built.[110] It follows that art's theological power of utterance should be considered more seriously than theologians generally do.[111] This is to acknowledge the necessity of the majority of

---

has described this in his book *L'Amour des lettres et le désir de Dieu* (Paris: Cerf, 1957). We are quoting from the German edition: *Wissenschaft und Gottverlangen* (Patmos, 1963). On *desiderium*, cf. 14, 34, 65.

[109] *Sermones in Cantica* 8, 5-6 (PL 183, 812BD).

[110] PL 186, 1239-54.

[111] For an initial approach: Günter Wohlfahrt, *Denken der Sprache, Sprache und Kunst bei Vico, Hamann, Humboldt und Hegel* (Freiburg and Munich: Alber, 1984). On p. 36 he quotes Wittgenstein: "The understanding of a sentence in speech is much closer than we think to the understanding of a theme in music." He gives

theological approaches and insights; given that it is the Spirit who renders the theological data ever present and opens up the forward-looking, eschatological dimension of all theology (and since all past theology had this forward-looking thrust), our attention to the history of theology cannot really be backward-looking: rather it must be a conversation with thinkers and men of prayer in the ever-present communion of saints. For it is the communion of saints, gathered together above time in the Holy Spirit, which is immersed in the mystery of God in Jesus Christ —which is of all times. Finally, Christian faith is always a confession before the world on the part of the ecclesial community, rendered possible by the Holy Spirit; and since theology cannot be anything else but a meditative clarification of this confession of faith in order to understand it and make it intelligible to others, theology, too, can only be grounded, and can only unfold, in the Holy Spirit.

---

this formulation of Vico: "The *universale fantastico* is an intuition of the universal in the individual" (85); in the concrete and yet universal product of the imagination Vico sees a mediation between divine and human speech (106).

6

SUBJECTIVE SPIRIT

This expression must be understood in the context of the foregoing. We saw that *objective* and *subjective* in the theology of the Holy Spirit were not distinct spheres but the twofold manifestation of his one and indivisible Personhood. The Spirit's objective aspects, reflected in the Church, are to be seen, on the one hand, in connection with the Son's Incarnation and, on the other, in the Spirit's own essence as the encounter between Father and Son and as the fruit of, and testimony to, this encounter (that is, they must be regarded as inseparable from his hypostatic essence); correspondingly, the Spirit's subjective aspects, in their function of upbuilding and animating the Church and ecclesial man, must never be separated from the objective preconditions of this activity. Otherwise there is the danger of slipping into forms of subjectivistic or charismaticist pietism. A spiritual enthusiast is not necessarily a saint. But it is the task of the Holy Spirit, above all, within the fullness of divine and ecclesial gifts, to fashion genuine saints; and they need the Church's objective holiness if they are to dedicate themselves completely to the cause of Jesus Christ and, hence, of the triune God.

Once again we can only select a few central topics from the wealth of possible ones; and again, while selecting them, we must remember that they cannot be absolutely isolated from one another. Our guiding criterion is this: In what way, in the following instances, is the Holy Spirit the Interpreter of God's revelation in Christ?

a. Spirit and Prayer

The Son never encounters the Father, and the Father never encounters the Son, except in the Holy Spirit. So no prayer of Jesus is made to the Father except in the Holy Spirit. This is expressly emphasized in Luke 10:21: "In that same hour [Jesus] rejoiced in the Holy Spirit and said, 'I thank you, Father, Lord of heaven and earth, that you have hidden these things from the wise and understanding and revealed them to babes.'" Surely this praying "in the Spirit" must apply equally to the many other prayers of Jesus that we find in the Gospels,[1] particularly since he knows that his Father seeks "true worshipers" who "worship in spirit and truth" (Jn 4:24)? If God is called "spirit" here, this does not amount to defining him thus in a philosophical sense. Rather, this passage "asserts that God discloses himself in the Spirit; it is in this sense that God 'is' spirit. That is also why the true worshipper can only worship God 'in spirit'."[2*] All the words of Jesus addressed to men, words that are "spirit and life" (Jn 6:63), are always addressed to the Father, too; thus, for instance, the high priestly prayer to the Father is spoken in the presence of the listening disciples and is (perhaps like no other) spoken in the worshipping Spirit. The prayer Jesus teaches his disciples begins with the word he uses to address his Father and which, after he has completed his work on earth, the Holy Spirit puts into the disciples' hearts and minds: "Abba" (Mk 14:36 = Rom 8:15; Gal 4:6). This is both astonishing and yet intelligible, for it is not the Spirit himself (as the third Person in God) who can utter this cry: but the Spirit enables the cry of the Son to resound in the hearts of the children who are "born of God".

"Abba" is not, first and foremost, a cry of petition; rather, it is the cry that understands itself as a child, its whole existence dependent on another; it is the sound made by "self as gift", which we may surmise to be the very first word uttered in the eternal and incarnate Son.[3] It may also express that puzzling "hearing" whereby he receives his being from the Father as the Word uttered by him (Jn 3:32; 8:26; 8:40; 15:15), and whereby we, too,

---

[1] "There is hardly one of the more significant events in Jesus' life that is not connected with a prayer" (J. Jeremias, "Das Gebetsleben Jesu", ZNW 25 [1926]: 131).

[2] H. Schlier, "Zum Begriff des Geistes nach dem Johannesevangelium", in *Besinnung auf das Neue Testament* (Herder, 1964), 264.

[*] All German nouns are capitalized, which means that the distinction in English between "Spirit" and "spirit" does not exist in German; the translator has no choice but to use both upper-case and lower-case initials in English, but in certain instances it is extremely hard to tell which—"Spirit" or "spirit"—is more apt. —Trans.

[3] On self as gift, cf. TD II, 284–88.

"hearing" him, are meant to receive him as the Father's Word (Jn 6:45; 8:43, 47)—which, in turn, presupposes that we are "of God" (8:47), that we are "of the truth" (18:37), that is, that the Holy Spirit is present in us as "hearers". But this presence has already been given to us in baptism (-confirmation), enabling us to hear the Word and to engage in dialogue with God: it was already given, in advance, when "God's love [was] poured into our hearts through the Holy Spirit who has been given to us" (Rom 5:5). So the Spirit can always witness, because of the cry "Abba" that continues to resound in our hearts (Rom 8:16), that "we are children of God". The Spirit, given to us as a gift, enables us not only to speak as creatures in God, but to enter into God's personal dialogue, which is the Spirit.

The origin of all biblical "hearing" of God is that hearing whereby we receive ourselves as gift, together with our hearing of the Word proceeding from the Father. We are accustomed to call this "contemplation" [*Kontemplation, Betrachtung*]—with all the nuances suggested by this term, which is borrowed from the Greek milieu rather than that of the Bible, whereas the biblical "Hear, O Israel" (and make sure you continually reflect on what you have heard in all life's dimensions—Deut 6:4–9) signals a more personal relation to the Word.[4] There can be no Christian prayer that is not an answer, in the Spirit of Christ, to the Word spoken to us by the Father in Christ, in which he reveals and gives himself. But the word that the Spirit places on our tongues is not his word but that of the divine Word, Jesus; the Spirit arouses and mediates the dialogue but does not himself utter the word: he is wordless (*alalētos*: Rom 8:26), but he knows the right word and can bring it forth where it is not yet adequately known.

However, our word does not come first: it is merely an answering word. First comes "the Spirit [who] searches . . . the depths of God", the "Spirit which is from God", who introduces us into these depths, so that we "might understand the gifts bestowed on us by God" (1 Cor 2:10–12, 16). Just as the

---

[4] Cf. my *Prayer* (San Francisco: Ignatius Press, 1986), 24: "This unwavering 'beholding', moreover, is also and always a 'hearing', because what is beheld is the free and infinite Person who, from the depths of his freedom, can give himself in a way that is ever new, unsuspected and unpredictable."

Son, in receiving the gift of himself from the Father, recognizes —in the Spirit—the unfathomable depths of the Father's love and returns him thanks in the equally unfathomable Eucharist, every Christian prayer begins by acknowledging what the Spirit bears "witness with our spirit[:] that we are children of God" and so "heirs of God and fellow heirs with Christ" (Rom 8:16f.), that is, people who have been showered with God's inexhaustible riches, the whole "fullness of deity": "you have come to fulness of life in him" (Col 2:10). This means that, in eternity, "hearing" and "reflecting" are progressive, because God's sources are inexhaustible, his "light is a draught that can never be drained". Initially it might seem that the words that "the Spirit says to the Church" (Rev 2:7, 11, 17, and so on) are clearly adumbrated and definable, but soon it becomes apparent that the Spirit's ever more profound interpretation of the Word of God—which is Christ—transcends every limited form of words; for the Father who utters, the uttered Word and the interpreting Spirit are absolutely infinite. So we can understand Gregory the Great when he says, "the speech of the Spirit resounds wordlessly in the ear of the heart";[5] "May our silence cry to him, and let our cry come to him in silence";[6] and "God's voice is heard in quiet."[7] We must also recall the fact of revelation, that the Word of God has become flesh, that is, he speaks to all that is human: first through his entire action, his life, suffering, and death, and through his word in the narrower sense: in all the dimensions of human speech, from gesture to image, symbol and parable, right up to the explicit word. This unlimited language is once more interpreted, in an infinite panorama, by the Spirit. It follows that the dialogue of prayer, too, acquires unforeseeable dimensions, which the interpreting Spirit opens up to limitless possibilities.

Since Christ is "the truth", he is "always heard" (see Jn 11:42) when he prays to the Father, and, knowing this, he expressly gives thanks in his prayer for having been heard (v. 41). When he plumbs his own prayer in order to teach some of it to us, he

---

[5] *Moralia* 5, 20.

[6] Ibid., 34, 48.

[7] Ibid., 5, 75. These and other texts can be found in P. Catry, O.S.B., "L'Esprit chez Saint Grégoire le Grand", in *Parole de Dieu, Amour et Esprit Saint chez S. Grégoire le Grand*, Vie monastique 17 (Bellefontaine, 1984), 186.

knows precisely what he is asking for when he begs the Father that his "name be hallowed", that his "kingdom come" and that his "will be done on earth just as it is in heaven". These things are clearly present to his contemplation before he formulates them as a request. He asks for what is dear to the Father's heart but no less to the Son's. Prayer of this kind (which is by no means a tautology) is infallibly heard. He bids us get into step with this prayer. It is what he calls "asking in his name"; and, once the Son is again with the Father, it will be all the same whether the Son infallibly does it (Jn 14:14) or the Father infallibly grants it (Jn 15:7; Mt 18:19). Asking in the name of Jesus means asking in his Spirit, in the adoration and thanksgiving he offers to the Father, and this prayer is "always heard". Not only subsequently, either, but—in the context of the Trinity—synchronically: "Therefore I tell you, whatever you ask in prayer, believe that you receive it, and you will" (Mk 11:24). "And this is the confidence which we have in him, that if we ask anything according to his will he hears us. And if we know that he hears us in whatever we ask, we know that we have obtained the requests made of him" (1 Jn 5:14–15). There is an infinite progression between our hearing of our children's requests and the Father's hearing of ours: "How much more will your Father who is in heaven give good things to those who ask him!" (Mt 7:11); in Luke these "good things" are "the Holy Spirit" (Lk 11:13). As Christians, we already possess the Holy Spirit, but he will be communicated to us in such a way that our prayer-dialogue with the Father, in Christ, will be infallibly effective.

In prayer we know, of course, that we do not attain to that fully adequate insight and petition which belongs to the Son. So the teaching of Romans 8:17–30 and the role of the Holy Spirit in our prayer acquire considerable importance. This text speaks of a twofold or actually threefold inadequacy. First the Spirit witnesses to us that we are children of God and hence fellow heirs with Christ, "provided we suffer with him". But do we suffer with him sufficiently? It goes on to say that, because of man's sin, the creation has been subjected to "futility" by God and "has been groaning in travail together until now" with "eager longing for the revealing of the sons of God". But we too, surely, are part of this creation that groans in futility and are unable to redeem ourselves? And finally, we are what creation is waiting for: it is waiting for us to be manifested in the promised glory of the new world, so that we may draw the "groaning" world into the glory for which it is hoping. Although possessing the pledge of the Spirit, however, we, too, are groaning and sighing, "for we do not know how to pray as we ought" (8:26). Christ knew well what he meant by the Father's "name", his "kingdom", and his "will", but do we know what this means? And even if we did know, would we really will it and ask for it "as we ought"? We may ask for things for ourselves, but do we ask for this whole creation, groaning in futility, of which we are undeniably a part? What is meant here is, not only blind and deaf human beings, but also the subhuman cosmos, which is looking for something it cannot envisage (which is why the text speaks not of *elpis*, hope, but *apokaradokia*, indistinct expectation); we are that "something", which is why we have a deep-down solidarity with the subhuman cosmos. We, too, are waiting for "the substance of what is hoped for" (here it is *elpis*), but we cannot describe it. We, too, therefore, do not get beyond the universal groaning of the creation. It does indeed have a particular direction, otherwise creation would not have the awareness of being under some compulsion; if it had no "hope" (v. 20), it would not feel the "travail" (v. 22) that signals a delivery. But this hope, as Paul so insists, does not know what it hopes for; and we, too, the sighing sons of God, cannot describe it, either, so all we can do is wait patiently (v. 24–25). And here again the question is: Are we waiting in the proper patience, which is meant to be a sharing in Christ's Passion?

At this point "the Spirit helps us in our weakness" and "intercedes for us with sighs too deep for words" (v. 26).[8] Of course, since we are "saved" in view of a hope (*tē elpidi*), we cannot yet see the infinite, superabundant good for which we are destined. But the Spirit transforms from within our inadequate sighing (which is all too lacking in hope) and makes it adequate. He

---

[8] It is highly unlikely that this is a reference to the glossolalia that was practiced by the Roman congregation and successfully supported by the Spirit, as H. Schlier, *Römer*, 269, and U. Wilckens, *Römer* (EKK, 1980), 161, rightly maintain against Käsemann, *Römer* (1973), 230. There are no parallels to "speaking in the Spirit" in 1 Corinthians 14:2.

adopts it and gives it the power to become a plea that is—christologically—sufficient; thus the Father, attending to the Spirit's intention (*phronēma*) in us, recognizes the proper content of this "sighing" prayer and is able to grant it. The prayer is heard: "We know that in everything God works for good with those who love him" (v. 28). Much follows from this. For it refers back to the inadequacy of our sharing of Christ's suffering (v. 17) and also to the great inarticulate suffering of creation, "groaning" in its subjection to futility: it is our task to enter into this twofold suffering so that everything will turn out "for good". If the Spirit is to render our prayer effective with God, we need to declare our solidarity with the suffering of creation and with Christ's suffering for creation. In our search for salvation, all that is purely private has been rendered obsolete by the Spirit.

More must be said, however. It is not merely a case of entrusting the success of our efforts to the Spirit and being resigned to our inadequacy and weakness. At this point 1 Corinthians 14 supplies what is lacking, for Paul insists that unintelligible spiritual speech (glossolalia) must be refashioned by an interpretation (prophecy) intelligible to and for the benefit of all and that, as far as the good of the Church is concerned, "he who prophesies is greater than he who speaks in tongues" (1 Cor 14:5). This is true not only of the community but also of the individual person praying, for if he merely prays in the Spirit, "my mind is unfruitful" (14:14). Ecstasies can be fruitful for a man's spiritual development if he is thereby taken to depths of prayer he would otherwise never have imagined possible, but these depths must also bring forth fruit for his practical apostolic life. "The mind" must have a share in this. "I will pray with the spirit and I will pray with the mind also" (14:15). "While the Spirit's exclusivity is important, he cannot do without the mind. The bridge between the two is found in man's will, whereby he submits in faith to God's will and so makes his human will docile. Man is able, by his obedience, to make his mind a useful tool for the Holy Spirit; through obedience, pure contemplation guarantees the possibility of action, and only in this way can it be fully what God desires: something of benefit for all. . . . Man must pray until his mind is so seized by the Spirit that, like a twin sister, it follows the Spirit wherever it is required."[9] On the one hand, this may have consequences that are highly relevant today, where a "mystic" is speaking in the Church: it may be "that God is speaking to the Church, through someone's prayer, in a 'language' that is not understood by the Church at that time; perhaps the Church does not want to and cannot accept it. The message will have to be interpreted."[10] But it may also have consequences for the individual "mystic" himself: "God's fullness is communicated in the interpretation; his view, his light is imparted to man in such superabundance that he forgets himself. But if, at the moment when he is speaking with God, he brings his entire self with him, planting these things in his rational 'I' without thereby intending to diminish the Spirit, his mind acquires a share in the Spirit."[11] If he fails to do this, he will not be able to give an adequate account of the insights and tasks he received in the Spirit. For, in Christian terms, even the "mystic" is never an isolated individual; praying in the Spirit (glossolalia) and praying in the mind (prophecy) are here envisaged as a unity, in the context of the charisms that are to be fruitful for the Church in various ways. "To each is given the manifestation of the Spirit for the common good" (1 Cor 12:7). This benefit can be purely internal, as when graces of prayer are given that are for the good of the Church in ways we cannot ascertain (as Thérèse of Lisieux attests); or it can be in the form of a command given by God to be communicated to the Church (as we see in the case of Catherine of Siena, for example).

In any case, as we have already said in the context of "theology": even the most intelligible discourse about divine things, addressed to the Church, can be fruitful only if it comes from prayer or, what is the same thing, from the sphere of the Holy Spirit.

---

[9] A. von Speyr, *Korinther* I (Einsiedeln: Johannesverlag, 1956), 443-44.
[10] Ibid., 450f.
[11] Ibid., 459.

b. Forgiveness

The importance of forgiveness in the New Testament[12] is clear from the phrase in the Our Father: "as we forgive those who trespass against us". This does not mean that God's forgiveness depends on our reciprocally forgiving each other but that this divine initiative (which is always primary) can only become effective in us if we make a path for its effectiveness by forgiving others. "If you do not forgive men their trespasses, neither will (—and we could add, neither *can*) your Father forgive your trespasses" (Mt 6:15).

In forgiveness we transcend the spheres of both cosmic[13] and social justice. The Greeks were well acquainted with the concept of ex-culpation, which depends solely on understanding how an apparently or really guilty person could not have acted differently, given his views or situation: such a person is recognized and pronounced to be not culpable.[14] Generally, the civil ethical order requires that crimes should attract punishment by way of restitution and as a restoring of equilibrium. When Seneca defined *clementia* as "self-control in the exercise of vengeance or leniency when sentencing", he nonetheless knew that "the wise man will not prescribe forgiveness in the sense of the remission of a deserved punishment."[15] Simplicius accuses the Christians thus: "Some of our contemporaries even attribute to God the

[12] In the Old Covenant, it is true, we find in the Psalms the plea for forgiveness and the certainty that God can grant it, but not until the Wisdom literature do we come across a recognition of the reciprocity between divine and human forgiveness: Wisdom 12:22 and especially Sirach 28:2–4: "Forgive your neighbor the wrong he has done, and then your sins will be pardoned when you pray. Does a man harbor anger against another, and yet seek for healing from the Lord? Does he have no mercy toward a man like himself, and yet pray for his own sins?" In Qumran, by contrast, everyone should direct his love or his hatred according to God's attitude: he should love the sons of light alone and hate the sons of darkness (1QS I, 3–4; 9–11; *Hymn.* XIV, 9–11; 18–21; XVII, 24; 1QS X, 20–21).

[13] Hans Heinrich Schmid, *Gerechtigkeit als Weltordnung: Hintergrund und Geschichte des alttestamentlichen Gerechtigkeitsbegriffs* (Tübingen, 1968).

[14] On this issue, cf. L. Oeing-Hanhoff, "Verzeihen, Ent-schuldigen, Wiedergutmachung", *Gießener Universitätsblätter* XI (1978): 68–80, from which we have quoted in what follows. Cf. also *Theo-Logic* I, 244, on "creative forgetting".

[15] *De clementia*, II, 7.

irrational attitude of simply pardoning offenses instead of having restitution made."[16] "Let the objection of Simplicius stand: If an offense and the guilt of it is evidence of a spiritual illness and a pathological condition of the soul, is not pardoning it a refusal to restore and heal the sick soul, just as if a doctor, confronted with an ulcer, were to say: 'It's nothing, nothing serious at least', instead of burning it out?"[17] One might suggest that a considerable proportion of modern analytical therapy has not progressed beyond the Greek model, trying as it does to explain away and eradicate (alleged) culpability through psychological understanding.

Christian forgiveness goes beyond the sphere of cosmic and social justice, without vitiating the latter's sphere of competence (although this has been relativized). We have already seen this in the area of canon law. It is clear, even from the Old Testament, that the covenant law prescribed by God, and hence the covenant justice lived out (if possible) by man, results from the freest divine condescension; when this covenant is fulfilled in Christ, it transpires that the "expiation" (*hilasmos, hilastērion*) he performs on the Cross is motivated, not by penal justice, but purely by love (1 Jn 4:10; Heb 2:17; this is how Romans 3:25 should be understood). This aspect of (suspended) justice, which is at home in the love between the Father and the incarnate Son, clears a path for the outpouring of the Spirit of love into our hearts; we are to understand the Cross as the work of divine, pardoning love and respond to it by forgiving others. Just as God's work of forgiving took place "while we were enemies" (Rom 5:10), the Christian response to it is the eager forgiving of the brother who "has something against you" (Mt 5:23), which is itself part of the command to love your enemy (Mt 5:43ff.); this is explicitly an imitation of God (Mt 5:42; Lk 6:36). M. Scheler is no doubt right, in philosophical terms, when he defines the guilty man's repentance as "the restoration of the full capacity to love";[18] but, just as God's readiness to forgive does not wait for man's repentance, the Christian who follows

[16] *Comm. in Epict. enchir.*, ed. Dübner, 106, 13.

[17] Oeing-Hanhoff, "Verzeihen", 72.

[18] *Reue und Wiedergeburt*, in *Works* V, (1954), 27f.

him does not make his forgiveness dependent on the repentance of the guilty. God, on his Son's Cross, not only demonstrates his forgiveness symbolically but operates as what we have termed "original righteousness", the readiness to send his Spirit into the hearts of sinners; this being so, the course of action urged by the Sermon on the Mount, that is, not to resist evil, to offer the other cheek, to part with one's cloak, to go the further mile, are all possible ways of discipleship of the Cross. Along with prayer and penance on behalf of the hard of heart, this is the most effective means man has of moving the "wicked" toward repentance and conversion. What we do, in our following of the Cross, to achieve the conversion of others is not the exerting of some kind of psychological pressure but a sharing—in the Holy Spirit—in the Son's attitude on the Cross (and, as Ephesians 4:32–5:2 shows, it is the Father's attitude, also). "Spiritual men" (*pneumatikoi*) are able to "restore in a spirit of gentleness" anyone who has fallen (Gal 6:1). And, lest the spiritual man should think that he has personal possession of this "spirit of gentleness", Paul immediately adds: "Look to yourself, lest you too be tempted." On the other hand, ministering to the fallen brother in the spirit of gentleness is only one example of "[walking] by the Spirit" (5:25); it is a following of the Cross by "[bearing] one another's burdens" (6:2). It has nothing to do with boasting of one's achievements but is a humble bearing of "one's own load" and a "[fulfilling of] the law of Christ" (6:2). This is the only way in which Christian forgiveness can express "the law of the Spirit of life in Christ Jesus" (Rom 8:2).[19]

c. *Experience of the Spirit*

Can a man know whether the Holy Spirit indwells him, whether "uncreated Love" is producing in him the grace of "created love"? The Fathers, long ago, were exercised by this question. Montanism and Messalianism, with their unguarded affirmations, forced the Fathers to confront the issue and adopt positions that, while cautious, are not simply a rejection (Diadochus of Photike,

[19] The best treatment of this is found in Luigi Giussani, *Alla ricerca del volto umano* (Jaca Book, 1984), 75ff.

the sermons of Leo the Great). The question teased the Middle Ages, provoking it to draw subtle distinctions. When the Reformers also strongly affirmed the indwelling of the Spirit, without going into the nuances of this doctrine, the Council of Trent was obliged to meet their position with a highly nuanced refutation.[20] The question, although it has been settled at the level of theology, nonetheless continues to flicker into life again; in our time it does so quite openly, since, in a secularized world, some element of faith experience seems essential if children and adults are to acquire and keep the Christian faith. "Experience" —however ambiguous and imprecise the word may be—is one of today's big words. Much of what is to be briefly noted here anticipates the topic of our next section: the discernment of spirits. Here the straight question is this: Can a Christian experience in himself the gracious presence of the Holy Spirit?

The fundamental problem arises in St. Thomas' demonstration that the Holy Spirit can operate in our spiritual nature only if we already have a created ability to love. "Nor can we forget that the Holy Spirit, who is uncreated Love, can move the soul of a man (who possesses a created love) to an act of love; just as God moves all beings to their acts, while they themselves are inclined to such acts on the basis of their own ability. So he gently causes all things to operate in concert: he gives to all beings their (natural) abilities and powers that incline them to do what he moves them to do; thus they strive for these things freely (*sponte*), not by compulsion."[21] Since a man is moved in this way, will he be able to know whether he is moved by his natural inclination or by a supernatural impulsion? Thomas' answer is clear: "Someone who has supernatural love can suppose, on the basis of probable signs, that he has Love . . . , but no

[20] "But neither is this to be asserted, that they who are truly justified must, without any doubting whatever, settle within themselves that they are justified, . . . as though whoever does not have this belief doubts of the promises of God and of the efficacy of the death and Resurrection of Christ. For even as no pious person ought to doubt of the mercy of God, of the merit of Christ, and of the virtue and efficacy of the sacraments, even so each one, when he regards himself and his own weakness and indisposition, may have fear and apprehension touching his own grace; since no one can know with a certainty of faith, which cannot be subject to error, that he has obtained the grace of God" (DS 1534).

[21] *De Car.*, q. and a. 1, c in fine.

one can know it with certainty unless God himself reveals it to him",[22] and this uncertainty arises "because of the similarity between natural love and that which is given by grace".[23] Even the delight (*delectatio*) with which he performs this act "is not an adequate proof".[24] For instance, he may know with certainty that he loves a fellow man, "but he does not know with ultimate certainty that this love is *caritas* [that is, a love fostered by the Holy Spirit]".[25] It could just as well be a *habitus acquisitus*. Thomas gives a clear summary of what Scholasticism has said, before and after him, albeit to some extent using different modes of expression.[26]

This teaching cannot be countered by quoting St. Thomas' presentation of the "gifts of the Holy Spirit" that are given to the divine and natural virtues, granted to the justified man so that he can "obey the Holy Spirit promptly and with joy",[27] and that, following Aristotle, are called *instinctus divinus*. They, too, essentially, are based on the fundamental attitude of faith and so exclude any critical reflection on their origin. Such faith would have to be understood in a Pauline sense, as a life that has died with Christ and been raised with him; here the Spirit given to us, crying "Abba", leads us to be more and more profoundly a child "with Christ". This internal evidence of the Spirit, namely, that we are in Christ, arises solely from the whole thrust of our believing and surrendered existence. The same thing applies to the doctrine developed in the First Letter of John: on the one hand,

[22] *De Ver.* 10, 10c.

[23] Ibid., ad. 1.

[24] Ibid., ad 2.

[25] Ibid., ad 3, cf. *De Ver.* 6, 5 ad 3.

[26] Thus the *Summa* of Alexander of Hales distinguishes between a speculative certainty that is unattainable and a *scientia experimentalis* that is accessible; the former is reached only through special revelation (m. 7, a. 3). Cf. Albert in his *Summa* I, 17, a. 5; Bonaventure: Grace can be recognized *in universali*, but its existence *in speciali* cannot. He, too, insists on the similarity between natural and supernatural love, so that only a *probabilis cognitio* of grace can be attained (1, d. 17, p. 1, a. and 93). Further texts in J. Auer, *Die Entwicklung der Gnadenlehre in der Hochscholastik* I (Herder, 1942), 312–36. The particular relationship between grace and love in the Duns Scotus tradition does not change the disposition of the problems.

[27] *S. Th.* I/II, 68, 3; 68, 1: "homo disponitur, ut efficiatur prompte mobilis ab inspiratione divina".

the "knowledge" given to us through the "anointing" of the
Spirit appears to be infallible; and yet it is always linked to very
concrete conditions of Christian living, for example, active love
of neighbor, keeping the Commandments, also the awareness of
one's own sinfulness and need of forgiveness, the necessity of
"abiding" in the doctrine in the face of all trials—and all this,
it is strongly stressed, in faith. It is utterly impossible for the
Christian to be taught by the Spirit and to receive his testimony
unless he is carrying out the commandment of love in his whole
life.

We must agree, therefore, with Jean Mouroux[28] when he carefully distinguishes three degrees in the concept of Christian experience of the Spirit. He insists that Christian experience (and
he affirms that it exists) can be securely established only on the
basis of a man's total attitude. The three levels are: "empirical
experience", with its symptoms (consolation, enthusiasm, and
every form of emotional experience of the divine), which always
remain ambiguous: "Religious experience appears to be a spe-
cially structured experience; it cannot be described as something
elemental and simple. Most importantly, it cannot be restricted
to the sphere of the feelings (*sentir*)."[29] The second level is that of
"experimental experience", based on a consciously applied tech-
nique, that is, it is an experience produced (*provoquée*) by the
subject himself. This would include the oriental methods for
achieving particular "religious" experiences (which Mouroux
does not deal with), but also, no doubt, much of what takes
place in the realm of the Church. The third level—the only
level that counts here—is what he calls *expérientiel*, which is
hard to translate but becomes clear from his definition: "an experience that arises from the totality of the person's life".[30] This

---

[28] In his foundational work *L'Expérience chrétienne: Introduction à une théologie*
(Paris: Aubier, 1952). On the same subject: D. Mollat, *L'Expérience du Saint-Esprit
dans le Nouveau Testament* (Paris: Éd. du Renouveau, 1975). For a broad basis for
"religious experience" (not only Christian), cf. the thorough treatment in the
article "Expérience religieuse", by Pinard de la Boullaye, in DTC V/2 (1913),
1786–1868.

[29] Mouroux, *Expérience chrétienne*, 35. On p. 50 he gives Messalianism, Lutheran-
ism, and Quietism as examples.

[30] Ibid., 24, 348–54, illustrated by references from Leo I and Bernard.

totality can only be read as such, as a whole, through a convergence of many "signs" that are "hierarchically structured and
integrated"[31] and thus enter "into the simplicity" of a life lived
for God (and hence for his work in the world), a simplicity
that integrates everything that comes to it, from within or from
without. This is what is meant by living by faith (understood
in a Pauline sense); but, as Thomas maintained (and contrary to
the Reformers' faith-certainty), this faith must not be taken in
isolation to be an infallible criterion[32] but has to prove itself in
the various expressions of a lived life of faith; that is, it must
show itself to be genuine through signs.

It is clear that the Holy Spirit is very much involved here,
because the Church as a whole, with the incarnate Word who is
now her heavenly Head, is always in need of the Spirit to interpret the Word, so that she can pursue her habitual path and do
what is laid upon her here and now. The Church of the Word
is necessarily the Church of the Spirit, and the individual in the
Church, together with his entire existence, will live and move
under this same leadership and its spiritual interpretation. Paul
addresses the community, in the name of the Church, in these
terms: "For our gospel came to you not only in word, but also
in power and in the Holy Spirit. . . . And you became imitators of us and of the Lord, for you received the word in much
affliction, with joy inspired by the Holy Spirit" (1 Thess 1:5–
6). Again we see here that the objective, ecclesial Spirit and the

---

[31] Ibid., 25f.

[32] Cf. Mouroux' detailed presentation, ibid., 57–88. Again we find the same
reservations in Thomas (cf. 66–69: while it is quite possible for there to be *certitudo* regarding a *fides informis* where someone is certain that he is assenting to the
Church's faith, this does not yield any certainty about *fides formata caritate*: *In 2 Cor.*
13, 15); Cajetan goes so far as to admit a *certitudo* regarding the *donum infusum fidei*,
but with the restrictions formulated by the Council of Trent (In I/II 112, 5 ad
2). Suarez opposes the assertion of a *certitudo moralis* (which is admitted by many
writers) by maintaining the contrary thesis, that there is no sure sign that would
permit an "acquired natural faith" to be distinguished from a supernatural infused
faith (Mouroux, *Expérience Chrétienne*, 70). On this question, cf. R. Aubert, *Le
Problème de l'acte de foi* (Louvain, 1945), 69. Suarez is thinking particularly of the
case of a heretic, who can have lost the infused faith but retains an "acquired faith".
On the indirect nature of experience, cf. also K. Rahner "On the Experience of
Grace" (*Theological Investigations* 3 [Baltimore and London, 1967].

subjective Holy Spirit are one; and the Church as an organization can only understand herself if she manifestly surrenders herself to the interpreting Spirit. The Church as a whole, like the individual Christian, walks in the darkness of faith, in "mirrors and riddles", so that "there is a substantial darkness enveloping every experience of the Spirit, however simple it may seem to be: and this is the darkness of faith. We have no way of grasping the Spirit except through the mediation of his signs." What the signs have in common is "a unity of life", in other words: "There is an essential correspondence between the gift of the Holy Spirit and the human spirit who receives it; thus there is a spiritual unity between them."[33]

It follows that the references to "spiritual feeling" or "tasting" (*sapere, delectatio*) that one finds throughout the Christian tradition must be assessed along these lines. At the first, lowest level such concepts are definitely ambivalent, but if they are raised to the third level they can change and be refined, forfeiting their primitive immediacy. Then, as an individual element within a total structure they can acquire a new valence. "La structure juge l'élément."[34]

It is possible to speak of "archetypical experiences" in the history of Christianity (as we did in the first volume of *The Glory of the Lord*),[35] but the Gospels teach us that they, too, were experiences in faith, and (in the case of Mary and the disciples) it was a faith that did not understand, a faith that, in the first ending of St. John's Gospel, is called "blessed" and contrasted with the desire to see and to experience. Philip naïvely wished to see the Father face to face and had to be pointed to the vision afforded by faith in Christ. Similarly, Magdalen at the graveside was denied tangible experience. According to John, this is the only way to hear, see, and touch the Word of life; this is the only mode of experience that is passed on to later generations. Jesus' admonition—that we should recognize the decisive Christian experiences from the "fruits" they show—is the key and sum of all that we have said on this topic (Mt 7:16f.). This takes us

---

[33] Mouroux, *Expérience chrétienne*, 157.

[34] Ibid., 307.

[35] *The Glory of the Lord*, I (301–65).

far away from the criterion of *delectatio*, with its ambiguity and capacity for gradual transformation, and points us toward the total achievement, the total stance, of a life.

A life of this kind, guided by the Spirit, will exhibit two features; and we shall conclude this section with them. The first is that the Spirit, who is the Interpreter of Christ, will always point to the bearing of witness (martyrdom). Now as always, it is not the enthusiasts but the genuine martyrs who are most authentically the spiritual locus for the experience of the Spirit in the Church of Christ.[36] The second feature is the way in which every Christian experience is open to the eschatological future. As G. Sauter remarks, the Church and Christ confirm their claims, not by insisting on their own experience, but in the calm and modest way in which they encounter historical reality. "Pneumatology" will prove itself in our sober grappling with our particular history; we should speak about the "Whole" only out of an attitude of hopeful expectation.[37]

d. Discernment of Spirits

The wide-ranging topic of the "discernment of spirits" follows on directly from the foregoing; much of what we have learned will be of profit in what follows. Here we cannot give a thorough treatment of the shape it has taken in history, for the present work is concerned, not with "spirits", but with the Holy Spirit. Yet wherever there is a doctrine of "spirits", God's Holy Spirit must be there in the background. This is so both where society and the Church are concerned with distinguishing the nature and operation of the true Spirit of God from that of other spirits (perhaps hostile to God) and also where the individual must discern the genuine Spirit of God so that he can choose and decide correctly. In this context we can distinguish three problematical areas. First there is that of the dualism of the divine Spirit and the spirit that is hostile to God; we find this dualism in the Bible

---

[36] Cf. M.J. Le Guillou, *Les Témoins sont parmi nous: L'Expérience de Dieu dans l'Esprit Saint* (Paris: Fayard, 1976).

[37] *Erwartung und Erfahrung*, Theol. Bücherei 47 (Munich: Kaiser, 1972), 283–308. See also his *Zukunft und Verheißung* (Zürich: Zwingli, 1965).

of the Old and New Covenants, and it continues right up to the
"discernment of spirits" of Ignatius and his commentators. Then
there is the theme of the Pauline charisms, which, though they
are allotted by a divine Spirit, are nonetheless—particularly in
view of the way they are exhibited by "charismatics"—in need
of a process of "discernment of spirits". Finally, and linked with
the first topic, there is the problem of how the "spirits" that
guide the Church as a whole, in her inner life and in her missionary activity, are related to one another.

1. In the Old Covenant, from paradise on, man is faced with a
choice between the Spirit of God and the spirit of the serpent.
According to the primitive account leading up to Noah, this
choice continues in the form of a life with or without God. In
Deuteronomy 30:15ff. Yahweh himself faces Israel with the possible alternative paths of "life and happiness or death and mis-
fortune". In themselves these paths are clearly distinct, but for
man, living in the darkness of faith, where evil can clothe itself
in a seductive light and where he himself cannot know his own
heart and assess the consequences of his deeds, a process of spiritual discernment is imperative, allowing him to choose between
what are in fact opposites. In the prophets, we see emerging
with difficulty and much pain a distinction between true and
false "prophecy": both kinds of prophets claim to be speaking
by the Spirit of God, and criteria need to be found to separate
truth from falsehood. Those are suspect who predict peace and
success where God must punish or test his servants (Jer 23),
for God sends his prophets to reveal man's blindness, attempting, as he does, to use God's gifts and signs (the Tabernacle,
the Temple) as insurances against him. The criterion (from the
great writing prophets right up to Paul) is the testimony of an
express divine call, together with a life that is in accord with
this vocation. There is also the fulfillment (or non-fulfillment)
of what is predicted. There is also faithfulness to the spirit of the
covenant and its tradition (just as Paul will hold fast to the tradition and base himself upon it). In the Old Covenant the doctrine of the two paths produces the contrast between the paths
of the wise man and the fool; ultimately there is no bridge, no
communication possible between these two.

In the apocalyptic, inter-testamental literature this leads to the doctrine of two opposed empires, presided over respectively by a good and an evil spirit; these two spirits accompany each individual man. (There are embryonic stages of this in Greek and Latin antiquity,[38] and some Iranian influence is possible.) In the testaments of the patriarchs we read of both "two paths"[39] and "two spirits".[40] This may be due in part to the influence of Qumran, where there was a systematic elaboration of the two-spirits doctrine: God "created man to rule the world and appointed two spirits for him, so that he would walk in them, . . . these are the spirits of truth and of wrong . . . , the spirits of light and of darkness";[41] they may also be called the "fleshly spirit" and the "holy spirit";[42] there can be an alternation of singular ("spirit of truth") and plural ("spirits of truth").[43] Since they were originally created by God, they are angelic princes. "Spirits" and "paths" can be used interchangeably: "There are two paths in the world, watched over by two angels: one is the angel of righteousness, the other the angel of wickedness".[44] The idea passes across into Jewish-Christian literature and those writings influenced by the latter;[45] in Pseudo-Barnabas we are presented more with angelic beings; in the *Shepherd* of Hermas, more with the Holy Spirit of God.[46] Where it is a case of distinguishing

[38] P. Boyancé, "Les Deux Démons personnels dans l'antiquité grecque et latine", *Revue de Philologie*, 1935, 189ff.

[39] *Test. Aser* I, 3‒4.

[40] *Test. Juda* 20: "Two spirits concern themselves with man, the spirit of truth and the spirit of error; man's reason stands between them and can bend this way or that, as he will."

[41] 1QS IV, 18f., 25.

[42] 1QS XIII, 13; XVIII, 25; XVII, 26.

[43] 1QS IV, 21 and 23 ("Until then the spirits of truth and of wrong wrestle in the heart of man").

[44] *De Duobus Viis* (Fribourg, 1900), 8.

[45] J. Daniélou, "Une Source de spiritualité judéo-chrétienne: La Doctrine des deux esprits", *Dieu Vivant*, 1953, 127‒36; also his "Esprit Saint et Prince des Lumières", in *Théologie du Judéo-Christianisme* I (1958), 192‒96.

[46] Cf. James 3:17: "But the wisdom from above is first pure, then peaceable, gentle, open to reason, full of mercy and good fruits, without uncertainty or insincerity"—which is clearly in the tradition of the biblical wisdom literature. The expression "from above" will acquire a particular significance in Ignatius of Loyola.

between false and true prophets, "Hermas" speaks of the "divine Spirit"[47] and lists criteria. But he is also acquainted with the doctrine of the "two angels accompanying man, the one of righteousness, the other of evil",[48] a view that is taken up by Origen (explicitly basing himself on "Hermas") and "spreads thence into all monastic spirituality": the good spirit inspires man to good and heavenly deeds, whereas the evil spirit is recognized by "confusion and lack of mental power".[49] Gregory of Nyssa takes up the doctrine of the two angels; Athanasius expands the doctrine of the discernment of spirits in his *Life of Antony*; Diadochus uses it against the Messalians; in the West, Cassian and Gregory the Great will finally settle it.[50]

Although this very concrete notion of the two angels or spirits accompanying man throughout his whole life is elaborated by Origen and his followers[51] and persists into the Middle Ages (up to the great summary of this tradition that we find in *De discretione spirituum* by Dionysius the Carthusian),[52] it should by rights have paled into oblivion in the face of the New Testament requirement for a "discernment of spirits". Paul expressly speaks of this as a charism of the one Holy Spirit (1 Cor 12:10), as the practical art of distinguishing, *dokimazein*, for which he calls on several occasions (Rom 12:2; Eph 5:7, 11; Phil 1:9–10). John, in his First Letter, urges his readers to "test the spirits to see

[47] *Mand.* XI, 7–17 (SC 53 bis, 195f.).

[48] Ibid., IV, 1.

[49] *Peri Archon* III, 3, 4.

[50] Examples are given in the detailed article "Discernement des Esprits" in DSp III (1957), 1222–91. On the discernment of spirits in spiritual direction: I. Hausherr, *Direction spirituelle en Orient autrefois* (Rome, 1955). On tradition in the prehistory of the "rules for the discernment of spirits" in the Exercises: H. Rahner, "'Werdet kundige Geldwechsler': Zur Geschichte der Lehre des Heiligen Ignatius von der Unterscheidung der Geister", in *Ignatius von Loyola*, ed. F. Wulf (Würzburg, 1956), 301–41.

[51] The origin of this idea is first found in Qumran, where the two spirits are understood to be explicitly created by God. However, this idea goes back to the ancient Israelitic notion according to which both the good and the evil spirit proceed from Yahweh (esp. 1 Kings 22:19–23, but also Judg 9:28; 1 Sam 16:14–23; 18:10; 19:9; 2 Kings 19:7; Is 19:14; 29:10).

[52] *Works* XL. Ignatius can speak of "God and his angels" in the traditional sense (Ex. 320, passim); Thomas, too, ascribes to the latter the power of acting on man's mind (*S. Th.* I/II 5, 6 ad 3; 9, 6 ad 2).

whether they are of God" (4:1); the spirits he means here are
clearly the Spirit of God and the spirit "of this world", or "of the
Antichrist", or plainly "of Satan". When writers like Bernard,
Richard of St. Victor, or Thomas Aquinas speak of *discretio* (*spirituum*), they are thinking of this New Testament either-or, and
the same is true of the Ignatian rules for the discernment of spirits. Paul's express concern is "to know [God's] will and approve
what is excellent" (Rom 2:18), which is something that must
be learned, because it can only be done by those who are mature in the Spirit (Heb 5:13–14), or, as Paul likes to say, "the
spiritual". When Paul includes "discernment of spirits" among
the charisms of the Holy Spirit, it is, after all, a power that is
entrusted to each Christian, to be cultivated in inner vigilance,
sensitivity, and with a sense of the Church. He urges the entire Corinthian community not to be led astray by the serpent,
like Eve, and "receive a different spirit" (*pneuma heteron*, 2 Cor
11:3–4), different from the Spirit of God (*pneuma theou*, Rom
8:9) who "dwells within you". There are numerous criteria for
this Spirit of God in the community: the list of the "fruits of
the Spirit", speaking with boldness, living in peace with one another, brotherly love, obedience to the Lord; but also authority
in the Church (2 Cor 10), adherence to the incarnate Christ:
"No one speaking by the Spirit of God ever says '[the earthly]
Jesus be cursed!' and no one can say 'Jesus is Lord' except by
the Holy Spirit" (1 Cor 12:3). This brings us to the central affirmation of the First Letter of John: while the entire Gospel
was a battle between faith and unbelief, over the Word of God
having become flesh, the Letter has only one criterion for distinguishing between truth and the lie: the confession or denial
that Jesus is the Son of God (1 Jn 2:22). Like Paul, and perhaps
even more explicitly than he, John is acquainted with an inner
witness of the Spirit of truth (1 Jn 3:24; 4:13), an inner certainty
that is based on the anointing of the Spirit (2:27). However, discernment, *discretio*, acknowledges this inner witness as genuine
only if it is one both with "what you heard from the beginning"
(2:24) and with the practice of brotherly love: "By this it may
be seen who are the children of God, and who are the children
of the devil: whoever does not do right is not of God, nor he
who does not love his brother" (3:10).

It is important to remember this before we proceed to the Ignatian rules for discerning spirits (Ex. 314–36), which are for the purpose of making a "choice" (of the will of God, of a path in life). We know that the rules for discerning spirits constitute the primary core of the Exercises that Ignatius tested out in Manresa: the experiences of consolation and desolation came over him like "a new and alien life",[53] as he saw "in bright daylight a wondrous appearance like a snake with many points shining like eyes, which gave him great consolation . . . , and the more he looked at it, the more his inner consolation became".[54] Simultaneously, however, he became aware of the difficulties of the life for God that he had chosen. He felt no attraction to attend Holy Mass and other exercises of prayer and found himself "plagued with scruples". Finally he recognized the enchanting thing as the devil's mirage; but later, too, he was tempted to abandon his studies by great inner consolations.[55] We must bear in mind experiences such as these when reading the first description of consolation and desolation (Ex. 315), for even at this early stage "it is typical of the evil spirit to cause regret and sadness, using fallacious arguments to disturb them"—which matches the effects of the devilish phenomenon in Manresa, whereas the "consolation" he felt when he looked at it was not at all the "spiritual consolation" described in rule 3 (Ex. 316). Hence the instructions Ignatius gives in his first rules (Ex. 314–27), particularly his warning that we must hold fast and go against inimical influences (*agere contra*) during a period of desolation (Ex. 318–19, 323–24), his explanation of why God allows desolation (Ex. 320–22), and his unmasking of satanic ploys and his prescriptions for repulsing them (Ex. 325–27). Thus the second series of rules (Ex. 328–36) makes the ambiguity of consolations even clearer; not, that is, of those that come from God and are produced in devoted souls "exclusively" by him who is their cause (Ex. 320), but of those for which some psychological antecedent can be found. In such a case the task of discernment will be to find out what is the goal of this particular consolation (Ex. 331),

---

[53] *Pilgrim's Report*, no. 21.
[54] Ibid., no. 19.
[55] Ibid., no. 54.

which means that great attention must be paid to the "entire train of thought" (Ex. 333). The direction taken by the evil spirit is chosen to bring him closer to his own goals (Ex. 332), and he is recognized "by his snake's tail" (Ex. 324). Even the ways in which consolation enters the soul are different: that which leads to good is "soft, light, and gentle" (Ex. 335), encouraging positive movements ("quietly, like a man coming into his own house when the door is open"), whereas that which leads to evil is "rough, accompanied by noise and disturbance", with the aim of obstructing and reversing the movement toward God through the use of noise and force. Ignatius' final precautionary measure concerns the transition between the consolation that comes directly from God (which Ignatius does not question in any way) and the "subsequent stage" when the soul is still glowing and yet in which it can already draw independent conclusions from its consolation: since, at this stage, it is resting in itself rather than directly in God, vigilance is once again called for, since its conclusions may drive it off course (Ex. 336).

All these instructions are primarily directed toward the central event of the Exercises, the choice of each individual man's God-appointed path in life. This choice should emerge cleanly out of a unity between divine and human freedom: the whole purpose is "to prepare ourselves to achieve perfection in whatever state of life our Lord God shall grant us to choose" (Ex. 135). This delicate consonance between God's most free offer and man's most free acceptance, a consonance that is "clear and pure" (*pura y limpida*) and yet threatened by human impurity, must not be clouded by anything if it is truly to come about. This is the whole aim of the Exercises. The discernment of spirits is evidently highly subjective; accordingly the retreat master is forbidden to interpose his own opinions into the dialogue between God and the soul (Ex. 15). At the same time, since what is to be chosen is a way of life within the realm of "our holy Mother the hierarchical Church" (Ex. 170, 353), some control of this subjectivity must be exercised by the objective side of the official Church, in the person of the retreat master, who must apply the Church's understanding of the discernment of spirits to the particular exercitant, testing the discernment that the latter has made (Ex. 8–10, 14). It will not do here to say simply that, for this, "the human mind is sufficient, but it is supported and enlightened by the light of faith, which comes from God, and the one cannot contradict the other, since truth necessarily agrees with truth";[56] this "light of faith" must be more closely defined as the grace of discernment, specifically imparted to the retreat master by the Holy Spirit. This gift is connected with the objective spirit of office in the Church, so that in fact subjective and objective spirit cannot contradict each other, if both are attending to the inspirations of the Spirit of God. H. Rahner has demonstrated how balanced this teaching is, how futile the attempts of those who attack the Exercises, and how shrewdly the Exercises have been defended by men (primarily Nadal and later Jesuits, of whom Suarez was the most prominent) who could rightly cite the great tradition of the Fathers.

2. Since the "Charismatic Movement" is centrally concerned with the Holy Spirit and his charisms, and since one of these charisms proclaims itself explicitly to be the discernment of spirits (1 Cor 12:10), we cannot avoid applying the discernment of spirits to this movement itself, at least briefly. We shall have to restrict ourselves to a few essential themes.[57] The term "Charismatic Movement" or "Charismatic Renewal" has often been criticized on the grounds that there are many other movements of renewal in the Church, no doubt equally inspired and sustained by the Holy Spirit. In Paul, for instance, the word "charism" has a much wider spectrum of meaning than that found in the special list of charisms in 1 Corinthians 12–14, Romans 12, and Ephesians 4. Many of these other initiatives and spontaneously generated movements are aware that they owe their existence to the Holy Spirit, without making him the central object or criterion of their spirituality, as the "charismatics" do. We must maintain,

---

[56] *Directorium* of 1599 (28, 5), quoted from H. Rahner, "Werdet kundige", 321.

[57] There is no end to the bibliography here. Particular selections can be found in Y. Congar, *Je crois en l'Esprit Saint* II (Paris: Cerf, 1980), 189f., 209f. (= ES in what follows). Norbert Baumert, *Gabe des Geistes Jesu: Das Charismatische in der Kirche* (Styria, 1986), 195 (= B). Often quoted is F. A. Sullivan, *Die charismatische Erneuerung: Die biblischen und theologischen Grundlagen*, 2d ed. (Styria, 1986) (= S). K. G. Rey, *Gotteserlebnisse im Schnellverfahren: Suggestion als Gefahr und Charisma* (Munich: Kösel, 1985) (= R). See also the relevant works of H. Mühlen in the series Toposbücherei (Mainz: Grünewald), vols. 40, 49, 90.

on the other hand, that the discernment of spirits appears in Paul as a specific charism, although, as we have said, this ability to distinguish "in the Spirit" can be attributed to the community as a whole (1 Cor 14:29; 1 Thess 5:21; 1 Jn 4:1; *Didache* 11).

There can be no doubt that the charismatic prayer groups, which have spread throughout the whole world and embrace millions of Catholics, constitute a genuine departure in the Church, particularly if they are guided by competent spiritual leaders. The Council has explicitly recognized this (LG 12, 2). An essential criterion of the genuineness of these groups will be that they fit into and bear fruit in the surrounding Church and, in particular, the parish community. This follows from the fundamental thrust of our theological reflection; namely, that the Holy Spirit does not carry out his own work but rather fosters and develops the work of Christ as its Interpreter.[58] "The soundness of a Pneumatology is seen in the way it points to Christ."[59] The Spirit teaches us to confess that "Jesus is the Lord" (1 Cor 12:3). His "charisms" have no other purpose, therefore, than to build up the "body of Christ" (see 1 Cor 12:12). This being so, when we read that the Spirit distributes his gifts to Christian people for their "common good" (v. 7) as members of the Body of Christ, this can only mean "for the common good of all the others". So the apparent exception in 1 Corinthians 14:4 ("He who speaks in a tongue edifies himself") must indicate that the value of this gift is less when it is exercised outside the context of the community. The whole point is to "build up" the community (1 Cor 14:12).[60]

The strange thing is that the charism to which Paul alludes, and which seemed so important to the isolated Corinthian community—although he himself regarded it, in social terms, as the

[58] A priest gives his testimony: "I had to be broken in order to find the Holy Spirit. And what I found was *Jesus*. There was nothing strange about this: 'He will call to your mind all the things I have told you'" (B 75).

[59] ES 267.

[60] This contradicts the attempt to undermine the social character of the charisms in 1 Corinthians 12, as we find in Sullivan (S 30) and also in Baumert (B 148), who asserts that certain charisms are given "for one's own edification" and not "for the service of others" (B 151). Paul's vision of the mutual interrelationship of the members of the Body seems to argue against this view.

most insignificant—is so highly prized in charismatic groups. The first Pentecostalist (Charles Fox Parham, in Kansas, 1900) taught his followers "that the only sure and scriptural sign that a man has been baptized in the Holy Spirit is the gift of speaking in other tongues" and that the apostles' experience on the day of Pentecost "was the normal experience of all believers in the early Church and that, even today, all believers have the pledge of such an experience and should seriously seek it".[61] There are several criticisms to be made here. First, the Pentecost phenomenon as Luke describes it was not "speaking in tongues" but intelligible speech in several languages (*xenoglossia*); for Luke, no doubt, this was a theological sign rather than a historical accreditation. The other references to *glossolalia* in the Acts of the Apostles seem to be more stereotypical (the one on whom the Spirit descends speaks "in tongues": Acts 10:46; 19:6). Nothing of this kind is mentioned in the case of any community other than that of Corinth, so that it is quite wrong to speak of *glossolalia* as if it were universal in "primitive Christianity". Nor is it specifically Christian: there are similar phenomena among the shamans, in Mesopotamia, in Qumran, and in Greece.[62]

Speaking in tongues plays a strangely dominant role in the new Protestant and Catholic movements. An immense amount has been written on it, but its religious fruitfulness is very questionable. Since this speaking in tongues was unintelligible, Paul strictly required that there be an "interpreter" for the congregation and even for the speaker himself (1 Cor 14); but most contemporary meetings lack an interpreter of this kind.[63] Nor is it ecstatic speech; it remains subject to the free will of the speaker.[64] Why does speaking in tongues exercise such a fascination? Some point to the natural wish to "relax" control over one's

---

[61] S 55–56.

[62] J. D. G. Dunn, *Jesus and the Spirit: A Study of the Religious and Charismatic Experience . . . as reflected in the New Testament* (London, 1975), 304 (cf. 441, no. 19).

[63] According to Sullivan, in no case has it really been proved that "speaking in tongues" is a speaking in a foreign language, i.e., foreign to those present (S 147, 148).

[64] S 142f. It emerges from a wealth of testimonies that "the use of this gift is not normally accompanied by ecstasy or trance. On the contrary, . . . the speakers can start and stop at will; they determine whether they speak in an audible or inaudible way, whether they pray or sing, etc. . . . . The person exercising his gift is perfectly in control of himself and his feelings" (ibid., 152–53).

own speech; others refer to the wish to respond to the expectation of the group, for whom speaking in tongues is "the physical sign of fully committed incorporation into the Charismatic Renewal".[65] K. G. Rey goes into detail on the role of (auto-) suggestion, although he does not want to deny a connection with religious receptivity.[66] Others have spoken of a "compulsion to experience", a "fascination with experience", a "psychic craving" (Congar) for "the unusual".[67] "The phenomenon of speaking in tongues, as such, is not a sign of the authenticity of spiritual renewal."[68] "My view is that only in very rare cases does God wish to tell us something through *glossolalia*. . . . We should therefore maintain a certain reserve about this practice of speaking in tongues, particularly in public worship, where it only causes trouble".[69]

There is no need to go into detail to show that something similar can be said of the charism of healing. We must not deny that it may exist as a charismatic gift, but what is unacceptable is the view that, since Jesus "bore our diseases" (Mt 8:17, after Is 53:4) in the same sense in which he bore our sin, the charism of healing is somehow a normal form of Christian discipleship. Jesus' bodily healings are always a sign of his redemption of souls, operating proleptically in anticipation of the Cross. The patient acceptance of serious suffering and death can be more fruitful for the Kingdom of God than restored health (which can also be due to the doctor). At this point Rey again points to the enormous effect of what is often nothing more than a temporary hypnosis;[70] his witty title, *Express Experiences of God*, is well chosen for both phenomena.

---

[65] S 156–57; cf. B 93.

[66] R 9f., 72ff., 133ff.

[67] ES 216, 223.

[68] S 158–59.

[69] R 22.

[70] R 97–122. Rey analyzes the new phenomenon of "falling down" found in charismatic groups, particularly in the context of the laying on of hands (24, 123ff.), but here, too, he mentions the widespread effect of suggestion ("If I hadn't resisted, I would have fallen down": 32). Rey concludes wisely: "We do not renew the Church by falling down. It would be better—this is what I have learned from Teresa of Avila and Johannes Tauler—to carry out the central requirements of the gospel in our everyday lives, with both our feet on the ground" (54–55).

The third "extraordinary" charism, which Paul presents to the Corinthians as most highly to be prized, is "prophecy". In the narrower sense this refers to some instruction communicated to an individual by the Holy Spirit for the benefit of the assembled community; more broadly it is what is called "inspiration", the gift given to the community's teachers, preachers, catechists, "evangelists", and, naturally, to the Apostle. Since it is through this charism that the Spirit builds up the community, it is highest of them all (14:1), but, like them, it is worthless without love (13:2).

Once we have got beyond the distortions that result inevitably from Paul's dealings with an isolated, difficult, and far from exemplary community—for the other lists of charisms are quite different—we can ask what an authentic new departure of Christian living in the Holy Spirit would look like. Such a reflection would have to take account of two things in particular. First, the Church does not begin with the experience of Pentecost (as Luke suggests); Pentecost only gives the disciples the strength and courage to be bold in declaring the reality of Jesus to the whole world, partly through their proclamation and partly by following him to the Cross. Second, the Spirit of Christ sends out and accompanies the whole Church into the world—with her objective and subjective spiritual dimensions constituting her a single Whole (corresponding to the twofold aspect of the one Holy Spirit). Here we can distinguish five aspects.

First, the Spirit of Jesus is always directing attention, in a new way, to his central deed: the Cross and the Resurrection that is only accessible through the Cross. From Pentecost on, the Church is persecuted, and the apostles are glad to suffer shame for Jesus (Acts 5:41). Paul, who saw the glorified Lord, no doubt also saw the Crucified One within that glory, for in Corinth he wants to know nothing, and speak of nothing, but the folly of the Cross. This, together with the Resurrection, of course, must always be at the center of "charismatic" contemplation of Scripture: only on this basis can there be offered to the Father that perfect worship his love deserves. Every kind of spirituality, personal or communitarian, that would lead its practitioners to try to avoid this instead of being steeped in it—as all true saints did and still do—will drop out of the center and be banished to a meaningless periphery.

Second, according to Paul, all Christians only have value in virtue of the "super-eminent way" of love. Without this all men, and even angelic voices, are nothing but "a noisy gong or a clanging cymbal" (1 Cor 13:1). That is why great theology like that of Aquinas understood the "gifts of the Spirit" as a perfection given by the Holy Spirit to the man with a lively faith, hope, and love, imparting an *instinctus divinus* to him, making him "disposed to become amenable to the divine inspiration".[71] "The gifts are perfections of man, whereby he becomes amenable to the promptings of the Holy Ghost."[72] To this elevation of the "divine virtues" by the gifts of the Spirit, Thomas adds the acquisition of certain "charisms": thus, for instance, he says that, when the Spirit is "sent" into the believer's heart, a new knowledge of the Son is also communicated, which "implies a certain experimental knowledge",[73] or, in the case of the acquisition of a "new state of grace", for instance, there is "the gift of miracles or of prophecy".[74] Such gifts are "non-manipulable"[75] because the essential gifts of grace that, according to Thomas, they accompany were also essentially non-manipulable.

Third, the Holy Spirit given at Pentecost is primarily a Spirit of power for the worldwide mission. Unfortunately, where the new movements of the Spirit are concerned, the continual complaint is that the groups become inward-looking and the "social involvement decreases" (Congar).[76] Not as if the Acts of the Apostles did not show the Church after Pentecost assembled in prayer and in the breaking of bread, but she is (at least) equally portrayed engaged in toilsome apostolic endeavors, in which she is explicitly led by the Spirit. People pray not only in private assemblies but also on all the roads of the world. And in all this the Spirit is never the object of the proclamation: they pray in the Spirit, through Christ, to the Father; in the Spirit, they proclaim Christ as the Messiah of the Jews, sent by the Father, and also as the Savior of the Gentiles. We never find the Church's worship

---

[71] *S. Th.* I/II, 68, 1.

[72] *S. Th.* I/II, 68, 3.

[73] *S. Th.* I, 43, 5 ad 2.

[74] *S. Th.* I, 43, 6 ad 2; "quando . . . notio per inspirationem elevatur ut etiam divina mysteria cognoscat, sic datur in dono prophetiae" (1, d. 15, q. 5, a. 1, sol 2).

[75] S 33; B 25.

[76] ES 217–20.

concentrating on the Spirit; it is by the Spirit that due prayer is made and by the Spirit that there is a correct proclamation of God the Father, who has revealed himself in Jesus and is extolled for Jesus' sake. By contrast, a concentration on the Spirit (as the object of worship) only leads to a pietistic "Jesusism" that is so prevalent today in the churches and among young people. People have the idea that in charismatic circles they can "experience" something of the Spirit and of Jesus in an "immediate" (unmediated) way; but as we have said, the genuine experience of faith is only given to those who patiently persevere in the Christian life. We are not questioning the fact that young people need a certain existential "experience" of Christianity in their surroundings or meetings if they are eventually to make up their minds to leave the nest and fly by faith; nor are we denying that adults need certain contacts if they are to keep their faith alive. But the continual inclination to remain in the inward-looking group can be a symptom of an infantile stagnation, particularly nowadays.

Fourth, on the basis of Pentecost the Church goes out to the world as a single unity that is both objective and subjective, both "juridical" and "charismatic". The early Church never separated the two sides of her organic unity. (It was the Montanists, Messalians, Donatists, and Joachimites who tried to play off "subjective" holiness against the holiness of office.) Paul, for instance, "proves" his objective apostolate by referring to his subjective sufferings for Christ. Unless it is led by good priests or religious the charismatic approach is often in danger of slipping into a subjective concept of the Church that lacks all structure. The various groups should be encouraged to create "as few structures of their own as possible", so that they can better integrate themselves into the Church's overarching structure[77] and not "imagine that they are something special, distinct from the community as a whole".[78] Under proper leadership the group will succeed in the difficult task of integrating itself into a parish that is somehow felt to be lacking in the spiritual dimension or in the more difficult task of being, in and beyond the parish, what Christ wills: the leaven, the salt of the earth. This will be even harder if the final point is taken seriously.

[77] B 26f.: "Their ministry remains orientated to the office of the priests and the relevant diocesan bishop."
[78] B 120.

Fifth, very many groups have an ecumenical orientation and are inclined to think, on the basis of their experience, that where there is prayer in common (and even in a liturgical context), church unity has already been granted from above, brought about by the Holy Spirit himself. Congar put his finger specifically on this point. "At a prayer meeting, where people open up and dedicate themselves to Jesus and the Spirit, there can naturally arise a unity at the level of fruits and spiritual realities. People are united with great intensity in the same Lord and the same Spirit. Thus a unity is reached above the denominational allegiances and divisions. . . . And yet unity is not attained. The Church is sacrament, not merely a communion in and through the Spirit."[79] She is not only the Church of the heart, but also the Church of objective structure. Can it be said that the Charismatic Movement is fostering a "spiritual ecumenism"?[80] Yet one hears views such as this: "The present movement, brought about by the Holy Spirit, is in the process of creating a totally new Church in the West, which will be neither Catholic nor Protestant, but simply evangelical."[81]

None of these five points presents a dire threat, but everyone would need to take very seriously what has become a gigantic Charismatic Movement; we should all engage in the task of discerning the spirits according to the Spirit of the whole Church. Properly speaking, it is only the whole Church of Jesus Christ that is "charismatic", for in her every member has his gift from the Spirit. She alone, because of Christ's promise and gift, can boast of possessing (but not being able to manipulate) the Spirit; and the Spirit "apportions to *each* one individually as he wills" (1 Cor 12:11).

3. A further question arises in the context of the "discernment of spirits", namely, the relationship between the Spirit of Christ and power. The situation is always critical when it is a case of the relationship between the Christian and the Church and worldly power. We do not need to go into the legitimacy, necessity, and limitations of worldly power here. But since the Christian and

[79] ES 264.
[80] B 62.
[81] J.-P. Gabus, quoted by Congar, ES 262, n. 64.

the Church are "in the world" (Jn 17:11; 1 Cor 5:10), the question of their relationship to worldly power cannot be avoided.

We must take Christ's example as our starting point. He speaks and acts as someone who has plenary power (*exousia*), but he always speaks of it as something *given* to him. When people become aware that Jesus "has" power (in his words, Mt 7:29; in forgiving sins, Mt 9:6), he explicitly states that this power comes to him as the Father's gift. It is the Father who gives him power to execute judgment; he gives the Son power to have life in himself (Jn 5:26f.); he gives him power over all flesh (Jn 17:2); and when Jesus says that he has power to lay down his life, he describes this power as a "charge" he has received from his Father (Jn 10:18). Even at the Transfiguration, when he possesses "all authority in heaven and earth", he declares that it has been "given" him (Mt 28:18). In the temptations it is suggested to him that he should wield his power as Messiah; he refuses, because that is not why the Father gave him power. He does have power, and he does exercise it, but in obedience to the will of the Father. His response to what has been given him is to use it solely in the service of the Father's Kingdom, like the servants in the Parable of the Talents. Even as the Resurrected One with sovereign authority, he aims "to be subjected to him who put all things under him, that God may be everything to every one" (1 Cor 15:24–28). This "power" that the Son has is entirely governed by his receptivity toward the Father, so much so that it can even adopt the paradoxical form of the powerlessness of the Cross, where (*sub contrario*) the power to reconcile the world with God takes on its perfect form. This is where the "powers" of this world are "stripped of power" and their prince is dethroned. This ultimate powerlessness, which is in fact the highest power (but entirely hidden in the Father and wielded by him), is Paul's watchword: "power [*dynamis*] is made perfect in weakness" (2 Cor 12:9).

The disciples, who are "given" power from the Lord (to preach, to heal, to cast out demons), are well aware that this power is for a particular task and must be used in obedience. Furthermore they are instructed to exercise it without relying on any worldly power whatever (Mt 10). They have to face the same questions that were put to Jesus: "By whose authority do you do these things?" And the answer they are to give is the same: by the authority of him who gave them this power (Acts 4:10–12). When they are persecuted (in Acts) and deprived for a time of their concrete power to preach, they will not see this as a lacuna in the exercise of their plenary authority, but on the contrary they will rejoice "to be counted worthy to suffer dishonor for the name [of Jesus]" (Acts 5:41). They understand the powerlessness they have to experience for a time, and perhaps until death (Paul), as a fulfilling of part of their mission, as a following in the footsteps of the Lord who commissioned them.

Jesus received plenary power from the Father, and in the Holy Spirit (who is breathed into the disciples) he entrusts this plenary power to the Church; this is inseparably bound up with Jesus' teaching that the greater (the one with authority and power to command) must act as the "youngest", as the "one who serves" all (Lk 22:26–27). So it is evident to the one in command (*hegoúmenos*) that what he has received in the Holy Spirit can only be transmitted in the Holy Spirit; it cannot be acquired with money, as the magician Simon thought (Acts 8:18f.). And if the leadership of the Church decides something that is binding on everyone, it can only do so in the same Spirit by whom it has received this plenary power from the Lord: "It has seemed good to the Holy Spirit and to us . . ." (Acts 15:28). Therefore when Paul, as the leader of the communities he founded, has to take decisions that require the response of obedience, he always cites his call by the Lord and the Holy Spirit that he then received (Acts 9:17): "In my judgment. . . . And I think that I have the Spirit of God" (1 Cor 7:40). For him, however, in contrast to the Old Testament (Jer 1:10; 31:28), Spirit and plenary power are only for building up, as he emphasizes on two occasions, and not for tearing down (2 Cor 10:8; 13:16). At the same time this shows that the power of binding and loosing given to the Eleven can only be meant in a positive sense: it is a binding with a view to the amendment of life, as when Paul removes the profligate from the community and hands him over "to Satan for the destruction of the flesh, that his spirit may be saved in the day of the Lord Jesus" (1 Cor 5:4). There is no other way of understanding a punishment administered by the Church, except when the Church simply ratifies the individual's free decision no longer to submit to Church order. The power exercised by the leadership of the Church is nothing other than the concrete communication of the mind of Christ. The Apostle's final dispute with the Corinthians (2 Cor 13) shows this in detail.

Believers receive their spiritual authority in baptism (and the other sacraments), which is given to them by the Holy Spirit, fundamentally liberating them from all slavery to the "principalities and powers" of the cosmos, which have been "disarmed" (Col 2:15). Authority, however,—and hence freedom—is given for building the Church up, not for bringing her into danger; it is a power to be exercised for service, and so it uses the criterion of the "weaker brother" (see Rom 14:13—15:1; 1 Cor 8:7-13), or, in other words, that which ministers to the "common good" for the sake of Christ (1 Cor 6:12; 12:7). All this is based on the "power to become children of God" (Jn 1:12), given by Christ, empowering them to be infallibly heard when they make their requests to God according to Christ's wishes, endowing them with the "mind of Christ", giving them "wisdom as the Spirit teaches", and enabling them to judge correctly about all things, while they themselves cannot be judged (correctly) by anyone, "for who has known the mind of the Lord?" (1 Cor 2:13-16). Paul can even go so far as to say that a person equipped with the gift of prophecy is not at the mercy of this gift but rather that "the spirits of prophets are subject to prophets" (1 Cor 14:32). All this is part of what is meant by "power" within the realm of Christ and within the community he has willed and which he inhabits. It is not self-sufficient but must bear witness in the face of the world and its different kind of power—and this witness can be most victorious and fruitful when it is rejected and violently suppressed by the world (cf. the fate of the two witnesses in Revelation 11). Those who witness to Jesus have taken the Beatitudes to heart, which means that there is no mention of using temporal power to extend the spiritual realm of Christ's authority. The paradoxical picture of Christians being sent into the world "as lambs in the midst of wolves" (Lk 10:3) says it clearly enough. Jesus himself laid down the course of action to be followed when the Christian testimony meets with the world's rejection: they are to move on (Mt 10:14). Moreover, as the example of Paul shows, they are not to go beyond the appointed limits of their task (2 Cor 10:13).

All this helps us to practice the discernment of spirits where plenary spiritual power clashes with worldly power. It is not our purpose here to trace the dramatic, and often tragic, history of this conflict through the history of the Church or to accuse the Church of the many wrongheaded undertakings that, in part, were practically unavoidable (as a result of the profound inter-penetration of Church and State since Constantine and in the Middle Ages). We are simply offering a few basic considerations for today's situation.

First of all, we must take seriously the New Testament's as-sertion that "there is no authority [*exousia*] except from God" (Rom 13:1). This applies even to the *exousia* of the anti-Christian world powers; the Book of Revelation uses the words: "and *ex-ousia* was given to it (him)", both in the case of the angelic beings that inflict harm on the creation and in the case of the beasts that oppose God—primarily the devil-dragon who is said to be in a position to "give *exousia*" to the "beast"—for a period of time. The power of governing all the powers of world history lies with God (Rev 16:9), which means that, according to his sovereign providence and with a view to his Last Judgment, he also rules the conflicts between sacred power and unholy power.[82] What

---

[82] Jesus' words to Pilate, "You would have no power over me unless it had been given you from above" (Jn 19:11), is applied to the present concrete situation. Cf. H. von Campenhausen, "Macht, mich zu entlassen oder zu kreuzigen", in "Zum Verständnis von Joh 19, 11", *Theol. Literaturzeitung* 73 (1948): 387–92. See also R. Schnackenburg, *Johannes* III, 301–2. Here the meaning of *exousia* is close to that of the "power of darkness" (Lk 22:53). Here we do not need to raise the vast question of the legitimacy of worldly power (e.g., Rom 13:1–7; 1 Pet 2:13f.); cf. Lutz Pohle, *Die Christen und der Staat nach Römer 13* (Mainz, 1984). The central Catholic axiom is that the natural order (which is not totally destroyed by sin) must contain a divinely willed social order, the *bonum commune*, which in turn calls for "appropriate acts to promote the common good and a corresponding organization of state power". Unlike the individual, the state has no transcendent goal, which means that there is a constant and insoluble tension: If the state is responsible for people's immanent well-being, how can it tolerate within it some-thing such as the Church, which has a transcendent goal and yet which, while acknowledging state power and its coercive function within its proper realm, criticizes its "totalitarian" trespassing and in extreme cases actually has to re-sist it, albeit "nonviolently"? For a discussion of a Protestant doctrine of the state

is required of the saints—who may also be "vanquished" by the powers hostile to God (Rev 13:7)—is "steadfastness" unto death; they must hold fast to their duty to bear witness. It is not they who will fight the last battle but the Logos himself in his "robe dipped in blood" (Rev 19:13). The disciple of Jesus is never asked to do more than give witness: this would be the place to speak of that "freedom of religion" which belongs to man and his dignity, even if the Apocalypse only paints a black-and-white picture of "faith or blindness". In Christian terms, surely, the only way to meet this freedom is with the example of a total life—which alone can be a convincing witness. In Jesus' own apologetical activity, this witness consists ultimately in ecclesial love, which as such renders plausible Jesus' trinitarian and soteriological love for the world (Jn 17:23).

This brings into focus an aspect of the Church that is rarely considered. The Church, as compared with most of the sects, does not engage in propaganda on her own behalf. She does not campaign for herself but prefers to let her witness exert its influence. She simply considers what form of witness is most

---

(which denies that the natural order was not destroyed by sin) and its totalitarian consequences, cf. Richard Hauser, *Autorität und Macht: Die staatliche Autorität in der neueren protestantischen Ethik und in der katholischen Gesellschaftslehre* (Heidelberg, 1949). See also his *Was des Kaisers ist: Zehn Kapitel christlicher Ethik des Politischen* (Frankfurt, 1968). "Per fidem Jesu Christi non tollitur ordo justitiae, sed magis firmatur."—"Jus divinum, quod est ex gratia, non tollit jus humanum, quod est ex naturali ratione": Thomas Aquinas, II/II, 104, 6; 10, 10c.—It is important to see that, while state *exousia* differs from the *exousia* of the Church, the "power" in both cases is anchored in the *bonum* and, ultimately, in love, as P. Tillich points out in his two lectures, "Das Evangelium und der Staat", *Works* IX (Stuttgart, 1967), 193–232: "Power, love and justice are not mutually opposed: in the ultimate ground of being they are one" (232). Strangely enough we can see this in the origin of the concept of *auctoritas* among the Romans, who worked out the law of the state in such detail: it refers to the the stature of a person in whom the people willingly put their trust and for whom they had regard: "Every Roman citizen constantly had the strong feeling that he freely and for his own advantage left decisions to the superior personality of the prince" (H. Heinze, "Auctoritas", *Hermes* 26 [1925]: 348–66, here 357). So we should "not forget that *auctoritas*, in its true essence, does not limit freedom" (364). "*Auctoritas* in this [moral] sense does not restrict anyone's freedom but is always dependent on people affirming it interiorly and freely following it" (T. G. Ring, *Auctoritas bei Tertullian, Cyprian und Ambrosius*, Cassiacum 2, [Würzburg, 1975], 149).

authentic according to the mind of Christ; this is not the "most effective" one by worldly standards. This is both a theological datum and a serious warning in an age of propaganda, advertising, and marketing, when people are promoting themselves with all means available. The most powerful attraction the Church has is that she does not seek to promote herself at all. This is very relevant at present, because young "movements" in the Church (in contrast to the great, old-established orders, which were content to give witness) are strongly inclined to advertise themselves, naïvely convinced that they represent the authentically Catholic line in today's confusion in the Church.

Members of this tendency can distance themselves, with a good conscience, from Augustine's ultimate appeal to the "secular arm" to step in against the marauding attacks of the Donatists, from the Inquisition's practice of handing delinquents against orthodoxy over to the "secular arm" for burning, and from all the other pacts between spiritual and secular power that seem so scandalous to us today. All the same they should ask themselves if they are not perhaps perpetuating the same dubious situation: for instance, by making their prime aim the attainment of positions of worldly power—in order to spread the gospel more effectively, of course—are they not following the very path, universally condemned today, along which the conquistadors sent the sword to prepare the ground for the Cross? It may be that the discernment of spirits is nowhere more relevant today than in this sector. "He charged them to take nothing for their journey except a staff; no bread, no bag, no money in their belts; but to wear sandals and not put on two tunics" (Mk 6:8–9).

e. The Witness of Life

We have already spoken of witness as one of the marks of the Holy Spirit[83] and of "proclamation" as one of the aspects of the Church on the side of "objective Spirit". In both contexts we observed that the Christian witness is far more than "information": it is the taking over of the believer's entire existence. The

---

[83] Cf. above pp. 242ff.

testimony that it gives, together with the Spirit, is nothing other than the love of God that bears witness to itself in Christ; accordingly, the credibility of such a life cannot ultimately consist in anything other than ecclesial love. Thus Jesus asks the Father, "that they may become perfectly one, *so that* the world may know that you have sent me and have loved them even as you have loved me" (Jn 17:23). It is only because the Spirit is the personal love of Father and Son that he can witness to this love; if Christ's human witnesses are required to witness together with the Spirit (Jn 15:26f.), the power and center of their witness can only come from a love that is a surrendering of their life (1 Jn 3:16). In this final section of the chapter on "The Spirit and the Church" we cannot undertake an exhaustive analysis of the concept of "witness"; all we can do is examine the essential connection between witness and the Holy Spirit.

The concept of "witness", in the specifically theological sense, ascends from the common Synoptic sources to Paul (who largely adopts the usage of the LXX) and Luke, who restricts it to a particular function in his twofold work, until it attains its broadest development in John (including the Apocalypse). We shall focus upon this.

As far as the Synoptics are concerned, we must refer back to Jesus' instruction to the effect that when the disciples are brought to court to testify (that is, in a life-threatening situation) they may rely on the Holy Spirit speaking through them (Mt 10:20). Thus they will "witness" before the judges, be they Jews or Gentiles (cf. also Mk 13:9–11; in Luke it is not only an objective witness but the disciples' personal witness: 21:13). In a similar way the healings performed by Jesus in the Holy Spirit are "for a witness" to the Jews, proving Jesus' power in the Spirit (Mk 1:44; Mt 8:4; Lk 5:14). In Paul the "witness" is to Christ's Resurrection (1 Cor 15:15), but he can also describe the gospel itself as a "witness" ("the testimony of God", 1 Cor 2:1; 2 Thess 1:10) that is confirmed by the Apostle. In the elliptical and "almost unintelligible"[84] expression of 1 Timothy 2:6 ("Christ Jesus . . . gave himself as a ransom for all, the testimony to which was borne at the proper time"), the context suggests

---

[84] Cf. C. Spicq, *Les Pastorales*, 4th ed. (1969), I, 368.

that it is God's testimony, mediated by the Apostle—namely, that God wishes to grant his salvation to all men, through the death of Christ, at the appropriate time.[85] In Luke the witnesses empowered by the Holy Spirit are the first apostles (including Matthias and particularly Paul), who are eyewitnesses of Christ's Resurrection to all the world.[86] The witness of the Spirit and of the apostles is one, as is emphasized in the Pentecost event and in Acts 5:32: "we are witnesses of these things, and so is the Holy Spirit." The martyr Stephen (who saw the Lord as he was dying) is an exception: he, too, is reckoned among the witnesses (Acts 22:20).

In John it is Jesus himself who is at the center, giving witness. In Revelation 1:5; 3:14, he is described as "the faithful witness". In the Gospel he is continually witnessing to the fact that he is the truth or that "it is he." He attests this by his whole existence, for the latter is identical with his witness that he is the truth, the exposition of the Father. So it is the same thing whether, speaking of himself, he says that he is giving true testimony (Jn 8:14) because he *knows* whence he comes and whither he is going or whether he says that there are two who witness concerning him, the Father and he himself (Jn 5:17–18), because these two are one (Jn 10:30). It is essential to remember at this point that Jesus gives this witness in the Holy Spirit (and precisely in John's Gospel). As far as the Baptist is concerned, Jesus is accredited because John "saw the Spirit descend as a dove from heaven, and remain on him"—which is why he will also "baptize . . . with the Holy Spirit" (1:32–33). And since the Baptist simultaneously recognizes Jesus as "the Lamb of God who takes away the sin of the world", he has also grasped in its fullness the witness that Jesus will give: he will witness to the Father through his death on man's behalf, and his heart will be opened, as the other John solemnly attests: "He who saw it has borne witness—his testimony is true, and he *knows* that he tells the truth" (19:35). Between these two attestations there is Jesus' own witness to himself: he has "the Spirit without measure" (see 3:34) and so

---

[85] In Hebrews, similarly, it is God himself who gives "witness" to believers (under the Old Covenant): Heb 11:2, 4, 5, 39.

[86] N. Brox, "Zeugnis", in HThG II, 903–11. K. Hemmerle, "Wahrheit und Zeugnis", in *Theologie als Wissenschaft*, QD (1970), 54–72.

he can witness to what he has "seen and heard" in the bosom of the Father and what he *"knows"* (3:32; 3:10; 7:29; 8:14). When his task is accomplished, when his heart is opened, he will be in a position to give the Spirit to the world along with the water and the blood. Thus all three, water, blood, and Spirit, will become a joint witness that comes from him and is for him (1 Jn 5:7f.): it will be God's witness (v. 9). So Jesus, looking ahead, can describe his body as a well from which believers will drink the Spirit (Jn 7:39), which is a draught "of living water" that not only refreshes the one who drinks it but transforms him into a spring of water welling up to eternal life (4:14). This is nothing other than his being drawn into the well of God's being, which can be described as being "born . . . of God" (1:13) or being "born of the Spirit" (3:8). We can grasp how utterly mysterious this is from the image of the untamable Spirit-wind (3:8) into which the "reborn" man is drawn: "That which is born of the Spirit is spirit" (3:6). As we have already said, when Jesus tells the woman that "God is spirit" (4:24), this is no philosophical definition: he is asserting that God makes himself present for us in the pneumatic mystery that comes to us in Jesus' unity with the Holy Spirit. In the expression "true worshipers will worship the Father in spirit and truth" (4:22), we have a trinitarian formula, for "spirit" points to the Holy Spirit, and "truth" to the Son. Jesus himself says that his word is "spirit" (6:63); it is this Spirit that he breathes into the Church at Easter (20:22).

Jesus, the "faithful witness", is surrounded by those who witness to him and point to *his* witness, which stands on its own feet and has its own full validity. Jesus does not need them to substantiate his own self-evident status (as we showed in the first volume of *The Glory of the Lord*). He does not need others to bear witness to him, for "he himself knew what was in man" (2:25). He acknowledges the witness of the Old Testament writings, for they speak of him; but he does not say that he needs it (5:45–47). Compared with Jesus' own witness to himself, even the Baptist's witness has a twilight quality: it has its validity, because it comes from God (prologue) and is a "burning and shining lamp" (5:35), but as a merely human testimony it does not come near the testimony given by the Father (5:31, 33). The "disciple whom Jesus loved", who attests the piercing of Jesus' side and—like Jesus—proclaims that he knows the truth of his own witness, is here, basically, nothing more than the famous finger in Grünewald's painting, pointing to the self-evident witness of Spirit-water-blood or to the Father's love, which, in the Son, "loved them to the end" (13:1).[87]

As Christ himself said, the believer's witness to him takes over his whole life: if a man is not willing to give up everything, even his life, he "is not worthy of me" (Mt 10:37ff.). There is no need, therefore, to draw a distinction between the dedication of a whole life, on the one hand, and "blood martyrdom", on the other. From the Gospel perspective, those who were later called "martyrs" are not more important than those whose whole life is a daily mortification (Rom 8:36; 2 Cor 4:10–11). Even in the Apocalypse, as N. Brox has proved (contrary to the usual interpretation), the martyrs are not yet understood as blood martyrs in the narrower sense: "They died as martyrs because they were witnesses, as Revelation 11:3–7 makes it abundantly clear, even terminologically."[88] It is significant, however, that, on the one hand, the Apocalypse designates all the "offspring" of the woman, the Church, as those who "bear testimony to Jesus" (Rev 12:17) and, on the other hand, draws a distinction between the "blood of the saints" and the "blood of the martyrs of Jesus" (17:6) drunk by the Whore of Babylon; for here "martyrs" (in the narrower sense) means the apocalyptic "prophets" (Rev 1:1–3; 19:10; 22:9; also 11:6–7). But the earlier prophets, according to Jesus' own words (Mt 23:29–37), suffered death for their testimony. Here we have the beginning of that usage of the word witness (*martys*) to mean "blood martyr" which came to the fore in the second century: the martyr gave a proof of the reality of Christ's sufferings (against the Docetists).[89] In his study "Zeuge der Wahrheit",[90] Erik Petersen criticized the view of Hans von Campenhausen[91] and suggested that the

---

[87] See also Jn 21:24; 1 Jn 1:2; 4:14. In John 12:17 the crowd attests the fact of the raising of Lazarus; in 4:39 the Samaritan woman bears witness to the fact that Jesus is the Messiah.

[88] Brox, "Zeugnis", 910. In more detail: N. Brox, *Zeuge und Märtyrer Untersuchungen zur frühchristlichen Zeugnis-Terminologie* (Munich, 1961, with bibliography). In Revelation 2:13, Antipas, who was killed, is described as "my witness, my faithful one".

[89] Literally in Irenaeus, *Adv. Haer.* III, 18, 15; also in Ignatius, *Sm.* 5, 3.

[90] Included in *Theologische Traktate* (Munich: Kösel, 1951), 167–224, here 223.

[91] *Die Idee des Martyriums in der alten Kirche* (Göttingen, 1936), 50–51.

"testimony" (*martyrein*) in 1 Timothy 6:13: "Christ Jesus who in his testimony before Pontius Pilate made the good confession" already includes his death.[92]

It should not be forgotten, on the basis of Jesus' demand that those who believe in him should give testimony in their lives, that such a testimony in the context of discipleship is meaningful only if Jesus' own life testimony is seen expressly as a revelation of the love of the Father and of the Trinity. Jesus' obedience "unto death . . . on a cross" (Phil 2:8) only makes sense as a making present of God's love in and for the world; the promise to Peter that he will be crucified is the ultimate consequence of his profession of love. So, according to the express will of Christ, the individual life testimony is first and foremost a realization of the brotherly love that characterizes the Church, for it is by this that the Church as a whole gives witness to the credibility of God's love in Christ, to and for the world. This is the whole aim of the ecclesial exhortation we find in Paul and John, and it is also why the Holy Spirit distributes charisms to all the members of the Body of Christ. By receiving the gift of the Holy Spirit, the baptized become joined into a single people, just as the ancient people were bound together by the law (Phil 2:1; 3:3; 2 Cor 3:6–11).

From outside it may seem that the spread of Christianity has been the work of individuals—"apostles, . . . prophets, . . . teachers" (1 Cor 12:28)—and not that of communities with their own internal coherence. This appearance, however, is illusory. In the first place, the breakthrough into the totality of the pagan world (Peter in Joppa, Stephen, the Hellenists, the preachers in Antioch, Paul) constituted the preliminary phase of an entirely

---

[92] Petersen always understands the word "martyr", *martyrion* in the Gospel to signify the full surrender of one's life, which is required of those who are sent out as sheep among wolves. For him it means sharing "the eschatological community of suffering and destiny" ("Zeuge der Wahrheit", 171) with Christ. "How can we expect the wolves not to attack the sheep?" (176). While Peter (Jn 21:19) and all the apostles (Jn 16:2) are promised a martyr's death, subsequent developments must necessarily have introduced a distinction between apostolic office and martyrdom. Martyrdom becomes a charism without which the Church is unthinkable (175). Peterson's reference to Kierkegaard's concept of the truth-witness is entirely appropriate as is his reference to Christ's royal priesthood, in which Christians have a share (in 1 Pet 2:9 and in Rev).

new consciousness embracing the whole world; that is why Paul, proclaiming to the world the commandment of love, saw "in his small communities, where each bore the burden of the others, a new humanity already present in the Spirit. . . . These communities had left behind, as a mirage without substance, the distinctions of Jews and Gentiles, barbarians and Greeks, high and low, rich and poor. A new humanity had come into being."[93] And this was no illusion. Paul's preaching, which regarded with equal seriousness concern for the individual and concern for the community, was something unheard of and new for the ancient world: the commandment of love, as the communities endeavored to live it, was a political reality: people

> could only admire the solution given to one of the most difficult problems of every large-scale organization, namely, how to maintain the complete independence of the local community at the same time as a strong and united system of order that embraced the entire empire and would gradually become a comprehensive constitution. What security would such a body give to the individual! What a power of attraction would it not have had to exert once its whole thrust was understood! It, not this or that evangelist, was the most effective missionary. We may take it as certain that it was, above all, the mere existence and constant activity of the individual communities that brought about the spread of Christianity.[94]

But as early as Matthew 25, the parable of judgment, with its criterion of effective love shown to "the least of my brethren"— which meant, not merely members of the Christian community, but every man[95]—elevated Christian love, following the example of Christ, to the universal norm of the Good: ultimately, giving one's own life for one's fellowmen, in conscious or unconscious following of Christ, will be the hallmark of every human ethics, including atheistic ethics.

---

[93] A. von Harnack, *Die Mission und Ausbreitung des Christentums in den ersten drei Jahrhunderten* (Leipzig, 1902), 108.

[94] Ibid., 311.

[95] Gerhard Lohfink, "Universalismus und Exklusivität des Heils im Neuen Testament", in *Absolutheit des Christentums*, QD 79 (1977), 63–82, esp. 79ff.: "Ein folgenreiches Interpretationsproblem".

VI. SPIRIT AND WORLD

I

THE WORLD DIMENSION

We have examined in detail the intimate relationship between the Holy Spirit and the Church of Christ; this should not cause us to forget our earlier observations on the Spirit's worldwide operation. It is not necessary to insist that the "spirit" of God brooding over the chaos in Genesis 1:1 is the third Divine Person; but there can be no question—since the world was created with a view to the Son, who was to be born as a man and to die as the Lamb of God; and that this incarnate Son was shown to be a product of ("conceived by") the Holy Spirit—that the Spirit must have been active in the creation, explicitly or implicitly, as a Person; all the more so since Christ's redemptive work was universal, which means that it is impossible to restrict the Spirit's sphere of activity to the realm of the Church.[1] For the present we can leave aside what has already been said about the Old Covenant and the visibly close connection in it between the word of Yahweh and the spirit of Yahweh[2]—although the Creed affirms that the prophets spoke in the Spirit and that the Psalms expressly speak of the Spirit's operation in nature and human life —but his activity in universalizing the Son's Person and work has already become too vast to encompass.[3] God the Father has always been at work in the world with "his two hands" at the same time.[4]

Today no theologian will any longer maintain the patristic thesis that there can be no salvation outside the Church (even if it was admitted at that time that heretics could administer valid sacraments). On the other hand, no theologian will agree with the theses of Joachim of Fiore that the age of the Spirit is still in the future and that we must wait until the clerical Church has been superseded. The Church has always resisted this

[1] Cf. pp. 169–70 above.
[2] Cf. pp. 37ff. above.
[3] Cf. pp. 196ff. above.
[4] Cf. pp. 165–207 above.

"seduction by the Spirit".[5] It has abundantly been shown, how-ever, that "Church" exists only when she is ready to transcend herself by going into the world in missionary mode.[6] In the world she will find *spermata pneumatika*, but this Church, all too human as she is, is always "afraid of the Spirit",[7] which, nonetheless, has been "poured out on all flesh". She is afraid of taking risks and of having to "resist the opposition of the multitude, whether traditionalist or progressivist".[8] W. Kasper has shown that the necessary corrections to a concept of the Church that was all too closed (from the Fathers, right up to *Mystici Corporis*) have already been applied. In the first place, the Church now knows that she is an "interim reality" since she is "only" the sacrament of the world's salvation; secondly, she who is the *Catholica* has acknowledged that other ecclesial communities most definitely can communicate the Holy Spirit in their sacraments. Ultimately, as Augustine himself put it, many are "inside" who "seem to be outside".[9]

The Spirit impels, not only the Church to her perfection, but the world (which is in principle redeemed by Christ) as well. The "sighs too deep for words", attributed to the Spirit by Paul, do not relate only to the perfection of Christians but, in and through them, to "all creation, groaning in travail" in its enforced "sub-jection to futility", as it looks forward to an all-embracing re-demption (Rom 8:20ff.). After all, the nature of the world, even in its tiniest particles, seems to bear the stamp of its trinitarian origins.[10] Furthermore, the Spirit's "sighs too deep for words" are not in vain; Paul goes on to show that they constitute an immense motive power: God the Father understands this "mind

[5] H. Cox, *The Seduction of the Spirit: The Use and Misuse of People's Religion* (New York: Simon and Schuster, 1973).

[6] Cf. pp. 255-66 above.

[7] K. Rahner, "Angst vor dem Geist", in *Chancen des Glaubens* (Herder, 1971), 52-57.

[8] Ibid., 56.

[9] W. Kasper, "Kirche also Sakrament des Geistes", in W. Kasper and G. Sauter, *Kirche als Ort des Geistes* (Herder, 1976), 44-53.

[10] A. Haas, "Die Stilähnlichkeit christlicher Glaubenstatsachen mit den beiden Lebensakten der Entwicklung", in *Gott in Welt*, Festschrift Karl Rahner, II (Herder, 1964), 756-78.

of the Spirit" and causes all whom he has predetermined and chosen "according to his purpose" to reach "glory".

The Fathers, and in particular the Greeks, most strongly emphasized the universal significance of the Incarnation of the Logos for the whole of mankind and for the whole cosmos. Augustine's eschatology caused this universalism to be obscured for an entire epoch, but in more recent times (one only need recall de Lubac's *Catholicism*) it has experienced a resurgence.[11] The Church is now seen as an "inner circle" through which the hypostatic union, and hence the *communio* in the Holy Spirit, reaches outward; what is "intensive", closely united in the Church, must become "extensive" in humanity and in the creation.[12] Of course, if this idea is taken in an absolute sense, it is hard to resist the pull of Joachimism. Thus in Petrus Olivi's *Postilla super Apocalypsim* the Holy Spirit is the "engine for change in history and in social life",[13] showing that the Spiritual Franciscans become the predecessors of the liberation theologians. Calvin, in his Pneumatology, pays more attention to the creation as a whole; thus, starting from the beginning of Genesis, he portrays "the Spirit of God poured out over the abysses", thereby lending the world its ordered beauty; "for it is the Spirit who, everywhere diffused, sustains all things, causes them to grow, and quickens them in heaven and in earth. Because he is circumscribed by no limits, he is exempted from the category of creatures, but in transfusing into all things his energy and breathing into them essence, life, and movement, he is indeed plainly divine."[14]

At this point—prior to all the confusion in which Old Testament legends concerning the "spirit" in relation to man's natural life (Gen 2:7) are mixed up with the ("supernatural") spirit of God given to the prophets and those dedicated to God— the question arises as to whether the trinitarian Spirit does not

[11] W. Kern, "Eine Wirklinie Hegels in deutscher Theologie", ZThK 93 (1971), 1–28; H. Thielicke, *Theologie des Geistes* (Tübingen, 1978), 552–623.

[12] T. F. Torrance, "La Mission de l'Église", in ES 275–94.

[13] C. Schütz, *Einführung in die Pneumatologie* (Darmstadt, 1985), 100; cf. E. Benz, *Ecclesia Spiritualis* (Stuttgart, 1934), which contains a thorough analysis of the "Postilla": 265–332.

[14] *Institutes* I, 13, 14; similarly Beza, *Opera* I, 6 (Ghent, 1582). For references to the Spirit in Luther's late works, see R. Prenter, *Spiritus Creator* (Münster, 1954).

have a particular relationship to the creation of the world as a whole, particularly if the latter is seen in modern terms, as a total history embracing both nature and the human race. Such an interpretation of the cosmos as a whole will no longer be able to avoid the notion of evolution, however it may be conceived in the particular case, whether nature is read as following a development toward consciously historical humanity or humanity (together with its prehuman infrastructure) is taken as a single natural history. As regards the particular world view of Hegel, we have already said that there can be no question of equating what he calls "world spirit" [*Weltgeist*], in its totality, with the trinitarian Holy Spirit.[15] But might not this be bound up with the particular form of his thought on the Trinity? Karl Barth, who can by no means be suspected of pantheism, expressly and fully spoke of the Holy Spirit as the Divine Person "who makes the existence of the creature as such possible, permitting it to exist, maintaining it in its existence, and forming the point of reference of its existence".[16] This is because the Son of God, from all eternity, has been foreseen by God's wisdom as he who was to become incarnate; so much so that "it was not only appropriate and worthy but *necessary* that God should be the Creator. If this was God's eternal counsel in the freedom of his love, . . . it was . . . essential for God to be the Creator."[17] In that case there never was a *logos asarkos*. It follows, furthermore, that being a creature, outside (that is, not) God, on the basis of that Spirit through whom the Logos will become flesh, is not something suspect but something excellent. This means that Barth can understand the Old Testament references to the Spirit, which are "no doubt intended cosmologically", as direct antecedents of soteriological and eschatological texts.[18] Moreover, he can read the creation as a single salvation history reaching from the development of nature up to mankind and from mankind up to Christ (*creatio continua*), in which nature is always orientated toward and surrounded by grace, and the creature's apportioned time is allotted

[15] Cf. above pp. 44ff.
[16] *Church Dogmatics* III/1 (Edinburgh, 1958), 56.
[17] Ibid., 51.
[18] Ibid., 57.

to it from God's eternally triune time and history.[19] From this vantage point, without getting involved in Hegel's *Weltgeist*, the question of the Holy Spirit as the "soul of the world" once again acquires contemporary relevance.

[19] Ibid., 60–94. Barth is so drawn by the idea of salvation history that he fails to deduce the world's space from God along the same lines. There is a brief reference on p. 163.

2

IS THE SPIRIT THE SOUL
OF THE WORLD?

The Greeks—Pythagoras, Plato in the *Timaeus* (34AB), the Stoics (Cicero, Marcus Aurelius), Plotinus—and subsequently the Arabs from Al-Kindi to Averroës, had postulated a "world soul". Augustine was not sure whether he should adopt this notion but was quite sure that, if it existed, it would not be divine but created.[1] Theologians of the school of Chartres in the twelfth century—Thierry of Chartres, Bernard Silvestris, and William of Conches—were the first to identify the world soul with the Holy Spirit or one of his emanations.[2] This was part of their attempt to bring about a rapprochement between theology and cosmology. It was Abelard who had to pay the bill: his assertion "quod Spiritus Sanctus sit anima mundi" was condemned at the Council of Sens (DS 722).[3] Later ideas on the world soul do not concern us here, since they do not contain any reference to the Holy Spirit.[4]

However, the topic undergoes a strange resurrection in Wolfhart Pannenberg's cosmological theories, particularly in his attempt to offer a pneumatological supplement to Teilhard de

[1] *De Gen. Lib. imp.* IV, 17 (PL 34, 226). *Retract.* I, 53 (PL 32, 591) corrects *De Immort. Animae* XV, 24. *Retract.* I, 11, 4 (PL 32, 602) corrects *De Musica* VI, 14, 34. At all events the *anima mundi* would be "non Deus, sed a Deo facta atque insita creatura". But it could still be what is termed *spiritus Dei* in Genesis 1:2.

[2] Examples in Geyer, *Die patristische und scholastische Philosophie*, 12th ed. (Basel, 1951), 233–38.

[3] In his revised *Dialectic*, however, Abelard expressly rejects this view; on the one hand, he says that the Holy Spirit, although omnipresent, only apportions his gifts to the just; and, on the other hand, he acknowledges that, even in the *Timaeus*, the "world soul" is not God but something created by the world's Creator (*Ouvrages inédits d'Abélard*, ed. Cousin [Paris, 1836], 475). Cf. also the article "Abélard", in DTC I (Portalié), 46.

[4] Most importantly Giordano Bruno, Schelling ("Von der Weltseele" [1798]; "Bruno" [1802]), Goethe ("Weltseele" [ca. 1800]), and Fechner. (Herder preferred to speak of the "world spirit" [*Weltgeist*]: here, restricted reality participates in the unlimited "I".) Cf. H. Glockner, "Drei philosophische Gedichte Goethes", in *Gesammelte Schriften* 4 (1968).

Chardin's evolutionary theology. Pannenberg, too, is animated by the justified concern to build a bridge over the alienation between science and theology. He is acquainted with the English[5] and American[6] prehistory of this alienation, little known on the continent, and also knows and uses the dispute between Newton/Clarke and Leibniz on God's eternal omnipresence as the "medium" for the existence of finite things, that is, that which gives them space.[7] He finds the concretion of Clarke's notion in the concept of "field" (from Faraday to Einstein),[8] which should be interpreted as the "field of force" and the "frame of reference" for "the divine operation that is present in the process of evolution". He goes on to insist that, since the whole process must reach its zenith in man, and in God becoming man, this presence of God facilitating evolution (a presence that is not to be understood in a pantheistic sense) must be seen in a trinitarian context. Like Barth, he sees this resting on the continuity between the Old Testament *ruach Yahweh* and the New Testament *pneuma theou*; but Barth does not move outside the biblical framework and does not engage with science. Pannenberg rejects Tillich's all-too-naturalistic theology, according to which the emergent "spirit" goes through anorganic, organic, and psychic stages, before hovering ambiguously between the divine and the human. Then he deals with Teilhard's twofold concept of energy, in which life's evolution into spirit is, he feels, couched in one-sidedly christological terms: what is missing is the concept of the "energy field", to which Teilhard gives too little attention and which is necessary to guarantee the possibility of living things experiencing self-transcendence: "The field is orientated to the future." Pannenberg sees the pneumatological element of evolution in this "field". "A contemporary Christian theology of creation will employ the possibilities latent in the doctrine of the Trinity to describe the transcendence/immanence

[5] Summary in A. M. Ramsey, *From Gore to Temple* (1960).

[6] E. C. Rust, *Evolutionary Philosophies and Contemporary Theology* (Philadelphia, 1969). For a short summary, see W. Pannenberg, "Gott und die Natur", *Theologie und Philosophie* 58 (1983): 489f.

[7] Ibid., 491–500.

[8] W. Berkson, *Fields of Force. The Development of a Worldview from Faraday to Einstein* (New York: Wiley, 1974).

relationship of God in creation and salvation history. Perhaps it will combine the ancient Christian doctrine of the Logos with the concept of 'information' and come to see the operation of the divine Spirit in life's self-transcendence and evolution."[9] This operation grounds the "contingency" (by which he means what is not a necessary consequence of the past)[10] of that evolution which simultaneously leads to self-affirmation (consciousness) and self-transcendence: "Life's self-transcendence presents itself simultaneously as an activity on the part of the living thing and as the effect of a power that tirelessly lifts this living thing beyond its own limitations, thereby guaranteeing its life."[11]

Unfortunately, a doctrine of creation that is structured in this way in trinitarian terms is in danger of ironing out the difference between the Old Testament's largely cosmological concept of the Spirit and the New Testament's soteriological one. As a result, the Old Testament view predominates and, roughly speaking, tends toward a certain identity between the transcending human spirit and the divine Spirit that is understood—somehow or other—as the "world soul". This view still depends on Tillich, however much Pannenberg tries to distance himself from him. Man's ecstatic self-transcendence is a participation in the divine Spirit; but ecstasis is part and parcel of the human spirit's essence. "There is no need, nor would it be meaningful, to posit a fundamental separation between human and divine Spirit. . . . The creature participates in the divine Spirit when it transcends itself", although Pannenberg insists that this ecstatic element should not be regarded as belonging "to man's natural capacity".[12]

One must have similar reservations about John V. Taylor's "The Holy Spirit and His Operation in the World":[13] like

[9] "Gott und die Natur", 300.

[10] W. Pannenberg, "Kontingenz und Naturgesetz", in A. M. Müller and W. Pannenberg, *Erwägungen zur einer Theologie der Natur* (Gütersloh, 1970), 75.

[11] W. Pannenberg, "Der Geist des Lebens", in *Glaube und Wirklichkeit* (Munich: Kaiser, 1975), 31–56, here 43–56.

[12] W. Pannenberg, "Ekstatische Selbstüberschritte als Teilnahme am göttlichen Geist", in HM (1974), 176–92.

[13] The Go-Between God (London, 1972).

Pannenberg (and Charles G. Raven)[14] he understands the power of evolution, drawing development onward from the Eschaton (or the Omega), as the Old Testament *ruach* in modern guise; this is meant to serve as an interpretation of the New Testament experience of *pneuma*. Indeed, only the man who has the *pneuma* of Christ really belongs to him, so the author is very critical of the official Church and discerns the Spirit's presence in all religions.[15]

---

[14] *The Creator Spirit* (1962). Here Jesus' death and Resurrection is understood as only the highest instance of the natural law of "dying in order to become".

[15] Moltmann, in his *Gott in der Schöpfung* (Munich, 1985), has also taken steps in this direction, although for him the central theological datum remains the Cross, seen as a revelation of the Trinity. Yet, like Pannenberg, he would like to see God and nature united, though not in a pantheistic amalgam; he goes so far as to say: "God the Spirit is also the spirit, total consonance, structure, information, and energy of the universe. . . . The universe's evolutions and catastrophes are also the motions and the experiences of the Spirit of the creation" (30).

3

REFLECTION

It must be admitted that the speculations here presented on the relationship between the Holy Spirit and his pancosmic and universal, historical operation seem to go beyond the limits set by Christian revelation. We find these limits in the pretrinitarian mode of speech of the Old Covenant, where it speaks of the Spirit of Yahweh at the creation of the world and (in the Book of Wisdom) in the order of the world and in providence. No doubt there are fluid transitions here between the cosmological side of the divine Spirit and his specific, sanctifying function in Yahweh's covenant relationship with Israel; this covenant is expressed in terms that anticipate that relationship in the Spirit which will be set forth in the New Testament. But the fluid transitions between Yahweh's "word" and "Spirit" mean that it would be improper to give an automatically trinitarian interpretation of Old Testament passages, even if it is felt that what we see in the New Covenant, that is, the distinguishable functions of the Divine Persons cooperating in the creation of the world and its history, must be traceable back to distinctions already existing in the Old Covenant. Such reservations are only confirmed if we leave aside the passages that speak of God breathing the breath of life into man (Gen 2:7)—which Paul expressly calls the purely natural life principle, distinguishing it from the *pneuma* of the "second Adam" (1 Cor 15:45)—and go on to those "endowments" bestowed by the Spirit of Yahweh, such as the leader's political ability in Joshua, judicial talent in the judges, artistic gifts in those who made the Ark of the Covenant, economic enterprise (such as Pharaoh praised in Joseph), right up to the art of government (thus Saul, moved by the Spirit, joins in the dancing of the prophets). We are bound to ask what all this has to do with the Holy Spirit whom we know from Jesus. Such endowments may be dispensed by God as natural gifts in the order of creation and of providence, even if they have a role to play within the narrower field of salvation history. At all events they cannot be described—like the Christian Spirit of the Cross

—as the "overthrowing of the natural spirit" that, "self-enclosed and in self-admiration, always proceeds on the basis of its own dignity, its own merit and its own human abilities (which it thinks are its own work)".[1] It is a long way from such abilities to the prophetic spirit with which an Elijah or Elisha is filled, to Micah's utterance: "I am filled with power, with the Spirit of the Lord, and with justice and might, to declare to Jacob his transgression and to Israel his sin." True, the political events by which Israel was liberated from its oppressors and enemies are hard to evaluate: they are a sign of Israel's election and of the accompanying presence of the God who protects it (and to that extent they are "anticipatory images", *typikōs*, 1 Cor 10:11, of what happens to the Christian community), but they remain within the realm of what Pascal calls the "figure" ("All that does not end in love is a prefiguring"; we must "resist the exaggerated use of the figurative");[2] and so he also urges us not to overlook the ambivalence of the word "enemy".[3]

If the interpretation of Scripture must follow Scripture's own movement toward the fulfillment of the "figures" in Christ— that is, in the case of Jesus himself, the evangelists, and Paul— it would be just as wrong to conceive the Holy Spirit on the basis of the early cosmological texts as to make a "liberation-theological" interpretation of the notion of "enemy" on the basis of the Old Testament types. We can put this in more concrete terms. In the New Covenant, the Spirit, who is the Spirit of Christ, is a Spirit of humility, of service, of taking the lowest place, of giving his life as an expiation for all men; this being so, it will hardly be possible to refashion this Spirit, within the evolution of the created universe, and turn him into the motor of ascent, of the self-transcendence of the (logos-) forms; the Spirit of Christ can hardly turn out, for good or ill, to be the "spirit of power" and of the triumph of the stronger. Nor will it do,

---

[1] Hans Joachim Kraus, *Heiliger Geist: Gottes befreiende Gegenwart* (Kösel, 1986), 21–22.

[2] Pascal, *Pensées*, nos. 583, 551.

[3] Ibid: "I shall prove that a Messiah was promised who would free [them] from their enemies but that one has come to free them from their sins, and not from their enemies . . . , for in reality it is not the Egyptians who are their enemies, but their sins. Thus the word 'enemy' is ambivalent."

however, to combine this necessary cosmic prehistory of man with some kind of cosmic principle of guilt and fall, supposed to have frustrated the Creator's plans. Rather, this slow, planned ascent (achieved at the cost of vast sacrifices) up to the point at which the Spirit's "spark" could jump is the only way in which we can envisage the Creator's world plan. Pannenberg could be right when he urges us to adopt the notion of a "field" that depends on, embraces, and animates the forms [Gestalten], but, given what we know of the uniqueness of this Spirit in the New Testament, it seems wayward to ascribe this to the presence of the Holy Spirit in particular rather than to the plan of creation of the one God. He may distance himself from Hegel, but the distance seems to be insufficient. We observed concerning Hegel, in the first chapter, that he saw the highest stage as "Holy Spirit" but also felt able to regard the preliminary stages as instances of "objective" Spirit in nature, characterized by its striving to ascend. We can say the same thing here, with greater emphasis: with the manifestation of the Holy Spirit of God and of Jesus, we discern a tendency that contradicts the upward-striving natural "spirit". This is quite clear in the New Testament, and it is there in embryonic form in Israel, too.

It is not necessary, therefore, to reproach the spirit of evolution for its rectilinear thrust and to see it as an egoistic and self-enclosed heresy (cf. above). Quite simply, it strives, in the prehuman realm, toward a position at which God wishes to engage with man in a free, ethical history. However, the driving principle, in whatever way it is described, must be seen, not as a divine, trinitarian principle, but as a principle inherent to creation, as Augustine clearly assumed—despite all his vacillation over the notion of a "world soul". Accordingly, Clement is also right to distinguish a natural *pneuma* and a grace-bringing *pneuma* in man.[4] So one must be careful not to regard the upward-striving principle of evolution as something that aspires solely to the "I" and to see it as opposed to the "selfless", descending principle of grace. In this regard it may be helpful to reflect on Teilhard de Chardin's "centrology": he regarded the tendency

---

[4] W.-D. Hauschild, *Gottes Geist und der Mensch: Studien zur frühchristlichen Pneumatologie* (Munich, 1972), 27f.

toward consciousness as being also a tendency toward sociabil-
ity—obviously within the limits imposed by the particular context, but nonetheless it clearly constituted a preliminary stage
of the simultaneity of the "I" and the "we" in the human being, which in turn achieves fulfillment in the christological and
ecclesiological realm. We notice a corresponding structure in
mankind's historical stages, as we saw in connection with the
"I writ large": it is not the case that the individual "I" emerges
only gradually from an internal relationship to a central "I" that
gives him form and shape; the legend of Cain's flight (Gen 4:15)
fittingly illustrates this.

We should also note that, for the most part, Pneumatologies
devote a brief chapter to the Spirit's relation to nature before
quickly—and rightly—moving on to a more detailed study of
the context in which the Holy Spirit acquires his distinctive soteriological countenance.[5] In the totality of his world plan, God
has designed nature, not only with a view to man, but so that
nature, as the precondition for man's becoming and existence,
will be brought together with man into the final Kingdom of
God. If we bear this in mind as we try to expand the range of
topics of theological Pneumatology toward the sciences, it will
be clear that projecting the intrahistorical events of salvation
backward onto evolution is not a suitable means of elucidating
the unity of the divine plan. Here, too, we should take Paul's
words seriously: to him grace was given "to make all men see
what is the plan of the mystery hidden for ages in God who
created all things" (Eph 3:9); this "light" initially refers to the
historical nations of the world and can also be extended, if one
wishes, to the history of nature. As regards the nations it certainly means that they thereby step into the light of the mystery
of Christ and, hence, of his Cross and Resurrection; but we can
hardly say that this light extends effectively to nature's law of
"die and become". Paul, and Christ himself, may use the "dying and becoming" of the grain of wheat as a metaphor of the
central event of salvation history; but this does not mean that
Cross and Resurrection become the intelligible peak instance of

---

[5] Typical of many is Christian Schütz's *Einführung in die Pneumatologie* (Darmstadt, 1985), 28–30.

a natural religion or some fundamental law of human history; neither Good Friday nor Easter nor Pentecost can be turned into a speculative principle. What we have here is, not the uppermost level of transcendence, but the overcoming (by God alone) of the contradiction between God's love and man's sin. Here alone do we see, finally, what Holy Spirit is: "Receive the Holy Spirit; those whose sins you remit. . . ." "How much more will the blood of Christ, who through the eternal Spirit offered himself a spotless sacrifice to God, cleanse our consciences."[6] What is most creative about the Holy Spirit (*Creator Spiritus*) must be marked by the stigma of Cross and Resurrection as it spreads all over the world.

---

[6] This unique event cannot be understood on the basis of laws of nature; nor can it be understood by sociological laws, either, as René Girard tried to do (*Les Choses cachées depuis la fondation du monde* [Grasset, 1978]), even if he is definitely aware of the fact that the sociology of redemption goes beyond that of world history ("En subissant la violence jusqu'au bout, le Christ révèle et déracine la matrice structurale de toute religion" [201]).

VII. "UPWARD AND ONWARD TO THE FATHER!"

I

THE RETURN

"There is a living stream murmuring within me and saying 'Upward and onward to the Father'" (Ignatius).[1] "Past now the taste for foreign lands, / We seek the Father's home and hands" (Novalis).[2] Is not Jesus' whole desire, as he carries out his Father's will, the yearning to be on the way back to him? "If you loved me, you would have rejoiced, because I go to the Father; for the Father is greater than I" (Jn 14:28). And, once in the bosom of the Father, he will not rest until, together with the entire world that is subordinated to him, he is able to submit to the Father, so "that God may be everything to every one" (1 Cor 15:28). For as long as the world lasts, the Father "is working", and "with both his hands", and the Son only does "what he sees the Father doing" (Jn 5:19): in this, the Father is working with a view to a Sabbath in which, not only man will rest from his labors, but God himself rests from his (Heb 4:10). This Sabbath will not be inactivity, for the work of trinitarian love in God himself and in the saints will never rest. On the other hand, the groaning of creation, which has been subjected to futility against its will, and the deeper sighing of the children of God and the even deeper sighing of the Holy Spirit, by which we "wait patiently" (Rom 8), will be soothed and silenced once God "will wipe away every tear from their eyes", "and death shall be no more, neither shall there be mourning nor crying nor pain any more, for the former things have passed away" (Rev 21:4). Here we have the return, not only of Son and Spirit to the Father, but of the whole creation together with them and in them. This yearning for our origin in the Father is not, therefore, a flight from the world. At the end of our long journey of reflection we must say something about this return home, for it could have no other destination.

[1] *Ad Rom.* 7, 2.
[2] *Sehnsucht nach dem Tode* (Seelig, 1945, I, 23).

Before we examine in more detail the Holy Spirit's relationship to this return home to the Father, we can take a look at
that urge which is present in the created human being, driving him to embrace his origin—which, often enough, he calls
"father".[3] The more reflection a religion has undergone, the
clearer the conviction becomes that the Many, the plurality of
non-identical things, cannot be ultimate but must owe its existence to some ultimate, unitary source—in which alone it can
find rest. There have been numerous attempts to recognize, in
this One that sustains the Many, the final, all-embracing reality.
Sometimes the Many is experienced as diminished being, that is,
diminished to the level of mere illusion (Buddhism, Parmenides);
sometimes the contradictions found in the world are reconciled
in an all-embracing *logos* (Heraclitus); sometimes the world of
appearances is concentrated in ideas that are in turn sublimated
and unified by the superexistent Good (Plato); sometimes the
pure One is found beyond the unity of being and spirit—as its
source—and yet abiding in itself, independently of it (Plotinus);
and sometimes the isolated, individual thing as such—or perhaps
only in its idea, its higher truth—is thought of as returning to
its origin and its home. We should not be too quick to dismiss
these attempts as "pantheism". In the end all these expressions
are only the different facets of an ultimate drive on the part of
world being in its thought process [*des denkenden Weltseins*], unable to envisage any higher goal than the unity of its origin—
which by no means implies that the whole movement of coming forth and return (*egressus-regressus*) has been meaningless and

[3] For the concept in the context of the ancient, Indo-European and Greek/
Roman civilization, cf. Schrenk's article "Pater", ThW V, 946–59; in religion
generally, cf. RGG, 3d ed., VI, 1232f. Also Bertholet and Lehmann, *Lehrbuch für
Religionsgeschichte*, 4th ed. (1925), under "Gott-Vater". We know that, among the
civilizations surrounding Israel, the word "father" was applied to the god who
was regarded as responsible for the world; and that this was one reason why the
Old Covenant is hesitant to call God by the name "Father". We also know that
Israel's God has maternal attributes—this has no sexual connotations whatsoever
—which means that in what follows we can prescind from all the feminist problems surrounding the use of the word "Father" for God. "From the most ancient
times, for oriental man, the word "father" as applied to God embraces something
of what "mother" means for us" (J. Jeremias, *Abba: Studien zur neutestamentlichen
Theologie und Zeitgeschichte* [Göttingen, 1966], 15).

nugatory. One can refuse to utter the meaning of this coming forth (as Buddha reputedly did), but it does not follow that there *is* no meaning; some notions can presuppose that what flows from the source, or perhaps even the source itself, undergoes an enrichment: either the source goes to the limits of the void in unfolding its whole wealth (Plotinus) or else the origin, which stands in need of no enrichment, is—in biblical language —"glorified" by what acknowledges it and flows back to it.

Staying in the realm of man's fundamental religious constitution, the question arises of whether what flows forth from its source in the One—thereby necessarily distancing itself from it—possesses within it the element of its own turning back or conversion (in Neoplatonic terms, *epistrophē*), so that it takes a decision, an effort, an ascetical program to turn it around and set it on the way home to its origin; or whether from the very outset, in virtue of its origin (since all thinking is *re-flection*), it contains within itself the element of conversion.[4] No religious system would tolerate the idea that that which comes forth (unreflectingly) from its origin, and thus distances itself from it, could decide to engage in such reflection simply on its own initiative; there must be some indwelling memory of its origin, acting as a goad, however much this may also depend on the experience of nothingness [*Nichtigkeit*] toward which—precisely in coming forth—it is hastening.

In the Old Testament this goad of memory, in the context of salvation history, means that Israel cannot forget the origin to which it owes its existence. The memory of its hour of birth in the miracle of the Sea of Reeds is too deeply engrained; Israel cannot forget it, even when faithlessly abandoning God. Even if

---

[4] On Plotinus: "Absolute thought is identical with thinking the One"; this "orders thinking toward an integrated form that is pure activity. This unity, which is in itself limited, defining itself through the most intensive life (because it defines itself in thinking the One), comes about through the joint operation of the *dynamis* that comes from the One and the movement of return that comes from the procession of the Second. The 'impetus' for this return actually originates in the principle itself."—"If the first phase of the procession from the One is a kind of indefinite outward movement, the conversion or return whereby this movement seeks its beginning is like a self-definition insofar as, on its inward path, it 'comes to a stop' in acknowledgment of the One" (W. Beierwaltes, *Denken des Einen* [Frankfurt: Klostermann, 1985], 53–54).

the individual tried to stop his ears to this constant call, the voice of the Torah, insistently repeated by the prophets' reproachful tones, would prevent him from forgetting it entirely. The relationship to God, as we have said, was rarely expressed in "father-son" terms in the Old Covenant because the surrounding nations used such terms in a mythological context;[5] yet God the Father is the merciful One who is called upon in distress and to whom obedience is due and who is addressed as "my Father" in Hellenistic (not Palestinian) Judaism,[6] and here this term never has a mythological-sexual connotation; here the background is God's historical act of adoption. And while initially Israel's historical destination is the Promised Land, it is God who is called "my rest" (Ps 95:11). This expression is interpreted in Hebrews 3:11 and 4:3, 5, as referring to the eschatological arrival of the pilgrim People of God at his (God's) heavenly rest; the tentative prophecies found in the Old Covenant, to the effect that all nations will share in Israel's ultimate salvation, are expanded in the New Covenant, promising a pilgrimage to God's rest on the part of the whole human race.

Paradoxically, this comes about by Jesus claiming God's Fatherhood entirely for himself, the Son.[7] Thus he both singularizes and intensifies Israel's relationship to its Father, while, at the same time, Israel's racial destiny is exploded to become the destiny and transcendent goal of all mankind: these two are so bound up with each other that all who believe in Jesus can become sons of God in the Son (Eph 1:3–5). There can be no cosmic return without this very specific "I am the way . . . , no one comes to the Father except by me" (Jn 14:6). If the world is to return to its origin, the trail must be blazed by him who has already completed, emphatically and archetypically, the

---

[5] Texts in W. Marchel, *Abba, Père! La Prière du Christ et des Chrétiens*, Analecta Biblica 19 (Rome, 1963), 9–44.

[6] The words "my father" in the Greek text of Sirach (23:1, 4) can be traced back to a Hebrew "God of my father" (Jeremias, *Abba*, 32).

[7] We cannot ignore the fact that the oldest sources only rarely refer to Jesus addressing the Father thus. It is Matthew and John who multiply these instances. Nonetheless it cannot be denied that he used the family term "Abba" (which is not, however, a childish term) and commended it to the disciples (as is attested by Galatians 4:6 and Romans 8:15).

circle of coming forth and return: "I came from the Father and have come into the world; again, I am leaving the world and going to the Father" (Jn 16:28). He is the "Way", that is, he is the "forerunner" (Heb 6:20) and "pioneer" (Heb 12:2): he prepares not only the path but also the arrival at the Father: "In my Father's house are many rooms; if it were not so, would I have told you that I go to prepare a place for you? And when I go and prepare a place for you, I will come again and will take you to myself, that where I am you may be also" (Jn 14:2–3). This going to the Father is also paradoxical, for, in Jesus, the linear Jewish "forward" of the Messianic hope changes into a mission to all the world (and to all its future) that is also characterized by a linear "forward", so that the path of discipleship of Christ, leading to the Father, goes simultaneously in two directions: vertically upward, and horizontally into the world in the proclamation of salvation to all nations and in the transformation of the world according to the Christian commandment of love. The Second Vatican Council went as far as it possibly could in integrating these two paths, without equating proclamation of the gospel and the preparing of the eschatological Kingdom of God with the fashioning of a more humane world.[8] The universality of the salvation brought by Christ also involves mankind in its own history: it is not only individuals but the whole of world history that is to be brought home to the Father's mansions.

The Council insistently urged on us a dialogue in which the "return" tendencies—we have identified them in the various religions—feature as entirely commendable blueprints, whereas the positivisms and atheisms that reject any notion of an Omega that is transcendent in history are incapable of dialogue. It is worth noting that religious paths that apparently reject the world can overcome their one-sidedness as they seek to return to their origin. What seems to be the radical religious nihilism of Zen Buddhism (with its philosophical basis in the Mahayana) arrives at a double negation: if the Absolute is not anything of this world (which, in itself, is nothing), this worldly nothingness can be ultimately identical with the nothingness of Nirvana; once the egoistic "I" has eventually succeeded in annihilating itself by

---

[8] The whole of *Gaudium et spes*, esp. 40–45, 77–93.

embracing the open vastness, the egoless or selfless subject is ready to encounter all worldly reality in ultimate peace. The same thing could happen in a radically consistent Neoplatonism (in its innumerable variants): if the sage can find the One not only in rare ecstasy but in all the emanations that symbolize the One and are due to it, his stance "cannot automatically be equated with flight from the world or distaste for it".[9] Even more astonishing than Plotinus in late antiquity is the equilibrium we find in Plato himself between the striving for the divine and for love and the desire to shape the earthly world.[10] In the dialogue with Christians, all these outlines of an eschatological path back to the origin are like models that lack only one thing if they are to live (something the world cannot guess or construct), namely, the trinitarian love that is the essence of all being and that has become visible in Jesus Christ: the Father, a wellspring of reciprocal love. He is this wellspring in the realm of the Absolute; but this outpouring is proved to be selfless love in that the Son freely surrenders himself for the world that is alienated and that *therefore* is to be brought home. Thus Aquinas organized his mighty *Summa* according to the religious framework of the *egressus-regressus*—although he may not have been entirely consistent in its execution.

But even when this dialogue seems to be going well, we are brought up with a jolt as we realize that, in Christian terms, the final unity can never be attained perfectly: the final step, where the Alpha of the world's origin should coincide with the Omega of its ultimate destiny, is always obstructed by the doctrine of the Trinity. Does not Christ himself claim this Alpha and Omega as his own (Rev 1:17; 22:13)? Would we not have to follow Meister Eckhart as he looks behind the trinitarian face of God that is turned toward the world and peers at the featureless abyss of his essence, resembling nothing so much as a desert? Here, it seems, the Christian is faced with the most difficult dialogue with the fanatics of absolute unity, be they Jewish or Moslem, for whom Jesus becomes only a mediating, go-between, prophetic figure

---

[9] Beierwaltes, *Denken des Einen*, 24.

[10] This has been emphasized by R. Guardini in his book *Der Tod des Sokrates* (Berlin, 1944), 183, 222. Cf. my own study *Romano Guardini* (Munich, 1970), 57.

(of however exalted a dignity). What price such a unity? The distinction between Lord and servant cannot be effaced (and in spite of its "election", the creation remains a servant);[11] and it remains unprovable that the divine Father is more than "favor", "faithfulness", and "mercy"—namely, substantial love in himself (and not merely vis-à-vis the creature). This means that he needs the Beloved who is begotten in self-surrender; furthermore, the "Third"—the fruit and witness of this unity of generative and receptive love—is necessary to attest the perfect selflessness of their union. In the Christian dispensation, the origin remains inaccessible except through this unity beyond number.

---

[11] In spite of the fact that in the Old Testament the titles of "son" (and even "gods") were applied to the kings or the people as a whole.

2

"THE SPIRIT SEARCHES
THE DEPTHS OF GOD"

This statement (1 Cor 2:10) is astonishing, for the Spirit himself is God. If he searches himself, he must plunge into his own depths and know that he who is love owes his existence to love. Primarily (*principaliter*) he owes his existence to the love of this unfathomable origin who bears the name of Father. Then to the love of the Beloved, whose delight is in his grateful love for the origin whom he loves with no less love. In searching these depths, the Spirit acts as the witness and the fruit of this reciprocal love; but he is not an observer here: he himself *is* this love. No wonder, then, that this unimaginable mystery occupies him for a whole eternity—and occupies us, too, who "have received . . . the Spirit which is from God" (1 Cor 2:12). For if love, as such, is genuine, it has no other ground but itself; this love that has its source in the Father is, initially, the Father himself (since, as Father, he is nothing other than the pure surrender of himself; the Father does not "have" love, he "is" love); this being so, it is impossible to discover the ground of this groundless love. Or *can* we, perhaps, discover the ground of the love of the Son —begotten of the Father in groundless love—in the fact that he owes his entire existence to the Father and therefore "owes" him love? (Richard of St. Victor calls the Son's love *amor debitus*).[1] Can we not say that the Son's self-offering to the Father, which goes "to the end" (Jn 13:1) of all possible love, that is, to the extreme of forsakenness by God in utter pain, somehow has its "ground" in the groundlessness of the Father's love? This would be intelligible if the Son were a second God beside the Father; but since he is the same God (the Father's self-utterance, his "Word"), this Word evinces the same original groundlessness of love—and it does so even if, for the present, it adopts the mode of infinite gratitude and devoted self-oblation. The Spirit

[1] *De Trin.* V, 16 and 18.

441

searches the depths of this love but does not discover in it any "ground" that would give us a key for our conceptualizing of it.

It is the mystery of love, however, that—itself groundless— grounds everything else. In its invisible light everything else becomes manifest and intelligible. To use a word from the Old Covenant, it becomes "wisdom". Nothing on earth or in heaven could be known if God had not "given wisdom and sent [his] holy Spirit from on high" (Wis 9:16-17). "In your light do we see light" (Ps 36:9). Thus love is not unreasonable, since it is the source of all rationality. But if knowledge is ultimately based on wisdom, wisdom is based on love. So we can say, with the spiritual theology of the Middle Ages, on the foundations laid by Gregory the Great: "It is through love that we attain knowledge."[2] Indeed, "love itself is knowledge."[3] Love's ultimate evidence is within it, and all reasoning knowledge is dependent on it.

Only now does it become clear that the irreducibility of love, which wells up in the Father's act of being, is not something irrational, obliging us to adopt a stance of resignation and a purely apophatic theology. We must look closely at Paul's hymnic outburst: "O the depth of the riches and wisdom and knowledge of God! How unsearchable are his judgments and how inscrutable his ways!" (Rom 11:33).[4] The translation "unsearchable" would suggest that further searching is vain; theology would give up. But such a translation clearly contradicts the earlier assertion, which is one of adoration and wonder at the riches of God's wisdom and knowledge (*gnōsis*). It also contradicts Ephesians, which summons the Christian "with all the saints" to "know" (*gnōnai*) all the dimensions of "the love of Christ which surpasses knowledge, that you may be filled with all the fulness of God" (Eph 3:18-19). What remains for us, therefore—together with the searching Spirit—is a never-concluded, ever-deeper penetration (possible only to love) into the miracle of the groundless love of the Father (and of the Son and the Spirit that flows from it). This love, as such, hands itself over to the searching of

[2] *Moralia* 10, 63; 31, 101.

[3] *In Evang.* 27, 4.

[4] Cf. Markus Barth, "Theologie—ein Gebet", *Theol. Zeitschrift* 41 (Basel, 1985): 336-37.

gnōsis, or "wisdom". "To know the love of Christ which surpasses knowledge" (Eph 3:19) is therefore only superficially a
paradox, for love offers itself to be known; to be known, of
course, not by a knowledge that is enclosed in its own principles, but by a knowledge that remains open to the miracle of
that love which wells up, eternally groundless, from within itself. Gregory of Nyssa saw and formulated this perfectly.[5]

Given this Christian understanding of the originating Father,
Jesus' whole behavior is transparent: it is one single act of pointing to the Father.[6] According to John, in his concluding statements, Jesus is nothing other than the interpretation of the Father, making visible him who is invisible;[7] he says categorically
that "no one has ever seen God" (Jn 1:18; solemnly repeated
in 1 Tim 6:16) and that anyone who sees him (Jesus—as the
One he really is), sees the Father (Jn 14:9). Again and again the
Johannine Jesus insists that he does not speak of himself, that
his teaching is not his own but the Father's, that he does only
what he sees the Father doing (and the Father shows him everything). This Johannine view, however, is already laid down in
the Synoptics. It is there in the prayer to the Father that Jesus
teaches his disciples as his very own prayer; it is there in the
warning against using the word "father" on earth (since only
the Father in heaven is worthy of it); it is there in the assertion
that his ultimate destiny is hidden from him, known only to the
Father. Paul concludes the hymn to Christ in Philippians 2:6–11
by saying that the glorification of Jesus in the entire cosmos re-
dounds "to the glory of God the Father", just as, in 1 Corinthians 15:28, the Son finally puts all things beneath the Father's
feet so "that God [the Father] may be everything to every one".
This can only mean one thing: ultimately the groundless Source
will be present and recognized, not only in the Son, but—as the
all-pervading and all-ruling principle—in every created reality.

---

[5] Cf. our selection from the commentary on the Song of Songs: *Der versiegelte
Quell*, 3d ed., Christliche Meister 23 (Einsiedeln: Johannesverlag, 1984).

[6] On Jesus' relationship with the Father, cf. the bibliography in Gnilka's article
"Vater", in LThK 10 (1965): 621; E. Schillebeeckx, *Jesus*, 2d ed. (Herder, 1974),
227; and the remarks of Schrenk, ThW V, 981–1001, and Marchel, *Abba, Père!*
101–77.

[7] L. Bouyer's book on the Father is entitled *Le Père invisible* (Cerf, 1976).

This Source, however, as set forth consistently in the First Letter of John, can never be grasped in isolation, separate from him who streams forth. We cannot "have" the Father without the Son. "No one who denies the Son has the Father. He who confesses the Son has the Father also" (1 Jn 2:23). "Any one who goes ahead and does not abide in the doctrine of Christ does not have God; he who abides in the doctrine has both the Father and the Son" (2 Jn 9). That is why, in spite of many requests for it, the Church has always refused to admit a "feast of the Father" into the Calendar.[8]

The assertion that the Spirit searches the depths of God (the Father) and that this Spirit is given to us as the Spirit of Christ (1 Cor 2:10–16), is "clearly and definitely trinitarian".[9] The whole context shows that this searching on the part of the divine Spirit in the abyss of the Father's love can (and must) also be *our* searching, in virtue of the Spirit of Christ that has been given to us. Furthermore, such searching on our part is not in vain: in the first place, we are meant thereby to "understand the gifts bestowed on us by God" and effectively communicate this to those who, like us, have received the Spirit; and in the second place, we are assured that, in searching together with the Holy Spirit, each Christian and his wisdom is removed from all purely human judgment, whereas he himself is able to judge all earthly wisdom on the basis of the heavenly. No religious philosophy

[8] For a thorough treatment of these requests made to Rome, first from France and then by the Spanish king, cf. M. Caillat, "La Dévotion à Dieu le Père: Une Discussion au XVII siècle", *Revue d'Ascétique et de Mystique* 20 (1939): 35–49, 136–57. The theological sources for this kind of particular devotion were Suarez and, especially, Théophile Raynaud, S.J. (in his *Heteroclita spiritualia et anomalia pietatis* [Grenoble, 1646]); paradoxically, he first lists all the reasons in favor of instituting such a feast, but then he goes on to say that it would be undesirable, not only because Urban VIII had already rejected the idea, but because it would be theologically incorrect to introduce feasts for the individual Divine Persons outside the framework of the existing economy. The fact that Raynaud "openly contradicts himself" (*Heteroclita* 140) in the two parts of his work need not delay us here. It should be said, however, that there should be no more petitions today for "the introduction of a feast of Our Father's Fatherhood", such as T. Styczen makes ("Gott ist Vater", *Münchener theol. Zeitschrift* 35 [1984]: 290). On "devotion to the Father", cf. E. Bertaud and A. Rayez, "Dévotion au Père", DSp III (1957), 763f.

[9] H.-D. Wendland, *Die Briefe an die Korinther*, 14th ed., NTD 7 (1978), 31.

invented by man could dare to make the bold Johannine statement that "God is love."

In the end, all that we have said here shows that the concluding statements of the first volume of this *Theo-Logic*, which were formulated purely philosophically, are heightened and confirmed in a trinitarian context in the assertions of the second and third volumes. This vindicates the old maxim that grace perfects what is given in nature, while nature itself, by its own efforts, can neither attain nor even dream of such perfection.

3

THE INVISIBLE FATHER

It is with considerable reticence that we raise one final question: What can it mean to "behold" the groundless abyss of love that the Father is? Our beholding always requires an object [*Gegen-stand*], but this groundless abyss can be neither "over-against" [*gegen*] nor something that "stands" [*Stand*]; at its highest it could be our becoming aware of the miracle that such a source exists.

The Old Testament knew that man cannot see God, and the New Testament insists upon it in many places. "No one has ever seen God" (Jn 1:18); "Not that any one has seen the Father except him who is from God" (Jn 6:46); "No man has ever seen God" (1 Jn 4:12); only indirectly can God's "invisible nature" be "perceived in the things that have been made" (Rom 1:20); he himself "dwells in unapproachable light" (1 Tim 6:16; he is wrapped in light as in a garment: Ps 104:2; cf. Job 37:22f.). Only one passage seems to contradict this: 1 Jn 3:2: "Beloved, we are God's children now; it does not yet appear what we shall be, but we know that when he appears we shall be like him, for we shall see him as he is." Can the "he" whom we shall see be God the Father? Grammatically speaking it is the most probable interpretation. Yet "the idea of assimilation through vision would be unique in Johannine writings."[1] According to Paul, the ability to see divine things seems to presuppose that the beholder has been endowed with "splendor" (*doxa*) (2 Cor 3:7ff., 18), but in each case it is the glory of Christ, not of the Father. The same is clear in John: the "glory" the disciples saw is "the glory [*doxa*] as of the only-begotten Son from the Father" (Jn 1:14). So Jesus prays to the Father: "I desire that they also, whom you have given me, may be with me where I am, to behold my glory which you have given me . . . before the foundation of the world" (Jn 17:24). These two passages speak of different glories. The first can be beheld in this world, in the Son (Jn 2:11); the other is the heavenly glory that the Son has with the Father, "the glory which I had with you before the

---

[1] R. Schnackenburg, *Die Johannesbriefe* (Herder, 1953), 152.

world was made" (Jn 17:5). The latter pertains to the divine
glory, and the "Kyrios Jesus Christ" has it "to the glory of God
the Father" (Phil 2:11). It is Jesus' wish that, one day, his disciples shall be assimilated to this glory, so that they will see him
"as he is", in the *doxa* given him by the Father before the world
was made.

This is really divine glory, and on Tabor the disciples were
given a preliminary burst of it, which threw them into a stupor.
Accordingly we are bound to agree with Thomas Aquinas when
he says that we must have a direct participation in the divine
essence if we are to be able to behold him.[2] Nonetheless, the
same Thomas says that the blessed see God as "infinitum, sed
non infinite, totum, sed non totaliter", because he is "infinite
cognoscibilis".[3] However, he immediately adds—in a way that
is entirely in accord with the Fathers of the fourth century—
that if by seeing and understanding we mean "embracing totally"
(*includere*), then "sic nullo modo Deus comprehenditur, . . . cum
sit infinitus". Infinite love will not be caught and held, but the
more love there is, the more it can penetrate what exceeds its
grasp; "plus autem participabit lumine gloriae, qui plus habet de
caritate".[4] In the Apocalypse, the One who sits on the throne is
invisible—no doubt even to the heavenly ones—and can only
be described in feeble metaphors (Rev 4:3). The "great voice
from the throne" (Rev 21:3) is audible and intelligible, and all
heaven is bathed in the light of the "glory of God" and of the
Lamb (Rev 21:23); but those who dwell in the light, beholding
and understanding all that they see in it, do not need to look
into the abyss of the light's source. Through the Son's glory we
glimpse the abyss of the invisible Father's love-glory in the Holy
Spirit's twofold love. Born of the Spirit as we are, we exist in
the fire of love in which Father and Son encounter each other;
thus, together with the Spirit, we simultaneously bear witness
and give glory to this love.

---

[2] "Divina essentia unitur intellectui creato ut intellectum in actu, per seipsam
faciens intellectum in actu" (*S. Th.* I, 12, 2 ad 3). Otherwise, i.e., by means of a
mere created cognitive image, God could not be seen "as he is" (I, 12, 2; *Contr.
Gent.* III, 49; *De Ver.* 8, 1; 18, 1 ad 1).

[3] *S. Th.* I, 12, 7c.

[4] *S. Th.* I, 12, 6.

INDEX